The Language of Greek Comedy

The Language of Greek Comedy

◆

EDITED BY

ANDREAS WILLI

OXFORD
UNIVERSITY PRESS

OXFORD
UNIVERSITY PRESS

Great Clarendon Street, Oxford OX2 6DP

Oxford University Press is a department of the University of Oxford.
It furthers the University's objective of excellence in research, scholarship,
and education by publishing worldwide in

Oxford New York
Auckland Bangkok Buenos Aires Cape Town Chennai
Dar es Salaam Delhi Hong Kong Istanbul Karachi Kolkata
Kuala Lumpur Madrid Melbourne Mexico City Mumbai Nairobi
São Paulo Shanghai Singapore Taipei Tokyo Toronto

Published in the United States
by Oxford University Press Inc., New York

First published 2002

British Library Cataloguing in Publication Data
Data available

Library of Congress Cataloging in Publication Data
The language of Greek comedy / edited by Andreas Willi.
p. cm.
Includes bibliographical references and indexes.
(acid-free paper)
1. Greek drama (Comedy)—History and criticism. 2. Language and culture—Greece. 3.
Greek language—Style. I. Willi, Andreas.
PA3166.L36 2002
882'.0109–dc21 2002019043

ISBN 0–19–924547–9

1 3 5 7 9 10 8 6 4 2

Typeset in Imprint and Porson Greek
by Joshua Associates Ltd., Oxford
Printed in Great Britain
on acid-free paper by
Biddles Ltd, Guildford and King's Lynn

Preface

Since the middle of the twentieth century linguistics and literary scholarship in the field of classical studies have rapidly grown apart. Although this development was not actively encouraged by anyone, it could hardly be avoided as both sides became ever more specialized. Very few scholars were able to invest their energies into the courageous attempt to keep abreast with the rapid progress on both sides of the rift. Nevertheless, many classicists intuitively still feel that a reunification of the two branches—and in fact more than that, for historical and archaeological research should also be integrated—is an ideal to be striven for today no less than in the 1920s, when Wilamowitz, having a similar vision for his *Klassische Philologie*, wrote that 'its division into . . . separate disciplines . . . can be justified only as a concession to the limitations of human capacity and must not be allowed to stifle awareness of the whole' (Wilamowitz 1982: 1). It is out of such a spirit of unity that the contributions to this volume have been born.

Most of the essays published here were first delivered as papers to the Corpus Christi Classical Seminar on 'The Language of Greek Comedy' at the University of Oxford in Michaelmas Term 1999, and several of the contributors have deliberately chosen to retain some signals of orality that betray this origin. The positive response to the Seminar greatly encouraged me to envisage a subsequent publication and we are all very grateful to the Delegates of Oxford University Press for having made this possible.

The Classical Seminar itself was generously supported by the Corpus Christi College Centre for the Study of Greek and Roman Antiquity and by the Faculty of Literae Humaniores of the University of Oxford. In particular I must mention Robin Osborne and Michael Winterbottom, who, as directors of the Centre, first suggested and then actively contributed to the organization of this semi-interdisciplinary Seminar.

In the editorial work, too, I have profited from the help and advice of many people. Here I should like to name especially Anna Morpurgo Davies and Nan Dunbar, both at Somerville College Oxford, Hilary O'Shea and Jenny Wagstaffe at Oxford University Press, and above all Leofranc Holford-Strevens, whose unique erudition and experience in copy-editing prevented more blunders than is comfortable to admit.

Finally, it is a pleasure to acknowledge the great friendship, patience, and cooperation I have experienced as a novice editor from all the contributors. Without their trust, I should not have dared to disregard Aristophanes' advice: *ἐρέτην χρῆναι πρῶτα γενέσθαι πρὶν πηδαλίοις ἐπιχειρεῖν*. For comedy usually knows what is right.

A. W.

Corpus Christi College, Oxford
1 July 2001

Contents

Abbreviations

Abbreviations are generally those used in the *Oxford Classical Dictionary* (3rd edn., Oxford and New York, 1996) and, for journals, in *L'Année Philologique*. All fragments of Greek comedy are numbered according to the edition by Kassel and Austin (*Poetae Comici Graeci*, Berlin and New York, 1983–).

Notes on Contributors

W. Geoffrey Arnott FBA was Professor of Greek Language and Literature at the University of Leeds (1968–91, now Emeritus). His publications include *Menander, Plautus, Terence* (Oxford, 1975), *Menander* (LCL, 3 vols., 1979, 1996, 2000), and *Alexis: A Commentary* (Cambridge, 1996), as well as papers and reviews in various classical journals.

Ewen Bowie is E. P. Warren Praelector in Classics at Corpus Christi College, Oxford, and Reader in Classical Languages and Literature in the University of Oxford. He has made a number of contributions to the study of early Greek elegiac and iambic poetry, Attic comedy, and Hellenistic poetry, but the majority of his work has been on the Greek literature and society of the high Roman Empire (Pausanias, Philostratus, Heliodorus). He is currently completing a commentary on Longus, *Daphnis and Chloe*.

Albio C. Cassio is Professor of Greek and Latin Grammar at the University of Rome 'La Sapienza'. He has worked on Attic Comedy, the language of the Greek epics, and the ancient dialects of Sicily and Magna Graecia. He is the author of *Commedia e partecipazione: la* Pace *di Aristofane* (Naples, 1985) and the editor of *Katà Diálekton* (Proceedings of the Third International Congress of Greek Dialectology, Naples, 1997). He is currently working on the latest phases of Homer from a linguistic perspective.

Gregory W. Dobrov is Assistant Professor of Classical Studies at Loyola University, Chicago. His interests include classical theatre, linguistics, Byzantine hymnography, and the Second Sophistic. Select publications: *Beyond Aristophanes* (Atlanta, 1995), *The City as Comedy* (Chapel Hill, 1997), *Figures of Play* (Oxford, 2001). His Ph.D. is from Cornell and he has taught at Syracuse University and the University of Michigan.

SIR KENNETH DOVER FBA was Professor of Greek at the University of St Andrews from 1955 to 1976 and President of Corpus Christi College, Oxford, from 1976 to 1986. Since 1981 he has been Chancellor of the University of St Andrews. His numerous publications include *Aristophanic Comedy* (Berkeley and Los Angeles, 1972) as well as commentaries on Aristophanes' *Clouds* (Oxford, 1968) and *Frogs* (Oxford, 1993).

RENÉ NÜNLIST is Assistant Professor of Classics at Brown University. His areas of interest (besides Menander) include Homer, early Greek lyric poetry, narratology, and papyrology. He is the author of *Poetologische Bildersprache in der frühgriechischen Dichtung* (Stuttgart and Leipzig, 1998), co-author of the new Basel commentary on the *Iliad* (Munich and Leipzig, 2000), and editor of two substantial fragments of Menander (P. Oxy. LXVIII, forthcoming).

SIMON R. SLINGS has taught Greek at the Free University in Amsterdam, where he currently holds the chair of Greek language and literature. His research interests include Greek linguistics, especially pragmatics, early Greek lyric, and Plato.

ALAN H. SOMMERSTEIN is Professor of Greek and Director of the Centre for Ancient Drama and its Reception (CADRE), University of Nottingham. He has produced editions of the eleven comedies of Aristophanes (Warminster, 1980–2001) and of Aeschylus' *Eumenides* (Cambridge, 1989), and is the author of *Aeschylean Tragedy* (Bari, 1996). He is at present, with three collaborators, preparing an edition with translation and commentary of selected fragmentary plays of Sophocles.

ANDREAS WILLI was Charles Oldham Graduate Scholar at Corpus Christi College, Oxford (1998–2001), where he wrote a doctoral thesis on linguistic variation in Aristophanic comedy. He is currently Research Assistant in the Department of Classics at the University of Basel. His research interests include historical linguistics of Greek and Latin, Greek sociolinguistics and dialectology, and comparative philology.

I

The Language of Greek Comedy: Introduction and Bibliographical Sketch

ANDREAS WILLI

λέγεται δὲ καὶ Μενάνδρῳ τῶν συνήθων τις εἰπεῖν· "ἐγγὺς οὖν, Μένανδρε, τὰ Διονύσια, καὶ σὺ τὴν κωμῳδίαν οὐ πεποίηκας;" τὸν δ' ἀποκρίνασθαι "νὴ τοὺς θεούς, ἔγωγε πεποίηκα τὴν κωμῳδίαν. ᾠκονόμηται γὰρ ἡ διάθεσις, δεῖ δ' αὐτῇ τὰ στιχίδια ἐπᾷσαι" (Plut. *Mor.* 347 E = Men. test. 70).

Allegedly a friend of Menander's once said to him: 'The Dionysia are already close, Menander, and you haven't made your comedy!' To which the latter replied: 'Yes, of course I have made my comedy. Its structure is all arranged, there's just the verses left to compose.'

Menander, it appears, knew the value of a good story. If he had got a neatly structured plot, what else could he need to win the favour of his audience?

But then: imagine Aristophanes saying this in 421 BC, shortly before the City Dionysia when *Peace* was first performed. Would he have been as confident as Menander? After all, what Aristophanes would have had was about this much: an Attic farmer who is tired of war flies to heaven, liberates the imprisoned goddess Peace with the help of a chorus of Greek peasants, then returns home, and all ends in a huge feast. Unlike Menander, Aristophanes would have had good reasons for worrying about time running out.

The crucial point in Plutarch's anecdote about Menander is the relegation of the comic *signifiant*, the level of comic form and expression, to the second rank. Structure and plot, the things which are moulded from the *signifiant*, are all that matters. With only a little exaggeration we may say that in an Aristophanic comedy like *Peace* it is exactly the other way round: the comic *signifié* is insubstantial, but the *signifiant* creates a masterpiece.

Of course this is a very crude statement about comic literary history, but it is a statement which shows that changes within a literary genre are often most closely related to changes in form and expression. It is therefore somewhat surprising and paradoxical how little attention literary historians usually pay to language as the most basic aspect of form and expression.

The paradox becomes even greater if we turn to fragmentary texts, authors, and genres. For Doric and Middle Comedy, for example, the fragments provide us with rich evidence on the *signifiant* side, but we are frequently tapping in the dark when we ask for a coherent *signifié*, for entire plots and themes. So why should we not turn the tables for a change and think of literary history as the history of the *signifiant* as much as that of the *signifié*?

The contributions in this volume all centre around the idea of creating a 'linguistic literary history' of comedy, a literary history of comic form and expression. To write a comprehensive account of these matters is a task for the future. What we attempt to do is to outline the agenda, to give ideas, and to establish possible viewpoints. The diversity of approaches represented here shows how large a field this is to turn over. But it also shows how fascinating such work can be even for scholars who do not, or not in the first place, regard themselves as linguists.

The present introduction will not only point out the conceptual links between the different papers in this book, but it will also try to help further research along similar lines by presenting in clearly separated paragraphs (some of) the work that has been done by others, on whose shoulders we all stand. Unfortunately, bibliographical completeness is a goal that is increasingly hard to reach and certainly not reached here. Nevertheless, I hope that the introduction thus becomes a useful contribution in its own right.[1]

[1] The bibliography includes, with very few exceptions, neither notes on textual criticism and articles dealing with single words or lines nor editions and commentaries (although much important material is 'hidden' there; for a recent survey see Zimmermann 1992*a*: 161–82). The compilation would have been impossible without such wonderful tools as *L'Année Philologique* and *Gnomon* supplemented by *Dissertation Abstracts International* (= *DA*), the surveys by Murphy (1955/6), (1972), Dover (1957), Mette (1965), (1966), (1968), (1971/2), Kraus (1971), (1973), Newiger (1975), Storey (1987), (1992), Zimmermann (1992*a*), (1994), and the Menander bibliographies by Corbato (1963) on *Dyskolos* and by Katsouris (1995). Those items which I have not seen myself are marked by an asterisk (*); this concerns in particular several unpublished (but microfilmed) American theses, for which I am basing myself on the summaries given in *DA*.

§1. Basic tools: grammars and indices. Apart from the standard grammars—especially Kühner–Gerth (1898–1904), Schwyzer (1939), and Schwyzer–Debrunner (1950)—word indexes and concordances are indispensable for many linguistic approaches to Greek literature.

For Menander there is a recent lexicon with Latin translations and metrical indications by Pompella (1996; cf. also *Georgescu 1971). For Aristophanes there is an index by Todd (1932), based on the Oxford edition by Hall and Geldart, as well as a line concordance by Dunbar–Marzullo (1973). Until the final volume of *Poetae Comici Graeci* (Kassel–Austin 1983–) appears, Jacobi (1857) must still be consulted for the comic fragments (based on Meineke's edition).

The hermeneutic potential of a literary history of the *signifiant* is best illustrated by an example. Let us look at personal names. Suppose we had only fragments of all Greek literary genres, but fragments which present a broad range of genre-specific personal names. How much could we learn from them?

We should see, for instance, that many of the names found in Homeric epic return in Attic tragedy, despite the fundamental change from narrative to dialogue. This would suggest that tragedy took up and transformed a group of (presumably fictional) stories that had first taken literary form in epic. Next we should discover that iambic poetry and Old Comedy resemble each other in using a mixture of names, which includes both names of historical individuals (or at least individuals who are presented as historical figures) and apparently invented speaking names with a comic point. In comedy names of personifications and some of the epic–tragic names would complete the picture. Finally in New Comedy there would be a last major group of names which repeat themselves although they do not belong to the epic–tragic tradition: their frequency would indicate that they may be stock character names.

On the basis of so little linguistic evidence, we might conclude, like Aristotle in the fourth chapter of his *Poetics*, that there is a typological similarity between epic and tragedy on the one hand, and between iambus and comedy on the other, and further that there must be a substantial break between Old Comedy and New Comedy. We could also infer that literary tradition is more important in tragedy than in comedy and that the latter is more directly related to present-day issues. The curious name mixture in Old Comedy might even lead us to the conclusion that comedy must have created a fantasy-world in which intertextuality played an important role (given the inclusion of epic–tragic names). The stock names of New Comedy would naturally be compared with those of the *Commedia dell'Arte* and their unoriginality would point to a loss of importance of the *signifiant* when compared with Old Comedy. On the other hand, we might suspect from the apparent absence of historical names that New Comedy enjoyed considerable freedom in plot construction.

§2. Comic names: speaking names (Old Comedy). The choice of names as an example of a language-focused approach to literary history is not entirely accidental. There is no other linguistic aspect of Greek comedy to which so many articles and even books have been devoted.

For Old Comedy, *Steiger (1888), *Fröhde (1898), and *Peppler (1902) initiated the functional and thematic explanation of 'speaking names'. Among the more recent publications one may list articles on the names of 'Dikaiopolis' in *Acharnians* (E. L. Bowie 1988), 'Peisetairos' in *Birds* (Kapp 1928, Marzullo 1970, Corsini 1993), 'Strepsiades' and 'Pheidippides' in *Clouds* (Marzullo 1953, Panagl 1983), 'Praxagora' and 'Blepyros' in *Ecclesiazusae* (Paganelli 1978/9), or 'Marikas' in Eupolis (Cassio 1985*b*, Morgan 1986) and 'Ankylion' in Eubulus (Rosen 1989). With contextually insignificant names such as 'Theoros' in *Wasps* (Andrisano 1984/5) and 'Dexinikos' in *Plutus* (Di Marco 1981, Bonanno 1984/5), the search for far-reaching implications may sometimes be exaggerated.

The most important theoretical discussion of names in Old Comedy is found in Marzullo (1953), who not only retraces the history of speaking names in other literary genres but distinguishes in comedy between the 'ominous' speaking name, which indicates the distinctive features of a character to the audience (e.g. that 'Praxagora' is active (*πραξ-*) in the male domain of the *ἀγορά*), and the 'punning' name, which is used for the sake of a momentary comic effect (e.g. the semi-obscene 'Kinesias' in *Lysistrata*, a play full of such names: Funaioli 1984/5). The comic function of the second group is comparable to that of puns on real names like that of Lamachus (*Ach.* 1071; cf. Lewis 1955 on Lysistrata and in general Taillardat 1956, *P. I. Kakridis 1972, *Ghiron-Bistagne 1989; for Aristophanic prosopographies see *Molitor 1969, Holden 1902, and the literature cited by Zimmermann 1992*a*: 183). Bonanno (1987) underlines that neither 'ominous' nor 'punning' names need to be freely invented since the poet often applies the technique of semantically 'reloading' existing names (so that for instance *Lysistrata* brings out the sexual connotations inherent in the conventional name 'Myrrhine').

§3. Comic names: naming conventions (Old Comedy). Olson (1992) discusses the dramaturgical modalities of naming in Aristophanes. For example, heroes and heroines are usually named late in the play so that their name comes as a climactic point in the development of their characterization and allows them to keep control over it (cf. also Sommerstein 1980*a* on the reluctance to name women). The function of diminutive names is treated by Mikołajczyk (1979; cf. F. Schmid 1954), whereas *Holmes (1990) looks at the use of demotics, the non-patronymic application of names in -*ίδης*, and the type-names of slaves (which may have formed a literary tradition since the frequency of certain slave-names in New Comedy does not always correspond to the frequency in the epigraphic attestations: K. Treu 1983; Lascu 1969 points out that slaves are named only in comedy, not in tragedy).

§4. Comic names: epithets and other forms of address. Being firmly established, divine names provide less scope for literary manipulation, but C. A. Anderson (1995) shows how the use of epithets takes part in the thematic development of several Aristophanic comedies and is closely related to contextual circumstances. Similarly, human forms of address show a great variety in Aristophanes because they serve dramatic functions, whereas simple names are relatively rare as address-forms; their frequency increases in New Comedy, whose usage thus agrees with that in philosophical dialogue and probably reproduces actual address practices more faithfully (Dickey 1995; cf. Dickey 1996; earlier e.g. Brunius-Nilsson 1955: 82–97 on *δαιμόνιε*, de Vries 1966 and Szemerényi 1987: 569–78 on *ὦ τᾶν*).

§5. Comic names: New Comedy. 'Speaking names' are not entirely absent from New Comedy (and Doric comedy: Albini 1984), even though they are often less straightforward, as the example of 'Knemon' shows (from *κνήμη* 'shin-bone' or from *κνάω* 'to scratch'?: see e.g. Macleod 1981, Cavallero 1994). One difference between Old and New Comedy lies in the fact that speaking names such as 'Polemon' for a soldier produce no comic effect (Poland 1914). According to Fantuzzi (1978/9) Menander's speaking names—unlike those of Aristophanes—are 'macrostructural': they do not indicate the role of a figure but the fact that a figure belongs to a Theophrastean character type (e.g. 'Smikrines' corresponds to Theophrastus' 'petty-minded' *μικρολόγος*).

This relationship between character names and character types has been hotly debated. In a series of articles MacCary (1969, 1970, 1972) argued that the naming practice of New Comedy is comparable to that of the *Commedia dell'Arte* because names, masks, and character features form a firmly established triad: a slave called Daos would always wear the same mask, have a leading role, and be πανοῦργος 'cunning'; only by modulating *within* this framework would Menander add some individuality. MacCary's position has been challenged by P. G. McC. Brown (1987), who points out that, for instance, the two characters named 'Chaireas' in *Dyskolos* and *Aspis* are entirely different from each other; by bestowing a new individuality to a traditional name the poet creates a surprise effect (Poland 1914; cf. also Webster 1974: 94–9 and on the issue of masks Wiles 1991).

The preceding thought experiment on the heuristic value of 'reading' comic names summarizes only one of two fruitful approaches to a literary history of linguistic forms. This first approach entails a comparative analysis of one particular type of *signifiant* feature (here personal names) throughout various genres. Of course some features are more promising than others, but even less promising ones may yield important results. It is not excluded, for example, that a quantitative and qualitative comparison of potential optatives or first person singular forms in different genres would teach us something essential about the construction and intentions of these genres.

Whereas the first approach concentrates on one feature in a plurality of genres, the second approach deals with a plurality of features within one genre. Here partial or complete inventories of the *signifiant* features of a genre are compiled in order to understand its specificity, its functioning and purpose. If we recognize, for instance, that tragedy is full of artificial linguistic features that did not belong to contemporary spoken Greek, it becomes clear that tragedy conventionally operated with a defamiliarizing or dequotidianizing code which, at least originally, aimed at a 'deautomatization' of audience reactions.

Since a comprehensive literary history of linguistic forms would have to combine both approaches, the essays in this book also exemplify the two types. Thus, the papers by Nünlist (reported speech in comedy, tragedy, and epic), Slings (figures of speech in comedy and non-literary language), Sommerstein ('comic' vocabulary in tragedy), Dover (evaluative words in comedy and general language), and Bowie (especially on the lexicon of comedy and iambus) primarily belong to the first type, which compares different genres with regard to one particular feature or one narrowly defined group of features, whereas the papers by Cassio (Doric comedy), Arnott (New Comedy), and myself (Old Comedy) concentrate on the co-occurrence of different features in one genre.

Ewen Bowie reconsiders the old problem of the relationship between comedy and iambic poetry. By comparing three possible hypotheses of dependence he voices objections to the view of Rosen (1988), according to whom Cratinus introduced into Attic comedy certain iambic features which then continued to live there throughout the epoch of Old Comedy. Before entering a detailed discussion of several lexical points of contact between iambus and comedy, Bowie underlines the substantial differences between the two genres on the macroscopic level of discourse parameters such as length, audience, performers and mode of performance, and presence of narrative. Since these differences speak against a close affiliation of iambus and comedy, it is difficult to lay much stress on the superficial lexical overlap, which exists especially in the field of obscenity or *aischrologia*. Bowie also stresses that Aristotle in the *Poetics* does not suggest a genetic link between iambus and comedy. Where there are similarities, we should rather regard them as the natural, independent, developments of two verbal genres in which a mixed tradition of narrative and abuse was endowed with a social or political function.

The last point raises a methodological question which is important not just for comedy: how much structural, thematic, or linguistic overlap do we need in order to postulate a genetic affiliation (whether partial or complete) between two genres? Is it possible, for instance, to adapt a methodology like that of linguistic reconstruction to the culturally determined domain of literature? And if so, to which constituents should we pay particular attention? No literary scholar will be convinced by mere lexical statistics: even if two genres employ a similar range of vocabulary, they may still be entirely different in social function, but a category such as 'social function' is far more difficult to handle because it cannot simply be quantified. Bowie's focus on performers and audience shows that some help may come from linguistic anthropology. Since the time when Malinowski (1923: 465–70) developed the concept of a 'context of situation', this field has become increasingly important in cultural studies. It stresses the relation between social setting—and in particular 'participation frameworks'—and textual forms or genres. If two genres have a similar 'context of situation' (i.e. if the addressors and addressees as well as the modes and aims of communication are similar), a genetic link can be postulated more easily.

In the case of literature, such a concept of similarity appropriately leaves considerable space to the inventiveness and originality of individual artists. Because the 'context of situation' and the 'participation framework' did not fundamentally change between the tragedies of Aeschylus and those of Euripides, they are rightly regarded as representatives of one and the same genre, in spite of all the divergences on the formal (linguistic) and the ideological level. On the other hand, from this perspective it is problematic to see in New Comedy a direct continuation of Old Comedy. Even if we disregard the different appearance in linguistic and formal matters (for instance the loss of structural elements like the parabasis, the elimination of metrical variety, and the reduction of stylistic heterogeneity), we must admit a crucial remodelling of the participation framework. If we apply Goffman's terminology (1981: 124–57; cf. Duranti 1997: 295–307), the *demos*, for instance, is both 'principal' and 'ratified primary recipient' in Old Comedy: it is both the institution whose views are (meant to be) represented and the audience which is aimed at by the comic poet who acts as 'author' on behalf of the *demos*. In New Comedy the *demos* loses its role as principal; this automatically affects the authorial role of the comic poet, who withdraws from the language and world of his plays (Dobrov 1995*a*). It may be that the participation framework of Doric comedy presented greater similarities to that of Middle or New Comedy, but it is impossible to prove this (old) view (to which we shall come back later).

§6. Comedy and linguistic anthropology. An anthropological and often also typological approach to tragic discourse has become quite common over the past few years (cf. e.g. Dover 1979 on 'song-language'; Goldhill 1997 defines tragic language as a combination of a literary, a ritual, a political, and a rhetorical linguistic code) and it seems that a similar development is now taking place in research on comedy. Like Rosen (1988), Degani (1993; cf. Degani 1987: 37–8) pays attention mainly to microstructural and formal similarities such as scatology, metaphor, and especially parody when he sees Hipponax as a precursor of Old Comedy (cf. *Lee 1993; also M. Treu 1999: 79–105 on the forms of *ψόγος* in the choral parts of comedy). Henderson (1990; cf. Henderson 1998), on the other hand, gives a broad outline of the participation framework of comedy within the *polis* as he argues that the comic poet's voice (or at least one of his voices: Carey 1994: 80–2) acts as the voice of the *demos*, but Henderson does not stress the 'demotic' aspects of the linguistic mode and form. A first step towards intertwining the two threads of form and framework is made by Goldhill (1991: 167–222), for whom the carnivalesque poet's voice is closely linked to the mode of parody.

Anthropological considerations have played a crucial role in determining the function of one major linguistic layer in Old Comedy: obscenity and *aischrologia*. The reference work for this area is Henderson (1991), which is also of great practical value because it lists and groups all the relevant lexical items. More recently McClure (1999: 215–18) has raised anthropological objections against the theory that comic *aischrologia* reflects the ritual origins of comedy; she points out that ritual *aischrologia* is a female verbal genre, whereas comedy is essentially male. Nevertheless, it seems clear that comic freedom of speech had a special status in the democratic organization of classical Athens precisely because it belonged closely together with ritual or festive (Dionysiac) celebrations (Halliwell 1991: 66–70).

If Bowie is correct in suggesting that the partial similarity between iambus and comedy, especially with respect to their lexical material, results from an independent crossing of narrative and abuse, we may ask in how far the resulting mixture is culture-specific. When we take the abusive lexicon, it is obvious that it belongs to one particular historical society, but is it equally obvious that its basic constituents are similarly restricted? Or are there areas of the lexicon which are exploited for verbal abuse in most, if not all, cultures and societies? Relatively little cross-cultural sociolinguistic research on the constitution of lexical fields has been done so far and the diachronic perspective with which **Kenneth Dover** takes up one aspect of this huge complex is particularly exciting because the gap between ancient Greek society and our modern industrialized societies is both chronologically and culturally large enough to exclude extensive interdependence.

Dover first establishes what range of evaluative strategies is found in Greek comedy and then concentrates on explicit lexical evaluation in comedy. With his discussion of various evaluative words he further elaborates some of the observations made in his work on Greek popular morality (Dover 1974). Perhaps the most interesting point to be learnt from the peculiar composition of the comic evaluative vocabulary is the fact that negative evaluation through the metaphoric application of sexual and scatological words is conspicuously absent (the only exception to this 'rule' being the occasional use of lexical items referring to oral and anal sex). The absence of this group of words—Dover speaks of a 'semantic niche'—is all the more striking if we compare their importance in modern negative evaluation.

Since comedy does use both basic and 'deviant' (i.e. oral or anal) obscenity in a non-metaphorical way and since oral and anal obscenity *is* used metaphorically, it is difficult to find a straightforward explanation. *If* it is legitimate to speak of a linguistic taboo in this case, one is reminded of Henderson's (perhaps slightly exaggerated) claim (1991: 4–5) that in ancient Greece language was never regarded as 'obscene' by itself. Words were taboo (i.e. they should be kept to oneself) only if they referred to taboo actions, domains of life that would or should not be exposed to the public. In our modern societies (as in ancient Rome), on the other hand, language as such can be taboo so that it is possible to speak without obscenity about taboo actions and also, at least in theory, to speak in an obscene manner about actions that are not taboo. In this sense there was a narrower link between language taboo and action taboo in ancient Greek society. Because negative evaluation typically seeks the strongest possible form, it would naturally turn to those areas where the action taboo is strongest: oral and anal sexual practice.

§7. Obscenity, vulgarity, and terms of abuse (Aristophanes). There is a large literature on obscene words and expressions in comedy, but the obvious starting-point is the 'lexicon' in Henderson (1991; cf. *Marston 1973, Komornicka 1981). Opelt (1975) on terms of abuse in Lysias also contains Aristophanic material and supplements *G. Hoffmann (1892) and especially A. Müller (1913), where comic terms of abuse are listed under headings such as 'external appearance', 'lack of intellect', 'animal names', etc. (cf. also Fraenkel 1963 on a 'rhetorical' form of abuse, Moulton 1979 on 'lyrics of abuse', and Brzóstkowska 1983 on the abusive use of slavery terminology).

The fascination of the lower ranges of the comic lexicon is revealed by the amount of literature written on simple words such as *βινεῖν* 'to fuck' (Collard 1979, Sommerstein 1980*b*, Baldwin 1981, Jocelyn 1980*a*, Bain 1991*a*; cf. further Pascucci 1959, Jocelyn 1980*b*, Bain 1991*b*). In many cases it seems as if it depended on the 'imagination' of modern scholars whether an expression is really 'dirty' or not (cf. e.g. the discussions on *μέγας* by Calder 1970 and 1971, Marcovich 1971, and Stone 1978, on the famous *ληκύθιον ἀπώλεσεν* 'he lost his flask' by Whitman 1969, Griffith 1970, Henderson 1972, Snell 1979, G. Anderson 1981, Beck 1982, Robertson 1982, Bain 1985, Nieddu 1989, and Borthwick 1993, or on *κῳδάριον* 'fleece' by Penella 1973 and 1974 and Henderson 1974*a*; on other 'hidden' obscenities see e.g. Dickerson 1974, Henderson 1973, 1974*b*, A. M. Wilson 1974, Ruck 1975, McLeish 1977, Perpillou 1984*a*, Di Marco 1987, E. L. Bowie 1990).

De Wit-Tak (1968; cf. de Wit-Tak 1967) underlines that obscenity is not just a traditional ingredient in comedy but can acquire a dramatic function either in the intrigue (e.g. when a character wants to be aggressive) or as a means of characterization. A. T. Edwards (1991) even regards scatology as part of the 'poetics' of comedy.

§8. Vulgarity in other comic authors. The ancient opinion, promoted by Aristophanes himself (Bremer 1993: 144–9) and reflected in Platonius, that Aristophanes reduced the amount of vulgarity (*φορτικόν*) and that his language—like that of the 'charming' (*χαρίεις*) Eupolis (cf. *Sarati 1996)—was less 'violent' than that of Cratinus is not confirmed by the fragments: Cratinus uses rather less strong words, except in some invectives against homosexuals (Beta 1992; cf. *Pieters 1946, *Farioli 1996; see also Sommerstein 1999 on euphemism in Aristophanic comedy). This may either serve as a reminder that the fragmentary transmission can seriously distort the picture or warn against putting too much trust in critical statements by ancient authors. In later comedy (Menander) obscenities (and other *φορτικά*: e.g. punning without a specific aim) are increasingly rare, though not completely absent (Legrand 1910: 598–613, Katsouris 1975*b*, Cavallero 1994: 90–1).

§9. Non-abusive evaluative terms. Selected non-abusive evaluative terms in Aristophanic comedy have been discussed by Moorhouse (1947: 41–2) on *μικρός* and *ὀλίγος*, by *Freeman (1968) on *καλός*, by J. R. Wilson (1971) on *τάλας*, and by Turasiewicz (1981) on καλός κἀγαθός and (1986) on ἀστεῖος (cf. also Maquieira Rodríguez 1987 on ἀγαθός/κακός vs. χρηστός/πονηρός in Menander). A more comprehensive treatment might be worthwhile and should include certain aspects of word-formation (cf. e.g. Kronasser 1960 and Richardson 1961 on the magnifying prefixes βου- and κολο- in comedy).

§10. Other studies on the comic lexicon. The lexicon of Greek comedy as a whole (as well as that of single plays and epochs: *Jungius 1897, *Selvers 1909, *Guss 1962) deserves more attention not just from the linguist but also from the cultural historian (cf. *Johannes 1963, *Mactoux 1978/9 and 1999, Brzóstkowska 1983, *Zanetto 1999), not least because lexical aspects often enrich the literary interpretation. For instance, Adkins (1970; contested by de Vries 1973) argued that Aristophanes' use of mystery terminology in *Clouds* made Socrates appear as a blasphemous desecrator of mysteries. Others have looked at the use of 'mental' and 'intellectual' words such as νοῦς or φρονεῖν in the same comedy and elsewhere in Aristophanes (Handley 1956, Stewart 1968, Byl 1981; cf. Huart 1973; also J. Ferguson 1979 on δῖνος in *Clouds*).

Because of its peculiar subject-matter, comedy sometimes preserves lexical and idiomatic elements that are hardly or not at all attested elsewhere (cf. Meerwaldt 1928, M. L. West 1970, and Stephanopoulos 1983 on 'baby words', Komornicka 1996 on banquet toasts). Mattingly (1977) correctly points out that vocabulary change may help in the absolute or relative dating of fragments, but his example is unconvincing (πέρυσι in Cratinus).

The issue of semantic niches and linguistic taboos is further complicated by the fact that such empty spaces do not necessarily affect a culture as a whole. Instead, they can be restricted to certain social circumstances or textual environments: particular areas of culture can have their particular taboos. In a wider sense it is possible to speak of a linguistic taboo also when, for instance, we avoid a direct address to the readership in an academic article or when we end a formal letter with 'best regards' rather than 'love'. Such cases show that an anthropological perspective on language often overlaps with register or text linguistics, which concentrate on the 'do's' and 'don't's' of styles and genres. The paper by **Alan Sommerstein** illustrates how such a genre-based approach can enrich the literary interpretation of ancient texts.

Sommerstein starts from the more or less obvious premise that there are linguistic features which are common in comedy but either unknown or at least exceedingly rare in tragedy. In a close analysis of Aeschylus' *Oresteia* he demonstrates that such 'comic' features, which are normally taboo in tragic poetry, begin to appear with some frequency after the slaying of Agamemnon and Kassandra. By using them, Klytaimestra and Aigisthos, who have broken the rules of legitimate marriage, also break the rules of language. Moreover, the violation of linguistic decency is constantly associated with the sphere of the Erinyes, those goddesses who are themselves the prime representatives of all that is taboo in the Greek imagination. The violation of linguistic decency continues throughout the *Oresteia* up to the liberating vote of the Areopagus tribunal, which ends the spell of kinship murder. Thus, 'comic' language does not, as is sometimes believed, function as a dramaturgical means of relief but on the contrary heightens the darkness of crime.

These findings do not only throw an interesting new light on the literary interpretation of Aeschylus. Sommerstein notes that they must also be taken into account in assessing the difficult question of how fragments of satyr plays can be distinguished from fragments of tragedy: the mere occurrence of a comic feature cannot be a decisive argument in favour of satyr drama.

On an even more general level we also need to reconsider the relationship of comedy and tragedy. Even though Sommerstein's 'comic' features are not necessarily exclusive to comedy—they include for example vulgarisms that must have been part of the most informal registers of Attic Greek—the common situational context of tragedy and comedy as dramatic genres performed at the same festival for the same audience suggests that they function as comic (and not just generally vulgar) intruders into tragedy. This is the exact reversal of the intrusion of tragic features into comedy: there, too, the relevant features are rarely exclusive to tragedy and more often shared with other genres of serious poetry, but we perceive them as tragic nevertheless because *on stage* they appear in tragedy only. Just as we speak of 'paratragedy' when comedy makes use of tragic language, we may therefore regard Aeschylus' procedure in the *Oresteia* as an instance of 'paracomedy'. *Mutatis mutandis* the dramatic function of this paracomedy is the same as that of paratragedy: both indirectly strengthen the nature and laws of the respective genre. By breaking the linguistic norms of comedy (i.e. the reproduction of unpretentious everyday language), paratragedy enhances the comicity of comedy. Conversely, paracomedy in the *Oresteia* heightens the tragic tension by breaking the linguistic rules of tragedy.

§11. Paratragic (and paracomic) language. The literature on paratragedy is immense, but there is no systematic linguistic discussion of the phenomenon, which is often elusive because of the absence of a source text (cf. J. Z. Kakridis 1970). However, the excellent monograph by Rau (1967) includes extensive linguistic commentaries on several paratragic passages in Aristophanes. Rau cites earlier literature and especially refers to Mitsdörffer 1954 and Pucci 1961 but regrets the incompleteness of the index of parodic words by *Hope 1906 and the mere listing of parodic passages by Schlesinger 1936 and 1937; see also H. W. Miller 1942 and Sardiello 1983*a* on the function and stylistic effect of tragic vs. comic three-word trimeters, and Komornicka 1967 for a classification of Aristophanic parody. Contrariwise, the use of colloquialisms in the major tragic poets has been treated by Amati (1901), Stevens (1937, 1945, 1976), and M. L. West (1990*b*), but simple colloquialisms must be distinguished from the comic features observed in Sommerstein's paper. Note also that Aristophanes may be unique in his concentration on paratragedy: in Cratinus, for example, para-epic seems more prominent (cf. Silk 2000*b*: 302–6).

§12. Tragic language in Middle and New Comedy. Tragic elements continue to appear in the language of Middle and New Comedy, but their function changes: paratragedy as such disappears, not least because tragedy itself lost its paradigmatic status in fourth-century literature. According to Hurst (1990) tragic language has two almost diametrically opposed functions in Menander: either it marks feelings and situations as 'artificial' and distances the audience from them (for instance in the scene with the fake doctor in *Aspis*, where the tragic artificiality of Daos' language corresponds to the metatheatrical setting: Paduano 1978) or it enhances the emotionality of a given scene and creates greater empathy. In the former function tragic language retains some of its comic potential (cf. Oliva 1968: 51–3; Webster 1974: 56–67), whereas in the latter it is comparable to the use of elevated style in Euripides (Katsouris 1975*a*: 152–6; cf. Zagagi 1995: 51–4). It is quite possible that Menander's technique in this respect is directly influenced by Euripides (cf. Arnott 1986, Nesselrath 1993).

In spite of the preceding remarks on 'paratragedy' and 'paracomedy' it would be an exaggeration to claim that the interaction between tragedy and comedy is exactly balanced. It is true, as Silk (2000*a*: 97) has recently stressed, that comedy does not depend on a serious point of reference such as tragedy more than any other genre does and that the dependence of Aristophanic comedy on tragedy is freely chosen. Nevertheless, Old Comedy (as we have it) is unparalleled in its 'parasitism', which finds its linguistic expression in an extreme stylistic mobility. Unlike other genres, Old Comedy does not know 'differential stability', i.e. it does not restrict linguistic variation to a regular and predictable pattern (Silk 2000*a*: 102–20). For Sommerstein it is possible to interpret the intrusion of comic features in the *Oresteia* precisely because they follow an intrinsic logic that aims at a contrast with the surrounding usual linguistic code of tragedy. But is there a corresponding 'usual linguistic code' of comedy, a level of expression that is unmarked and serves as the background in front of which stylistic mobility can be enacted less randomly? And if so, how is this background style defined? Is it a literary language like that of tragedy or is it simply the language of average Athenian everyday conversation—if such a thing existed at all? From different angles these questions are looked at in both Slings's and my own contribution.

In his paper on figures of speech in Aristophanes **Simon Slings** illustrates some of the problems which arise when we try to separate literary and non-literary language. First, a very large part of our evidence for classical Greek is actually literary evidence. Because there are few ancient texts that do not betray a relatively high degree of (pre-)planning, des Places (1934) suggested a long time ago that we should distinguish between an unmediated 'spoken style' and a pre-planned 'oral style': genres such as Greek comedy would then represent 'oral style' but not 'spoken style'.

Second, in order to avoid circularity in establishing what is purely 'literary' and what is 'oral' at least in such a limited sense, we must operate with an independent point of reference. Slings finds such a point in functional pragmatics, which is based on the axiomatic assumption that it is the principal goal of non-literary language to convey information in a well-structured manner. If we do not object to this axiom and if we further agree that the logical operations of the human mind are not fundamentally different in different places and societies, we may make inferences about the functioning of an ancient language by comparing how modern languages structure information.

Slings argues that a figure of speech such as chiasmus (and similarly anaphora) is a natural (or universal) means to package complex information. As long as it fulfils this primary aim, a chiasmus is therefore not a literary embellishment. If, on the other hand, the information complexity is minor so that the chiasmus is functionally 'unnecessary', the addressee will perceive it as a literary figure. Interestingly, most of the Aristophanic examples of chiasmus and anaphora are not 'justified' by an excessive information complexity. This leads to the conclusion that Aristophanes' style is in this respect more literate than oral. However, it remains imperative to reconstruct the audience response in every single case before we can confidently label any figure of speech as 'literary' (cf. Loepfe 1940: 138–44 and Del Corno 1975: 38–9, who reach similar conclusions for the question of colloquial and poetic hyperbata).

§13. Figures and tropes: metaphors and personifications. The problem of distinguishing the natural or 'automatic' from the conscious literary configuration is even more acute in the case of tropes because a functional approach is less promising with semantic (rather than syntactic) variation. The issue has been carefully discussed by Taillardat (1965: 5–29, elaborating on Taillardat 1961) in his great compendium of Aristophanic imagery. According to Taillardat images are most likely to be original when they are unique and rejuvenate a traditional image (cf. Bonanno 1987) without being either vulgar in tone or part of an entire series of metaphors. Komornicka (1963) adds as criteria for originality the presence of allusions to recent events, social developments (cf. Burelli 1973 on the novelty and frequency of financial images in Aristophanes), or historical figures.

Komornicka (1964; cf. already *Blümner 1891) gives a detailed description of the dramatic and thematic function of metaphors, personifications, and comparisons in each Aristophanic play (cf. in general *Staples 1978, Moulton 1981; Landfester 1967, *Littlefield 1968, and *Scholtz 1997 on the—often erotic—imagery of *Knights*, *Banks 1973 on *Wasps*, Dobrov *1988 and 1997*a* on *Birds*, where Peisetairos gains mastery over metaphorical language). D. Müller (1974) points out that the original metaphors of Aristophanes are often used for parodic purposes rather than because of their intrinsic value as images (e.g. in the portrayals of Agathon and Socrates:

Morenilla-Talens 1988, Nevola 1990/3). Moreover, metaphors are frequently comicized through their material representation on stage (cf. Silk 2000*a*: 121–3). They acquire particular importance as personifications (although personifications as such are a traditional literary styleme and not exclusive to comedy: Lever 1952/3). Newiger (1957) distinguishes 'normal personifications' which concretize an abstract thought or concept (e.g. the figure of Demos in *Knights*) and 'rhetorical personifications' (such as the two Logoi in *Clouds* or Penia in *Plutus*), which teach directly rather than by their mere scenic representation.

§14. Other figures and tropes: comic stylistics. The comic use of figures and tropes other than metaphors and personifications is much less well studied. Both *Kronauer (1954) and Michaël (1981) (with useful lists of examples) include some relevant material in their typologies of Aristophanic humour and verbal play (on which see also Schmid–Staehlin 1929–48: 2.533–4, 4.53–7, Ferrante 1965: 483–9, Diller 1978 with examples from *Acharnians*, *Kloss 2001).

Morenilla-Talens (1987; cf. Morenilla-Talens 1985, *Guido–Filippo 1988) discusses the function of word-responsions and sound-responsions in comic lyrics where they seem to be used in imitation of elevated style. In a wider sense the widespread accumulation technique also belongs to the domain of comic stylistics (see especially Spyropoulos 1974 and also Osmun 1953/4, Ferrari 1996; cf. *Kann 1909, Miller 1944 and 1945*a*, and François 1977 on comic repetitions of lines, phrases, and single words as leitmotifs and key words). *Campagnolo (1991/2) bases his discussion of comic style on the fragments of Eubulus, which foreshadow New Comedy (Argenio 1964).

The language of New Comedy loses the strong metaphorical colouring of earlier comedy. Metaphors appear only as occasional stylistic embellishments (e.g. imprisonment and insanity metaphors to express a state of desperate love: Flury 1968: 20, 86–7), not as essential links between the language and the action of a play. Chiarini (1983) draws a distinction between 'mainly metaphorical authors' such as Aeschylus, Aristophanes, and Plautus and 'mainly metonymical authors' such as Euripides and Menander (but the latter need not stand for all authors of New Comedy: according to *Astorga 1990, Diphilus is closer to Aristophanes). Aristophanes and Plautus are also opposed to Menander by Lilja (1979): they employ animal imagery for more specific characterizing effects (on animal imagery cf. *Ewbank 1980).

Slings' view that comic language can be distinctly literate even in those passages which pretend to reproduce 'pure' orality agrees with my own argument about the position of Aristophanes' unmarked 'background'-style in the system of literary codes in classical Athens (**Andreas Willi**). Various linguistic details of morphology and syntax show that Aristophanes' language is an artificial or literary construct, although a comparison with non-comic data proves the obvious point that this literary language is much closer to spoken Attic than, for instance, the language of tragedy.

However, because comic language is 'artificial' too, its closeness to 'real' Attic must be regarded as a deliberate choice. Since Aristophanic comedy constantly defines itself by contrast to tragedy, its greater linguistic realism contributes to the configuration of comedy as 'trygedy' or anti-tragedy. At a time when poetic realism becomes a desirable quality even in tragedy, the comic mode of expression supports Aristophanes' claim that comedy should replace tragedy as the literary paradigm of the *polis*. This *polis*-centred ideology of comedy is further enhanced by the distinctly local character of comic language (as opposed to all 'serious' poetic genres and to some degree even to Attic prose, which both tend to avoid excessive Atticness).

Once the stylistically unmarked language of comedy is established as a *polis*-code and has defined Athenian identity on a linguistic level, Aristophanes can go a step further by introducing marked styles, which make the comic discourse of identity more complex. The 'politics' of foreign dialect on the Attic stage has recently received due attention in a comprehensive treatment by Colvin (1999; cf. Colvin 2000). Following Anagnostopoulos (1925), Dover (1976), and Halliwell (1990), Colvin has corrected the simplistic view that the Aristophanic passages in Megarian, Boeotian, or Laconian dialect primarily aim at a derision of the linguistic Other (cf. e.g. Janssens 1952).

Instead, the representation of dialects other than Attic belongs to the realistic features of comic dramaturgy. In a short interpretation of *Lysistrata* I argue that Aristophanes not only does not deride the Laconian dialect but that he exploits its cultural connotations as both the language of the enemy and the language of traditional lyric poetry. By gradually shifting from the former to the latter, the linguistic level of the play contributes to the reconciliation plot, which forms its ideological heart. Thus, language helps to establish a wider concept of Athenian identity as part of a unified Greek civilization.

And finally, this panhellenic identity gains additional contours by being contrasted, again both in dramatic action and in language, with the non-Greek world as represented by Persians, Triballians, or Scythians, whose imperfect command of Greek stigmatizes them as true barbarians—though even there we may detect traces of a differentiation between the civilized and the non-civilized barbarian.

Like Slings, I try to integrate a cross-linguistic perspective into my interpretations. Since we often have very few direct clues of how to reconstruct the primary response to the linguistic shape of a comedy, I suggest supplementing them by typological parallels provided by modern sociolinguistic research. My basic contention is that language has contributed to the construction of social identity not only since the time of the nineteenth-century Romantic movement, when it became the prime indicator of national consciousness. Similar ideas were present, though perhaps less emphasized, in ancient Greek thinking and inevitably promoted a culture in which 'the medium became part of the message'.

§15. Foreign dialects and accents. Contributions on non-Attic dialects and the Greek of foreigners in comedy have long been numerous, but most of them have paid little attention to the cultural implications of these styles and concentrated on textual and grammatical rather than on sociolinguistic and literary aspects (Solmsen 1908, Elliott 1914: 207–41, Friedrich 1918, Crönert 1922, Whatmough 1952, *Floyd 1986, Brixhe 1988, Verbaarschot 1988, Morenilla-Talens 1989, Palumbo-Stracca 1991/2, Colvin 1995, Bettarini 1998). It is one of the merits of Colvin's work (1999, 2000) to have broadened the perspective (but cf. already Rosen 1984 and Cassio 1985*a*: 105–15 on the Ionian passages in *Peace*, *Cassio 1998 on dialect-based humour in *Lysistrata*, and E. Hall 1989*b* and Sier 1992 on the role of the barbarian in Aristophanes). Ethnicity and cultural identity are issues that have been addressed by classical scholars only recently (see e.g. Long 1986, E. Hall 1989*a*, J. M. Hall 1997) so that much work remains to be done on the socio-historic place and function of linguistic codes in literature.

§16. Foreign languages. A disproportionate amount of ink has been spilt over the one Persian sentence in Aristophanes' *Acharnians*, but even so the question whether this is real Old Persian or simply a comic imitation of Old Persian sound patterns has not yet been definitely settled (cf. Tolman 1906, Friedrich 1921, Wackernagel 1921, *Lesný 1923, O. Hansen 1956, Dover 1963, Brandenstein 1964, M. L. West 1968, and Schmitt 1984). A curiosity is the suggestion by Margoliouth (1887) that Aristophanes' original was a Sanskrit phrase.

It is obvious that a literary and sociocultural interpretation of linguistic forms like that presented in my paper is possible only if we already possess a wealth of data. In the first place we need some idea of how Athenian people spoke in real life in order to decide where there are divergences from, and similarities with, a transmitted literary style. Since we have no tape recordings, we can only extrapolate this from a comparison of various written sources, one of which is comedy itself (and others include oratory or prose dialogue). Such an extrapolation is a dangerous and difficult task, for we need to decide time and again how much 'value' as evidence for 'real' language we attach to this or that form, syntagm, or idiom.

But even if all the features were already labelled as 'colloquial', 'vulgar', 'high-flown', etc., one problem would remain: that of textual transmission. It is easily forgotten that linguistic work on ancient texts always demands that the linguist should also take on some responsibility as a textual critic. In other words the linguist cannot simply rely on a modern printed text but must be aware of the principles involved in constituting such a text. Of course, in practice this often means to trust the editors' judgements since one cannot always do everything from scratch again.

Nevertheless, a suspicion sometimes remains that we are stuck in a vicious circle. Editors and textual critics constitute a text among other things on the basis of what they know from linguistic handbooks. Those handbooks in turn are not based uniquely on uncorrupted epigraphic evidence but also take into account what is commonly read in literary texts from a given period. Editors who learn from all but the most extensive reference grammars that a potential optative must be accompanied by *ἄν* in fifth-century Attic will have doubts about some isolated occurrences without *ἄν* and feel prompted to change the text. Linguists who come across these editors' texts will then find their opinion confirmed that potential optatives never occur without *ἄν*. Even if they read in the critical apparatus that the manuscripts had no *ἄν* in the passage they are looking at, the editor's emendation will usually look sound enough—and the linguistic rule will find its way into the next grammar as well.

The problem is particularly acute with phonological matters. For reasons of space there are few critical apparatuses that can afford to list all the minor orthographic divergences between the manuscripts of an ancient text. It would therefore be a great help to the linguist who works with literary material if the controversial phenomena were presented more often in a comprehensive manner, as in the paper by **Geoffrey Arnott** on orthographic variation in the fragments of Middle and New Comedy (and, for some points, already in Rosenstrauch 1967: 58–80 and Arnott 2001*a*, 2001*b*).

Arnott's contribution clearly shows how quickly we reach the limits of our knowledge even in a linguistic variety that is as well-represented as Attic Greek. It would be linguistically and culturally most interesting to know exactly how much Koine influence there is in a writer like Menander, but how can we ever form a definitive judgment on the matter if cases like that of *οὐδείς* vs. *οὐθείς* only demonstrate that orthographic developments may be independent of phonetic ones? And this is only the tip of the iceberg: in few literary genres does our evidence (in the form of papyri) reach back almost to the original texts themselves. Thus both editors and linguists may read Arnott's remarks as a healthy reminder: the former of how desirable it is to produce textual apparatus that aim at total completeness even when things look straightforward enough (and when publishers are reluctant to accord more space), and the latter of how uncertain even the most 'obvious' rules and generalizations turn out to be if they are looked at in detail.

§17. Menander and Koine Greek: word-formation and lexicon. Since the summaries of Wilamowitz (1925: 153–61) and Körte (1931)—cf. already *Galante (1914); later Horrocks (1997: 52–5)—the traditional view has been that Menander is essentially a (late) Attic writer and that Koine features are comparatively rare in his comedies. It is unlikely that a comprehensive analysis of the more recent evidence (not least the entire *Dyskolos*) would fundamentally alter the picture, but a new study on the relationship between Menander's language, classical Attic, and Koine Greek nevertheless remains a desideratum.

Much useful material on word-formation in Menander has been compiled by Rosenstrauch (1967), who points out, for instance, that Menander, unlike Koine authors, uses relatively few nouns in -μός (cf. already Rosenstrauch 1964) or adjectives in -ώδης and -ικός. The old adjectival lexicon of Menander by Klaus (1936; supplemented for *Dyskolos* by Brescia 1960) may still be consulted because of its interesting semantic and statistic observations and comparisons with other authors (e.g. that εὐπρεπής and ὡραῖος qualify women but not men, or that 90 per cent of Menander's adjectives are already attested in or before the fifth century). A similar list of Menander's compound verbs was compiled by Giannini–Pallara (1983), who agree that linguistic innovation is limited (cf. further Pascucci 1971, 1972, and Grandolini 1976/7 on *hapax legomena* in the comic fragments).

The view of the ancient Atticist grammarians Phrynichus and Pollux, who condemned Menander's language as impure (whereas Aelius Dionysius was less negative: De Falco 1930), was challenged in an original way by Bruhn (1910) and Durham (1913): both compared Menander's vocabulary with that of some exemplary writers of Attic Greek (e.g. Plato, Thucydides, and Aristophanes: for a list of Aristophanic lines highlighted as 'proper Attic' in the scholia see Rosenkranz 1964) and noted that Menander frequently employs words which are explicitly approved by the Atticists themselves. Durham (1913: 22–102) also showed that with every single lexical group there is a 'good' Attic writer whose usage is *more* Koine-like than that of Menander (e.g. Aristophanes has more adjectives in -ικός). Nevertheless, Durham is able to list more than 300 Menandrean words that are not found in the authors of the Atticist canon (cf. Körte 1929 on ὑπόχρυσος 'gilded' and Boscherini 1959 and Danker 1960/1 on the curious phrase ὀδύνης υἱός; an example of late morphology is οἴκει 'at home', which, *pace* Hamp 1970, can hardly be a fossilized form of the original Proto-Greek locative). The suggestion by Osmun (1954) that most of Menander's 'late' words occur in the dialogue of slaves has been challenged by Krieter-Spiro (1997: 215–16). Conversely, Zini (1938) believed that some figures like Charisios in *Epitrepontes* were characterized by a particularly pure form of Attic.

§18. Menander and Koine Greek: syntax. Menander's syntax has received much less scholarly attention than his vocabulary, probably because syntactic topics tend to be more difficult to handle. The title of *Husquinet 1945 promises a relevant study, but I have not been able to locate a copy of this thesis (which in any case predates the discovery of *Dyskolos*; the later article by Tacho-Godi 1965*b* is almost exclusively concerned with conditional clauses).

Just as the most common prepositions (ἀπό, εἰς, διά, etc.) increase in frequency between Aristophanes and Menander (Kelly 1962*a*; cf. also *Teykowski 1940, Kelly 1962*b*), González Merino (1981/3) observes that the variety of particles and particle combinations is much smaller in Menander than in Aristophanes (so that their meaning becomes less stable: Provolo 1960/1) and that urban Athenians use more particles than other Menandrean characters.

A diachronic comparison of some syntactic issues in Aristophanes and Menander is also found in Poultney (1963), who deals with the gradual (but not complete: Humpers 1922) loss of the dual and the increasing use of the subjunctive after secondary tenses (on the latter cf. also the cautionary remarks by De Falco 1949). On the whole, however, Menander's syntax is not 'Koineized' either (*pace* Ghedini 1944 on the alleged use of ἵνα as a future particle; the comparative construction discussed by Fraenkel 1961 is rare but not necessarily late).

§19. Aristophanes (and Old Comedy): grammatical surveys, syntax, word order. When we turn to Aristophanic grammar, we find a similar patchwork of studies but no comprehensive treatment. In this case older works have not been outdated by substantial new finds. Thus grammatical compilations like those by Sobolewski (1890; cf. *Senger 1888) on prepositional usage and Sobolewski (1891) on subordinate clauses are still extremely useful. Moreover, there are several good surveys on the language of Aristophanes or Old Comedy. Most of these unfortunately focus on morphology, morphosyntax, and word-formation, but leave out more complex fields such as clause syntax: Anagnostopoulos (1925), Hoffmann–Debrunner–Scherer (1969: 116–26), Hiersche (1970: 163–77), López Eire (1986). More detailed information must be collected from the literature on particular grammatical topics (for recent bibliographical details see Meier-Brügger 1992*a*).

A few grammatical contributions focus specifically on comedy or drama in general: see A. R. Anderson (1913) on repudiative questions, Basset (1997) on ἀλλά, Björck (1950) on non-Attic phonology (which can serve as a criterion to distinguish between lyric and recitative verse: Pretagostini 1976*a*), Campbell (1943) on οὐ μή constructions, Hasse (1891) on the dual, Lattimore (1979) on optatives of refusal, Peppler (1933) and Nickau (1993) on verbal aspect, Perpillou (1984*b*) on the pronunciation of αι, A. L. Post (1938) on the imperative, Poultney (1936) and Morris (1960) on case syntax, Prause (1876) on πρίν, Ricca (1989) and Martín de Lucas (1996) on deictic adverbs and adjectives, Walker (1894) and (1906) on 'Doric' futures, *Zaragoza (1964) on the infinitive.

One may particularly highlight the morphological contributions by Lautensach (1896, 1899, 1911, 1912, 1916, 1917, 1918, 1921) with useful statistics on metrically conditioned variants (cf. also *Sachtschal 1908), the observations on particle usage by Duhoux (1997), or the discussion of comic word order by Dover (1985: especially on postponed particles and the positioning of the intensifying adverbs *πάνυ* and *σφόδρα*; cf. (Menander) Loepfe 1940 and Heap 1992, who see word order as a means to express psychological aspects such as emotion and affect, Werner 1969, who underlines the final position of certain words as comic 'coups', Dover 1971, *Baechle 1993).

§20. Aristophanes (and Old Comedy): word formation. Because Aristophanes' originality is most palpable in the field of word-formation, several studies have been devoted to this subject, especially by Peppler, who discussed most of the 'comic' simplicia (Peppler 1910, 1916, 1918, 1921; cf. already Uckermann 1879, later Handley 1953 on *-σις* nouns, P. Chantraine 1962 on *-ικεύομαι*, Goldberg 1976 on *-τήριον*, Mawet 1983). The stylistic and thematic impact of the comic compounds has been treated by Meyer (1923: 119–32) and Ramalho (1952). Bonanno (1972: 54) underlines the frequency of *hapax legomena* and comic compounds in Crates, and Rehrenböck (1987) elucidates certain comic formations in Pherecrates, especially his words for an invented currency in Hades.

§21. Aristophanes and Menander: colloquial language (incl. oaths). According to López Eire (1991, 1993) the development of several features which were later going to characterize Koine Greek originated in the colloquial language portrayed by Aristophanic comedy. The literary isolation of such a stylistic level has stimulated a particular interest in the colloquial aspect of comic language since the time of *Bauck (1880), Lottich (1881), and *Setti (1885). The most comprehensive treatment of colloquial (and predominantly 'oral') linguistic features in Aristophanes (e.g. ellipsis, use of interjections, phonetic simplifications such as crasis, prodelision, etc.) is now found in a recent monograph by López Eire (1996*b*; cf. López Eire 1997*a*, 1998*a*, 1998*b*). For some of the material, however, the presentation by Dittmar (1933), which incorporates and compares material from Menander, is still equally convenient (e.g. exclamations, interjections, ellipsis; cf. also *Schinck 1873 and *Labiano Ilundain 2000 on Aristophanic interjections, Biraud 1991 on exclamatory *οἶος*, Miller 1944/5 on colloquial phrases in Aristophanes, Platnauer 1960 on prodelision, *Bachmann 1961 and *Smith 1992 on ellipsis, Luck 1965 on *ἥν/ἤν* and Macleod 1970 on *νή* in Menander, Heubeck 1970 and Bain 1981 on Menander's calls for assistance). Dittmar shows that Menander's language is much quieter and less emotional (for a similar conclusion based on Menander's vocabulary see Tacho-Godi 1965*a* and 1965*c*).

To the literature on colloquialism one may add various treatments of oaths and formulaic invocations in comedy. In Menander oaths become more frequent when a character is in an emotional state, but the use also depends on the character of the speaker (Feneron 1974 against Wright 1913; cf. Wright *1911, 1912, Secknus 1927: 5–11, *Feneron 1976). Menander may use oaths to reveal hidden feelings or subconscious thoughts (de Kat Eliassen 1975), but the adaptation of the oath to a character never goes as far as with Aristophanes, who invents comic oaths in order to ridicule or stigmatize stage figures (Dillon 1995; cf. also *Pfeiffner 1931, *Blaszczak 1932, *Werres 1936).

In his paper on Doric comedy, **Albio Cassio** too is facing the problem of transmission, though on a much more elemental level. Whereas Attic comedy is surrounded by the most diverse literary genres, all of which are quite well-known to us, the fragments of Epicharmus occupy a virtually empty linguistic, literary, and cultural space—not historically but in the eyes of the modern interpreter. The Doric dialect of fifth-century Syracuse, for instance, is extremely poorly attested outside the Epicharmean fragments (which are scanty enough in themselves). The vexed question of the digamma and the presence of Italic loanwords are just two out of many dialectological issues Cassio takes up and discusses in greater detail.

Moreover, with fragments in Doric the textual transmission is particularly problematic since interferences from scribes with a Koine background created far more serious dialectal distortions than in the case of Attic literature. Stylistic comparisons are therefore fraught with difficulties, but Cassio demonstrates that they are not impossible. His aim is not only to give an outline of Epicharmean grammar but also to assign to Epicharmus the place that is due to him in the linguistic history of Greek literature. Epicharmus' language becomes the key to a complicated tissue of textual layers and styles, which are as subtly manipulated as in the works of any Attic playwright. It is partly a consequence of Greek political history that our view of Greek literature has become Athenocentric, but that must not fool us into believing that literature outside Athens was second-class literature by definition.

Cassio even shows that we must keep an open mind in the old

dispute whether Attic comedy (both as non-Aristophanic Old Comedy and as Middle and New Comedy from Alexis onwards) was influenced by Doric comedy or not. If we do not let ourselves be misled by Aristophanes' apparent obsession with tragedy as his anti-genre but allow for more variety in the intertextual relations between Old Comedy and serious literature, the case for an affiliation between Attic and Doric comedy seems far stronger than for the one (refuted in Bowie's paper) between Attic comedy and Ionic iambus (or even the one between Old and New Comedy as they manifest themselves in the surviving plays). Just like Old Comedy, Doric comedy played with the literary tradition and Epicharmus appears to have been particularly fascinated by Homeric themes and language (and to have locally accommodated the latter). We are tempted to wonder if this intertextuality did not have a more vital cultural function in fifth-century Syracuse than in fifth-century Athens: the danger of losing one's roots must have presented itself as a more serious threat to the Greeks in the far West than to those in the mother country.

§22. Epicharmus: language, style, and literary impact. The first description of Epicharmus' language was given by Lorenz (1864: 148–56) who even ventured to individuate elements of colloquial or vulgar Syracusan although sociolectal classifications of this sort are particularly problematic in such a poorly attested dialect (cf. Francis 1973 on an Epicharmean verbal form whose stylistic level is difficult to assess). In his monograph on Epicharmus, Berk (1964: 42–70) paid special attention to the poet's stylistic devices (antithesis, anaphora, climax, etc.) and to the frequency of proverbial sayings (Epicharmus is already qualified as *γνωμικός* in ancient criticism: cf. Nesselrath 1990: 49–52). Berk, too, recognized a complex structure of intertextual relations (including philosophical allusions, e.g. to Xenophanes, and according to Demand 1971 even to the Sicilian sophist Gorgias).

The importance of Epicharmus in Greek literary history is debated and this debate is also based on linguistic aspects. Thus Wüst (1950) wanted to separate Epicharmus' comedy from Attic Old Comedy among other things because of the absence of an *ἰαμβικὴ ἰδέα*. On the other hand, Kamel (1952; cf. also Gil–Rodríguez Alfageme 1972: 56–9, Rossi 1977) stressed that Epicharmus used the same comic stylemes as the writers of Old Comedy (parody, wordplay, word-coinage, diminutives, significant proper names; cf. Albini 1984, Rodríguez-Noriega Guillén 1992 on compounds) and saw Epicharmus as the true forerunner of both Attic character comedy (Phrynichus) and of mythological comedy (Cratinus). Accordingly the political comedy *à la* Aristophanes and Eupolis would have to be regarded as an ephemeral sideline (cf. also Cassio 1985*c*: 39–43, against François 1978). Such an early link between the comedies of Sicily and Attica would of course lessen the mediating role of the South Italic comic poet Alexis (Olivieri 1939; cf. Gigante 1969), whose influence on Menander seems clear (Gil 1970).

We must keep in mind Cassio's observations on the intertextual relationship between Doric comedy and Homeric epic as well as the parallel intertextual plays of Aristophanic comedy with tragedy in order to become fully aware of the deep linguistic change which comedy undergoes after 400 BC. What happens is not just another replacement of the linguistic antibody (as when Epicharmus' Homer is replaced by Aristophanes' Euripides) but a functional reorientation of the relationship with this antibody.

In his paper on the riddling and dithyrambic language of the cook in Middle Comedy **Gregory Dobrov** points out that Aristophanic paratragedy is not simply turned into paradithyramb. As a genre, dithyramb has no importance for comedy, so that it becomes difficult to speak of parody or even intertextuality. It is only the verbal art of dithyramb which is transferred into comedy and becomes a new 'special effect'. Whereas in Old Comedy virtually every character can have a paratragic line or two, in Middle Comedy dithyrambic style becomes a prerogative of one particular type of speaker: cooks and servants (cf. Nesselrath 1990: 241–66, Dobrov–Urios-Aparisi 1995: 164–73). By speaking in riddles the cook appropriates a verbal genre that 'belongs' to the upper classes who meet at symposia, and by using a dithyrambic medium in the formulation of these riddles he gives his social pretension or *ἀλαζονεία* expression also on a linguistic level. Thus, in the cook's language the poets of Middle Comedy already encode that collapse of social boundaries which is later, in both Greek and Roman New Comedy, institutionalized in the figure of the *servus callidus*.

The fascination of this process lies in the parallelism between the emergence of a character type with a distinctive character language (cf. Arnott 1970: 5–7 on a cook in Alexis) and a changing attitude of comedy towards its literary competitors and their linguistic codes. In this light Dobrov's paper can also be read as an invitation to investigate further whether there might be a link between the spread of continuous linguistic characterization (which is still largely unknown in Old Comedy but reaches an impressive degree of refinement in New Comedy) and the gradual loss of generic parody.

§23. Parody of non-tragic literary styles and parody of special languages. When dithyrambic poetry is parodied in Old Comedy, its linguistic shape is just one of the aspects that are highlighted; it seems that the musical dimension of dithyrambic parody was at least as important as the linguistic one. Moreover, dithyrambic language is not treated as a status symbol but rather as the (misguided) idiolect of derided poetasters who break the rules of traditional *paideia* (cf. in general Zimmermann 1992*b*: 117–28, 1997).

If it were possible to detect in Old Comedy substantial traces of technical languages, their dramatic function as a stylistic 'quarry' from which isolated elements can be borrowed for specific characterizing purposes would not be dissimilar from the use of dithyrambic language in the mouth of cooks in Middle Comedy. However, despite the work of Denniston (1927) and Dover (1992) on the terminology of literary criticism, of *Sens (1991) on juridical language, of *Camacho Maxia (1996) on the nautical lexicon, or of Miller (1945*b*), *Southard (1970), Byl (1990), and Zimmermann (1992*c*) on medical words (cf. Kudlien 1970), it remains doubtful whether a meaningful definition of 'technical languages' allows us to classify these lexical groups as technical.

Only in a wider sense do we find 'special languages', which may also be termed registers or 'styles' (see in general Dover 1970 and 1972: 72–7; note that not every passage with special or poetic words is necessarily parodic: cf. Mastromarco 1987 on the poetic language of the parabasis). Such 'special languages' appear in the parody of prayers and ritual language (cf. Kleinknecht 1937 and 1939, Horn 1970), hymns (Dieterich 1893, Adami 1901, Conti Bizzarro 1998), oracles (*Muecke 1998, Suárez de la Torre 1998), public ceremonies and political oratory (Burckhardt 1924, Haldane 1965, Heath 1997: 231–4; cf. also López Eire 1997*b*), or epic cosmology (Bernabé 1995). Aristophanes' occasional attacks (for instance in *Clouds*) against sophistic language and linguistic research (cf. Rosenstrauch 1961, Delaunois 1986, Noël 1997) as well as his critical attitude towards the art of rhetoric (cf. Murphy 1938, Bonanno 1983, Rothwell 1990, O'Regan 1992) are closely related to these phenomena (see also Pöhlmann 1971, Rosen 1999, and Ruijgh 2001 on the paralinguistic ABC play by Callias). According to the Bakhtinian reading by

Platter (1993; cf. Carrière 1979, Goldhill 1991: 176–88, Möllendorff 1995) the resulting variation in comic language is ultimately destabilizing or carnivalesque since it challenges the 'authority' of the parodied speech genres.

§24. Linguistic characterization: Aristophanes. The absence of continuous linguistic characterization in Old Comedy was first commented upon by Plutarch (*Mor.* 853c-d) and has been treated more systematically by Dover (1976; cf. Silk 1990: 153–4 and 2000*a*: 209–15). Dover stresses that the language of Aristophanes' characters is conditioned by the dramatic context rather than by some kind of 'ethos'. Linguistic continuity is found only with the language of non-Athenians, who speak their own dialects, and with minor stage figures (e.g. dithyrambic poets). Even there, however, it is not possible to speak of complete dramatic realism. (Rather funnily Aristophanes has been praised for his realism in the imitation of animal voices: Horowski 1966; cf. also Haury 1960, Allen 1968, and on the linguistic imitation of thunder and lightning *Pais 1966.)

Del Corno (1997) slightly modifies Dover's remarks by observing that Aristophanes often antithetically opposes the language of two figures (e.g. Philokleon with extravagant images vs. Bdelykleon with a very concrete style; cf. de Wit-Tak 1968: 362–5 on the characterizing use of obscenities). Furthermore, there are occasional indications that a character has a peculiar voice quality or speech defect (Halliwell 1990: 75–7, Vetta 1993: 715–18; Vickers 1989*a* and 1989*b* goes too far when he claims to discover in *Birds* and *Thesmophoriazusae* a hidden layer of meanings based on Alcibiades' lambdacism).

§25. Linguistic characterization: Middle and New Comedy. In New Comedy and its Roman adaptation the picture changes completely (cf. already C. R. Post 1913: 143–4). Characterizing techniques include the recurrence of keywords attached to a figure, the presence of possessive and personal pronouns to indicate selfishness, or the use of oaths and tragic reminiscences. The first entrance of a character is of crucial importance to introduce the specific tone (Webster 1974: 103–10, Katsouris 1975*a*). Sandbach (1970; cf. Brenk 1987 on the language of young lovers, *Grasso 1995 on the language of old men) portrays the styles of Menander's major characters: for example, Gorgias in *Dyskolos* talks stiffly like a book and Onesimos in *Epitrepontes* has a predilection for nouns in -*μός* and adjectives in -*ικός*.

There is a certain difference between the language of cooks in Middle Comedy and linguistic characterization in New Comedy. Menander, at least, tends to create idiolects rather than 'sociolects'

> or group languages (cf. Krieter-Spiro 1997: 201–50), even though these idiolects may be inspired by Theophrastus' psychological character categories (Del Corno 1975: 21–5). However, with well-defined groups such as cooks (see in general Dohm 1964 and Wilkins 2000: 379–414) and doctors (cf. Gigante 1969, *Stepanov 1987; this type originates in Old Comedy: Gil–Rodríguez Alfageme 1972, Rossi 1977) even New Comedy prefers group or type language.
>
> Similarly there are some linguistic characteristics typical of women: e.g. the use of specific oaths, vocabulary items, and forms of address (Bain 1984; cf. Adams 1984). In his three women plays Aristophanes is a forerunner of such gender-linguistic differentiation (Sommerstein 1995; cf. also McClure 1999).

The question of linguistic characterization forms part of a larger complex dealing with the interaction of language and dramatic technique. In the last paper of this collection **René Nünlist** takes up another aspect of this wide field when he describes the dramatic use of 'speech within speech' (i.e. the quotation by one person of the words of another person).

Nünlist's contribution paradigmatically combines a diachronic and a synchronic approach. He starts with a historical review that stretches from Homer down to Hellenistic literature and he then goes on to work out the specific role 'speech within speech' takes on in New Comedy. By distinguishing factual and imagined quoted speech Nünlist is able to show that Menander's usage is closer to that of Euripides than to that of Aristophanes even though the absolute frequency of quoted speech is comparable in all three authors—a conclusion which resembles that reached by Bain (1977: 148) on the basis of the dramatic use of asides.

Since the demarcation of 'speech within speech' passages is gradually deformalized from the fifth century onward, they must have demanded more and more performance skills. The linguistic configuration of drama may thus reflect the growing professionalism of acting (cf. Lamagna 1998). Quoted speech also allowed the dramatist to retain some unity of space and to stage dramaturgically difficult scenes. However, Nünlist argues that such functional explanations do not fully account for the prominence of quoted speech in New Comedy. Apparently quoted speech had become a literary technique which writers began to exploit for its own sake so as to display their artistic virtuosity.

At the same time, one may look at the disappearance of external signals for quoted speech from a theoretical perspective. When all 'disruptive' elements are removed, the narrative becomes smoother. In this sense, the increasing refinement of 'speech within speech' goes hand in hand with a general reinforcement of narrativity, a trend which is observable also, or even more clearly, in other authors of New Comedy (cf. Guido 1983 on Philemon).

We are thus led back to our starting-point: discourse parameters and the concept of a literary history of linguistic forms. Only one of Bowie's two modes of comic discourse managed to survive into New Comedy, but the loss of the abusive mode was amply compensated by the sophistication of its narrative counterpart. Where Old Comedy favoured *paradigmatic* links and focused on linguistic *items* that would establish links to alternative elements of a similar order *outside* the text, New Comedy decided to concentrate on *syntagmatic* links *within* the text and to select those elements that could combine into the ideal linguistic *structure*.

§26. Language and dramatic technique. The recognition by Nünlist and Lamagna (1998) of more complex motivations for 'speech within speech' refines the views of Legrand (1910: 339–40) and Osmun (1952; cf. *Osmun 1953), who saw these passages mainly as a means to achieve greater vividness.

The interaction of language and dramatic technique is observable in various other domains, too. For instance, monologues are further diversified by the use of self-addresses (especially in serious passages) and by imaginary addresses, which add warmth to the expression of the speaker's feelings (Blundell 1980: 65–82; cf. also Swoboda 1971: 63–5). A similar psychological dimension is recognizable in the use of aposiopesis, where silence does not imply a lack of communication but becomes a linguistic act in its own right (Ricotilli 1984).

Often these issues have implications for editorial practice. Asking when we may regard a dramatic utterance as a question, Turner (1980) argues that we should do so as frequently as possible since questions, too, help to avoid monotony and add vivacity.

Emotional scenes traditionally show a high incidence of short paratactic and asyndetic sentences (Zucker 1955). Conversely, the number of asyndeta in prologues is extremely low (Ferrero 1976). Because they must present a large amount of information in a concise form, prologues are in general characterized by greater syntactic complexity and the frequent use of hypotactic structures, or, when 'abstract' divinities are speaking, participial constructions

(Del Corno 1994); on prologue structuring see also Holzberg (1974: 81–6) and for Aristophanes, whose verbal play is concentrated at the opening of the plays, Arnott (1993). Interestingly, more complex sentences are also typical of the first appearance of characters later in the play (Ireland 1981).

Menander's mastery in combining linguistic form and dramatic technique is further visible in his ability to insert sentences into dialogue quite naturally (Waltz 1911) and to adapt the formulaic end of his comedies to individual situations and appropriate characters (Dworacki 1977; cf. Katsouris 1976).

§27. Language, stage directions, and staging practice. Another technical peculiarity of comic language is the integration of important stage directions into the words of the dramatic characters (Taplin 1977*a* after Pretagostini 1976*b*). This may help the audience to imagine scenes whose staging is complex, but it probably also implies that the practical realization of a given scene is unimportant whenever such implicit stage directions are missing (Del Corno 1986). In this way a linguistic analysis of comedy may give clues about staging practices (cf. Petersmann 1971, who wished to support with philological arguments the highly problematic view that the stage door opened outwards).

At the beginning of this introduction we set out from the 'archaic' open text of Old Comedy, which invites an anthropological approach to its form and language (Bowie, Dover) and which, like Doric comedy (Cassio), comes to full life only if we recognize the interplay with different styles and forms of expression (Sommerstein, Willi). This in turn raises questions about the link between the literary code of comedy and its linguistic surroundings in the real world (Slings, Arnott). Almost imperceptibly we are drawn into an atmosphere of dramatic realism in which stage characters begin to appear as individuals (Dobrov), who take it into their own hands to tell, and retell, the comic story as *they* witnessed it (Nünlist).

Have we then reached the point where the comic author takes leave? Yes and no. As web of words—as *text*—his work has become autonomous and will not tolerate his intrusion any longer. But as web of action—as *drama*—all is still his, prepared and tightly held behind the scene. And this is why, before the Dionysia, Menander was not worrying although he had no comedy—or had he?

2

Ionian *Iambos* and Attic *Komoidia*: Father and Daughter, or Just Cousins?

EWEN BOWIE

Sitting comfortably? 'It were a dark and stormy night'. Spot the genre. Anacreon had said, after all, that it would be a dark and stormy night. When he had seen the clouds on the horizon he had not been able to resist quoting his favourite poet Archilochus:[1]

> *Γλαῦχ' ὅρα, βαθὺς γὰρ ἤδη κύμασιν ταράσσεται*
> *πόντος, ἀμφὶ δ' ἄκρα Γυρέων ὀρθὸν ἵσταται νέφος,*
> *σῆμα χειμῶνος, κιχάνει δ' ἐξ ἀελπτίης φόβος.*
>
> (Archilochus fr. 105 W.)

[1] No verdict on Archilochus is stated in the fragments of Anacreon, and although P. A. Rosenmeyer (1992: 21 and 42) draws attention to the Archilochian side of Anacreon she does not follow it up. Anacreon's interest in Archilochus might be argued for on the basis of some apparent echoes: (*a*) Anacreon fr. 346.8–9 (3) *PMG* *δῶρα πάρεστι Πιερίδων* 'there are here the gifts of the Pierian Muses' and Archil. fr. 1.2 W. *Μουσέων ἐρατὸν δῶρον* 'the lovely gift of the Muses'; (*b*) Anacreon fr. 347.1–2 *PMG* *καὶ κόμης, ἥ τοι κατ' ἁβρὸν | ἐσκίαζεν αὐχένα* 'and of your hair, which shaded | your soft neck': compare Archil. fr. 31 W. *ἡ δέ οἱ κόμη | ὤμους κατεσκίαζε καὶ μετάφρενα* 'and her hair | shaded her shoulders and back'; (*c*) Anacreon *iamb.* 5 (spoken by a woman) *κνυζή τις ἤδη καὶ πέπειρα γίνομαι | σὴν διὰ μαργοσύνην* 'Now I am become wrinkled and over-ripe | because of your lust': compare Archil. fr. 196A.26–7 W. *αἰαῖ, πέπειρα, δὶς τόση | ἄν]θος δ' ἀπερρύηκε παρθενήιον | κ]αὶ χάρις ἣ πρὶν ἐπῆν. | κόρον γὰρ οὐκ* ['Ah! She's over-ripe, twice your age, | and her maidenhood's flower has lost its bloom | as has the charm that she once had. | For she did not [. . .] satiety.' Note too that the metre of Anacreon *iamb.* 5 is identical with that of ll. 1 and 2 of the unit used in Archil. fr. 196a, and seems to recur in Anacreon *iamb.* 7. The metre of Archil. fr. 195 (as we know from Hephaestion) was used for whole poems by Anacreon (fr. 394 *PMG*). The metre of Archil. fr. 105 W. (trochaic tetrameters catalectic) is used in Anacreon, *iamb.* frr. 2–4. The polyptoton of Anacreon fr. 359 *PMG* has a precedent only in Archil. fr. 115 W. For terms of abuse in Anacreon cf. fr. 446 *PMG*, and for discussion of the invective against Artemon in fr. 388 *PMG* see C. Brown (1983).

Look Glaucus, the sea is now stirred up with waves
to its depths, and on the Gyraean heights a cloud stands right above them,
the sign of a storm, and from the unexpected comes fear.

Anacreon hadn't even needed to change the vocative. Bathyllus, after all, had fine grey-green eyes.

But despite his forecast, the next morning had dawned bright and clear. So now they were having an easy voyage back to Athens from Amorgos. It had been Anacreon's idea to take the chorusmen to Amorgos, get some contact with the Muse of *iambos* by visiting the cities founded by Semonides—and revisit some of these Samian wines that he had come to like at the court of Polycrates and that were only available in Samos and its colonies on Amorgos. Today's journey reminded him of his first trip in an Athenian penteconter—the one Hipparchus, Peisistratus' son, had sent to evacuate him from Samos when Polycrates was assassinated and things began to turn nasty ([Pl.] *Hipparch.* 228 B–C). That was decades ago, and nowadays Anacreon's hairs were all grey, not just some of them. Hipparchus too had been assassinated, and now the leading families of Athens had established an elaborate system of government which persuaded the *demos* that they were running the place.

This voyage wouldn't have happened otherwise. The new form of Dionysia set up in Athens by Cleisthenes and his friends gave hundreds of citizens a chance to sing a dithyramb in huge male-voice choirs, and one of the dithyramb's aristocratic backers had been attracted by Anacreon's idea—an idea he had had on a Tuesday afternoon the previous July, while ruminating on the lack of punch and zap in the Dionysia. Everybody else thought he had just had the eccentric notion of taking off a men's dithyrambic chorus to get some advanced training in peace and quiet on Naxos, which had some rather special Dionysiac associations: fifty men rowing a penteconter, what else could it be but a dithyrambic chorus going off for rehearsals? But Naxos had not been his real destination. First Paros, and then Amorgos, had been the stop-off points, so that he and his singers could pick up a range of iambic metres, tunes, words, and themes different from the few that had survived to the end of the tyranny in Attica. The Pisistratids hadn't been tolerant of abusive poetry, and though they found the storytelling side of the genre entertaining, *iambos* was now much less vigorous than it had been in Solon's Athens, when even Solon himself had used it regularly.

Well, he might have succeeded, but it was perhaps too early to congratulate himself. What a surprise the Athenians would get when he got back! They'd know something unusual was happening at the Dionysia because of the extra day, but not what that something was. Anacreon had sworn to secrecy all fifty oarsmen and the ship's *aulos*-player, so that they were the only Athenian citizens who knew what speech, song, and dance routines he had trained them to perform (after dividing them into two choruses of twenty-four), or what sort of plot he was going to have the remaining two oarsmen act out with each chorus. Had anybody noticed that two of his oarsmen had done some goat-song acting? A pity he hadn't been able to take one or two more such experienced men without arousing suspicion: as it was the actors, like the *aulos*-player, would have to perform in both dramas. Just as well they had had a bit of experience in these boring dramatic performances they called goat-songs and that had been up and running for a few years. Having only two choruses of twenty-four men competing with each other might also be a bit of a problem, but if the idea caught on he could reasonably hope that more choruses might be trained and allowed to compete next year. Meanwhile there was still the problem of the name: what was he to call them? Bathyllus had suggested *komos*-songs, but Anacreon wondered if Bathyllus was pulling his leg—it seemed too much like the sort of late-night singing Anacreon had become notorious for.

Almost there! The ship was making good time along the coast of Attica, despite the spring swell which occasionally threw it about. Perhaps they could start drinking soon, and sing the Archilochian elegy which an old man living in West Paros had claimed was meant to be sung on a boat (Archil. fr. 4 W.; cf. M. L. West 1974: 11). Anacreon patted his phallus to make sure it was sitting comfortably. It was a big one, and it would be a shame if it came to harm at this stage, after so many successful performances in Amorgos and Paros. He had had it specially made in Amorgos by the best phallus-maker in town, and he was sure he would be able to work in a procession with a phallus-pole to mark his new creation as specially suited to a festival for Dionysus, and perhaps there would even be an opportunity for a short hymn to Dionysus or Phales that might allow him to play around (not for the first time) with mock cult-titles. Meanwhile there was just time for his late afternoon nap before they made land. . . . Zzzz.

Fiction? Well, of course, though all history is reconstruction, and much that is written about both *iambos* and about the development of comedy is also fiction, though it is not always conscious of being such. And as in Old Comedy, there are some serious arguments buried in the admittedly self-indulgent romp. What I now wish to do in a more sober and scholarly genre is to examine how many similarities there are between early *iambos* and comedy, and what sort of case might be made for saying that comedy in any sense developed—or was developed?—out of *iambos* or was significantly influenced by *iambos*.

There are several hypotheses that could be advanced on this question. Either: (1) When Attic comedy developed, late in the sixth or early in the fifth century, one of the genres drawn upon by its creator or creators was Ionian *iambos*. This is the position implied by my *μῦθος* about Anacreon.

Or: (2) Early comedy did not have the sort of political abuse that we find in both Ionian *iambos* and later comedy, but it was brought in by Cratinus from Ionian *iambos* and was retained by his late fifth-century successors. This is a crude statement of Rosen's position (Rosen 1988).

Or: (3) The similarities between Ionian *iambos* and Attic comedy are limited, and those that there are come from a crossing of the abusive and narrative habits of Greeks in many private and public contexts with the political function (in a quite broad sense of political) that each of these two genres acquired.

Any attempt to choose between these positions has to acknowledge the extent of our ignorance. We know very little indeed about Attic comedy before Cratinus. We know rather more about Ionian *iambos*, in the sense that we have quite substantial remains, but it is still debated what sort of performance *iambos* was and what the identifying features of the genre were (M. L. West 1974: 22–39, Carey 1986, Bartol 1993: 61–74). I have recently tried to argue that narrative, in the sense of telling things that one claims have happened or narrates as if they had happened, whether to oneself or to others, is an important generic feature of early *iambos* (E. L. Bowie 2001). My conclusions can be summarized as follows:

Iambos was a form of poetry in which a number of identifying features regularly appeared: narrative, speeches embedded in narrative, ψόγος ('vituperation') either in the narrative frame or in such speeches, self-defence that naturally led to criticism of others, just occasionally reflection or exhortation. Any of these might be addressed to an individual, sometimes to a group. No one of these features needed to be present for a poem to be recognized as (an) *iambos*, and in some metrical types or in some poets certain features may have been commoner than in others, as αἶνοι seem to be commoner in Archilochus' epodes than in his other *iamboi*. With such an *à la carte* menu for the components of an *iambos*, it may not always have been easy for either poet or audience to perceive immediately when existing patterns were being varied.

If my arguments were to be correct, their relevance to this paper's arguments would be to diminish the importance within *iambos* of that element which has most often been seen as linking it closely with comedy, abuse.

Let me turn, then, to a swift and hence very schematic review of the respects in which *iambos* and comedy are similar and are different. Some features I consider may seem very obvious: but the obvious and the elusive have to be taken together in any assessment.

Length

To judge from the earliest complete texts to survive, the *Acharnians* of 425 BC, the *Knights* of 424 BC, and the *Clouds* of 423 BC, comedies in the 420s were expected to run to 1200–1500 lines.[2] Perhaps earlier comedies were shorter, but it is hard to imagine that they were less than, say, 700 lines. *Iamboi* were of such a length as allowed several to be grouped by Hellenistic editors in a single book.[3] Occasionally we have more precise evidence of

[2] Ar. *Ach.* 1232, *Eq.* 1408, *Nub.* 1510: of course it could be claimed that the greater length of *Clouds* is partly due to our (second) version, being a revision (though hardly, as some have thought, a revision not intended for staging).

[3] It is just possible that the first *iambos* of Hipponax and the first book of his *iamboi* were co-extensive, but that is not the inevitable conclusion of citations that are sometimes to the first *iambos* (frr. 2, 3, 6 W., all Tzetzes) and sometimes to the

length. If we consider the trimeters of Archilochus, the eighteen lines of fr. 24 W. are almost certainly a complete poem. Archilochus fr. 23 W. seems likely to have been between twenty-two lines (those on our papyrus) and fifty lines.[4] An erotic narrative (fr. 48 W.) addressed to Glaucus extends to at least thirty lines on the papyrus that by beginning a fresh poem directly underneath gives a vital clue to its length.[5] If we turn to his epodes, 53 lines remain of the first Cologne poem; reconstructions of the lost beginning would add another 30 at the most. The longest trimeter fragment of his rough contemporary Semonides, fr. 7 W., albeit incomplete, is 117 lines. The longest choliambic fragment yet attested of Hipponax, a century later, is barely half that, but the length of the poem from which it comes is indeterminable (Hipponax fr. 104 W.). The military narratives of Archilochus in tetrameters may have been longer: fr. 91 W. was certainly more than forty-six lines, but again how many more we do not know.

A quite different sort of criterion may be worth taking into account. The regular address of *iamboi* to named individuals, sometimes, in Archilochus' case, to the same individuals as those addressed in his elegies,[6] suggests performance in a sympotic context where all or at least most of the participants were expected to take their turn. That could of course allow a performance as long as the longest speech in Plato's *Symposium*, that of Socrates, which occupies about 450 lines in a modern edition; but the others, at 90 to 200 lines, are probably better guides to what might be acceptable. It seems likely (though it cannot be proved) that the longest archaic *iambos* was some way short of the shortest fifth-century comedy.

Audience

I have already touched on audience. No doubt, especially for early comedy, a case could be made for informal performance before a small group. But from the time that it became a formal part of a festival in 486 BC, a larger and in principle *polis*-wide audience

first book of *iamboi* (frr. 2a, 20, 24 W., though in all but the first case the text is uncertain).

[4] For the problems of frr. 23 and 24 W. (which some have taken to constitute a single poem) see Bossi (1990: 88–113).

[5] *P. Oxy*. 2311. Two of these line-beginnings overlap with trimeters quoted by Athenaeus 15.688 C.

[6] Pericles: frr. 13, ?16, 124 W.; Glaucus: frr. 15, 48, 96, 105 W.

must be assumed.[7] By contrast the address of *iamboi* to individuals points, as I have just suggested, to small groups—groups that were either sympotic or so difficult to distinguish from sympotic that it makes little or no difference for this investigation.

Performers and mode of performance

There is nothing in the texts themselves to suggest that more than one person, far less a group organized as a *χορός*, ever performed *iamboi*. Athenaeus, drawing on the third-century BC writer *On Paians*, Semos of Delos, does offer a case of performers called *iamboi* who could be choral:[8]

οἱ αὐτοκάβδαλοι (φησὶ) καλούμενοι ἐστεφανωμένοι κιττῷ σχεδὸν ἐπέραινον ῥήσεις. ὕστερον δὲ ἴαμβοι ὠνομάσθησαν αὐτοί τε καὶ τὰ ποιήματα αὐτῶν.

The so-called 'Improvisers', he says, would simply deliver speeches, garlanded with ivy. And later the name *iamboi* was given both to them and to their poems.

Details in the description of the other performers whom Athenaeus goes on to mention, *ἰθύφαλλοι* and *φαλλοφόροι*, show that their performance was indeed choral. But the *ῥήσεις*, which seem to have been spoken and not sung by the people called *iamboi*, are most easily construed as lines spoken by individual speakers. Even if there were evidence suggesting these *iamboi* to be choral, we would still have no guarantee that the choral nature of the performance described by Semos went back as early as the beginning of the fifth century BC.

In comedy (though again we can only discuss the period when it has become visible) we have a complex mixture of song, recitative, and speech distributed between chorus and actors. Both of these are costumed to distance them from the 'real' world: the actors wear padding and masks, the actors and usually the chorus, at least if male, wear a leather phallus. I don't think there is any convincing evidence for a mask, a phallus, or any other disguising costume being worn by iambic poets or later archaic performers of their *iamboi*. A case can and has been made for some part of some *iamboi* being sung and/or being accompanied by music (Bartol

[7] 'In principle' is an important qualification. For the case against supposing an audience drawn equally from all social and economic sections of the city see Sommerstein (1997), E. L. Bowie (1998: 58–60).

[8] Semos of Delos, *περὶ παιάνων* ap. Athenaeum 14.622A–D = *FGrH* 396 F 24.

1992); and certainly the metrical pattern of epodes involves combination of sometimes diverse metres, though never building up a system of more than three units. This is very far from the great range of metres and presumably music deployed in comedy.

Narrative

There are also, of course, similarities. One of these is the vehement abuse directed against individuals, to which I return later. Given, however, that I have been claiming that telling stories is an important generic mark of *iambos*, I should also note that telling stories (sometimes called λόγοι) of various sorts can be claimed as another similarity between comedy and *iambos* (though of course it is one that links comedy and *iambos* with almost all other literary genres). Of many possible examples I think of the account of Philocleon's diseased behaviour offered by one of his slaves in the *prologos* of *Wasps* (87–135), or of his outrageous behaviour at the symposion (1299–1323): of the marvellous inventions about the unwashed Socrates as *psychagogos* in *Birds* (1553–64) or the similarly unwashed Cleomenes in *Lysistrata* (274–82). Moreover there is at least one type of story that turns up both in Archilochus' *Epodes* and in Philocleon's conduct at the party, viz. αἶνοι, animal fables. To these too I return shortly.

To me the differences so clearly outweigh the similarities that I would conclude that if hypothesis (1) were to be considered at all it would have to be in the very weakest possible version.

Another set of data might, however, shift this conclusion slightly: these are the passages in comedy where the poet has been claimed to make reference to iambographers and *iamboi* in a way which presents him as working in the same tradition. Rosen (1988) has made these claims, and his argument was largely accepted by Degani (1993). I am sceptical. It is clear, on the one hand, that both the names Archilochus and Hipponax and some of their poems were known to some comic poets and presumably to significant portions of their audiences, and that they were associated with expressions of aggression and abuse. Thus in *Lysistrata* 360–1 the phrase ἔκοψεν ὥσπερ Βουπάλου alludes to Hipponax fr. 120 W.[9] Five passages of Aristophanes quote

[9] εἰ νὴ Δί' ἤδη τὰς γνάθους τούτων τις ἢ δὶς ἢ τρὶς | ἔκοψεν ὥσπερ Βουπάλου, φωνὴν ἂν

Archilochus *verbatim* (in Rosen's words).[10] But it is questionable whether any one of these passages shows the comic poet acknowledging any generic debt to *iambos*.

The second of Aristophanes' allusions to Hipponax illustrates the tenuous nature of Rosen's argument:

> *Δι.* Ἄπολλον—ὅς που Δῆλον ἢ Πυθῶν' ἔχεις
> *Ξα.* ἤλγησεν—οὐκ ἤκουσας;
> *Δι.* οὐκ ἔγωγ', ἐπεὶ
> ἴαμβον Ἱππώνακτος ἀνεμιμνῃσκόμην.
>
> (Ar. *Ran.* 659–61)

Dionysus, tortured by Aeacus, roars out in pain Ἄπολλον. Then, wanting to cover up his suspiciously human reaction, he follows it up with a relative clause in ὕμνος κλητικός style so that he can pass off the whole line as a recollection of an *iambos* of Hipponax. There may be a quite sophisticated joke: the scholiast believes rather that the line was by Ananius, and if that is correct (which we have little chance of determining) then Aristophanes foists a mistake of attribution upon Dionysus. But that only slightly affects the main issue. Rosen argues that 'in choosing a line from Hipponax he [Dionysus] intends to explain away his painful outburst on the grounds that a cry of pain would be appropriate when quoting from that poet. This implies, of course, that the audience would immediately associate the Hipponactean *iambos* with poetic contexts that involved personal attack, exclamations of pain and the like.' (Rosen 1988: 16) But, to judge from allusion in *Lysistrata* 360–1 to Hipponax fr. 120 W., Aristophanes was likely to be familiar with lines of Hipponax that had a much more immediate link with the infliction of pain than that which he has Dionysus quote. If the scholiast is to be trusted, the next two lines of Ananius fr. 1 W. continued the ὕμνος κλητικός routine, and if there was any reference to infliction of pain in the poem it was some way away from the line quoted.[11]

οὐκ ἂν εἶχον, *Lys.* 360–1, linked by the *Suda* 1.487.10 Adler (presumably drawing on a Hellenistic or Graeco-Roman commentary) with Hipponax fr. 120 W., for which it is the only source: λάβετέ μεο ταἰμάτια, κόψω Βουπάλου τὸν ὀφθαλμόν.

[10] Rosen (1988: 17): Ar. *Ach.* 118–20, *Pax* 298, *Av.* 869, *Lys.* 1257, *Ran.* 704.

[11] Ἄπολλον, ὅς που Δῆλον ἢ Πυθῶν' ἔχεις | ἢ Νάξον ἢ Μίλητον ἢ θείην Κλάρον, | ἵκεο καθ' ἱρὸν ἢ Σκύθας ἀφίξεαι: Ananius fr. 1 W., quoted by the scholiast on Ar. *Ran.* 659–61. It is possible that shortly after these lines Apollo was requested to inflict violence on a human enemy of the poet (as I would suspect was the case in

The two passages where 'Aristophanes indicates how conscious he was of his iambographic heritage' (Rosen 1988: 24) are *Pax* 43–8 and *Ran.* 416–30, the entrance of the chorus of mystic initiates. I consider the *Frogs* passage first. As Rosen and commentators note, this passage is probably to be linked with the ritual abuse, *γεφυρισμός*, which took place during the annual procession to Eleusis, and a little earlier in *Frogs* the chorus had drawn attention to the ritual activity of abuse itself.[12] Rosen claims 'points of diction reminiscent of the iambos':

> Such iambic diction, combined with the fact that the chorus is reenacting a religious procession that was known to involve abusive *αἰσχρολογία*, suggests that Aristophanes had in mind the connection between the literary iambos and its ritual origins. (Rosen 1988: 25–6)

He goes on to examine the link set up between Eleusinian ritual and comic abuse in the anapaests of *Ran.* 354–71, and concludes:

> The fact, then, that this *ψόγος* employs diction that has its distinct provenance in the literary Ionian iambos implies that this genre is considered an intermediate, 'poetic' step in the development from ritual *ψόγος* to comic *ψόγος*. (Rosen 1988: 28)

As these two passages bring out, Rosen's argument depends heavily on the hypothesis that *iambos* had ritual origins, or at least that Aristophanes and his audience believed that they did. It does not help this argument that the poet seems to make no attempt here to link either comedy or *iambos* with pre-comic and specifically Dionysiac ritual abuse: the ritual abuse to which there seems to be allusion is in the first instance Eleusinian, uttered in the cult not of Dionysus but Demeter.[13] It is true that the metre of the abuse that follows in *Ran.* 385a–394 has been plausibly suggested to be that of 'traditional cult songs' (Dover 1993*a* on

Alcaeus fr. 45 L.–P.): but the absence of violence from the three lines quoted is important.

[12] *χώρει νῦν πᾶς ἀνδρείως | εἰς τοὺς εὐανθεῖς κόλπους | λειμώνων ἐγκρούων | κἀπισκώπτων | καὶ παίζων καὶ χλευάζων* (Ar. *Ran.* 372–5). Rosen does not remind us that the metre of that part of the choral song is (apparently) anapaestic, not a metre characteristic of *iambos*: for the identification of the metre see Dover (1993*a*) on 372–82, concluding 'the label "anapaestic" seems appropriate'.

[13] I say 'in the first instance' because the boundaries are not clearly drawn between terms which fit the chorus' role within the play as Eleusinian initiates and their role in the dramatic competition as a chorus honouring Dionysus. For a sensitive exploration of the problem see Dover (1993*b*) and (1993*a*) on 354–71.

385a, citing Fraenkel 1962: 201–2) and that the iambic metrical system of 416–30 is very similar to that used similarly for personal abuse by Eupolis fr. 99. But for somebody sceptical about the hypothesis that Ionian *iambos* had ritual origins the argument is necessarily weak, and must hinge entirely on the strength of the claim that there is 'diction that has its distinct provenance in the literary Ionian iambos'.[14]

How convincing is this claim? I consider Rosen's examples.

In Hipponax fr. 114a W. †ἔξ τίλλοι τις αὐτοῦ τὴν τράμιν †ὑποργάσαι 'evidently describes the same activity as the obscene phrase "plucking the anus" (πρωκτὸν τίλλειν, 423–4)' (Rosen 1988: 25). So indeed it does. It might also have been noted that the person who quotes this fragment, the doctor and grammarian Erotianus, who was active in the reign of Nero, also found τράμις in Archilochus (fr. 283 W.).[15] It was conjectured by Blaydes that the word was also in Hipponax fr. 51 W., where the manuscripts of Harpocration have τρόπιν and τρόπην (Harpocration s.v. μάλθη, p. 169 Keaney). But all that is common to *iambos* and comedy is reference to the practice and the use of the word τίλλειν. Rosen also notes ν]ενυχμένωι πρωκτῶ[ι (at Hipponax fr. 104.32 W.) but there the anus is not plucked but pierced (presumably by a penis rather than, as might now happen, by a piece of jewellery). If Aristophanes had wanted to allude unambiguously to Hipponax, or to the iambographers, it would have been better to use the rare word τράμιν. As it is there is the disturbing possibility that both the terms πρωκτός (which appears over 30 times in Aristophanes) and τίλλειν (9 times in Aristophanes, to say nothing of a dozen uses of this verb's compounds) are so familiar to members of the Attic audience in various imaginable (and perhaps unimaginable) contexts that they carry no scent of Ionian *iambos* at all.

Rosen's next word is κύσθος. 'κύσθου at 430 also represents a class of obscene words first found in iambographic diction' (Rosen 1988: 26). This is indeed the case. Johannes Tzetzes, commenting on the phrase ἄρτι παρατετιλμέναι in *Ran.* 516, explains that this plucking of hair relates to τὸν δορίαλλον, τὸν μύρτον, τὸν χοῖρον, τὸν κύσθον, καὶ ὅσα τοιαῦτα ὁ Σώφρων καὶ ὁ Ἱππῶναξ καὶ ἕτεροι λέγουσι.

[14] Ritual origins are argued for by West (1974: 22–39). The case against is well made by Carey (1986).

[15] Erotianus *lex. Hippocr.* τ 13 (p. 85.7 Nachmanson) is the source for both fragments.

In his commentary Dover displays a similar degree of scholarly interest in the practice, though of course from a more sophisticated standpoint. It is hard to be sure which term Tzetzes found in which source, but what we can be sure of is that Aristophanes' audience knew it from other passages in earlier plays (Ar. *Ach.* 782, 789; *Lys.* 1158), and, if they knew what it meant there, knew it from some register of their everyday speech. It is not easy to infer that they would associate it with iambographers.

Rosen goes on to say that 'The three puns on the proper names have a similar background.' Aristophanes' three puns here are obscene: *Σεβῖνον* and *τὸν Ἱπποβίνου* (both suggesting *βινῶ*) and *'Αναφλύστιος* (suggesting *ἀναφλᾶν* 'masturbate'; cf. Ar. *Lys.* 1099; Ar. fr. 37; Eupolis fr. 69). However, none of the Archilochian punning names listed by Rosen is obscene. They are: *Πασιφίλη* (fr. 331 W., suggestive perhaps, but far from obscene), *Λεώφιλος* (fr. 115 W.), *'Ερασμονίδης Χαρίλαος* (fr. 168 W.), and *Κηρυκίδης* (fr. 185 W.).[16] Of Hipponax's four allegedly punning names one is suggestive (*Πανδώρη*, fr. 104.48 W.) and two are indeed obscene: *Σάννος* (fr. 118.1 W.) and *Φλυήσιος* (in *τὸν Φλυησίων Ἑρμῆν*, fr. 47.2 W.). The fourth is neither (*Αἰσχυλίδης*, fr. 117.9 W.). I do not think it legitimate to extend the field of similarity to all punning names, whether obscene or not: this would allow us to adduce Homeric names like Thersites, Dolon, and Outis/Metis. That Aristophanes uses obscene punning names, and in particular uses *'Αναφλύστιος*, might conceivably evoke Hipponax's Phlyasios—if we could be sure that this was an invented name. It might also be claimed that the diminutive *Σαννίον* appeared in Eupolis, and might have evoked Hipponax's *Σάννος*.[17] Like the use of some anatomical terms, however, the obscene punning names in comedy seem to constitute a very weak link with *iambos*.

How much can in fact be done with words? As the title 'Words Apart' initially offered for this paper suggested, I had hoped that a major part of it might be devoted to an examination of the lexicon of iambographers and comedians. But this is an area where each yard has to be fought over for remarkably little gain, and a preliminary investigation has suggested a (perhaps) surprising

[16] On the punning names cf. Bonanno (1980: 65–88).

[17] LSJ, following Kock (fr. 440) attribute the word to Eupolis, but the text printed by Kassel–Austin fr. 471 makes it clear that *οὐρά* was the term found by the lexicographers in Eupolis.

lack of coincidence between the two. The greatest similarity is not in details but in the overall range of linguistic registers in each. Two examples illustrate the problem. An obscene use of ἀηδών for the female genitalia was found by Hesychius in Archilochus (fr. 263 W.) and the same sense of ἀηδών may appear in *Birds* and (perhaps) *Frogs*.[18] The obscene sense of ἀηδών has not been identified in any other archaic or classical text. Does it follow that its use in *Birds* may evoke the iambographers? The answer must surely be negative. So too with an even rarer word, not obscene, ἄθηλος 'unweaned'. It is used of a foal in a fragment of Semonides (fr. 5 W.) much quoted by Plutarch, then again of a baby in *Lysistrata* (881). That these are its only attestations constitutes no case for holding that Aristophanes alludes to Semonides. Both words clearly had a use in 'the real world', and that is where Aristophanes and his audiences will have encountered them.

If lexicographical investigation is not likely to help reach a solution, where else can we turn? The second passage where in Rosen's view 'Aristophanes indicates how conscious he was of his iambographic heritage' is *Pax* 43–8:

> οὐκοῦν ἂν ἤδη τῶν θεατῶν τις λέγοι
> νεανίας δοκησίσοφος "τόδε πρᾶγμα τί;
> ὁ κάνθαρος δὲ πρὸς τί;" κᾆτ' αὐτῷ γ' ἀνὴρ
> Ἰωνικός τίς φησι παρακαθήμενος
> "δοκέω μέν, ἐς Κλέωνα τοῦτ' αἰνίσσεται,
> ὡς κεῖνος ἀναιδέως τὴν σπατίλην ἐσθίει."

> So at this point one of the audience might say—
> a would-be-clever young man: 'What is going on here?
> What is the point of the dung-beetle?' And then to him
> there replies an Ionian seated beside him:
> 'It seems to me, this is a riddling reference to Cleon,
> since he shamelessly eats shit.'

Here the slave imagines that an Ionian in the audience suggests that the dung-beetle refers to Cleon, accused of shameless coprophagy. Many suggestions have been made as to why the slave specifies an Ionian.[19] Rosen finds the answer in the link with

[18] Ar. *Av.* 203, 208, 659, 664: Dunbar is canny on the possibility of double entendre at 203 and 208, and does not suggest it at all at 659 and 664; *Ran.* 683. For the Hesychius text see Bossi (1990: 253–6).

[19] As Rosen concedes, Cassio's explanations of the passage, taking the Ionian as an intellectual (Cassio 1981) but also as voicing the likely hostility of an Ionian

iambos. 'If we ask what the connection is between scatological obscenity and Ionia, the answer must be the Ionian iambos.' Rosen's reasons for this conclusion are the source of the beetle in Aesopic fable (as indicated by *Pax* 127–30) and the mention of dung-beetles at Hipponax fr. 92.7–13 W. Unfortunately the context in which Hipponax introduces dung-beetles seems to be a scabrous but non-abusive narrative of an unpleasant ritual, perhaps a cure for impotence, to which the narrator is being subjected by a lady whose oral accomplishments included a command of spoken Lydian.[20] The fact that Archilochus used fables in his *Epodes*, which Rosen goes on to discuss, is not perhaps as telling as he wishes. He points to Philocleon's use of fable in *Wasps* (1259, 1401 ff., 1446 ff.) as evidence of 'a fifth-century awareness of the use of fable for invective' (Rosen 1988: 32), and recently Giuseppe Zanetto (2001) has again examined the use of fable in *iambos* and in comedy to draw similar conclusions, viz. that in its use of fable comedy was looking back to *iambos*.

Once more I am sceptical. There is no doubt that fables were circulating in Greece as early as Hesiod, *Works and Days* (202–12), that they were at an early date associated with Aesop, and that Aesop was associated with Ionian Samos, at least by Herodotus (2.134) and presumably by others. It is also clear that in *Wasps* one, and perhaps the most important, reason for Philocleon telling fables is that they are thought appropriate to a symposium.[21] I would prefer to conclude that the link between the telling of fables by Archilochus (frr. 174, 185 W.) and by Philocleon in *Wasps* goes no further than the sympotic context of each, and that the supposed Ionian origins of Aesop, together with a known Aesopic fable about a dung-beetle, are enough to explain the choice of an Ionian at Ar. *Pax* 43–8.

The case for saying that comic poets were conscious of the importance of *iambos* for comedy is therefore weak. Furthermore, some positive points might be made against it. We have several *parabaseis* in plays of Aristophanes in which the speaker talks about the dramatic poet's career and one that sketches the

subject ally towards Cleon (Cassio 1985*a*: 105–6) are 'compelling', which might be taken to show that Rosen's own interpretation is redundant.

[20] Cf. also Hipponax fr. 78 W., where dung-beetles also figure (l. 12).

[21] Cf. *Vesp*. 1258–60: *ἢ λόγον ἔλεξας αὐτὸς ἀστεῖόν τινα, | Αἰσωπικὸν γελοῖον ἢ Συβαριτικόν, | ὧν ἔμαθες ἐν τῷ ξυμποσίῳ. κᾆτ' ἐς γέλων | τὸ πρᾶγμ' ἔτρεψας . . .*

development of Attic comedy as a whole (Ar. *Eq.* 518–40). Neither there nor in possibly parabatic fragments of other poets do we find hints that *iambos* is perceived as important. Secondly, in the passage of *Poetics* where some similarity between iambographers and comedians is noted, Aristotle never goes beyond noting similarity to claim influence. I regard the passage as significant enough to print in full:

διεσπάσθη δὲ κατὰ τὰ οἰκεῖα ἤθη ἡ ποίησις. οἱ μὲν γὰρ σεμνότεροι τὰς καλὰς ἐμιμοῦντο πράξεις καὶ τὰς τῶν τοιούτων, οἱ δὲ εὐτελέστεροι τὰς τῶν φαύλων, πρῶτον ψόγους ποιοῦντες, ὥσπερ ἕτεροι ὕμνους καὶ ἐγκώμια. τῶν μὲν οὖν πρὸ Ὁμήρου οὐδενὸς ἔχομεν εἰπεῖν τοιοῦτον ποίημα, εἰκὸς δὲ εἶναι πολλούς, ἀπὸ δὲ Ὁμήρου ἀρξαμένοις ἔστιν, οἷον ἐκείνου ὁ Μαργίτης καὶ τὰ τοιαῦτα. ἐν οἷς κατὰ τὸ ἁρμόττον καὶ τὸ ἰαμβεῖον ἦλθε μέτρον—διὸ καὶ ἰαμβεῖον καλεῖται νῦν, ὅτι ἐν τῷ μέτρῳ τούτῳ ἰάμβιζον ἀλλήλους. καὶ ἐγένοντο τῶν παλαιῶν οἱ μὲν ἡρωικῶν οἱ δὲ ἰάμβων ποιηταί. ὥσπερ δὲ καὶ τὰ σπουδαῖα μάλιστα ποιητὴς Ὅμηρος ἦν (μόνος γὰρ οὐχ ὅτι εὖ ἀλλὰ καὶ μιμήσεις δραματικὰς ἐποίησεν), οὕτως καὶ τὸ τῆς κωμῳδίας σχῆμα πρῶτος ὑπέδειξεν, οὐ ψόγον ἀλλὰ τὸ γελοῖον δραματοποιήσας. ὁ γὰρ Μαργίτης ἀνάλογον ἔχει, ὥσπερ Ἰλιὰς καὶ ἡ Ὀδύσσεια πρὸς τὰς τραγῳδίας, οὕτω καὶ οὗτος πρὸς τὰς κωμῳδίας. παραφανείσης δὲ τῆς τραγῳδίας καὶ κωμῳδίας οἱ ἐφ' ἑκάτερον τὴν ποίησιν ὁρμῶντες κατὰ τὴν οἰκείαν φύσιν οἱ μὲν ἀντὶ τῶν ἰάμβων κωμῳδοποιοὶ ἐγένοντο, οἱ δὲ ἀντὶ τῶν ἐπῶν τραγῳδοδιδάσκαλοι . . . (Arist. *Poet.* $1448^{b}24$–$1449^{a}5$)

Poetry split up, according to people's personal characters. For the more dignified imitated noble actions, and the actions of people of that sort, whereas those of lesser quality imitated the actions of low people, first composing vituperations, just as the other group composed hymns and encomia. For no poet before Homer can we point to a poem of this sort, but it is plausible that there were many poets, whereas beginning with Homer we can, such as that poet's *Margites* and poems of that sort. In this stage according to the principle of propriety there also developed the iambic trimeter as a metre—which is why it is in fact now called 'iambic trimeter', because it was in this metre that they used to utter *iamboi* against each other. And of the ancients some became poets of heroic poems and some of *iamboi*. And just as Homer was also pre-eminent as a poet in serious compositions (for he was the only one not simply to compose well but also to compose dramatic imitations) so too he was the first to give a glimpse of the form of comedy, by making a drama of what was laughable and not of vituperation. For just as the *Iliad* and *Odyssey* stand in relation to tragedies, so does the *Margites* to comedies. But when tragedy and comedy came into being the poets were drawn to each of the two types of poetry according to their own personality, and some, instead of composing *iamboi*, became comic poets, while others, instead of composing epic, became tragic playwrights . . .

The way Aristotle formulates the relationship between *iambos* and comedy would be very surprising if he thought there was a case for seeing the one as descended from the other. That he did not is further demonstrated by his total silence on Ionian *iambos* when a couple of sentences later he alludes (admittedly all too briefly) to the origins of Attic comedy in phallic choral performances.[22] When he returns to its early development a page later he takes it that initially comedy had an iambic character (*ἰαμβικὴ ἰδέα*) but no overarching plots (*καθόλου ποιεῖν λόγους καὶ μύθους*) and that these were an innovation of Crates. Again it would have been very easy for him to say explicitly that pre-Crates comedy was a direct descendant of *iamboi*, but instead he limits himself to attribution of an *ἰαμβικὴ ἰδέα*.[23] Finally he draws a distinction a few pages later

[22] Arist. *Poet*. 1449^{a}9–13: *γενομένη ⟨δ'⟩ οὖν ἀπ' ἀρχῆς αὐτοσχεδιαστική, καὶ αὐτὴ* (sc. tragedy) *καὶ ἡ κωμῳδία, καὶ ἡ μὲν ἀπὸ τῶν ἐξαρχόντων τὸν διθύραμβον, ἡ δὲ ἀπὸ τῶν τὰ φαλλικὰ ἃ ἔτι καὶ νῦν ἐν πολλαῖς τῶν πόλεων διαμένει νομιζόμενα. . . .* ‘Although it was to begin with a matter of improvisation, both tragedy itself and comedy, the one developing from those who led the singing of the dithyramb, and the other from those who led the singing of the phallic songs which even now are still performed in many cities . . .’.

[23] Arist. *Poet*. 1449^{a}37–^{b}9: *ἡ δὲ κωμῳδία διὰ τὸ μὴ σπουδάζεσθαι ἐξ ἀρχῆς ἔλαθεν. καὶ γὰρ χορὸν κωμῳδῶν ὀψέ ποτε ὁ ἄρχων ἔδωκεν, ἀλλ' ἐθελονταὶ ἦσαν. ἤδη δὲ σχήματά τινα αὐτῆς ἐχούσης οἱ λεγόμενοι αὐτῆς ποιηταὶ μνημονεύονται. τίς δὲ πρόσωπα ἀπέδωκεν ἢ προλόγους ἢ πλήθη ὑποκριτῶν καὶ ὅσα τοιαῦτα, ἠγνόηται. τὸ δὲ μύθους ποιεῖν [Ἐπίχαρμος καὶ Φόρμις] τὸ μὲν ἐξ ἀρχῆς ἐκ Σικελίας ἦλθε, τῶν δὲ Ἀθήνησιν Κράτης πρῶτος ἦρξεν ἀφέμενος τῆς ἰαμβικῆς ἰδέας καθόλου ποιεῖν λόγους καὶ μύθους.* ‘(The development of) comedy has remained obscure, in consequence of its not having been treated seriously from its beginnings. For in fact it was only very late that the *archon* granted a *choros* of comic performers, but they had been volunteers. And it is only when comedy already had some of its features that there is a tradition of those who are said to have been its poets. But who gave it its masks, or prologues, or the numbers of actors, and so on, this has ceased to be known. But as for writing plots [Epicharmus and Phormis], this originally came from Sicily, and of the poets in Athens Crates was first to abandon the iambic character and construct overarching stories and plots.’ Degani (1993: 5), like Rosen, may go too far in denying abusive comedy to Crates on the basis of this very sketchy point made by Aristotle. Crates fr. 15 (from the *Heroes*, according to Pollux 10.175) *ῥιπίδι κοπραγωγῷ*, ‘a dung-bearing fan’, has the scatological flavour that Rosen associates with Ionian *iambos* (though neither context nor chronology allows it to be claimed with any confidence as an example of pre-Cratinian political abuse). For other material in Crates that might be claimed (though in my view unconvincingly) to be similar to that of Ionian *iambos* cf. the possible farting Lamia of fr. 20. Closer to Aristophanic comedy than suggested by Degani is also the sexual play at fr. 43: *πάνυ γάρ ἐστιν ὡρικὰ | τὰ τιτθί' ὥσπερ μῆλα καὶ μιμαίκυλα* ‘for her tits are nicely developed, like apples and arbutus-fruits’ (perhaps describing a female character in a play) and at

between comedy's use of a plot with fictitious names by contrast with the iambographers' compositions concerned what happened to individuals.[24] Once more he writes as if the two genres had related features rather than the one being descended from or strongly influenced by the other.

This is a suitable point to return to the second of the hypotheses that I initially offered as possible explanations of the phenomena, i.e. that early comedy did not have the sort of political abuse that we find in both Ionian *iambos* and later comedy, but it was brought in by Cratinus from Ionian *iambos* and was retained by his late fifth-century successors—a thesis developed in a chapter of Rosen's book (Rosen 1988: 37–58, 'Cratinus'). That hypothesis seems to be completely at variance with the view of Aristotle just quoted that comedy up to Crates had an ἰαμβικὴ ἰδέα, and some of the points I have made above also count against its plausibility. I do not attempt to demolish it in detail here, not least because, as so often, we lack hard evidence: the ascription of the introduction of political abuse to Cratinus, although suggested by other ancient accounts of comedy,[25] cannot adequately be tested by our surviving material, because we can only guess whether his predecessors did or did

fr. 27 (possibly aimed at a real Athenian woman, or rather at her husband): παί|ζει δ' ἐν ἀνδρικοῖς χοροῖσι | τὴν κυνητίνδ' ὥσπερ εἰκός, | τοὺς καλοὺς φιλοῦσα 'she plays the kissing-game among the men's choruses, as you might expect, kissing the handsome young men'.

[24] Arist. *Poet.* 1451^{b}11–15: ἐπὶ μὲν οὖν τῆς κωμῳδίας ἤδη τοῦτο δῆλον γέγονεν. συστήσαντες γὰρ τὸν μῦθον διὰ τῶν εἰκότων οὕτω τὰ τυχόντα ὀνόματα ὑποτιθέασιν καὶ οὐχ ὥσπερ οἱ ἰαμβοποιοὶ περὶ τῶν καθ' ἕκαστον ποιοῦσιν. 'Now in the case of comedy this is immediately clear. For constructing their plot on the basis of the plausible they then attach random names, and do not, like the iambic poets, compose about what happened to an individual.'

[25] Two different claims need to be distinguished: (1) that of Platonius, *Diff. char.* (*Prolegomena de com.* II, 1, p. 6 Koster = Perusino (1989), 38.1–2 = Cratinus test. 17) that Cratinus emulated Archilochus in the harshness of his abuse: *Κρατῖνος* ὁ τῆς παλαιᾶς κωμῳδίας ποιητής, ἅτε δὴ κατὰ τὰς Ἀρχιλόχου ζηλώσεις, αὐστηρὸς μὲν ταῖς λοιδορίαις ἐστίν (for the problem of ζηλώσεις and a different text cf. Degani 1993: 16 n. 33, with the further literature he cites there); (2) that of Anon. *de com.* (*Prolegomena de com.* V, p. 14 Koster = Cratinus test. 19) that Cratinus (among other innovations) 'attached usefulness to the charm of comedy by lambasting malefactors and punishing them by comedy as if by a public whip': ἐπιγενόμενος δὲ ὁ Κρατῖνος . . . καὶ τῷ χαρίεντι τῆς κωμῳδίας τὸ ὠφέλιμον προσετέθεικε τοὺς κακῶς πράττοντας διαβάλλων καὶ ὥσπερ δημοσίᾳ μάστιγι τῇ κωμῳδίᾳ κολάζων . . . Combined, these claims would constitute an ancient view that Cratinus' Archilochian abuse was an innovation, but it is important to recall that they are not combined in our sources.

not have it, or how serious it was if they did.[26] It cannot be doubted that political abuse did play an important part in the comedies of Cratinus himself, and that in his *Archilochoi* it was very probably linked by Cratinus with Archilochus.[27] What Rosen, despite his claims, has not demonstrated is that Cratinus or any contemporary saw his plays as the first comedies to exploit vigorous political abuse, or that 'Cratinus was inspired by specific points of diction associated with iambographic invective'.[28]

That leaves me with my third possible hypothesis. The similarities between Ionian *iambos* and Attic comedy are limited, and those that there are come from a crossing of the abusive and narrative habits of Greeks in many private and public contexts with the political function that each of these two genres acquired. That seems to me better to explain the phenomena than any other hypothesis.

Anacreon suddenly woke up. Some noise had abruptly stopped. He began to recall his dreams. Birds, wasps, dung-beetles, gadflies, horsemen, women in assembly, priestesses. Not dreams, nightmares. Thank God he was awake again. He turned to his fellow-oarsman, Magnes, whose parents had given him that name in honour of Anacreon's prayer to Magnesian Artemis that they liked so much (Anacreon fr. 348 *PMG*). 'Come on, Magnes, let's go over that question-and-answer routine again, and then have some wine.'

[26] See, however, n. 23.

[27] This is on the whole well argued by Rosen (1988: 37–58).

[28] Rosen (1988: 47); iambographic diction is again the object of unsubstantiated claims at pp. 55 and 57.

3

The Language of Doric Comedy

ALBIO C. CASSIO

1. The study of Doric comedy is a risky enterprise, and much more difficult than the study of its Attic counterpart. The fragmentary state of the texts we possess never allows us to recover the plot of a play; nor have the papyri improved the situation significantly in this respect, as they are often too badly damaged to yield a coherent meaning. And there is more. Although we may regret the loss of complete plays of, say, Eupolis, in most cases we can easily put his fragments in a frame, as it were: we know in more or less detail the history of the period, we know what Attic tragedy and comedy were like, we are well informed about political and philosophical debates, state administration, and religious practice in contemporary Athens; we also possess a remarkable number of Attic inscriptions and we know the Attic dialect well—at least to the extent to which a dialect is recoverable from written sources.

By contrast, we know very little of the Sicilian, and especially Syracusan, environment in which Epicharmus, his colleague Phormis, and his pupil Deinolochus were active; as a consequence their fragments, along with those of the mimographer Sophron, are one of our main sources—often our only source—for social life, religion, and language in Syracuse between the late sixth and the fifth century BC. The information provided by inscriptions is minimal: those in verse or prose found in Syracuse and her sub-colonies, as well as in Greece proper, from the earliest times to Hieron's death in 466 BC amount to about 28.[1] The comparison with Athens is devastating: for the same period

[1] The texts of the Camarina archive (Cordano 1992) belong to a period later than 461 BC.

the verse dedications on the Athenian acropolis alone number about 94.[2]

Doric comedy is a colonial phenomenon. Doric comic traditions were imported into Sicily, where a number of decisive developments took place, also prompted by contacts with indigenous cultures and other Greek-speaking colonies in the West. At some point western comedy began to influence Attic comedy, as Aristotle tells us clearly.[3] Many scholars have maintained that the influence of Epicharmus on Attic comedy was minimal,[4] but on the one hand it is hard to sweep Aristotle's statement under the carpet,[5] and on the other hand we have no idea of what a complete Doric comedy looked like, and consequently any modern opinion on the matter is founded on sand. Copies of Epicharmus must have been available, and well known, outside Sicily in the fourth century BC: he is quoted seven times by Aristotle,[6] and Plato in the *Theaetetus*[7] values him as highly in the field of comedy as Homer in that of 'tragedy'—an opinion which would have sounded absurd if Epicharmus had been practically unknown at Athens. The general pattern of this colonial success reminds one of the history of Pythagoreanism: its origins are traceable to East Ionia, but the decisive developments took place in Magna Graecia, and it was in this 'westernized' form that the doctrine moved back to Greece proper and to the rest of the Hellenic world.

As Phormis and Deinolochus are represented by only a handful of fragments, in this paper I will mainly concentrate on Epicharmus. He may have been born about 530 BC (Handley 1985: 367 n. 5) either at Megara Hyblaea or at Krastos, a Sikanian town,[8] and apparently moved to Syracuse about 486 (Schmid-Staehlin

[2] The Syracusan inscriptions can be found in Dubois (1989: 89–141); for the verse dedications on the Acropolis see P. A. Hansen (1983: 99–157).

[3] Arist. *Poet.* 1449[b]6 ff. (Epich. test. 5 = Phormis test. 2) *τὸ δὲ μύθους ποιεῖν [Ἐπίχαρμος καὶ Φόρμις] τὸ μὲν ἐξ ἀρχῆς ἐκ Σικελίας ἦλθε, τῶν δὲ Ἀθήνησι Κράτης πρῶτος ἦρξεν ἀφέμενος τῆς ἰαμβικῆς ἰδέας καθόλου ποιεῖν λόγους καὶ μύθους.*

[4] See Arnott (1996*b*: 471) with previous bibliography.

[5] Lucas (1968: 91) rightly comments on *ἐκ Σικελίας ἦλθε* etc. 'this implies direct influence of Syracusan on Attic comedy'; see Cassio (1985*c*: 39–43).

[6] Arist. *Eth. Nic.* 1167[b]25; *Gen. an.* 724[a]28; *Metaph.* 1010[a]6, 1086[a]17; *Poet.* 1448[a]33; *Rh.* 1365[a]16, 1410[b]4. At *Poet.* 1449[b]6 (= Epich. test. 5) the words *Ἐπίχαρμος καὶ Φόρμις* are commonly regarded as spurious.

[7] Pl. *Tht.* 152E *καὶ τῶν ποιητῶν οἱ ἄκροι τῆς ποιήσεως ἑκατέρας, κωμῳδίας μὲν Ἐπίχαρμος, τραγῳδίας δὲ Ὅμηρος* (= Epich. test. 3 in Kassel–Austin 2001: 9).

[8] See Epich. test. 1. The location of Krastos is unknown. The birth on Kos may be an invention made on the basis of the initial assonance of *Κῶς* and *κωμῳδία*.

1929–48: 1.638–9); for us, he 'comes most clearly into focus as a comic writer in the Syracuse of Hieron I in the 470s' (Handley 1985: 367; see also Arnson Svarlien 1990/1). A detailed discussion of his role in the development of Greek comedy and Greek culture at large would take too much space; I will only recall that we possess some long and important fragments containing philosophical discussions (Pickard-Cambridge 1962: 247–55). Most of them were originally set in a comic frame,[9] but Aristotle clearly regarded some of the arguments used there as serious and worth mentioning;[10] their language was obviously influenced by the Ionic tradition of philosophy and philosophical poetry. It is hard to say whether Epicharmus was an original thinker or not, but his role as a popularizer of philosophical themes must have been remarkable, and he certainly deserves the twenty pages granted him by Diels–Kranz (1951/2); it is a pity that he disappeared from Kirk–Raven–Schofield (1983). He was fairly soon turned into a Pythagorean (Burkert 1972: 289 n. 58); a number of forgeries of philosophical, medical, and rhetorical content were circulated under his name in late classical and Hellenistic times, and even obscured the fame of the authentic plays (Pickard-Cambridge 1962: 239–47; Turner 1976). Their success is made clear by their surfacing in many Ptolemaic papyri[11] and by such works as Ennius' *Epicharmus*.

A detailed discussion of the linguistic features of Doric comedy (phonology, morphology, vocabulary, and syntax) will obviously require a whole book. In what follows I shall try to give an idea of the main problems posed by this remarkable literary language and discuss a number of points of detail that are interesting in themselves and may help to clarify some general issues. The numbers in round brackets refer to fragments of Epicharmus unless otherwise stated.

2. If we attempt to explore the nature of an ancient literary language based on a local dialect we must obviously form an opinion of what the latter was like. This is very difficult on many counts, because no local dialect has ever been a monolith; imports

[9] See e.g. Epich. fr. 275 and 276 (which I regard as genuine, see §3).

[10] Arist. *Metaph.* 1010^{a}5–7 (= Epich. fr. 143) *διὸ εἰκότως μὲν λέγουσιν, οὐκ ἀληθῆ δὲ λέγουσιν (οὕτω γὰρ ἁρμόττει μᾶλλον εἰπεῖν ἢ ὥσπερ Ἐπίχαρμος εἰς Ξενοφάνην).* See Pickard-Cambridge (1962: 244).

[11] See e.g. [Epich.] fr. 244, 245, 295.

from other dialects or even foreign languages have always been the order of the day, especially in colonial milieux.

Epicharmus' dialect has been described more than once in more or less detail.[12] For example, Pickard-Cambridge (1962: 283) following Bechtel (1923: 213, 268) regards it as a literary version of the Syracusan dialect, with an admixture of Rhodian dialect and Italic forms. This is acceptable as far as it goes, but there are several points to be considered. To begin with, Epicharmus was probably not a Syracusan by birth but a native of either Megara Hyblaea or Krastos, a Sikanian town (see §1), which means that non-Syracusan features in his language may be more numerous than we suspect. 'Italic' words (see §8 and §9) were certainly used in the Syracusan dialect, but many of them must have integrated into the dialect at an early stage to such a degree that they were no longer perceived as 'foreign'. Moreover some Ionic features may have already entered the dialect at high sociolinguistic levels (see §3).

The idea of the admixture of Rhodian dialect goes back to Ahrens (1843: 407) and has gained widespread acceptance.[13] It was based on the athematic infinitives in -*μειν* (e. g. *εἴμειν* 97.8), which are very frequently encountered in Epicharmus' text. We are told by Herodotus (7.156) that many inhabitants of Sicilian towns, among them the Geloans, were deported to Syracuse by Gelon in 485; since part of the original population of Gela was Rhodian, and -*μειν* infinitives are current in the Rhodian dialect (Buck 1955: §154.5), Ahrens thought that Epicharmus was influenced by this Rhodian element of the Geloan dialect. Now, since Epicharmus may have already been active as a playwright 'at a date before 500 BC' (Handley 1985: 367), and since the Geloan influence is conceivable only after 485 BC, on this theory every play featuring *εἴμειν*, *θέμειν*, and the like would automatically be later than 485 BC. It should be recalled, however, that -*μειν* is a banal innovation due to the influence of the thematic -*ειν* infinitives (like *φέρειν*, *λέγειν*) on the Doric athematic ending -*μεν* (Buck 1955: §154.5*a*); this means that *εἴμειν*, *θέμειν*, and the like may have originated independently in those Doric dialects whose thematic

[12] Schmid-Staehlin (1929–48: 1.648); Pickard-Cambridge (1962: 283); Hoffmann–Debrunner–Scherer (1969: 114–16).

[13] See Bechtel (1923: 213), Schmid–Staehlin (1929–48: 1.648), Hoffmann–Debrunner–Scherer (1969: 116).

infinitives ended in -ειν (not -ην), and may have been current in the Syracusan dialect much earlier than 485 BC. Unfortunately the early epigraphical occurrences of these forms are ambiguous; EMEN in a sixth-century inscription from Syracuse (Dubois 1989: 87) may represent either εἴμειν or εἶμεν. Note that εἶμεν is metrically guaranteed in Epicharmus (276.3).[14]

3. 'Comedy, alone of Greek literary genres, combines all the registers of Greek utterance which are known to us: at one extreme a solemnity evocative of heroic warfare and gorgeous processionals, at the other a vulgarity inadmissible in polite intercourse. The predominant register of dialogue is common to comedy, prose literature and documents; but even comic dialogue is poetry, and the comic poet does not deny himself the freedom of all poets to play with the language' (Dover 1972: 72). In Attic comedy we find widespread use of technical language (medical, administrative, and so on), mainly for humorous effects, and high literary levels, either with an aim at parodying a specific author or passage (Homer, the lyric poets, or the tragedians), or just for humorous elevation of language; we also find vulgar expressions as well as a high number of sheer verbal inventions. Moreover, Aristophanes makes some foreigners speak their own dialect (or non-Greek language), a topic on which we now have Stephen Colvin's valuable book (Colvin 1999).

We have every reason to believe that the same richness and variety obtained in Doric comedy, but here the data are far harder to interpret than those of its Attic counterpart. As I have already said, all we have of Doric comedy are fragments; their number is not impressive (300 including the forgeries; those of Cratinus alone are over 500), they are very short as a rule and frequently consist of isolated glosses in ancient lexica. Moreover, the language of Attic comedy can easily be compared with that of Attic tragedy and Attic prose; but no such thing as Syracusan (or generally Doric) tragedy has ever existed, and fifth-century Doric prose is lost. It did exist in Sicily in Epicharmus' times (Cassio 1989: 143–5): the physician Acron of Acragas wrote in Doric, and Athenaeus quotes a short fragment in Doric allegedly from the *Art of Cookery* by the famous

[14] Which I regard as genuine: see next section.

Syracusan cook Mithaikos,[15] mentioned by Plato in the *Gorgias*.[16] But this is all that we have. As a result, we cannot 'decide what we wish to take as the norm' (Colvin 1999: 22); it is very hard to identify different registers in what can be conventionally described as 'Syracusan dialect', and when we find Ionic phonology or morphology it is often difficult to say whether it was deliberately introduced by Epicharmus as a foreign dialect marker or it had already entered the dialect spoken (and written) by cultivated Syracusans (Schmid-Staehlin 1929–48: 1.648).

Homeric influences are easiest to detect because of the metre and well-known peculiarities in phonology, morphology and vocabulary. Homer is quoted and Epicharmus' comedies must have been interspersed with hexameters of his own making (the problem will be treated in full in §10). The Doric tradition of choral poetry may have been influential, too, although it is difficult to detect allusions to it in the fragments. Non-Homeric Ionic literature, both in verse and in prose, exerted a powerful influence on Epicharmus. The trochaic tetrameters and iambic trimeters in which most of Doric comedy was composed were an Ionic invention: the Ionic iambographer Ananius is quoted almost *verbatim* by Epicharmus, although in Doric translation.[17] Moreover, the philosophical discussions that played such an important role in the comedies were certainly rooted in the Ionic world: such famous and influential philosophers as Pythagoras, Parmenides, and Xenophanes had mainly been active in the Greek West. Epicharmus must have criticized Xenophanes more than once (Pickard-Cambridge 1962: 244).

This had obvious repercussions on the language, as the following example will show. Originally, the third person singular of the imperfect of the verb 'to be' was ἦς (< **ēs-t*) and the third plural ἦεν (< **ēs-ent*). The system was kept as such by the Doric dialects (but obviously at some point ἦεν contracted to ἦν). In the Ionic dialects this system was radically innovated: the third person plural ἦν was used for the third singular, and ἦσαν (with -σαν from the -σα aorists) was substituted for the old ἦεν (Sihler 1995:

[15] Ath. 7.325 F *Μίθαικος ἐν Ὀψαρτυτικῷ "ταινίαν", φησίν, "ἐκκοιλίξας, τὰν κεφαλὰν ἀποταμών, ἀποπλύνας καὶ ταμὼν τεμάχεα κατάχει τυρὸν καὶ ἔλαιον."*

[16] Pl. *Grg.* 518 B *Μίθαικος ὁ τὴν ὀψοποιΐαν συγγεγραφὼς τὴν Σικελικήν.*

[17] Epich. fr. 51 *καὶ σκιφίας χρόμις θ', ὃς ἐν τῷ ἦρι κὰτ τὸν Ἀνάνιον | ἰχθύων πάντων ἄριστος, ἀνθίας δὲ χείματι.* Cf. Anan. fr. 5.1 West *ἔαρι μὲν χρόμιος ἄριστος, ἀνθίης δὲ χειμῶνι.*

467). The forms actually found in Epicharmus are: 58 ἦν δ' ὑαινίδες τε βούγλωσσοί τε καὶ κίθαρος ἐνῆς . . ., 85.1 ἦν δ' ἐρωδιοί τε πολλοί . . ., 52.1 ἦν δὲ νάρκαι . . ., 122.6 φάσσαι τε τοσσαῦται παρῆν, 275.1 ἀλλ' ἀεὶ τοὶ θεοὶ παρῆσαν.

The latter is the only form of ἦσαν transmitted in Epicharmus' text so far; it is found in a fragment whose Epicharmean authorship has been doubted, but which I regard as genuine.[18] It can hardly be accidental that a local form is used in lists of fish or birds, but an Ionic one when it comes to an ambitious philosophical discourse on the eternal and immovable world of the gods in contrast to the changeable world of men—within a comic frame, as Bernays (1853) showed long ago, but no less philosophical for that. Ahrens (1843: 327) pointed out that παρῆσαν could easily be changed into παρῆν τε, but wisely did not recommend adoption of this conjecture, and Kaibel (1899: 121) left the text as it was transmitted, as now Kassel–Austin do (2001: fr. 275.1). Of course we do not know who spoke the lines: an article like Dover's 'Language and Character in Aristophanes' (1987: 237–48) is impossible to write for Epicharmus. Note that Kassel–Austin (2001) are probably right in leaving 115 πολλοὶ στατῆρες, ἀποδοτῆρες οὐδ' ἂν εἷς in the Ionic form in which it is transmitted. Attic comedy featured many speakers of non-Attic dialects (Colvin 1999), and speakers of Attic or Ionic may well have appeared as characters in Doric comedy.

[18] Fragments 275–80 are printed as *Pseudepicharmea* by Kassel–Austin (2001: 157–64) under the heading 'ex Alcimo', since they ultimately derive from Alcimus, a local historian of Sicily (*FGrH* 560) who in his *Πρὸς Ἀμύνταν* quoted a number of Epicharmean passages with an aim at 'proving' that Plato's philosophical ideas were 'copied' from the Sicilian playwright (see Cassio 1985*c*: 43–5). I personally regard at least 275 and 276 as authentic, in agreement with Bernays (1853), Körte (1911: 231), Pickard-Cambridge (1962: 251), and Berk (1964: 88–92); but probably 277–9 are also genuine (280 is certainly not 'ex Alcimo', see Kaibel 1899: 138 on his fr. 254). Not only are they 'lebhaftester dramatischer Dialog' in contrast to the spurious (and dull) treatises, but one wonders whether Alcimus could really afford to quote Epicharmean fakes if he wanted to carry his point (Körte 1911: 231). The idea that 277–9 are forged is closely linked with the notion that Epicharmus was more or less unknown in fourth-century Athens, which is far from being the case (see §1). At 275.1 ὑπέλιπον 'failed' has a meaning otherwise attested for the first time in Aristotle (LSJ 1940: 1887, s.v. ὑπολείπω I.3; Kassel–Austin 2001: 158 on 275.1), but this can hardly be used as an argument against the fragment's genuineness, in view of the enormous amount of archaic Greek literature that is lost to us. LSJ (1940: 728) quote a fragment of Eratosthenes (3rd c. BC) as the earliest example of εὔποτος in reference to vessels, 'good to drink from', but precisely this meaning has surfaced on 'Nestor's cup' of *c.*725 BC, εὔποτον ποτέριον (Hansen 1983: no. 454.1).

After Aeschylus' first Sicilian visit[19] Attic tragedy must have become very popular at Syracuse, and it was only too natural for Epicharmus to parody it exactly as his Athenian colleagues were to do many years later: in the papyrus commentaries on *Odysseus Automolos* there are a couple of comments on Epicharmean lines which alluded to, or parodied, tragic authors,[20] and according to a scholion on Aeschylus' *Eumenides* Epicharmus ridiculed the tragedian for his frequent use of the participle *τιμαλφούμενος*.[21] It is also possible that Doric comedy influenced Attic drama in its turn: some scholars believe that such Doric forms as *φίντων* or *θῶσθαι* found in Aeschylus' *Diktyoulkoi* are a consequence of his first visit to Sicily (Radt 1985: 161).

4. It is obviously the papyrus fragments which give us an idea of what an ancient edition of Epicharmus looked like. Gomperz (1889) published an important papyrus fragment of *Odysseus Automolos* datable to the first century BC, and fragments of other comedies surfaced seventy years later, when a batch of Oxyrhynchus papyri was published by Lobel (1959: 1–44). They represent ancient editions that must be more or less heavily indebted to the one prepared some time in the second century BC by Apollodorus of Athens, the last heir of the great Alexandrian scholarly tradition.[22]

A Hellenistic edition of an archaic author is an interpretation of an old text, either directly or through an intermediate, say late classical, text; Kaibel (1899: 90) regarded the latter alternative as the most probable for Epicharmus. A third-century or second-century editor was faced with the problem of preparing a new text on the basis of an older one according to the standard conventions of the time, i.e. use of the East Ionic alphabet (with ⟨Η⟩ = [ɛː] and ⟨Ω⟩ = [ɔː]) and the digraphs ⟨ΕΙ⟩ (= [eː]) and ⟨ΟΥ⟩ (= [uː] from an earlier [oː]).[23]

The problem may have been more or less thorny according to

[19] Between 472 and 468 BC (Herington 1967: 75–6).

[20] Epich. fr. 97 *schol.*, l. 2 (Kassel–Austin 2001: 61) *πάλιν πρὸ(ς) τοὺς τραγικοὺς λέγετ(αι)*; see also 98.48.

[21] Schol. vet. in Aesch. *Eum.* 626 (p. 61.9–10 Smith) *τιμαλφούμενον· συνεχὲς τὸ ὄνομα παρ' Αἰσχύλῳ, διὸ σκώπτει αὐτὸν Ἐπίχαρμος* (Epich. fr. 221 = Aesch. test. 115 Radt).

[22] Epich. test. 34; see Pfeiffer (1968: 252–66).

[23] The so-called 'spurious diphthongs', i.e. the result of contractions and compensatory lengthenings.

the type of alphabet and writing conventions used in an old manuscript. As is well known, in many archaic alphabets ⟨E⟩ stood for [e], [e:], and [ɛː]; ⟨O⟩ for [o], [o:], and [ɔː] (this was the prevailing system used for the official documents of classical Athens). If an archaic text employed this system, its Hellenistic edition must have been the result of interpretation based on prevailing notions of the phonology of each dialect. For example, an old ΦONETAI (3rd pers. sing. indic.) would have been rendered as ΦΩNEITAI if the author of the old text was an Athenian, but ΦΩNHTAI if the author was a Spartan. If the text to be copied was not really old but an 'intermediate' one (written, say, in the fourth century BC in the East Ionic alphabet), the interpretation of e.g. the old Spartan text would already have been made by the scribe of the intermediate text, and a Hellenistic editor already found ΦΩNHTAI in his model. In some cases, however, things were less easy; in an early fourth-century intermediate text of an old Athenian author *φωνεῖται* might still have been written as ΦΩNE-TAI, since the adoption of the East Ionic alphabet did not automatically entail use of the digraphs ⟨EI⟩ and ⟨OY⟩ (Wachter 1991: 111; Colvin 1999: 93–4). However, the digraphs ⟨EI⟩ and ⟨OY⟩ were occasionally used in some archaic Greek alphabets from very early times, and in an almost systematic manner at Corinth and especially in Corinthian colonies, where [e:] and [o:] were the result of contractions and compensatory lengthenings.[24] Obviously where ⟨EI⟩ and ⟨OY⟩ were in use, ⟨E⟩ and ⟨O⟩ were less ambiguous, since as a rule they could only stand for two sounds,[25] not three.

We must confess that we have no idea how a Sicilian literary text of the sixth or fifth centuries BC looked like. Scholars often explicitly or implicitly assume that the system used for writing literary texts in a given area was more or less the same as the one used in the local inscriptions (for instance the archaic Spartan alphabet in the case of Alcman.[26]) This, however, may not have always been the case; it has often been claimed, for example, that

[24] Thumb–Kieckers (1932: §126); Buck (1955: §254). The inscriptions written in the epichoric Corinthian alphabet feature not ⟨EI⟩ (as opposed to ⟨E⟩) , but ⟨E⟩ (as opposed to ⟨B⟩; at Corinth a letter very similar in shape to ⟨B⟩ = [b] in the Ionic alphabet was used for both [e] and [ɛː]).

[25] Respectively [e] and [ɛː], [o] and [ɔː].

[26] Cassio (1993) with previous bibliography; see also Wilamowitz (1922: 99–100) on Pindar.

early copies of Homer circulating in Athens were written in the East Ionic alphabet (Janko 1992: 20–38).

Nevertheless, Homer is in many ways a special case, that of an author of panhellenic import whose memorization and text were firmly in the hands of East Ionic bards by the sixth century. For a local literary genre like Doric comedy one would assume a writing system more or less close to that of the Syracusan inscriptions, namely one that did not employ eta and omega. As to the digraphs ⟨EI⟩ and ⟨OY⟩ for [e:] and [o:], they are sporadically attested quite early in the Syracusan colonies Camarina and Casmenae, and in other areas of South-East Sicily (possibly as a legacy of the 'Corinthian system');[27] this is, however, not an absolute rule (as we have seen, *εἴμειν* or *εἶμεν* is written EMEN in a sixth-century inscription from Syracuse). If this system was really used in early editions of Epicharmus, Deinolochus, etc. the task of a fourth- or third-century editor should have been relatively easy, because *εἴμειν* (Epich. fr. 97.8) appeared as EIMEIN, *Λευκάρου* (113.249) as ΛΕΥΚΑΡΟΥ and *προμαθεούμενος* (113.12) as ΠΡΟΜΑΘΕΟΥΜΕΝΟΣ.

But oscillations are the order of the day in our papyri (let alone the medieval manuscripts), and it is unlikely that the problem of the alphabet in which Epicharmus' plays were originally written will ever be settled satisfactorily, especially as far as the digraphs are concerned. At 97.11 the scribe wrote *ἐνθεὶν* (*sic*) but later the iota was deleted; this is strange if it was originally written ΕΝΘΕΙΝ, a form that we expect in the Syracusan dialect.[28] Fr. 113.142 is also puzzling: we should expect *κεντεῖν* (cf. 97.10 *ἐνθυμεῖν*) but what we actually find is *κεντῆν* corrected into *κεντέν* by a second hand, and again a second hand wrote an eta on top of the iota of *λέγειν* at 113.147. In these cases it is not clear to what extent the ambiguities of the archaic alphabets are to be blamed for these oscillations. In the Doric dialects infinitives like *ἔχεν* (and *οἰκέν*) are amply attested (García Ramón 1977), and *κεντῆν* might be a secondary consequence of the transfer of the

[27] Dubois (1989): no. 113 ΚΛΕΙΝΟΥΣ (gen. of *Κλεινώ*; Camarina, late 6th c. BC); no. 219 ΗΙΠΑΡΧΟΥ (SE Sicily, early 5th c. BC); no. 134.3 ΕΙΜΕΙΝ (Gela, early 5th c. BC). A genitive ending -ΟΥ is easily legible in a 6th-c. inscription from Monte Casale (Casmenae) (Dubois 1989: no. 103), but in the Camarina archive (Cordano 1992) the genitives of the thematic declension are as a rule written -Ο.

[28] Thumb–Kieckers (1932: §167.30a). Kassel–Austin (2001) print *ἐνθέν*.

-*άω* verbs to the -*έω* inflection, also very common in Doric dialects.[29]

In a papyrus fragment we read *τοῦ Λευκάρου* (113.249), but in another one (135.1) the genitive *τῶ* was corrected into *τοῦ* whereas the genitive *τούτω* of l. 3 was left untouched. As a consequence, both Kassel (1999: 30) and Bühler (1999: 338) have pointed out that the -*ω* genitives are no sufficient argument to regard the amusing trochaic tetrameter *θάσσον*[30] *ὁ τόκος Ἡρακλείτω* ⟨*τῶ*⟩ *Τεριναίω τρέχει* (*anon. Dor.* 20) as incompatible with Epicharmus' dialect[31] (this line might, however, represent a special case, see below). Obviously, if the oscillations *η*/*ει*, *ου*/*ω* are to be traced to the ambiguities of an archaic alphabet, it seems highly improbable that ⟨EI⟩ and ⟨OY⟩ for the 'spurious diphthongs' were employed in a fifth-century manuscript.

There is also the additional problem that dialect texts can be manipulated, whatever writing conventions were used in early texts (Cassio 1997). Even if they had EIMEIN we cannot be certain of *every εἴμειν* found in our text. The generally Doric *εἶμεν* was certainly used by Epicharmus; it is well attested in papyrus fragments (135.4) and is sometimes metrically guaranteed (276.3). He may have used *εἶμεν* more often than we think, but a later editor may have decided that *εἴμειν* was more 'typical' of the Syracusan dialect and may have written it wherever it was metrically indifferent, as at 97.8 *ε*]*ἴμειν ταῦτα*.

One might perhaps reason along the same lines in the interpretation of the fragment just mentioned, *θάσσον ὁ τόκος Ἡρακλείτω* ⟨*τῶ*⟩ *Τεριναίω τρέχει*. The -*ω* endings[32] are strangely appropriate for a citizen of Terina, a sub-colony of Croton where contractions of the *Doris severior* type are attested.[33] This in turn curiously recalls the problems posed by a (probably) Pindaric fragment where we find the genitives *Πυθαγγέλω* and

[29] Thumb–Kieckers (1932: §204.24); Buck (1955: §162.2). The infinitive *τιμεῖν* is attested at Akragas: Dubois (1989: no. 185.16). The transfer is often unsystematic (e.g. *συλέοντες* but infinitive *συλῆν*). If, for example, *τιμεῖν* existed alongside the 'regular' *τιμῆν*, *κεντῆν* may have been created beside the expected *κεντεῖν* and, by extension, *λέγην* beside *λέγειν*.

[30] To be printed with an acute accent: see below.

[31] A detailed discussion of this line and its interpretation can be found in Bühler (1999: 335–43). Wilamowitz (1922: 100 n. 1) had already argued that the -*ω* genitives were no obstacle to attributing the line 'der sizilischen Komödie'.

[32] Guaranteed by the source, Zenobius II.73 (Bühler 1999: 335).

[33] Schwyzer (1923: 224): no. 436.3 *ἀργυρίω*, *Ἱστιαίω*.

Ὀρχομενῶ (fr. 333(a), 6 and 8 Maehler), which are far from obvious in Pindar (Nöthiger 1971: 78) but very appropriate for a Boeotian *laudandus* and a Boeotian place-name. It is possible (although by no means certain) that in both cases an ancient editor using omega and eta decided to 'characterize' the dialect as far as the proper names were concerned. It should be noted, however, that, if this was the case (and if we can trust the manuscript tradition), in *anon. Dor.* 20 the operation was not carried out consistently, since a *Doris severior* dialect in which *η* and *ω* were used for secondary long *e* and *o* sounds would require *Ἡρακλήτω* (not *-είτω*).[34]

Our papyri are full of diacriticals and 'Doric' accents, which are likely to go back to Apollodorus' edition (Pfeiffer 1968: 264–5). Since the old texts bore no accents, and since all dialect features, including accents, change in the course of time, we are entitled to ask how Apollodorus knew that a fifth-century Syracusan actor pronounced e.g. *προτιμάσαι* (97.12), *ἀπαγγείλαι* (97.16), or *καλώς* (113.132). As a matter of fact it is unlikely that we shall ever know exactly how our texts in literary Doric came to be accented as they are:[35] basically the same system is used in the text of Doric comedy, western lyric poets (Stesichorus and Ibycus), and Alcman, and one has the impression of a standardized (and relatively late) grammatical doctrine imposed systematically on old texts in Doric (Colvin 1999: 180). At 113.26 *θᾰ́σσ*[with *alpha* marked as short and bearing an acute accent is interesting on two counts: (*a*) it is exactly what we expect from **thakh-i̯on*, *θᾶττον* with [a:] being an Attic innovation,[36] and is perfectly paralleled by *βᾰ́σσον* (176), the comparative of *βαθύς*;[37] (*b*) the quantity of [a] is irrelevant to the metre, and the marking of the *alpha* as short is solely meant to ensure a correct dialect pronunciation—a matter by which ancient Greek scholars obviously set great store. It is clear that in Epicharmus' Doric *θάσσων*, *-ον* had a short [a] and must be accented as *θάσσον* in the neuter.[38]

[34] As in the Heraclean tables: Schwyzer (1923) no. 62.4 *Ἀπολλώνιος Ηηρακλήτω*. *-κλειτος* or *-κλητος* derive from an older *-κλεϝετος*; see Risch (1974: 21).

[35] The best recent treatment of the problem is that of Colvin (1999: 180 ff.).

[36] Lagercrantz (1898: 32–44), Wackernagel (1914: 124–5), Sihler (1995: 193, 363).

[37] Hdn. *περὶ μονήρ. λέξ.* p. 942.17 ff. Lentz *τὰ εἰς ⟨σσ⟩ων λήγοντα συγκριτικὰ δισύλλαβα, εἰ ἔχοι πρὸ τέλους τὸ ἄλφα, συνεσταλμένον αὐτὸ ἔχει . . . ἔνθεν παρ' Ἐπιχάρμῳ* (176) *τὸ βάσσον*; see Sihler (1995: 361).

[38] *θάσσον* is accented correctly in Kerkhof's index under *ταχύ* (Kassel–Austin

5. The fate of [w] and its written counterpart ⟨ϝ⟩ is also interesting with regard to both the original dialect and Epicharmus' early written texts. In the spoken Syracusan dialect the sound must have gradually disappeared in all positions, but we do not know exactly what the situation was like at the beginning of the fifth century BC; since [w] was by then completely lost in the Ionic dialects, in theory its absence from a word used by Epicharmus may either reflect what was actually happening in the dialect or be due to the influence of spoken or literary Ionic.

The evidence (already discussed by Kaibel 1899: 90 and more recently by Hoffmann–Debrunner–Scherer 1969: 115) is often contradictory. If we accept *μόνος* (< *μόνϝος*: 32.1 and 113.8) and *φθΐνει* (< *φθίνϝει*: 276.7) as authentically Syracusan, as Thumb–Kieckers (1932: §166.7) did, [w] must already have disappeared in the [nw] clusters. Note however that there are oscillations in other clusters of a similar type: *δέρος* (< *δέρϝος*), metrically guaranteed at 135.3 is at variance with the Syracusan gloss *δερβιστήρ* (i.e. *δερϝιστήρ*);[39] see also *ὀλβάχ⟨ν⟩ιον* < *ὀλϝ-* at Deinolochus fr. 13. In theory both *Ἀτρέος* (97.15 < *Ἀτρῆϝος*) and *Προμαθέος* (113.14, < *Προμαθῆϝος*) might be literary forms,[40] but the elimination of intervocalic [w] and the consequent shortening of [ɛː] are very common at an early date in all Doric dialects (Buck 1955: §111). Note that *δᾱλός* appears as *δαελός* (< *δαϝελός*) in Sophron 4.13, and that according to an entry in Hesychius (*Glossar. Italiot.* 15) the Syracusans said *ἔβασον* (= Attic *ἔασον*), which means that in this case either [w] or the bilabial fricative [β] was actually pronounced. In our papyri we find indications that the ancient editors regarded as uncontracted certain vowel groups which were originally separated by [w], as in *ειδες*, *ειδε* (*ἔϊδες*, *ἔϊδε* 98.70 and 131).

What happened in word-initial position—where the [w] sound was most resistant—is also complicated. The prosodical treatment is twofold:

(*a*) there is hiatus where [w] was certainly present word-initially at an early stage of the dialect: 34 *ἐκάλεσε γάρ τύ τις* |

2001: 368) but not in the text itself (see e.g.149; at *anon. Dor.* 20 *θάσσον* is suggested in the apparatus).

39 *Glossar. Italiot.* 13 in Kassel–Austin (2001: 304).

40 *Ἀτρέος υἱός* and the like are often attested in Homer (e.g. *Il.* 3.37) and we read *Προμηθέα* in Hesiod (*Theog.* 510, etc.).

ἐπ' αἶκλον ἀέκων· τὺ δὲ ἑκὼν ὤχεο τρέχων, 61 *τε ἱέρακες*, 279 *καὶ ἀνδάνειν*;

(*b*) word-initial [w] is ignored and we find elisions and contractions: 49.3 *ταινίαι, λεπταὶ μέν, ἀδεῖαι δὲ κὠλίγου πυρός*; 122.8 *πάντας, ὀπτᾶντες δὲ χἀδύνοντες αὐτοὺς χναύομες*; 18.1 *αἴκ' ἔσθοντ' ἴδοις*; 277.3 *φέρ' ἴδω*; 278.6 *τόδ' οἶδεν*; 97.14 *ἐς ἄστυ*.

For the instances listed under (*a*) the main problem is to know whether our text reflects the original pronunciation faithfully (i.e. *τε ἱέρακες* with hiatus) or a [w] sound was originally pronounced and written as *ϝ* (i.e. *τε ϝιέρακες*) but the digamma was eliminated from later editions. It should be recalled that in early Syracusan inscriptions we do find word-initial digammas: *καλὰ ϝέργα* (Dubois 1989: no. 86, early sixth century BC), *ϝια(ν)θίς* (ibid. no. 87, late sixth century BC).

Kaibel (1899: 90) was inclined to the view that early editions of Epicharmus featured initial digammas, but that they were absent from Apollodorus' edition because it was based not on the early texts but on 'intermediate' ones in which the digammas were already absent.[41] As to the (*b*) set, Kaibel said 'poeta si ubique littera tum viva usus est, graviter corrupta videntur fr. 21 *αἴκ' ἔσθοντ' ἴδοις*' etc., but in his edition he fortunately refrained from emendations.

As a matter of fact it would be absurd to correct the lines of the (b) set, in which both meaning and metre are in order. They represent an innovative development in the Syracusan dialect which coincided with a long-established parallel development of the Ionic dialects. Probably word-initial [w] was still pronounced (and written?) by many in Epicharmus' time, but new pronunciations without [w] must have been gaining ground. Note that Kassel and Austin (2001: 298) print *anon. Dor.* 18 as *μάταια τἆλλα παρὰ Κρότωνα ϝάστεα*, a conjecture of V. Schmidt (*τἄστεα* codd.), who attributed the line to Epicharmus. Unfortunately the scanty fragments do not allow us to form an idea of how the 'old' and 'new' forms were connotated: was *δὲ ἑκών* perceived as old-fashioned and *φέρ' ἴδω* as brilliantly innovative? Note that *φέρ' ἴδω* is found in a 'philosophical' fragment (277) and in *λεπταὶ μέν, ἀδεῖαι δέ* (49.3) the particle *μέν* is imported from Ionic.[42]

[41] See also Schmid–Staehlin (1929–48: 1.648 n. 3).
[42] See Leumann (1949) and Morpurgo Davies (1997).

6. Mention should also be made of a phonological development typical of many Doric dialects which surfaced in the papyri published by Lobel (1959) and helped to recover a lost fragment of Doric comedy. In the Heraclean tables we read ΜΕΤΡΙΩΜΕΝΑΙ (Schwyzer 1923: no. 62.18), a development of an original *μετρε-όμεναι*. The best explanation of this and similar developments was provided by Méndez Dosuna (1993): in [eo] the first vowel became [i̯] and thus lost its syllabic value; the loss was counter-balanced by compensatory lengthening of the second vowel,[43] which became an [ɔː] as we expect in the Heraclean dialect.[44] This development is well attested especially in words that became longer by the addition of various suffixes, such as middle participles and Doric futures (Cassio 1999: 195).

Now two 'strange' new forms appeared in the Epicharmean papyri: 113.242 – ⏑ – × – *ἰαίνει θυμὸν εὐωχεουμένων*, with *-εου-* in synizesis, and 113.12]*ήσθαι προμᾱθεούμενος*, with disyllabic *-εού-*. Schmidt (1978) saw that *εὐωχεουμένων* was an authentic development of the dialect, of the *μετριώμεναι* type (*εὐωχεόμενος* > *εὐωχεούμενος*, with *-ου-* representing a secondary [oː], as expected in the Syracusan dialect,[45] and that *προμαθεούμενος* showed the same development but with secondary diaeresis, a very frequent device in Greek and many other poetic languages[46] whereby [e̯] or [i̯] developed a secondary syllabic value. It was then easy for him to realize that a fragment of Doric poetry, *ἁ κίττα τὰν Σειρῆνα μιμουμένα*, transmitted by Galen (8.632 Kühn) and attributed by Wilamowitz (1902: 325) to either Epicharmus or Sophron must be interpreted as an iambic trimeter, *ἁ κίσσα τὰν Σειρῆνα μιμ⟨ε⟩ουμένα*, with the same diaeresis as in *προμαθεούμενος*. Schmidt attributed (with caution) the fragment to Epicharmus; it now appears as fr. 8 among the *anonyma Dorica* (Kassel–Austin 2001: 295). Note that, if [oː] sounded the same in Syracusan as in Attic, in every middle present participle of *-έω* verbs there must have been a minimal

[43] This did not happen if the second vowel was in a closed syllable, as in the future ΑΝΑΝΓΕΛΙΟΝΤΙ < *ἀναγγελέοντι* (Schwyzer 1923: no. 62.118).

[44] Where the results of secondary lengthenings and contractions coincided with the inherited [ɛː] and [ɔː]: see Buck (1955: §246).

[45] Buck (1955: §254); see above, §4. We should expect the [e̯] in *-εου-* to have turned into [i̯], but in this case there might be either a phonetic or graphic restoration of an [e] sound conditioned by other forms of the same verb (to the best of my knowledge such forms as *εὐωχέομαι*, *εὐωχέονται* were left untouched in the Syracusan dialect).

[46] Schwyzer (1939: 104); Cassio (1997: 194 and n. 18).

difference between the Attic form, e.g. *φορούμενος* [phoro:menos] and its Syracusan counterpart *φορεούμενος* [phoreo:menos]; this might have eased, or even favoured, parody of Attic texts, as in the case of the Aeschylean *τιμαλφούμενος* (see §3).

7. Some of the vocabulary found in Epicharmus is common to all or most Greek dialects, like e.g. *καλέω*, *πίνω*, *σκότος*, *ἀγαθός*, just to quote some random examples from one fragment (32). Words used mainly, but not exlusively, in Doric texts include *μῶμαι* 'to seek' (*μῶται* 116; the verb is also found in tragedy;[47] *ἕρπω* (32.9) 'to go', a semantic innovation (Schmidt 1977: 52–3) very frequent in the Doric dialects and commonly used in tragedy;[48] *θῶμαι* 'to dine' (198 *θωσούμεθα*; cf. Aesch. fr. 47a, 818 Radt *θῶσθαι*);[49] *ἀννέμω* 'to read' (232, a verb also used in this sense in a Euboean inscription).[50] Other items of vocabulary seem to have been confined to the Doric dialects, like *αἶκλον* (34.2; cf. Alcman fr. 95b Davies) and *λῶ* 'to wish' (32.1, 49.1, etc.).[51]

In other cases we find words of diverse origin for which there is hardly a parallel in the rest of the Greek language. The verb *συνθυμεῖν* (209) 'to agree' looks deceptively banal, but is not found elsewhere and must be derived from a **σύνθυμος* which is never attested. The formation of *ῥογκιάω* (195) 'to snore' is clear enough,[52] but the verb is isolated. *Βιττάζω*, found in Epicharmus (171) and Sophron (110), is an obvious metathesis of *βαπτίζω* (Schwyzer 1939: 268) but, again, it is found nowhere else. *Ῥέζει* 'he/she dyes' (106) is also isolated but for totally different reasons: it belongs to an 'absterbende Wortgruppe' (Frisk 1960–72: 2.647) based on the Indo-European root **(s)reg-* 'to dye' (Rix 1998: 534). It is possible that *βιττάζω* was perceived by educated Syracusans as 'low' in comparison with the panhellenic *βαπτίζω*,

47 In lyrics and trimeters, Soph. *Trach.* 1136 *μωμένη*.

48 e.g. Soph. *Phil.* 730 *ἕρπ' εἰ θέλεις*.

49 Which might be due precisely to Aeschylus' familiarity with Sicilian Doric; see §3 and Radt (1985: 161).

50 P. A. Hansen (1983: no. 108.2): Eretria, 5th c. BC, *ἀνάνεμαι*. In the meaning 'to read' the verb is also found in Theocritus (18.48), Parthenius (*Suppl. Hellen.* no. 606), and in a 5th-c. Doric inscription from Erbessos (Sicily; Dubois 1989: no. 167).

51 Amply attested in Doric inscriptions and literary texts; see Frisk (1960–72: 2.150 s.v. *λῶ*) and Colvin (1999: 244). The root is the same as that of Latin *volo*; see Rix (1998: 618–19).

52 It is an *o*-grade 'frequentative' formation from the root of *ῥέγκω* 'nach den Krankheitsverba auf *-ιάω*' (Frisk 1960–72: 2.150, 647).

but it is impossible to surmise how they would have evaluated the local *ῥέζω* in relation to the far more widespread *βάπτω* (already attested in Homer).

The verb *ὀλισθράζω* (32.9)[53] = Attic *ὀλισθάνω* is not totally isolated, since it is found in a list of Hippocratic words compiled by Galen (19.126 Kühn). This does not mean, however, that *ὀλισθράζω* was current in Ionic. It is well known that some Hippocratic treatises show numerous Doric features because they were written by physicians native to Sicily and Magna Graecia (Schmidt 1977); we shall presently discuss another instance of this kind (*κυβιτίζω*). It is clear that *ὀλισθράζω* was not invented by Epicharmus for comic purposes, but must have been current in the Doric dialects of the Greek West, including that of Syracuse.

8. A number of words found in the fragments of Epicharmus and Sophron are never, or almost never, attested in the rest of Greek literature but closely resemble Latin words; they are usually supposed to derive from the language of the Sicels, who had migrated from central Italy to Sicily before the arrival of the Greeks.[54] However, this language is still mysterious in many ways; it must have belonged to the Indo-European group, but it is not clear whether it was an Italic language in the technical sense of the word (Penney 1988: 737). In what follows I shall use 'Italic' in a broad sense, with reference to features (usually vocabulary) foreign to Greek but attested in the Indo-European languages spoken in ancient Italy.

Let us examine some instances, starting from Epich. fr. 19 *ταῦτα δὲ (τὰ σιτοβόλια) ῥογοὺς Σικελιῶται ὠνόμαζον, καί ἐστι τοὔνομα ἐν Ἐπιχάρμου Βουσίριδι.* *Ῥογός* 'granary' is formally identical with Latin *rogus* 'funeral pyre', certainly a *nomen actionis* of inherited type, from a verb identical with Latin *rego* (in the sense of *erigo*), originally with the general meaning 'heap' (Leumann 1977: 276). *Κάρκαρον* was used by Sophron (fr. 145) and Rhinthon (fr. 17) and is clearly the same word as Latin *carcer* (also attested as *carcar*).

The system of coins and weights used at Syracuse was certainly of Italic origin (H. Chantraine 1962; Parise 1989). This is proved

[53] Possibly based on **ὄλισθρος*: Frisk (1960–72: 2.377).

[54] Schmoll (1958), Durante (1964/5), Holloway (1991: 42 and 86–96), Agostiniani (1988), Penney (1988).

by both linguistic and factual arguments: precisely as in the Roman system, the λῖτρα (Latin *lībra*) was divided into twelve ὀγκίαι (Latin *unciae*[55]). These names are attested at an early date both in Epicharmus (10.2 πεντόγκιον, 9.3 λίτραν, 10.2 δεκάλιτρος στατήρ) and in inscriptions (Dubois 1989: no. 20 δέκα λίτρας ἀποτεισάτō, from Megara Hyblaea, early sixth century BC). Latin *lībra* comes from **līdhra*, and the word must have reached Syracuse through a language of ancient Italy (Sicel?) in which *dh* > *th* > *t* (Leumann 1977: 171; Lejeune 1993: 11). Also interesting is ἑξᾶς, -ᾶντος 'the sixth part of a *litra*' = 2 ὀγκίαι; cf. lat. *sextans, -antis* (1/6 *as* = 2 *unciae*), which is implied by Epich. fr. 10.2 ἑξάντιον, and further names in -ᾶς, -ᾶντος are attested for other fractions of the λίτρα: τετρᾶς, -ᾶντος 'the fourth part of a λίτρα' = 3 ὀγκίαι (lat. *quadrans, -antis*: 1/4 *as* = 3 *unciae*) and τριᾶς, -ᾶντος 'the third part of a λίτρα' = 4 ὀγκίαι (lat. *triens, -entis*: 1/3 *as* = 4 *unciae*). They belong to an inflectional type which is comparatively rare in Greek, so that either a Sicel or a Latin model has occasionally been suggested. The latter option is, however, impossible for chronological reasons; that Latin was influenced by Greek is far more plausible.[56]

An interesting case is that of κυβιτίζω 'to nudge with the elbow', attested for Epicharmus (220) by the great physician Rufus of Ephesus (first century AD), who also says that the Dorians of Sicily call the elbow κύβιτον.[57] This word is certainly of Italic origin and

[55] 'Du groupe de *ūnus, ūnicus* etc.': Lejeune (1993: 3 n. 8).

[56] Τετρᾶς, ἑξᾶς, *quadrans, sextans*, etc. pose a number of complex problems that cannot be discussed in full here. The Greek forms found in Epicharmus cannot have been built on a Latin model because the beginnings of coinage in Rome do not predate 300 BC (H. Chantraine 1962: 55). -ᾶς, -ᾶντος has been traced back to the language of the Sicels (ibid. 57), but it is not clear why we cannot think of a Greek origin; Attic Greek has words like πελεκᾶς, -ᾶντος (Ar. *Av.* 882, 1155) or ἀλλᾶς, -ᾶντος (Ar. *passim*), although the origin of -ᾶς is controversial in both cases, and the *Kurznamen* in -ᾶς, which usually have a genitive in -ᾶ or -ᾶδος and a dative in -ᾳ or -ᾶδι, occasionally show -ᾶντος, -ᾶντι, etc. in the oblique cases, as in Δαμᾶντι: see Björck (1950: 268 ff.). Moreover, in the Doric dialects -ᾶς, -ᾶντος was the regular outcome of *-ᾱϝεντ-ς, *-ᾱ-ϝεντ-ος, as in Pind. *Ol.* 2.85 φωνᾶντα < *φωνᾱ́ϝεντα and the place-name Μολοχᾶς < *Μολοχᾱ́-ϝεντ-ς (Schwyzer 1939: 528): it is possible that in Doric areas -ᾶς, -ᾶντος was at some stage resegmented as a suffix in its own right. If so, it would also be possible that, as A. Morpurgo Davies suggests to me, forms like ἑξᾶς, -ᾶντος or τετρᾶς, -ᾶντος arose as abbreviated forms of compounds meaning 'consisting of *x* parts', e.g. τετρᾶς from τετραμερής 'quadripartite' (LSJ 1940: 1781). The matter requires further investigation.

[57] Ruf. Ephes. *De corp. hum. partium appellat.* pp. 45–6 Kowalski ἀγκών . . . οἱ δὲ ὀλέκρανον καλοῦσι· Δωριεῖς δὲ οἱ ἐν Σικελίᾳ κύβιτον· Ἐπίχαρμος δὲ καὶ τὸ παίειν τῷ ἀγκῶνι κυβιτίζειν ἔλεγεν.

corresponds to Lat. *cubitus* (*-um*), a word still alive in various Romance languages (Italian *gomito*, French *coude*, etc.). *Κύβιτον* is also found elsewhere, in the Hippocratic treatise *de locis in homine*, written in Ionic;[58] this does not mean, however, that *κύβιτον* was also current in Ionic. The *De locis* is one of those Hippocratic treatises, already discussed apropos of *ὀλισθράζω*, that show Doric features. So *κύβιτον* must have been current in the Greek West in place of the usual *ἀγκών* or *ὀλέκρανον*. But what about *κυβιτίζω* in Epicharmus? Was the verb a current one in Syracuse or is it a nonce-word for comic effects? I am inclined to accept the former solution but, again, the word is not attested elsewhere and no certainty is attainable.

9. There has been some discussion of *Λογίνα*, a fictional proper name that appears in the title of the Epicharmean comedy *Λόγος καὶ Λογίνα* (Kassel–Austin 2001: 52–3). Although nothing of the plot is recoverable from the scanty fragments, the title is usually taken to mean 'Mr and Mrs Logos', and a discussion of two allegorical figures is often assumed, in the fashion of the contrast between Right and Wrong in Aristophanes' *Clouds* (Pickard-Cambridge 1962: 272; Handley 1985: 370). If this is right, *-ίνα* (usually interpreted as *-ῑ́νᾱ*, not *-ῐ́νᾱ*) should indicate the female of the species: this function of the suffix is much more widespread in Latin (*gall-īna*, *reg-īna*, etc.: Leumann 1977: 327) than in Greek, where the real parallels are very few: especially *ἡρωΐνη* (*ἡρῷναι* in Ar. *Nub.* 315) and *ἐργαστίνη*. According to Kaibel (1899: 106) the suffix in *Λογίνα* is Italic in origin, and Hoenigswald (1941) came to the same conclusion after a thorough discussion of the linguistic data.

As a matter of fact, things are far from clear. To begin with, we know nothing of the plot; if *Λογίνα* was not Logos' wife or 'female Logos', but Logos' daughter, the force of the suffix was perfectly intelligible and well attested in classical Greek, since we find *Ἀδρηστίνη* 'the daughter of Adrastus' in Homer (*Il.* 5.412) and *Ὠκεανῖναι* 'the daughters of Okeanos' in Hesiod (*Theog.* 364; see Risch 1974: 101). And granted that we accept that the use of a feminine suffix in *-ῑ́νᾱ* was due to the pressure of a local language, we still have to understand how *Λογίνα* was perceived by the local

[58] Cf. Hippoc. *De loc. in hom.* 6.286.18 Littré *παρὰ τὸ τοῦ ὀστέου ἄρθρον ἤρθρωνται ἐς τὸ κύβιτον*; also 6.286.14, 6.288.2 Littré.

speakers. According to Hoenigswald (1941: 249) it was a hybrid name 'which may have recalled the word by which the barbarians around Syracuse called their hens . . . it no doubt added to the fun'. But if we admit that the Syracusans knew *gallina* (which is far from certain) I cannot see why they should not have known *regina*—surely a more dignified term. On the other hand, at Athens *ἡρωΐνη* and *ἐργαστίνη* had nothing ludicrous about them; moreover, the Syracusans were also familiar with such words as *Ταραντίνᾱ*, *Ἀκραγαντίνᾱ* in which *-ίνᾱ* had a different function[59] but still indicated a female human being and was by no means ridiculous.

My impression is that *Λογίνα* sounded comic not because of the suffix, whose use must have been widespread at Syracuse, but simply because it was the (invented) feminine form of a masculine word that had no feminine counterpart; an Attic **Λόγαινα* (cf. *μαγείραινα* in Pherecrates fr. 70.4) would have produced the same effect, as would in Italian **la discorsa* as the feminine version of *il discorso*.

10. Epic, and specifically Homeric, themes often provided a perfect foil for the plots of Doric comedy (Schmid–Staehlin 1929–48: 1.641; Handley 1985: 368–9); obviously imitation, or parody, of a Homeric plot could well imply imitation or parody of Homeric language. In some rare and fortunate instances one can detect precise parallels with the 'imitated' Homeric passages (see below on *Odysseus Automolos*). In other instances all we can say is that epic morphology and vocabulary are used, quite often for everyday or down-to-earth matters. A good example is provided by 150 *ὤεα χανὸς*[60] *κἀλεκτορίδων πετεηνῶν* 'eggs of geese and winged hens', where *πετεηνῶν* is obviously Homeric—usually interpreted as an artificial diektasis of an authentic *πετεινῶν* (Risch 1974: 100); note that the place at the end of the line is the most frequently attested in Homer. It is often easy to detect a Homeric model, far less so to guess what purposes it served. In 128 *Ζεὺς ἄναξ* †ΑΝΑΑΔΑΝ *ναίων Γάργαρα ἀγάννιφα*[61] a number of

[59] In *Ταραντ-ίνᾱ*, *-ίνᾱ* is the feminine of *-ῖνος*, a suffix commonly used for ethnics by the Western Greeks (Leumann 1977: 326).

[60] 'fort. *χανῶν*': Kaibel (1899: 199).

[61] Reconstructed by Kaibel (1899: fr. 130) as *Ζεὺς ἄναξ ἀν' ἄκρα ναίων Γαργάρων ἀγάννιφα*.

epic features are easily recognizable, most notably ἀγάννιφα; the tone is a very solemn one, but we do not know to what extent the line was meant as a parody.

Hexameters were occasionally used in comedy and iambus, and Epicharmus was no exception (test. 20 = Ath. 15.698 C κέχρηται δὲ καὶ Ἐπίχαρμος ὁ Συρακούσιος ἔν τινι τῶν δραμάτων ἐπ᾽ ὀλίγον). One of them is quoted, along with a Callimachean hexameter, by the T scholia on Homer (*Il.* 19.1 ἀπ᾽ Ὠκεανοῖο ῥοάων): Βοιώτιος ἡ φωνή. Καὶ ἀπὸ τῶν εἰς ες ἀρσενικῶν (καὶ θηλυκῶν Holford-Strevens)· "Ἄρτεμι Κρητάων πότνια τοξοφόρων" (Callim. fr. inc. 786 Pf.). "λαοὶ τοξοχίτωνες, ἀκούετε Σειρηνάων", Ἐπίχαρμος (121). Κρητάων (which must refer to the Cretans, not Crete as in the *Odyssey*, 14.199 = 16.62) was variously emended in the past, but should probably be accepted as such (Pfeiffer 1949: 487–8). As to the Epicharmean fragment, apart from τοξοχίτωνες (which is probably corrupt owing to the influence of τοξοφόρων in the preceding quotation) one would obviously expect Σειρήνων, not Σειρηνάων. 'Σειρήνα forma Italica videtur' said Kaibel (1899: 113) but archaic and classical Latin never used *Sirena*, *-ae*, which appears only in very late texts,[62] and nothing similar is attested in other Italic languages.[63] In my opinion Σειρηνάων is a purely Greek invention based on Homer: the Epicharmean line depends heavily on Hom. *Od.* 12.52 ὄφρα κε τερπόμενος ὄπ᾽ ἀκούσῃς Σειρήνοιϊν, where both the verb and the noun fill the same metrical slot at the end of the line.

In the *Odyssey* the Sirens appear in the dual also at 12.167 νῆσον Σειρήνοιϊν and at 12.185 νωϊτέρην, but are otherwise in the plural (e.g. 12.39 Σειρῆνας, 42 Σειρήνων, 44 Σειρῆνες, etc.). Whatever one may think about the number of the Homeric Sirens, they were certainly three by the time of the Hesiodic *Catalogue of Women* (fr. 27 Merkelbach–West), and presumably more than two by Epicharmus' time.

In my opinion Σειρηνάων is a bardic artificial form based on the Σειρήνοιϊν of *Od.* 12.52. Its creation was made possible because (*a*) the gen./dat. dual of the thematic declension (at an early stage -οιϊν, as in Homeric ὤμοιϊν) was also used for the athematic declension (Hom. ποδοῖϊν, later ποδοῖν; Rix 1976: 160), (*b*) feminine words belonging to the *-a* declension, like χώρᾱ or τιμή, originally had no special form for the dual and used the endings of the

[62] e.g. Hieronym. *epist*. 54.13 *Sirenarum carmina*.

[63] I am grateful to Dr J. H. W. Penney for helping me in this matter.

thematic declension (-ω, -οιϊν) instead.[64] This means that Σειρήνοιϊν was theoretically possible as the dual of both Σειρήν and *Σειρήνα. My impression is that either Epicharmus or an epic poet before him created a novel plural Σειρηνάων as a back-formation from the Homeric dual Σειρήνοιϊν; the new form enabled him to do away with an unwanted dual and at the same time to keep to the metrical shape of the model.[65]

Epicharmus also quoted actual Homeric hexameters; this is made clear by ἀφρ]άτωρ ἀθέμ[ιστος ἀ]νίστιος (113.415). These words are found in a context of (very badly damaged) trochaic tetrameters; however they 'do not get very kindly into a trochaic tetrameter but are presumably an interposed hexameter' (Lobel 1959: 26), obviously a quotation of Hom. *Il.* 9.63 ἀφρήτωρ ἀθέμιστος ἀνέστιός ἐστιν ἐκεῖνος κτλ. The Epicharmean quotation is accommodated to the Doric vocalic system (for ἀνίστιος cf. 32.4 τὸν ἱστιῶντ' ἐπαινέω). This might not look especially interesting at first sight, but becomes interesting once we cast a look at what we find in Aristophanes. The same Homeric line happens to be quoted at Ar. *Pax* 1097, and appears in the manuscripts precisely as it is in Homer, ἀφρήτωρ ἀθέμιστος ἀνέστιος. Ἀνέστιος could be Attic as well, but ἀφρήτωρ cannot: there were φρᾱ́τορες and φρᾱτρίαι in Athens, and one would expect ἀφρᾱ́τωρ in an Attic version of the line. Now, most of the Aristophanic hexameters (about 130 and never properly studied from a linguistic point of view) are of Aristophanes' own invention. In this case they show a remarkable number of Attic features in phonology, morphology, prosody, and vocabulary: suffice it to quote from the *Peace* ὦ κᾰτᾰ́ρᾱτε (1076b) and καὶ κᾰτᾰ́ρᾱτον (1272) which are clearly Attic (the Homeric form is ἄρητός and would be unmetrical). At *Av.* 971 πρῶτον Πανδώρᾳ θῦσαι λευκότριχα κριόν the dative Πανδώρᾳ has never been changed by modern editors into an Ionic Πανδώρῃ, and rightly so. Aristophanes seems to have drawn a sharp line between hexameters of his own making, very close to the Attic system, and actual quotations of Homer, which were left untouched. On the contrary

[64] This is made clear by Mycenaean, where the dual of τράπεζα appears as *to-pe-zo*, and *wa-na-so-i* (ϝανάσσοιιν) means 'den beiden Herrinnen' (Rix 1976: 135). In Hesiod (*Op.* 198–9) two female personifications, Aidos and Nemesis, καλυψαμένω χρόα καλὸν ἀθανάτων μετὰ φῦλον ἴτον προλιπόντ' ἀνθρώπους.

[65] The literary origin of Σειρηνάων was rightly perceived by Latte (1968: 110–11), who, however, envisaged the relationship between Σειρηνάων and the Homeric form Σειρήνοιϊν in wrong terms, as he recognized himself (110 n. 5).

Epicharmus, at least on the showing of ἀφρ]άτωρ and ἀ]νίστιος, seems to have accomodated the Homeric vocalism to that of his own dialect.

It is obviously hazardous to draw any conclusions from such scanty evidence. And yet that small scrap of papyrus with its Doricized ἀφρ]άτωρ ἀθέμ[ιστος ἀ]νίστιος reminds us of an important problem, familiar to those who study archaic Greek epigrams on stone: to what extent, and on what occasions, were the Ionic features of epic texts accommodated to the dialect of each Greek polis (obviously when metre allowed it)? At Athens Homer's Ionic text seems to have never been exposed to radical Attic tampering, in spite of various Atticisms discussed by Wackernagel (1916),[66] but the language of archaic Athenian stone epigrams is strongly influenced by the local dialect,[67] and according to Burkert (1994) Orphic hexameter poetry at Athens was also tinged with Attic, an idea I have recently tried to support with further arguments (Cassio 2000). What happened at Syracuse is unfathomable; Epicharmus' Doricized quotation might indicate an attitude of Doric comedy towards the epic tradition different from that of Aristophanes and his colleagues, but one might also suspect that Homeric recitations were more exposed to 'translation' into the local dialect at Syracuse than they were at Athens.

11. In what follows I offer some comments on a significant fragment (97) of the *Odysseus Automolos* ('Odysseus the Deserter'). Almost nothing was known about this comedy until Gomperz (1889) published a papyrus of the first century BC from the collection of Archduke Rainer that contained a fragment of commentary and a few trochaic tetrameters in Doric, which obviously belonged to a Doric comedy. The commentary made it clear that a character in the play had in mind to declare that he had carried out a mission which had never taken place[68] and Gomperz (1889: 3) suggested that it was in fact Odysseus, who had been instructed by the Achaeans to enter Troy disguised as a

[66] It should be recalled that many of the features labelled as Attic in that book are not *exclusively* Attic, and that 'irreducible Atticisms are very few' (S. West 1988: 38 n. 15).

[67] As it commonly happens in archaic stone epigrams, which, however, are also influenced by various literary traditions: see Mickey (1981).

[68] Epich. fr. 97, schol. l. 7 προσποιήσομ(αι) πάντ(α) διαπεπρᾶχθ(αι).

beggar (Hom. *Od.* 4.242 ff.). Here is the text of the papyrus without supplements:

]νθωντε̂ιδεθωκηcω̂τε· καιλεξου̂[
]ίμεινταυτα· καιτοιcδεξιωτεροιc[
]εμινδοκειτεπαγχυκαικατατροπ[
]οτωcεπευξασθ'άιτιcενθυμε̂ινγ[
]γ' ωφειλονὲνθὲνὖcπερεκελήc[
]ṭωναγαθϊκωνκακαπροτῑμᾱ́cαιθ[
]δυνοντελεccαι· καικλέοcθειονλ̣[
]νμολὼνεcαcτϋπανταδ' εὖcὰφα[
]νοcδίοιcτ' αχαιοιcπαιδίτ' ατρέοcφι[
]γέιλαιτατηνε̂ι· καυτοcαcκηθηc.[

5 ἐνθὲιν iota del.; 9 δῖ'οιc circumfl. del.

The interpretation of this fragment has a remarkably complicated story, and it is necessary to dwell on it briefly for clarity's sake. Gomperz (1889: 4) interpreted the text as information supplied by Odysseus to the inhabitants of the Troad, and reconstructed it as a semi-philosophical monologue, but his supplements were highly improbable, and were easily demolished by Blass (1889), who proposed different ones and interpreted the whole scene as a piece of information addressed to the audience in the prologue and expressed in the form of a wish:[69]

αἴθ' ἐγών] γ' ὤφειλον ἐνθὲν ὗσπερ ἐκελήσ[αντό με,
εἶτα μή τι] τῶν ἀγαθικῶν κακὰ προτιμάσαι θ[ανών
ἀλλὰ κίν]δυνον τελέσσαι καὶ κλέος θεῖον λ[αβέν.

Blass provided no translation, but one would guess that he took his text to mean 'may I go there where they told me, and not prefer evil conduct to courage[70] in such a way as to end up in death, but fulfil the dangerous task and win godlike glory'. The real trouble is that *αἴθ'* . . . *ὤφειλον* must refer to the *past*, and Blass himself had to admit (1889: 262) that the wish was expressed 'in eigentümlich gewählter Form'. Although Blass's interpretation is impossible as a whole, his reconstruction of 6 (*εἶτα μή τι] τῶν ἀγαθικῶν κτλ.*) was partially right and in any case far less wide of the mark than Kaibel's, as we shall see (§13).

[69] Blass (1889: 262): 'es gehört der exposition an, wohl dem prologe, in welchem der held in eigentümlich gewählter form des wünschens die zuschauer über das was vor sich gehen sollte in angemessener weise orientierte'.

[70] On the meaning of *ἀγαθικός* see §13.

A few years later, Kaibel (1899: 108–9) changed that interpretation radically: 'Ulixes explorandi causa Troiam missus metu praepeditus proficisci noluit. iam in media fabula solus in scaena sedens meditari videtur quam apud Achaeos habiturus est orationem'. As Kaibel reconstructed it, Odysseus' *Trugrede* to the Achaeans had a self-assured, almost defiant tone:

> τῆλ' ἀπε]νθὼν τεῖδε θωκησῶ τε καὶ λεξοῦ[μ' ὅπως
> πιστά κ' ε]ἴμειν ταῦτα καὶ τοῖς δεξιωτέροι[ς δοκῇ.
> "τοῖς θεοῖς] ἐμὶν δοκεῖτε πάγχυ καὶ κατὰ τρόπ[ον
> καὶ ἐοικό]τως ἐπεύξασθ', αἴ τις ἐνθυμεῖν γ[α λῇ,
> ὅσσ' ἐγών]γ' ὤφειλον ἐνθ[ὼ]ν ὕσπερ ἐκελή[σασθ' ἐμὲ
> τῶν παρ' ὑμέ]ων ἀγαθικῶν κακὰ προτιμάσαι θ' [ἅμα
> ἅμα τε κίν]δυνον τελέσσαι καὶ κλέος θεῖον [λαβεῖν,
> πολεμίω]ν μολὼν ἐς ἄστυ, πάντα δ' εὖ σαφα[νέως
> πυθόμε]νος δίοις τ' Ἀχαιοῖς παιδί τ' Ἀτρέος φί[λῳ
> ἄψ ἀπαγγ]εῖλαι τὰ τηνεῖ καὐτὸς ἀσκηθὴς [μολεῖν."

I will retire and sit down here, and consider how my story may seem true even to the sharper wits among them. 'It is, I deem, entirely right and proper that you should give thanks to heaven, if you will only consider how much misery I was obliged, by going where you told me, to prefer to your kindness, (in order) to fulfil a dangerous task, to win immortal glory by going to the foemen's city . . .'.[71]

This interpretation was reached by means of supplements very different from those of Blass, a different interpretation of ὤφειλον, and a correction of ἐνθὲν; moreover, the meaning of both ἀγαθικά and κακά is the reverse of that accepted by Blass (see §13).

12. Kaibel's text and interpretation were almost universally accepted[72] until Lobel (1959) published an Oxyrhynchus papyrus of the second century AD containing a commentary on a Doric comedy: in its initial section some new lines (now Epich. fr. 97.1–6) are quoted (and commented upon), but they are followed by Epicharmean lines already known from the Rainer papyrus. Its attribution to the *Odysseus automolos* was confirmed, but the previous interpretations and supplements were not.

Three things became clear: (1) the lines do not represent a continuous monologue, but two of them were delivered by a

[71] Page (1941: 195), translating Kaibel's text.

[72] Stanford (1950) did not agree with Kaibel (1899), but his own interpretation proved wrong in the light of the papyrus published by Lobel (1959); see below.

different actor;[73] (2) the Homeric 'model' of the comedy is likely to have been not *Odyssey* 4 but *Iliad* 10 (Lobel 1959: 42); (3) Odysseus does not want to go back because he is afraid of being beaten (97.6 *ο]ὐ γὰρ ἔμπα[λίν χ' ἀνύσ]αιμ' οὕτως ἀλοιῆσθαι κακόν*) by the Achaeans, who are near at hand (*τοίδε τωιχαιοὶ πέλας* 97.4; better *τω{ι}χαιοὶ*). Clearly Odysseus is no longer the self-confident liar imagined by Kaibel, but is dangerously near to a *redde rationem* and 'seems to be preparing some kind of cover story for an operation that has gone by no means according to plan' (Handley 1985: 369); in his speech there can be no room for triumphant tones.[74]

I append the text of Epich. fr. 97.7–16:

(*'Οδ.*) *ἐ]νθὼν τεῖδε θωκησῶ τε καὶ λεξοῦ[ ]ως*
ῥάιδιν' ε⌋ἵμειν ταῦτα καὶ τοῖς δεξιωτέροις ⌊ἐμεῦ[ς.—
(*B.*) *] ἐμὶν δοκεῖτε πάγχυ καὶ κατὰ τρόπ⌊ον*
καὶ ἐοικ⌋ότως ἐπεύξασθ', αἴ τις ἐνθυμεῖν γ[α λῆι.
(*'Οδ.*) *]γ' ὤφειλον ἐνθὲν ὗσπερ ἐκελήσ[*
]ṭων ἀγαθικῶν κακὰ προτιμάσαι θ[
κίν]δυνον τελέσσαι καὶ κλέος θεῖον λ̣[αβεῖν
]ν μολὼν ἐς ἄστυ, πάντα δ' εὖ σαφα[νέως
πυθόμε]νος δίοις τ' Ἀχαιοῖς παιδί τ' Ἀτρέος φί[λωι
ἄψ ἀπαγ]γ̣είλαι τὰ τηνεῖ καὐτὸς ἀσκηθὴς.[

I would suggest the following translation, based on some of the supplements recorded by Kassel and Austin in their apparatus (7 *λεξοῦ[μ' ὅπ]ως*, which seems inescapable to me;[75] 11 *αἴθ' ἐκελής[αντό με*, 13 *τόν τε*, 14 *Τρωϊκόν*, 16 *φυγεῖν*) and on Blass' (1889: 261) *εἶτα μή τι*] at 12 (see §13). Odysseus says: 'I'll go and sit here, and say that this (i.e. what I was told to do) was easy even for cleverer men than I', a surprise for 'perfect fools', as is made clear by the commentary.[76] Then a different actor delivers ll. 9 and 10:

[73] As stated in the Oxyrhynchus commentary (Epich. fr. 98.52) *ὁ ἕτερος τῶν ὑποκριτῶν*.

[74] Odysseus' brief 'rehearsal' of what he intends to say to the Achaeans reminds one of Sosia's words in Plautus' *Amphitruo* (201–2): *sed quo modo et verbis quibus me deceat fabularier, | prius ipse mecum etiam volo hic meditari. sic hoc proloquar*. I am grateful to A. M. Belardinelli for pointing out to me this parallel. The similarity between Odysseus' words in Epicharmus and Sosia's in Plautus had already been noticed by Sudhaus (Fraenkel 1960: 332 n. 3).

[75] For *ὅπως* followed by accusative and infinitive see Kühner–Gerth (1898–1904: 2.357–8).

[76] Epich. fr. 97, schol. l. 1; see Lobel (1959: 41).

'you (plural) seem to me to be entirely right in making (or: having made) prayers,[77] if one thinks about it'. At l. 11 Odysseus resumes: 'would that I had gone where they told me, not preferred dishonesty to virtuous conduct, but run the risk, obtained divine glory by entering the Trojan city, learnt everything clearly, brought the news back to the goodly Achaeans and the dear son of Atreus, and myself come unscathed.'

This translation differs from that of Webster in Pickard-Cambridge (1962: 256) in some important details. The meaning of *τῶν ἀγαθικῶν κακὰ προτιμάσαι* (l. 12) is hardly 'to prefer evils to camp comforts', as Webster supposed: see §13. And at ll. 9–10 *ἐμὶν δοκεῖτε πάγχυ . . . κατὰ τρόπ[ον] . . . ἐπεύξασθαι* cannot be addressed to Odysseus and mean 'you and your like seem to me to be entirely right in making prayers', as translated by Webster, who imagined an Odysseus 'praying' not to be punished; *δοκεῖτε* certainly refers to the Achaeans (Lobel 1959: 42) and *ἐπεύχομαι* cannot mean 'to make prayers' with the aim of being forgiven or pardoned.

Anyhow it is hard to say what ll. 9–10 really meant: apparently a different actor (Diomedes?) addressed the (absent) Achaeans as if they were present, probably rehearsing his own part of the cover story they both intended to tell. *Ἐπεύχομαι* basically means 'to make a vow' or 'to utter a curse', and might refer to vows made by the Achaeans before Odysseus' departure ('You were right to make vows because everything went off well'[78]). The tiresome insistence on the concept of righteousness (*πάγχυ καὶ κατὰ τρόπ[ον] [καὶ ἐοικ]ότως*) and the stilted prosody of *κατὰ τ'ρόπον* (see below) are in my opinion clear indications of a bitterly ironical remark.[79]

In the language the local Syracusan element is obviously prominent. This is evident in adverbs and pronouns, like 7 *τεῖδε* and 16 *τηνεῖ*, which are old locatives; at 8 *ἐμεῦς* and 9 *ἐμίν* are what we expect in the Syracusan dialect. *ὖσπερ* (11) is especially interesting; *ὖς* is the relative form of the adverb *πῦς* 'whither?', attested in Sophron (fr. 75), which is in turn a Greek manipulation of an inherited Indo-European form.[80] *θωκέω* is the expected form

[77] Or 'uttering curses', because *ἐπεύχομαι* is ambiguous.

[78] In this case *ἐπεύξασθαι* should refer to the past, as in e.g. Soph. *Ant.* 443 *φημὶ δρᾶσαι* 'I say that I did it'; see the commentary (Epich. fr. 98.53]*ηι εἰσόδωι εὐξαμένου τινά*).

[79] See also Luppe (1975: 197): 'gewiß ist diese Zwischenbemerkung höhnisch gemeint'.

[80] *πῦς* < *πυῖς* (Schwyzer 1939: 622). Apparently an inherited $*k^{w}u$ 'where' (cf.

in Doric.[81] The middle sigmatic aorist *ἐκελήσ[* is paralleled by 88.2 *κἠκελήσατο* and is attested in Pindar (*Ol.* 13.80 and *Pyth.* 4.159) and at Epidauros (Schwyzer 1923: no. 109.31). Some verbs are the same as those found in Ionic or Attic, but the opposite diathesis is used, like *λεξοῦμαι* (7): in Attic only *λέξω* (never *λέξομαι*) is used as the future of *λέγω* (Cassio 1997: 191); *ἐνθυμεῖν* (10) would have been *ἐνθυμεῖσθαι* in Attic. I dealt elsewhere at length with the problems posed by such Doric futures as *θωκησῶ* and *λεξοῦμαι* (Cassio 1997: 191); *-ῶ* and *-ου-* look like Attic contractions, but they are not, and were originated by the same phonological processes we already encountered in such forms as *εὐωχεουμένων*.[82]

As I said before, Lobel (1959: 42) noticed remarkable similarities—often exact verbal echoes—between Nestor's speech in *Iliad* 10 and the final lines of this Epicharmean fragment. They are set out in Table 1.

The correspondence is striking; clearly Epicharmus not only accepted the language of the Homeric passage he had in mind but even added further Homeric material, e.g. *δίοις τ' Ἀχαιοῖς* (*δῖοι Ἀχαιοί* is frequently found in the *Iliad*); also *παιδί τ' Ἀτρέος φίλωι* is a conflation of e.g. *παῖδα φίλον* (*Il.* 16.460) and *Ἀτρέος υἱός* (*Il.* 17.79). At l. 13 both *κλέος* and *θεῖον* are Homeric, but *κλέος θεῖον* (or *θεῖον κλέος*) is a different story: not only is it absent from Homer, but seems to be a unique expression in the Greek literature known to us. At l. 9 the prosody of *κατὰ τ'ρόπον* is certainly epic.[83]

It should be noted, however, that some of the Homeric vocabulary may have sounded less poetic to a Syracusan audience than it seems to us: for example *ἀσκηθής* (l. 16), which, incidentally, corresponds to English *unscathed* both etymologically and semantically, is attested in inscriptions of Tegea and Epidaurus (Frisk 1960–72: 1.164; LSJ 1940: 257, s.v.), and may have been current

Vedic *kúha*), which ought to have given **κυ* in Greek, was modified to **πυ* on the analogy of forms like *ποῖ* or *πῶ* (< **k*^{w}*oi*, **k*^{w}*ō*), then to *πυῖ* under the specific pressure of *ποῖ* 'whither?' Later on, *πυῖ* was 'mit -*ς* erweitert' (Schwyzer 1939: 621 n. 10).

[81] And Ionic; the Attic form is *θᾱκέω*: see Frisk (1960–72: 1.647–8).

[82] *λεξέομαι* > *λεξοῦμαι* in consequence of the following changes: [-séo-] > [-se̯ô:-] > [-si̯ô:-] and finally [-sô:-] with absorption of [i̯]. See Méndez Dosuna (1993), Cassio (1997: 192–7), Colvin (1999: 215–16).

[83] Contrast Epich. fr. 158.2 *μάρᾰθᾰ, 'τρᾱχέες τε κάκτοι κτλ.* (and 264.3 *οὐδὲ εἷς οὐδὲν μετ' ὀργᾶς κατὰ 'τρόπον βουλεύεται*, a line which, however, probably belongs to the *Pseudepicharmea*).

TABLE 3.1. *Comparison:* Iliad *10* ~ *Epich. fr. 97*

Hom. *Il.* 10.204–13	Epich. fr. 97
ὦ φίλοι οὐκ ἂν δή τις ἀνὴρ πεπίθοιθ' ἑῷ αὐτοῦ	
θυμῷ τολμήεντι μετὰ Τρῶας μεγαθύμους	(14 μολὼν ἐς ἄστυ)
ἐλθεῖν, εἴ τινά που δηΐων ἕλοι ἐσχατόωντα,	
ἤ τινά που καὶ φῆμιν ἐνὶ Τρώεσσι πύθοιτο	
ἅσσα τε μητιόωσι μετὰ σφίσιν, ἢ μεμάασιν	
αὖθι μένειν παρὰ νηυσὶν ἀπόπροθεν, ἦε πόλινδε	
ἂψ ἀναχωρήσουσιν, ἐπεὶ δαμάσαντό γ' Ἀχαιούς;	
ταῦτα τε πάντα πύθοιτο καὶ ἂψ εἰς ἡμέας ἔλθοι	14 ff. πάντα δ' εὖ . . . πυθόμενος . . . ἂψ ἀπαγγεῖλαι
ἀσκηθής· μέγα κέν οἱ ὑπουράνιον κλέος εἴη	. . . καὐτὸς ἀσκηθὴς (φυγεῖν)—13 κλέος θεῖον
πάντας ἐπ' ἀνθρώπους κτλ.	

in the Syracusan dialect. Moreover, the participle *μολών* at l. 14 has nothing poetic about it in Doric-speaking regions, as *ἔμολον* is used there as the aorist of *ἕρπω*, 'to go' (LSJ 1940: 692); *μολών* in Epicharmus interestingly correponds to a banal *ἐλθεῖν* in Homer. On the other hand, *ἐς ἄστυ* is semi-Homeric, as it were: in Homer we invariably find *εἰς ἄστυ*, which is a remodelling of an older **ἐς ϝάστυ* (obviously < **ἐνς ϝάστυ*) or an even older **ἐν ϝάστυ*. The general impression is that of an innovative and sophisticated combination of Homeric and local elements.

13. Two adjectives deserve special attention for different reasons: *ῥᾴδινος* and *ἀγαθικός*. At line 8 the neuter plural *ῥάιδιν(α)* 'easy' (guaranteed by the commentary, 98.45) in the place of the familiar *ῥάιδια* (*ῥᾴδια*) was an interesting surprise; it must be a Doric (especially Syracusan?) innovation. The *-ιδιος* suffix was very frequently used to derive adjectives from adverbs, as in *μαψίδιος* from *μάψ*, *ἐντοσθίδιος* from *ἔντοσθε*; both Homeric *ῥηΐδιος* and Attic *ῥᾴδιος* (< *ῥᾱΐδιος*) are developments of an older **ϝρᾱh-ίδιος*, which is in its turn derived from an adverb **ϝρᾱha*.[84] The easiest way to explain *ῥᾴδινος* is to admit that *ῥᾱ-ίδιος* was wrongly segmented as *ῥᾱίδ-ιος* (on the model of e.g. *ὑπασπίδ-ιος*), and *-ινος*, a suffix already attested in Homer (Risch 1974: 100) and very common in Greek, substituted for *-ιος*. After the publication of this papyrus fragment it became clear that *ῥᾴδινος* was virtually already known: the adverb *ῥᾳδίνως* was concealed in the *vox nihili* *ῥα δεινῶς* transmitted by the codex Marcianus of Athenaeus at Epich. fr. 31.2, which had been corrected a long time ago to the familiar *ῥαιδίως* (accepted by Kaibel 1899: 96, his fr. 34.2). Unfortunately, Kassel and Austin's apparatus is misleading on this point,[85] and neither *ῥᾴδινος* nor *ῥᾳδίνως* is recorded in Glare (1996).

[84] From **u̯rās-* or **u̯rāi̯-*: Frisk (1960–72: 2.636); cf. Hom. *ῥῆα* and *βρᾱϊδίως* (= *ϝρᾱ-*) in Alc. fr. 129.22 Voigt.

[85] They rightly put *ῥαιδίνως* in the text, but from what they print in the apparatus (Kassel–Austin 2001: 29, on Epich. fr. 31.2) '*ῥαιδίνως* Schweigh.: *ῥα δεινῶς* A.' one might get the impression that Schweighäuser (1802*a*) had already conjectured the right form, and wonder why on earth almost a century later Kaibel (1899: 96, his fr. 34.2) decided to adopt the Attic form *ῥαιδίως* instead. But in actual fact Schweighäuser (1802*a*: 405) had printed *ῥᾳδινῶς*, not *ῥαιδίνως*. The difference is not trivial, since he thought (Schweighäuser 1802*b*: 376) that the adverb must be connected with the adjective *ῥᾰδινός* 'slim, slender' and that its long first syllable (*ῥᾳδινῶς*) was justifiable on the basis of ancient etymologies connecting *ῥᾰδινός* with *ῥᾷον*—an obviously groundless surmise. In his opinion, 'si parasitum poeta *ῥαδινόν* diceret, id est macilentum et famelicum, haud incommodum foret epitheton'

At l. 12 ἀγαθικῶν has almost universally been misinterpreted in the twentieth century. The entry in Liddell and Scott (1940: 4) s.v. ἀγαθικός reads '= ἀγαθός, Epich. 99 [= 97.12]', and ἀγαθικά is usually translated as 'comforts'. This meaning is implied by Kaibel's supplements (1899: 108),

> τῶν παρ' ὑμέ]ων ἀγαθικῶν κακὰ προτιμάσαι θ' [ἅμα
> ἅμα τε κίν]δυνον τελέσσαι καὶ κλέος θεῖον λ̣[αβεῖν,

and is made explicit in translations based on Kaibel's text: 'to sacrifice the comforts of your camp to misery' (Page 1941: 195); 'quanti mali . . . dovetti preferire alle vostre comodità' (Barigazzi 1955: 124); 'preferring misery to comfort from you' (Phillips 1959: 59). The interpretation did not change after the publication of the Oxyrhynchus papyrus: 'would that I had gone, as you bade me, preferred evils to camp comforts, run the risk, obtained divine glory' (Webster in Pickard-Cambridge 1962: 256). In sum, ἀγαθικά seems to be commonly interpreted as 'comforts' in contrast with the κακά, the unpleasant situations Odysseus ought to have faced up to and decided to shun.

To my mind this interpretation is far from satisfactory. To begin with, if we assume that ἀγαθικός has the same meaning as ἀγαθός, as LSJ (1940) do, a translation 'comfortable' is by no means obvious, since ἀγαθός usually means 'noble', 'brave', 'morally good'. And there is more, since ἀγαθικός is not 'unattested' as Lobel (1959: 5) maintained: some ancient lexica have a special entry for the Epicharmean adjective, ἀγαθικά· τὰ σπουδαῖα,[86] already known to Gomperz (1889: 8). It was duly recorded in the *Thesaurus Graecae Linguae*, where it was translated with 'proba; recte et cum virtute facta vel dicta' (Stephanus 1865: 1.109), but was ignored by LSJ (1940)[87] and is still absent from the *Revised Supplement* (Glare 1996).

For an adjective derived from ἀγαθός a translation 'serious, honest' is infinitely more plausible than 'comfortable', and is also perfect as the opposite of κακός in its common meaning 'base'. In other words Odysseus is likely to say not, as is

(Schweighäuser 1802*b*: 376). Clearly he had not understood that the required meaning was 'easily'. His impossible ῥᾳδινῶς was corrected to ῥαιδίως by one of his reviewers and the correction accepted by Kaibel (1899: 96). Lobel (1959: 41) was the first to realize that ῥα δεινῶς must conceal ῥαιδίνως.

[86] Photius α 74 Theodoridis = *Anecd. Bekk.* 1.324.7 = *Suda* α 113 Adler.

[87] This is why Lobel (1959: 5) says that the word is 'otherwise unattested'.

commonly assumed, 'would that I had preferred harshness to comfort', but 'would that I had *not* preferred cowardice to virtuous conduct'. This solution, which seems to me the only possible one, had already been reached by Blass (1889: 261), who accepted the ancient explanation of *ἀγαθικά* and supplemented accordingly:

> *αἴθ ἐγών] γ' ὤφειλον ἐνθὲν ὗσπερ ἐκελήσ[αντό με,*
> *εἶτα μή τι] τῶν ἀγαθικῶν κακὰ προτιμάσαι θ[ανών*
> *ἀλλὰ κίν]δυνον τελέσσαι κτλ.*

As we have seen, Blass's interpretation was wrong in so far as he conceived of Odysseus' speech as a piece of information to the audience expressed in the form of a wish, but on this specific point he must have been right; apart from *θ[ανών*, which is clearly wrong,[88] the interpretation implied by Blass' supplements seem to me the only possible one: 'would that I had gone where they told me, *not* preferred dishonest to virtuous conduct, *but* run the risk . . .'. Unfortunately, it was not accepted by Kaibel (1899: 108–9) because it clashed with his own reconstruction of the scene: a soliloquy in which Odysseus exalted his bravery and merits, and in which there was obviously no room for statements like 'would that I had done my duty and not been dishonest'. Since the ancient explanation *ἀγαθικά· τὰ σπουδαῖα* ran counter to Kaibel's interpretation and supplements, he carefully avoided to quote it, and it was subsequently forgotten.

But the papyrus published by Lobel (1959) proved that Kaibel's reconstruction was wrong, and I personally feel certain that *ἀγαθικός* must be interpreted according to the ancient lexica: it must have carried a specialized meaning of *ἀγαθός* and gained some currency in Syracuse and in other Doric areas. Gomperz (1889: 8) compared 'das eng verwandte *ἀνδραγαθικός*' in the Hippocratic treatise *De articulis*,[89] which is, as it happens, very rich in Doric forms (Schmidt 1977: 55).

14. A few words by way of conclusion. It is always extremely difficult to provide a consistent picture of the language of an

[88] Gomperz's *θέλων* is possible as far as the meaning is concerned, but one expects *λῶ*, not *θέλω*, in Epicharmus' dialect, although *θέλω* would probably be acceptable as an importation from Ionic (or tragedy). Curiously enough, the main source here is Homer, in whom *θέλω* is almost non-existent.

[89] Ch. 78, 4.312.4 Littré *ἀνδραγαθικώτερον τοῦτο καὶ τεχνικώτερον*, 'cette règle est celle de l'honneur comme celle de l'art' (Littré 1844: 313).

author whose text is preserved only in fragments. In the case of Epicharmus we are faced with the paradoxical situation that his fragments are not just a witness to *his* language, but also our main source for his linguistic environment as a whole. As a consequence we constantly run the risk of mistaking personal idiosyncrasies for instances of common usage and vice versa; we simply have no idea of what a 'middle register' of literary Syracusan dialect looked like.

Yet there are at least two main reasons why one should not surrender without fighting. Firstly, Epicharmus' fragments open up a fascinating world often skirted round by students of Greek literature: that of a powerful colonial city whose traditions and institutions were profoundly different from those prevailing at Athens, and whose dialect, very different from Attic, was remarkably influenced by indigenous languages.

Secondly, Epicharmus provides a useful corrective to our 'Athenocentric' view of Greek drama. Doric comedy is a concept often consciously or unconsciously linked with obscure problems of 'origins' and 'popular farce', but its fragments are there to remind us that Greek comedy was at its zenith at Syracuse some fifty years (and probably more) before Aristophanes produced his first play: Epicharmus based some of his plots on Homeric material, could manipulate epic language in an extremely subtle manner, embarked on sophisticated philosophical discussions, and parodied Aeschylus precisely as Aristophanes was to parody Euripides many decades later. The linguistic analysis of his fragments undoubtedly presents a number of risks, yet it is certainly one of the most important tools at our disposal if we want to recover a glimpse of one of the most sophisticated literary genres of ancient Greece.[90]

[90] I am very grateful to C. Austin, A. M. Belardinelli, A. Morpurgo Davies, J. H. W. Penney, and A. Willi for suggestions and corrections.

4
Some Evaluative Terms in Aristophanes

KENNETH DOVER

> Bellamy, following him, had offered his services too, but had been told by Kenneth in a friendly way to 'fuck off'.
>
> Iris Murdoch, *The Green Knight*

For the proper understanding of anything that is uttered in our presence we need not only to hear the words but also to observe the pattern of stress, pause, and intonation, together with facial expression, gesture, and stance. Of all those ingredients, facial expression is the only one which was denied to ancient theatrical audiences, since the actors were masked, and combinations of the other ingredients could compensate for the loss. Every one of the ingredients, however, is denied to a reader of the text, from Hellenistic times to our own, except for such indications of pause and stress as can be inferred from the syntax. We do not even have authorial stage directions, which in modern plays help to bridge the gap between drama and narrative. Some of Shaw's and Barrie's amount to a commentary which almost closes the gap, though sometimes unhelpfully, e.g. (in Barrie) 'She looks round with an indescribable expression on her face'.

The intonations which express contempt, outrage, or wonder are not the same in all languages, and we have to remember this when we interpret Greek evaluations, especially since lexical tone existed in Greek, but in performing or discussing a text we can switch off the 'mind's ear' and simply use the intonations and stresses which correspond in our own language to our interpretation. There was an ancient theory that πονηρος was accented oxytone when it meant 'bad' but proparoxytone when it meant 'unfortunate' (Ammonius §405 Nickau, Herodian 1.197.19–20, Eustath. *Il.* 1.533.15–22 van der Valk), but it is clear from the sources that this was not agreed doctrine. Certainly the vocative of πονηρος can be used sympathetically, compassionately (as in *Av.* 1648, *Vesp.* 977, *Ran.* 852), but one may wonder how the accentuation of a word four or five generations before the invention of written accents could be known. Possibly theatrical tradition is the answer, since the vocative of πονηρος continued to be used in New Comedy—probably compassionate in Menander fr. 477 and *Dyskolos* 587, though in the latter πονηρά . . . γραῦ may be an exasperated 'Oh, you useless old woman!'.

Evaluation may be implicit in the choice between alternative verbs of motion, just as in English different ways of saying 'Go away!' occupy different points on a scale between 'Piss/fuck/sod off!' at one end and (e.g.) 'Don't you think perhaps it's time you thought about going?' at the other. In Greek, while (ἀπ)ιέναι and (ἀπ)ελθεῖν are neutral (the last word of the Periclean funeral speech in Thuc. 2.45.2 is the simple ἄπιτε), the use of (ἀπ)έρρειν implies contemptuous hostility. In *Nub.* 783 'That's drivel. ἄπερρε. I can't go on teaching you' conveys despairing impatience ('You're no use!'), and 'Get away!' is the point in *Pax* 1294 and *Eccl.* 169. The level of contempt implicit in ἔρρειν is demonstrated by *Lys.* 1240 οὐκ ἐρρήσετ' ὦ μαστιγίαι;, addressed to slaves who are in the way. Such an imperative (or negative interrogative future in imperatival sense) can be reinforced by the curse ἐς κόρακας, e.g. *Pax* 500, *Plut.* 604. The most curious verb of motion in comedy, always a problem for translators into any modern language, is φθείρεσθαι. The simple verb and its compound with ἀπο- can be rendered 'Piss/etc. off!', 'get out!', 'get the hell out of here!', etc., e.g. *Ach.* 460 φθείρου λαβών 'Here you are. Now get out!'. The other compounds call for a variety of treatments: *Av.* 916 κατὰ τί δεῦρ' ἀνεφθάρης; 'What the hell have you come up here for?', *Pax* 72 ἐκφθαρεὶς οὐκ οἶδ' ὅποι 'He buggered off somewhere, I don't know where . . .' (in a disgruntled voice) or 'He went off . . .' with the addition of a curse *sotto voce* (Olson 1998: ad loc.), *Eccl.* 248 ἢν Κέφαλός σοι λοιδορῆται προσφθαρείς 'If that shit Kephalos' ('that blasted Kephalos', Sommerstein 1998: ad loc.) 'comes up and starts abusing you . . .'.

The simplest expression of evaluation is by interjections. In current English, for example, 'Yu(c)k!' (replacing the earlier grapheme 'Ugh!' and generating the adjective 'yucky') expresses revulsion against something ugly or disgusting. The Greek equivalent is *αἰβοῖ*, as in *Ach.* 189–90, *Vesp.* 371, *Pax* 51 (all with reference to bad smells), *Vesp.* 973 (psychosomatic malaise); in *Nub.* 906–7 the evaluation is moral, but 'bring me a basin!' (*sc.* in which to vomit) follows immediately. There are however instances of *αἰβοῖ* used as a joyful exclamation: *Av.* 1342, ibid. 610 ('Oh, YES!'), and in *Pax* 1066 *αἰβοιβοῖ* represents laughter (the speaker explains, *ἥσθην κτλ.*). A similar spread is attested for *φεῦ* and *οἴμοι*, more commonly expressive of fear or sadness: *Nub.* 773 '*οἴμοι*, how delighted I am . . .!', *Av.* 162 '*φεῦ φεῦ*, I've a wonderful idea taking shape . . .!', ibid. 1723 '*ὢ φεῦ φεῦ*, her youth, her beauty!'. That last example may make us think of 'Pfwooaargh!', a favourable aesthetic appraisal highly charged with lust, though the same grapheme could plausibly represent the sound uttered by a sufferer from lumbago getting up from a chair; the difference, if no masks were worn, would be shown in the eyes and mouth, but could certainly be shown by gesture and posture. Between happy and unhappy *οἴμοι* the difference would have been analogous to the English differentiation of species of 'Oh dear!', which sometimes accompanies laughter, especially of a self-deprecating kind. So Hermes, tempted by a bribe, and indeed yielding to it, exclaims in *Pax* 424 '*οἴμοι*, what a soft spot I have . . .!'. López Eire (1996*b*: 90–1) compares Spanish *¡ay!*.

The validity of J. R. Firth's dictum that nothing 'means' anything without a context (I don't know if he ever said exactly that in print, but he said it to me, reprovingly, on an occasion at Oxford in 1946) depends on how far we extend or restrict 'context', and with any reasonable degree of restriction the dictum is vulnerable (cf. Langendoen 1968: 45–8, 64–5), but it makes an important point where evaluative words are concerned. Mere collocation is sometimes all the context that we need (e.g. *Nub.* 783 *ὑθλεῖς. ἄπερρε*), but evaluation abounds in paralinguistic ingredients. For instance, Dickey (1996: 95) acutely observes that on the only three occasions in Herodotus when the Persian king is addressed as *ὦ βασιλεῦ Μήδων* instead of the usual *ὦ βασιλεῦ* the speakers are subtly but defiantly demoting him.

The detection of sarcasm, in which a word which normally communicates a favourable evaluation is employed to convey the opposite, is seldom difficult, though the amount of context needed is variable. In *Ran.* 1154 'that great poet' (*ὁ σοφός*) 'Aeschylus has said the same thing twice' would be identifiable as sarcastic even if it were a one-line fragment, because good poets do not say the same thing twice. When Strepsiades in *Nub.* 8–10, tossing and turning, says of his son 'But this upstanding' (ὁ χρηστός) 'young man doesn't wake up at night. He farts away swaddled in five coverlets', although flatulence is perfectly compatible with virtue, untroubled sleep, given the circumstances, is not. Sarcasm is often expressed by γε after the leading word of an utterance (Denniston 1954: 129–30), e.g. *Av.* 139 καλῶς γέ μου τὸν υἱόν κτλ. 'That was a fine way to treat my son . . .!', *Nub.* 647 ταχύ γ' ἂν δύναιο κτλ., 'Oh yes, you'd soon be able . . .!', ibid. 1064 ἀστεῖόν γε κέρδος, 'A brilliant reward . . .!', Pherecrates fr. 159.2 καλόν γε δῶρον κτλ., 'A fine gift . . .!' (cf. 'This is a fine mess you've gotten me into!' in Laurel and Hardy films). In *Eq.* 344–5 'καλῶς γε you'd handle a case that fell to you . . . χρηστῶς', since the adverbs καλῶς and χρηστῶς are not coordinated, it looks as if χρηστῶς carries the weight and καλῶς signals sarcasm. Sometimes, though, an initial adjective followed by γε is plainly not sarcastic, e.g. *Eccl.* 70, in which the adjective is preceded by an oath, and γε is not always present, e.g. *Nub.* 8 (quoted above) and *Av.* 91 ὦγάθ' ὡς ἀνδρεῖος εἶ, 'Why, you *are* brave!'.

In *Eq.* 346, immediately following the sarcastic passage cited above, the diminutive δικίδιον expresses contempt, 'some piddling lawsuit', and the same use of diminutives is manifest when an opprobrious adjective is added, as in *Ach.* 517 ἀνδράρια μοχθηρά. Yet a diminutive can also be pathetic, as when a widow in *Thesm.* 447 refers to her παιδάρια, or expressive of enthusiastic affection, the verbal equivalent of an impulsive embrace, as in *Nub.* 746, where Strepsiades is struck by a good idea and cries ὦ Σωκρατίδιον φίλτατον. For the diminutive form of a proper name we may compare *Nub.* 79, where Strepsiades awakens his son with Φειδιππίδη Φειδιππίδιον, having decided that this will waken him ἥδιστα, ibid. 223 and 237, where he uses Σωκρατίδιον to lure Socrates down to the ground, together with *Ach.* 404 Εὐριπίδη Εὐριπίδιον and 475 Εὐριπίδιον ὦ γλυκύτατον καὶ φίλτατον used by Dikaiopolis begging from Euripides; Sommerstein (1995: 70–2) points out that γλυκύτατος, an endearment used by husband to wife and mother to baby (*Lys.* 872, 889–90) is a grotesque exaggeration for comic effect when used by Dikaiopolis. Even so, the use of 'Dear little . . .' and the like in English translations is usually no more appropriate than using it in translating Swiss

German words which are no more than formally diminutive. The English equivalent of vocative diminutives is the intonation associated with 'Oh, please!' and 'Oh, *do* . . . !'.

It would obviously be wrong to suppose that Dikaiopolis' affectionate diminutives express genuine affection on his part; the context indicates the opposite (cf. *Ach.* 457, 461), and, like the superabundant diminutives of colloquial Russian (not necessarily vocatives), *Εὐριπίδιον* and the like are 'tactical', designed to create in the addressee an attitude favourable to the speaker; *Nub.* 78 'Now, how can I wake him *ἥδιστα*?' implies as much, and even in *Nub.* 746 it may be that after the dialogue of 723–45 we are meant to think of Strepsiades as rather afraid of Socrates and anxious to appease him. A most striking example of tactical praise is the addressing of *ὦ γεννάδα* to Aeschylus in *Ran.* 997. In *Ran.* 179 *χρηστὸς εἶ καὶ γεννάδας* it denotes 'accommodating', 'helpful', referring to an attachment to fairness even at the cost of pain to oneself; so too 640, while in 738–9 it is 'easy-going', 'tolerant', 'lenient'. Aeschylus, however, throughout his contest with Euripides, shows the opposite characteristics, being bad-tempered, aggressive, anything but accommodating (cf. 1008, 1020). Yet the chorus still addresses him as *ὦ γεννάδα*, begging him not to let his anger run away with him when he replies to Euripides. After what they have heard from him (840–59, 936, 950–1, 955) they cannot conceivably imagine that he *is* *γεννάδας*, but in order to calm him down they address him *as if* they did think so. Similarly, while the vocatives *ὦγαθέ* and *ὦ βέλτιστε* often express the speaker's approval of the addressee (note especially *Eccl.* 213 'Well said, well said! Go on, go on, *ὦγαθέ*!', applauding a speech), they are also used tactically in an effort—appeasing, correcting, protesting—to make the addressee think and act in a way desired by the speaker. Such English expressions as 'My good fellow!' and 'My dear sir!' being now archaic, the nearest equivalent to tactical *ὦγαθέ* is 'Now, just think . . .' or 'But surely . . .' uttered with a soothing cadence. In *Plut.* 360 *παῦσαι φλυαρῶν ὦγαθέ*, 'Oh, stop all that nonsense!' *ὦγαθέ* has the effect of adding a friendly 'Come off it, now!' or 'Aw, c'mon!' to what would otherwise have been a harsh and insulting directive.

An illuminating example of tactical praise is provided by Plato, *Phdr.* 268 DE, where Socrates imagines a musician dealing with an obstinate ignoramus: 'He wouldn't say, coarsely' (*ἀγροίκως* Osann:

ἀγρίως codd.) '"*ὦ μοχθηρέ, μελαγχολᾷς*"' ("you daft bugger/silly sod/crazy jerk") 'but, as a cultured man' (*ἅτε μουσικὸς ὤν*) 'more mildly, "*ὦ ἄριστε, ἀνάγκη μέν. . .*"'. However 'cultured' the musician is, he can hardly help *thinking ὦ μοχθηρέ, μελαγχολᾷς*, but he refrains from *saying* it, because he (naturally) wants the ignoramus to see the truth, and he would be unlikely to achieve that purpose by launching straightway into coarse abuse. That is a principle which the Platonic Socrates himself keeps in mind, because, wanting to get at the truth, he handles his interlocutor as if the two of them were cooperating in that serious endeavour, and such cooperation demands civility and decorum (Halliwell 1995: 92, 106, 120, *al.*), even an occasional turning of the other cheek (e.g. *ὦ φίλε Μέλητε* in *Apol.* 26 D). Dickey (1996: 110–27) argues that complimentary modes of address in such circumstances are characteristic of the 'dominant' participant in an argument, who can afford magnanimity and no doubt is pleased to display it. That would account for some instances, but the contexts of *ὦγαθέ* and *ὦ βέλτιστε* are so varied that no one interpretation suits all of them (Halliwell 1999: 115–17). In Menander, *Aspis* 174 *ὦγαθέ* seeks sympathy for a complaint, in *Epit.* 443 it accompanies a bullying demand, while in *Dys.* 503 *βέλτιστε* reinforces an abject plea for mercy. In Demosthenes 52.27, 52.29, 56.40 *ὦ βέλτιστε* goes with a question addressed by the speaker to his opponent and triumphantly answered by the speaker himself; it seems here to have a formulaic character, which the speaker of 36.52 highlights by adding at once 'if you can be called that' and proceeding to *οὐ . . . παύσει;*. 'Dominance' there, certainly; but *ὦγαθοί* in *Ach.* 297, 305, *Vesp.* 415 and *ὦγαθαί* in *Lys.* 765, so far from being an expression of dominance, are a tactical effort to achieve a sufficient degree of it to get a hearing.

In *Nub.* 444–53 Strepsiades declares that if only he can be taught how to defeat his creditors in the courts he won't care if people regard him as—and then follow 21 nouns and adjectives, of which the first four are: *θρασύς, εὔγλωττος, τολμηρός, ἴτης*.

The adjective *θρασύς* or the noun *θράσος* appears in vituperation, coupled with *πονηρός* in *Eq.* 181, with *πανουργία* ibid. 33, and with the violently hostile *ὦ μιαρὲ καὶ βδελυρὲ κτλ.* ibid. 304; cf. *Nub.* 915, where *θρασὺς εἶ πολλοῦ* is part of Right's vehement abuse of Wrong. But whereas the old men in *Lys.* 318 pray for victory over the intolerable θράσος of the women, θράσος is one of the great virtues which the old women see in Lysistrata and her fellow-conspirators (*Lys.* 546).

εὔγλωττος is a rare word—laudatory in Eur. *Supp.* 775, where εὐγλώττῳ φρενί refers to a mind which can express itself well (and, in that instance, in a good cause), while Eur. fr. 56 and 206 convey implicit warning against the seductive power of εὐγλωττία. Different English intonations in 'he can speak' include one which conveys a serious judgement on oratorical skill, one with the implication 'but can't *do* anything' or 'but can't sing', another implying mistrust, and so on.

τολμηρός can certainly be used in vehement hostility; in *Pax* 182 and *Ran.* 465 it is joined with βδελυρός and ἀναίσχυντος, and the noun τόλμα goes with ἀναισχυντία in *Thesm.* 702. Cf. Antiphon iii.γ.1 ἀναιδὴς καὶ τολμηρός, ibid. 5 and iv.γ.6 τόλμης καὶ ἀναιδείας; and when Poverty rages at the two Athenians in *Plut.* 439 she says τόλμημα γὰρ τολμᾶτον οὐκ ἀνασχετόν. Not surprisingly, τόλμα normally figures in Thucydides as a military virtue, 'daring', and that fits with Dikaiopolis' encouragement to his own heart in *Ach.* 488 τόλμησον, ἴθι, χώρησον, 'Come on, be brave, get a move on!' and with the women's reference to their own bold plan as τόλμημα in *Eccl.* 106, 288. In Plato τόλμημα occurs only once and τολμηρός only twice. In *Leg.* 636 C, where homosexual acts are called a τόλμημα, I was wrong (Dover 1989: 165) to translate the word as 'crime' (see Nussbaum 1994: 1627–30 and 1647), associating it unconsciously with the allusion in 836c to the mythical Laios, who 'invented' homosexuality by abducting and raping Chrysippos, a crime by any standards. In *Leg.* 835 C the speaker declares that the desirable reform of festivals, in the absence of divine guidance, calls for someone who is τολμηρός and 'attaches the highest importance to speaking his mind (παρρησία)'; and in *Soph.* 267 D Socrates apologizes for inventing a (useful) compound noun which he fears may be τολμηρότερος, 'too bold'.

ἴτης appears from its occurrence in Pl. *Prot.* 349 E, 359 CD, *Symp.* 203 D to be synonymous with ἰταμός, 'energetic', 'enterprising', 'headstrong', and since that is coupled with ἀναιδής in Men. *Epit.* 537 and with τολμηρός in [Dem.] 25.24, we can see why ἴτης can take its place in Strepsiades' list of reproaches.

The daring which wins medals is very different from that which elicits a furious 'How *dare* you!', and the vocative τολμηρέ most commonly denotes the latter. When coupled with *μιαρέ*, as in *Pax* 182–4 and *Ran.* 465–6, it needs considerable strengthening in translation; the doorkeeper of the underworld in *Ran.* 465, believing his visitor to be none other than the Herakles who had carried off Cerberus, expresses in *τολμηρέ* what his modern equivalent might well put as 'You've got a fucking nerve!', while Hermes in *Pax* 182–4, outraged by the appearance of a mortal on Olympus, implies by *τολμηρέ* 'Who the hell are *you*?'.

Strife is more conspicuous in Old Comedy than mutual courtesy, so that adverse are commoner than favourable evaluations, and the modern translator has more occasion to draw upon rude words than on slang terms of praise; more on e.g. '*x* sucks' than on '*x* is cool' (or 'neat', or 'brill(iant)', 'terrific', 'fantastic', 'smashing', 'hot', 'wicked', 'ba-a-ad', etc.). Rapid change of fashion and (in English) immense dialectal variety complicate the translator's task. For instance, in some Scots dialects a 'pretty' man is anything but effeminate and a 'pretty' woman is more robust than—well, pretty.

Currently, at least in British English, while 'lovely' in 'lovely girl' is aesthetic, in 'lovely person' and 'lovely man' it is moral (I recently heard a general described by a warrant officer as 'a lovely man'). Metaphor at colloquial level in favourable evaluation is rather poorly represented in the language of comedy, though *χρυσίον* occurs twice (*Ach.* 1200, *Lys.* 930) as an erotic vocative (so too *χρυσομηλολόνθιον* in *Vesp.* 1341). In one passage, *Ran.* 745–53, we get an unusual glimpse of Attic slang: a slave responds positively to five successive questions of the form 'And do you enjoy . . . ?'. His first answer is *μάλλ' ἐποπτεύειν δοκῶ*, 'Why, I feel I'm seeing ⟨the sacred objects⟩ in the Mysteries!'. The second, third and fourth answers are banal, but the fifth is *κἀκμιαίνομαι* 'I really do have an orgasm!' ('I shoot my wad' would be too slangy a translation, since *ἐκμιαίνεσθαι* is a Hippocratic word). In current English 'It's orgasmic!' is not uncommon as a description of (e.g.) galloping on horseback or unearthing a legible inscription.

However, English differs from Greek in that the metaphors common in what was called in a recent libel case 'the language of the grown-up playground' have overwhelmed the taboos long arrayed against them. A foolish person is a 'cunt', 'twat', or (especially in cases of complacent folly) 'prick', while an oppressive, dishonest, or otherwise disagreeable person, when not a 'bastard' or 'bitch', is a 'shit', 'turd', or (US) 'asshole'. Varying degrees of hostility and/or contempt can be conveyed by 'wanker' or 'cocksucker'. 'Fuck/-ed, -ing, -er', daily infiltrating ever higher registers in its physiological sense, is all-pervasive in metaphor. It can approximate to a pronoun, as in 'the other fucker' = 'the other one', or function as an intensive infix, as in 'abso-fucking-lutely' (and I have read, but not heard, '*voi*-fucking-*là*!'). Such usage exists side by side with strong negative evaluation. Twenty years ago a good young actor, interviewed about his theatrical ambitions, might well have said 'I don't want to do weird stuff'; but now (*The Observer Magazine*, 19 November 2000): 'I don't want to do fucking weird shit'. Sometimes obscenity expresses the speaker's feelings not about the referent of the adjacent word but about the whole event or situation to which the utterance refers. So a Chancellor of the Exchequer is reported recently to have expostulated with his Prime Minister 'You've stolen my fucking Budget!'.

This phenomenon is shared with other modern European languages. In French *con* 'cunt' and *merde* 'shit' are acceptable as metaphor in a somewhat higher register than their English equivalents, and *foutre* 'fuck' is a permissible substitute for almost any common verb when the speaker wants to display contemptuous command of the situation. In Italian a whole range of vulgar terms for the male and female genitals are used (Galli de' Paratesi 1969: 59–61) to denote stupidity, folly, or misfortune. German usage is weighted in favour of excretion rather than sex, with *Arsch* 'arse' and *Scheiße* 'shit' often serving as first element in a derogatory compound word, e.g. *arschkalt*, *Scheißkerl*. Russian has a great wealth of metaphor based on *khui* and *kher* 'prick', including *ni khujá* 'nothing at all' (cf. the Glaswegian 'nae cunt' = 'no one'), *pizdá* 'cunt', *jebát'* 'fuck' and *govnó* 'shit'—also 'your mother' in the accusative, verb elided, rather as 'motherfucker' in American usage may be reduced to 'mother'. These idioms are of long standing in Russian; Olearius on Russian manners in the mid-seventeenth century observes (Baron 1967: 139): 'Little children who do not yet know the name of God, or father, or mother, already have on their lips "Fuck you!" and say it as well to their parents as their parents to them.'

In modern languages sexual and excretory metaphor is

deployed almost exclusively in hostile and contemptuous judgements, but not always, as we see from the exuberant English 'fucking great' and the French *foutrement bien.* In Italian *fottìo* (~ *fottere* 'fuck') can mean 'a great quantity', and in Russian the adjective *pizdátyj*, derived from *pizdá* 'cunt', means 'first-rate', 'in fine form' (Shlyakhov–Adler 1995: 148).

Where is the analogue to all this in Greek? Considering that Aristophanes exploits to the utmost the humour of excretion and every kind of genital friction, using in their literal sense words which are debarred from prose and tragedy, we may be surprised to find not a single instance of *βινεῖν* 'fuck', *κύσθος* 'cunt', *πέος* and *πόσθη* 'prick', *πρωκτός* 'arse(hole)', *σκῶρ* 'shit', or *πέλεθος* 'turd' used metaphorically (cf. Henderson 1991: 39–40). However, the situation is quite different with words denoting anal and oral sex. In *Nub.* 1325–30, where Strepsiades hurls abuse at his son, he begins by calling him *πατραλοίας*—correctly, since the young man has indeed struck his father—then *τοιχωρύχος* 'burglar', 'housebreaker', a vituperative metaphor which recurs in *Plut.* 909, 1141, and then, climactically, *λακκόπρωκτος*, a word formed from *λάκκος* 'cistern' and *πρωκτός* 'arse', and so akin to the commoner *εὐρύπρωκτος* 'wide-arsed', implying frequent subjection to sodomy, conduct not involved in the violence of which Strepsiades is complaining. In Cephisodorus fr. 3 someone is reproached as *λακκόπρωκτος* because he wants to put perfumed unguent on his feet, and in Eupolis fr. 385.4 the habit of drinking wine in the morning is called *λακκοπρωκτία*. Similarly *καταπύγων*, analysable as 'down-into-the-arse-man', is used in *Nub.* 529 simply as antonym of *σώφρων*, the most general epithet of anyone who stops to think, restrains the impulses to the pursuit of pleasure, and obeys the rules. The word can be used of women; Lysistrata, angry at the reluctance of the women to take part in her sex-strike, exclaims that the whole female sex is *παγκαταπύγων* (*Lys.* 137; cf. 776 *ὄρνεον . . . καταπυγωνέστερον*); there is also a feminine form *καταπύγαινα* (Dover 1989: 114). When Kleon in *Ach.* 664 is called *δειλὸς* ('cowardly'/'feeble') *καὶ λακαταπύγων* the context makes a specific reference to buggery unlikely. Someone in Ar. fr. 128 complains that side dishes and hors d'oeuvres are *καταπυγοσύνη* ('a load of crap') compared with a decent joint of meat. It must be remembered that *καταπύγων* does not correspond to English 'homosexual' or any of its synonyms in English usage, because

Greek society did not stigmatize the penetrator (Dover 1989: 61–8, 135–9), but only the person who is now (sometimes) called the 'penetratee' or 'insertee'. The same is true of the verb *λαικάζειν* and its agent-nouns *λαικαστής* and *λαικάστρια*, people who give 'blow-jobs'. *λαικάστρια* is used contemptuously to denote 'whore' in *Ach.* 529, 537, and we encounter it as an unjustified vocative, 'You whore!', in Men. *Pk.* 484–5. The curse *οὐχὶ λαικάσει;* corresponds to our 'Get fucked!' or 'Fuck you!' (Strato fr. 1.36), and *λαικάσομαι ἄρα* in Cephisodorus fr. 3.5 is uttered where we might say, with a mixture of indignation and ridicule, 'Never heard such nonsense!' or (more closely) 'Well, bugger me!' (Dover 1989: 204–5, correcting 113 and 142–3).

The inundation of colloquial English by the obscenities of the 'grown-up playground' has displaced expressions rooted in religion (Hughes 1991: 30, 171–2, 237), so that in 'God knows!', 'for God's sake', 'for heaven's sake', 'who/what/where/how the devil/hell . . .?', 'run like hell', etc., the elements 'God', 'heaven', 'devil', and 'hell' are increasingly replaced by 'fuck'. In Greek comedy and oratory the religious ingredient in the language of vilification is strong: there are in Aristophanes ten instances of *κατάρατος* 'accursed' (Photius records *λακατάρατος*) and eight of *θεοῖς ἐχθρός*. In New Comedy *ἱερόσυλος* 'temple-robber' serves as a general term of abuse (five times in *Epitrepontes* alone), rather like 'burglar' (see above); and the bizarre *ἱερόσυλα θηρία* is addressed to slaves in Men. *Pk.* 366. There is of course plenty of '(ac)cursed', 'damn(able/ed)', etc. in English-language drama, but it goes with reticence, often extreme reticence, in respect of sexual and excretory functions.

By far the commonest word with a religious base in Greek comedy is *μιαρός*, which serves throughout Aristophanes, especially in the vocative, as a vehemently opprobrious adjective. Although it appears with the connotation 'lustful' in Alcaeus fr. 347 'at this season women are *μιαρώταται*, but men are feeble' (Hesiod, *Op.* 586, purveying the same folk-wisdom, has *μαχλόταται*), it retains the specific sense 'pollut-ed/-ing', down into Hellenistic times, e.g. *SEG* 16.1306.25–6 (Teos, 3rd cent. BC) 'and whoever kills him, let that man not be *μιαρός*', i.e. 'he must not be treated as polluted by blood-guilt' (cf. Parker 1983: 2–5). *μιαίνειν*, *μίασμα*, *μιαρός*, *μιαρία* total 15 examples in a work contemporary with Aristophanes, the *Tetralogies* ascribed to

Antiphon, all concerned with the pollution incurred by homicide and the failure to detect and punish the killer (cf. Parker 1983: 104–10). In Eur. fr. 266.3 Auge, condemned for polluting the temple of Athena by giving birth in it, protests that the goddess herself does not reject as *μιαρός* the bloodstained spoils of war dedicated in her temple. The colloquial status of *μιαρός* as a very general term of vilification is shown by the fact that satyr-drama uses it in the same way as comedy, but tragedy does not: Soph. *Ichneutai* 197 *ἆ μιαρέ* (the satyrs of the chorus are quarrelling among themselves), Eur. *Cycl.* 676–7, where the blinded Cyclops calls Odysseus *ὁ μιαρός . . . ξένος*. A rarer word for 'polluted', *μυσαρός*, seems also to have become a general term of abuse: *Lys.* 340 *τὰς μυσαρὰς γυναῖκας*, 'quoting' what the old men say about the women, and 969 *παμβδελύρα καὶ παμμυσάρα* (note that the table in Hawtrey 1983: 59 omits these and some other *παν*-adjectives).

The English translator of Aristophanes may well feel that 'bastard', 'shit' and 'bitch' catch the tone of *μιαρός* best, e.g. *Thesm.* 1222 *ω μιαρο γρᾶο* 'Oh, the old bitch!' and *Lys.* 971 'What do you mean, "sweet"? She's a *bitch*!' (venomous repetition, *μιαρὰ μιαρά*). When *μιαρός* is heavily reinforced by *παμμίαρος* and *μιαρώτατος* its violence can be represented by stress, spacing, and colloquial obscenity; so in *Ran.* 465–6 'You bastard! You—fucking—*bastard*!', with deliberate stress on each word and spacing between words, and in *Pax* 182–4 (where the cause of anger is different; see above) 'You scum! You—fucking—*scum*!'.

μιαρός is not common in Plato. Twice it has strong religious associations: *Leg.* 716 E, where offerings and dedications *παρὰ μιαροῦ* are to be rejected because a bad man is *ἀκάθαρτος τὴν ψυχήν* but a good man *καθαρός*, and *Rep.* 559 C, where *μιαρώτατος* is coupled with *ἀθεώτατος* as characterizing the lowest part of the soul. Twice it occurs in passages which purport to represent the view of the man in the street: *Apol.* 23 D 'they say there's a *μιαρός* man called Socrates . . .' and *Rep.* 562 D on the democratic city's punishment of strict magistrates, 'accusing them of being *μιαρός* and oligarchic'. This is a kind of quotation, to which *Lys.* 340 (cited above) is relevant; so too is ibid. 252–3, a reference to women's 'being called *ἄμαχος* and *μιαρός*'. It is interesting that Plato also uses the vocative *μιαρέ* four times in a friendly way (Halliwell 1995: 113–15) which reminds us of the traditional cowboy riposte 'When you call me that, *smile*!'.

It would be easy to understand why the language of Aristophanes abstains from the use of 'basic' obscene metaphor in reproaching stupidity and unpleasantness *if* it abstained also from (1) the metaphorical use of 'deviant' obscenity and (2) the use of *both* basic *and* deviant obscene words in their literal meanings. But those conditions are not fulfilled, and we are left with something which resembles an ecological niche inexplicably unoccupied. Tempting though it might be (for a moment) to attribute this imbalance to pagan reverence for the genitals and respect for the penetrator, such a supposition would do nothing to explain the absence of metaphorical uses of 'shit'. We have to reconcile ourselves to the possibility that just as in any given language some syntactical niches are overcrowded and others vacant, the same is true of semantic niches.

5

Figures of Speech in Aristophanes

SIMON R. SLINGS

This paper has grown out of a long-standing dissatisfaction with the way we treat figures of speech in Greek poetry from Homer to Aristophanes. When we teach poetry from this era, or write commentaries about it, what we do is direct our students' or readers' attention to such phenomena, and normally we try to attach a special value to it, as if we were dealing with Virgil or Ovid, and, to my mind, with a signal lack of success.

In 1992, I was invited to read a paper, of a linguistic nature, on the *Electra* of Sophocles, to a conference of Dutch high-school Classics teachers, and I decided to choose figures of speech as my topic.[1] This paper eventually developed into my 1997 contribution to the volume *Grammar as Interpretation*, edited by E. J. Bakker. What I should like to do here is to apply the theoretical framework and the results of that study to Aristophanes, who plays only a minor part in the 1997 article.

I refer to that article for the theory, but a condensation of it must be given here if my statements are to be at all understandable. I use two major concepts of present-day pragmatics: Topic and Focus. Let me give a definition of each. A Topic is an entity or State of Affairs (action, event, state, process) that is known or inferrable within the discourse, and is used by the speaker to produce a predication that may be regarded as being 'about' the entity or State of Affairs. A constituent with Focus function presents the relatively most important or salient information of the clause or sentence; in spoken language, a Focus can often be recognized through its prominence in intonation patterns.[2] In her study of

[1] Published in Dutch: Slings (1993).

[2] Cf. Slings (1997: 170–1) for further references. In the sentence 'Is he a friend of yours?' *he* is Topic, *a friend of yours* Focus.

Greek word-order, Helma Dik showed that the standard order of the Greek main clause is Topic—Focus—Predicate (Dik 1995).

Furthermore, I tried to show that anaphora, chiasmus, and antithesis are all features of natural language use, but sometimes they have to be interpreted as 'literary', when the requirements for their use in natural language are not met. Let me illustrate this with two instances of question-word anaphora, which will not further be treated in this paper:

(1) *ὦ Ἡράκλεις τουτὶ τί ποτ' ἐστὶ θηρίον;*
τίς ἡ πτέρωσις; τίς ὁ τρόπος τῆς τριλοφίας;
(Ar. *Av.* 93–4)

Heracles, what kind of animal might this be? What's this plumage? What kind of triple crest is that?

(2) *ἄγε δὴ τίς ἔσται μηχανὴ σωτηρίας;*
τίς πεῖρα; τίς ἐπίνοι(α);
(Ar. *Thesm.* 765–6)

Come now, what device will be able to save me? what experiment, what idea?

The two questions in (1) are true questions bearing first on the identity of the bird, then on various aspects of its appearance. If they have a literary, in this case comic effect, it is because an answer to the first question would make it superfluous to ask the second and third questions. But the situation is different in (2): there the second and third questions add nothing because three nominal predicates (*μηχανή*, *πεῖρα*, *ἐπίνοια*) are practically synonymous. In natural language use, anaphora is typically a chunking device, that is to say a strategy used to split up information that otherwise would not be capable of being processed comfortably by the listener.[3] But in (2), the information load of the second and third questions is virtually nil, which leads to interpretation of the anaphora as 'literary'. Such forms of anaphora (rare in Homer, relatively frequent in tragedy)[4] are clearly recognizable as figures of speech, and in Aristophanes of course as *paratragodia*.

In 1997, I showed that anaphora is most normal when a speaker

[3] Cf. Slings (1997: 169 n. 3) and the literature cited there.

[4] In Slings (1997: 178) I gave some statistics, which, however, did not distinguish between literary and non-literary use of anaphora because the line between them is not always clear to draw.

is at liberty to develop his thoughts at length, and does not have to use what in pragmatics are called 'floor-holding devices'. If this analysis is correct it explains (or helps explain) why anaphora is frequent in epic and lyric, including choral lyric in tragedy (and in historic prose), relatively infrequent in tragic dialogue, virtually absent from Aristophanes, where the aggressiveness that characterizes most participants in dialogue is not a felicitous condition for anaphora to occur.

Aristophanes' liking for anaphora seems to grow somewhat with the years. In the earlier plays it is practically non-existent (I have counted two examples in all in the *Acharnians*, less than a handful in *Peace*), whereas it does raise its head a little in the mature plays (about ten in *Thesmophoriazusae*, and a similar number in the *Birds* and the *Frogs*). In the fourth-century plays hardly any instance is to be found. But compared with Euripides and especially Sophocles even the rate of the middle plays is virtually nothing. This throws an interesting light on what is probably the most famous anaphora from Aristophanes, the characterization of Sophocles:

(3) ὁ δ' εὔκολος μὲν ἐνθάδ', εὔκολος δ' ἐκεῖ (*Ran.* 82)

He is as easygoing in the next world as he was in this

I may be overplaying my hand here, but I suspect that the line is not only a tribute to Sophocles' character, but also to his style. Aristophanes goes out of his way to use a figure of speech that was more typical of Sophocles than of any other Greek poet. Besides, this line contains another phenomenon which is very typical of Sophocles himself, namely the simple juxtaposition of two clauses where the intended meaning is quite clearly a comparison. Let me just give one example:

(4) τυφλὸς τά τ' ὦτα τόν τε νοῦν τά τ' ὄμματ' εἶ (*OT* 371)

You are blind in your ears, in your mind, and in your eyes

This is of course a literal translation. But what Oedipus really means is: you are as much blind in your ears (i.e. deaf) and in your mind as you are in your eyes; you can't listen, and you can't think, any more than you can see. So in two aspects (3) is a very Sophoclean line, and I hope my claim that Aristophanes wanted it to be, as a salute to the master of fifth-century dramatic style, is not excessive.

A factor which is to be taken into account when pondering the relative frequency of anaphora in poetry is that poetry has a chunking device of its own, to wit line-end. This is why in poetry there are virtually no parallels for the following anaphora from Herodotus (4.95.1):

(5) *τὸν Σάλμοξιν τοῦτον ἐόντα ἄνθρωπον δουλεῦσαι ἐν Σάμῳ, δουλεῦσαι δὲ Πυθαγόρῃ τῷ Μνησάρχου*

This Salmoxis was a human being, a slave on Samos, and his master was Pythagoras, son of Mnesarchus

This non-serial anaphora enables the speaker to add a number of syntactically and informationally new constituents to a clause that is already syntactically and pragmatically complete (it has a Topic and a Focus); without the anaphora, the sentence would carry too heavy a load of new information, so a chunking device is necessary. This is natural language use, but it is hardly ever found in poetry, because line-end makes it superfluous. Curiously enough there may in fact be an instance in Aristophanes:

(6) *πρᾶγμα πρᾶγμα μέγα κεκίνηται, μέγα*
ἐν τοῖς νεκροῖσι
(*Ran.* 759–60)

A most extraordinary thing is going on, to wit among the dead

Dover prints a comma before the second *μέγα*. If this is correct the result is non-serial Herodotean anaphora, the comic effect being of course that there is nothing to chunk. The only thing that is added is *ἐν τοῖς νεκροῖσι*, which is hardly new information, since the reader/listener already knows that the scene is set in Hades. We are waiting for salient new information, but all we get is something we already knew.

In poetry, the most typical case of anaphora is when the repeated constituent is Topic, and the variant constituents Focus. Oddly enough, in Aristophanes, this type does not occur at all. The normal type in Aristophanes, apart from question-word anaphora, is illustrated by (3), the line about Sophocles. Here the article/pronoun *ὁ* is Topic and the first clause is a double Focus: he is easygoing, and he was so here. But I would guess that in the second clause *εὔκολος* has become Topic and *ἐκεῖ* is Focus. This is true of nearly all cases of anaphora in poetry which I have examined: the pragmatic status in the first clause may differ or be uncertain, but in the subsequent clauses the repeated constituent is Topic, the varying constituent Focus. This does not necessarily lead to the interpretation of this type of anaphora as 'literary'. Quite the contrary: two out of the five constituents in the clause complex contain brand-new information (the first εὔκολος and ἐνθάδε), of the remaining three, two are given (ὅ and the second εὔκολος) and one is more or less predictable (ἐκεῖ). Is the information load so heavy that the anaphora was needed as a chunking device? There is a thin line between what may and what may not have been interpreted as literary. But in similar cases in Aristophanes the anaphora has definitely a literary ring:

(7) ξυνευχόμεσθα τέλεα μὲν
πόλει τέλεα δὲ δήμῳ
τάδ' εὔγματα γενέσθαι

(*Thesm.* 352–4)

We join in prayer that these wishes
may be fulfilled for the city
and fulfilled for the people

Here *polis* and *demos* are so close together in meaning that the chunking seems entirely unneccessary. In other words an additive strategy is used where there is nothing to add. So a literary interpretation is beyond doubt. Of course the religious content of these words is another argument in this case. But such clear-cut cases are rare in epic, lyric, and comedy, and not even particularly frequent in tragedy, except for chorus songs.

Anaphora (A–B, A–B′) is related to two mutually exclusive ordering strategies in complex contrasts, antithesis[5] (A–B, A′–B′) and chiasmus (A–B, B′–A′); in fact anaphora can be a special case of either.

It may seem a paradox that both orders are treated as figures of speech by modern commentators; in antiquity, antithesis was treated as such from the fourth century BC onwards, chiasmus hardly ever (cf. Leeman 1963: 1.22). Leeman therefore holds that

[5] I use the term 'antithesis' for all cases of parallel order of two pairs of semantical parallel constituents in subsequent clauses: semantic opposition is a special kind of antithesis, but antithesis is not limited to it.

chiasmus is the basic order in Greek and Latin: antithesis is, he claims, normal for the modern, rational mind, but for the Greeks and Romans chiasmus was more natural.

And indeed, one may adduce many passages in which antithesis looks like an embellishment of the style. Consider the following passage from *Acharnians* (545–9):

(8) *ἦν δ' ἂν ἡ πόλις πλέα*
θορύβου στρατιωτῶν, περὶ τριηράρχους βοῆς,
μισθοῦ διδομένου, Παλλαδίων χρυσουμένων,
στοᾶς στεναχούσης, σιτίων μετρουμένων,
ἀσκῶν, τροπωτήρων . . .

The city would have been full of the hubbub of soldiers, noisy crowds surrounding ships' captains, pay being handed out, Pallas emblems being gilded, the Colonnade groaning, rations being measured out, leathers and oarloops . . .

Here we have the order noun–participle four times. According to Helma Dik's rule, in cases like this the nouns should be Topics and the participles Focus. That analysis seems to fit: all the nouns have to do with the war, which is the general Discourse Topic in this passage, and therefore one could say that the various clause Topics are if not given, at any rate inferrable. But the literary character is of course betrayed by the semantics of the passage: how can the city be full of pay being handed out, Pallas emblems being gilded, etc.? Besides, the list ends in a number of asyndetically connected nouns (all in the genitive), which are the hallmark of Aristophanes' style.

So it looks as if something could be said for Leeman's position that chiasmus is the natural order and antithesis the figure of speech. Yet his claim should be rejected for this very reason. Our analysis of anaphora shows that it is sometimes a feature of natural language use, sometimes a figure of speech. It would be counter-intuitive to assume that of the two orderings chiasmus and antithesis, one is always natural, the other always a figure of speech. And an appeal to the Greek and Roman mind as opposed to the rational modern mind smacks too much of an evolutionist and determinist view of language to be at all acceptable.

A more concrete argument is that there is simply no Greek author for whom it can be maintained that chiasmus is the natural order. In all samples from poetry, and even in a sample from inscriptions, antithesis is more frequent than chiasmus. In the *Acharnians* I have counted 29 antitheses as against 9 instances of chiasmus, roughly the same proportion as in Sophocles' *Electra* and in inscriptions (cf. Slings 1997: 186).

The choice between the two orderings of the constituents depends on the processing load of the two clauses. When the four constituents A–B, A′–B′ are comparatively simple in form, and not too unpredictable or focal *qua* content, parallel order is the rule; as they grow more complicated, the chances of a chiasmus become higher. This is nothing out of the ordinary: the rule goes for English as well. Consider the following replies to the question 'What kinds of drink do you like?':

(9a) Beer is nice, gin is awful.
(9b) Beer is nice, awful is gin.
(9c) Beer I actually like a lot, but a drink I really hate is gin.

At the moment when the speaker of (9a–c) starts replying, 'kinds of drinks' has been suggested by his partner as Topic. Normally such a Topic would appear in the sentence, but the speaker of (9a–c) opts for another strategy, by which the suggested Topic is split into two contrastive Topics, beer and gin. These Topics are not given but they are inferrable ('Sub-Topics'). As long as the Focuses are as manageable as they are in (9a), the sentence is clear enough.

The speaker of (9c) opts for another strategy: likewise, he selects an inferrable Topic (beer), but his Focus is much more complicated in form than 'is nice' (9a), it contains a phrase with a meaning that is focal by itself ('a lot'), and above all it introduces a first-person form: first persons tend to take over as Topics from third persons, especially inanimate ones (cf. Slings 1997: 98). This explains why from the Focus ('I actually like a lot'), the speaker derives a new inferrable Topic, his varying appreciation of drinks: 'gin' now becomes Focus rather than contrastive Topic as in (9a). It will be clear that (9b) has not the same complexity in information structure as (9c), which is why 'awful is' in (9b) is an illogical Topic.

The following general rule may be postulated: the more complex the information structure of two contrasted pairs of constituents, the greater, in natural language use, the chance of chiasmus. The following prediction can be derived from this rule: the less complex the information structure in a chiasmus, the stronger the probability that this chiasmus will be experienced as literary. (9b) is a good example of this. Any competent native reader of English will immediately recognize the literary register of this sentence: the author is trying to sound sophisticated, and signally fails to do so.

Here is an example from Aristophanes with a chiasmus which is easily understandable along these lines:

(10) πρὸς ταῦτα χρεὼν εἶναι μετ' ἐμοῦ
καὶ τοὺς ἄνδρας καὶ τοὺς παῖδας
καὶ τοῖς φαλακροῖσι παραινοῦμεν
ξυσπουδάζειν περὶ τῆς νίκης

(*Pax* 765–8)

In view of this, both the men
and the boys ought to be on my side.
And we advise all bald men
to join in striving for my victory.

The Focus of the first clause ('both the men and the boys') is rather a heavy one, so the Topic (χρεὼν εἶναι μετ' ἐμοῦ, 'ought to be on my side') has been lost sight of. Just as in (9c) a second Topic is derived from the first Focus ('all bald men'), and the inevitable option is that 'ought to be on my side' is replaced by a new verb plus depending constituents (παραινοῦμεν ξυσπουδάζειν περὶ τῆς νίκης). This is perfectly normal language use and there is no reason whatever to assume that Aristophanes is here using a figure of speech. What chiasmus has in common with anaphora is the fact that the two contrasted constituents in the second clause nearly always have the functions of Topic and Focus (in that order), whatever their pragmatic roles in the first. The same goes for antithesis.

Here is a candidate for use of chiasmus as a figure of speech:

(11) ὡς κωμῳδεῖ τὴν πόλιν ἡμῶν καὶ τὸν δῆμον καθυβρίζει (*Ach.* 631)

(claiming that he) ridicules our city and insults our people

The semantic relationship between τὴν πόλιν and τὸν δῆμον is very close, as we have already seen (cf. ex. 7), so there is no obvious reason why the latter should be Topic rather than Focus, as the former is. And besides, there is not a great deal of difference either between *κωμῳδεῖ* and *καθυβρίζει*. But there are many borderline cases:

(12) *στυγῶν μὲν ἄστυ, τὸν δ' ἐμὸν δῆμον ποθῶν* (*Ach.* 33)

loathing the town and longing for my village

As in (11), the two clauses are short, so the chiastic order is surprising. It could be accounted for by the double semantic opposition: loathing ~ longing for, town ~ village. Yet the hypothesis that in this instance the chiasmus is to be taken as a figure of speech is strengthened by a number of other factors. The two participles *στυγῶν* ('loathing') and *ποθῶν* ('longing for'), with their opposite meanings, are put at the beginning and the end of the line: dramatic poets, especially Sophocles and Aristophanes, like to place words which in whatever way are related to each other at the initial and final positions.[6] The two verbs are, besides, both disyllabic, and they rhyme. The two constituents in the accusative are juxtaposed, and the second is longer than the first (the so-called 'Gesetz der wachsenden Glieder'). The position of the words in the line and the chiasmus reinforce each other mutually.

It has to be noted, though, that indubitable use of chiasmus as a figure of speech is quite rare (statistics in Slings 1997: 191). The number for *Acharnians* is one or two out of nine, a relatively high one.

A similar reasoning applies to antithesis: it may reasonably be supposed to be taken as a figure of speech when there is no real difference between two contrasted constituents. There is one good instance in *Acharnians* (885–6):

(13) *ἦλθες ποθεινὴ μὲν τρυγῳδικοῖς χοροῖς*
φίλη δὲ Μορύχῳ

thou hast come—the heart's desire for comic choruses, and dear to Morychos

There is no real difference between *ποθεινή* and *φίλη*, so there is no pragmatic or functional reason why the second should have been used at all. Here it is the A′ constituent that is superfluous: we have therefore a figure close to anaphora.

When omissibility of the A′ or B′ constituent is used as a

[6] Cf. the analysis of Soph. *El.* 1027 *ζηλῶ σε τοῦ νοῦ τῆς δὲ δειλίας στυγῶ* in Slings (1997: 190).

criterion, antithesis is more often used as a figure of speech than chiasmus, especially in tragedy (cf. Slings 1997: 192 for statistics). The number is 3 out of 29 in *Acharnians*, which holds the middle between Homer and tragedy.

When at the end of this quest we set a step backwards and look at the net result, we are bound to conclude that for Aristophanes they are not very spectacular. There are remarkably few cases of anaphora, and the use of antithesis and chiasmus yields nothing out of the ordinary. But even this negative result is instructive enough. It has become quite clear that within the oral/written continuum, Aristophanes' style is, as far as his use of figures of speech goes, definitely a literate style. Although he had the opportunity of presenting people on stage in colloquial conversation, he did not avail himself of the opportunity in this respect.

This is quite an interesting result, because in other respects Aristophanes uses chunking strategies quite often (cf. Slings 1992: 104, 107, and n. 52): double *ἄν*, prolepsis, and various others. In the figures of speech as analysed here, he did not have much interest. I venture the suggestion that he did not because in his time, these figures were already well on their way of becoming truly literary devices. So if the results for Aristophanes are a bit meagre, that teaches us an important fact about the way in which the Greek literary language was developing at the end of the classical period. The way is now open for the Hellenistic poets, and above all the Roman poets, to use what were originally everyday chunking strategies as adornments of style, as true figures (*σχήματα*) of speech.

Let me finish by stating a thesis. It is useless, when dealing with classical Greek authors, to point out a figure of speech and leave it at that. The habit can become positively harmful when such a figure is invested with all sorts of meanings, although the harm is often diminished when on closer inspection such meanings turn out to be utterly vague ones like 'emphasis'. The only useful way of studying style is audience-oriented, linguistic, and more particularly pragmatic. We should start from the native reader (cf. T. R. Austin 1984, Slings 1997: 172–3), who is Chomsky's native speaker whose feeling for style is conditioned by having read or listened to a great amount of the literature of his own culture. We cannot be native speakers of Greek, but it is our duty as interpreters of Greek texts to come as close to them as possible by observing what goes on in natural language use in living languages. Only in this way can we hope to achieve anything fruitful at all.

6

Languages on Stage: Aristophanic Language, Cultural History, and Athenian Identity

ANDREAS WILLI

Si capisce come la nostra vita avrebbe tutt'altro aspetto se fosse detta nel nostro dialetto.

Italo Svevo, *La coscienza di Zeno*, ch. 8

1. INTRODUCTION: INTERPRETING LINGUISTIC CHOICE

A universal feature of all natural languages is their variability. What we commonly call 'a language' (English, Chinese, Greek, etc.) is in reality a bundle of overlapping languages or linguistic varieties. We can distinguish varieties associated with time, space (dialects), speaker's social place (sociolects), function (registers), or aesthetic value (styles). Every speaker commands an entire range of such subsystems. There is no utterance that is not preceded by a linguistic choice.

In most oral situations choosing a linguistic variety is a subconscious action. In the process of writing, however, the choice becomes conscious, as anybody who has ever formulated a job application, a love-letter, or an academic article will know. 'The actively literary consciousness at all times and everywhere . . . comes upon "languages", and not language. Consciousness finds itself inevitably facing the necessity of having to choose a language' (Bakhtin 1981: 295). It follows that language is never only the medium in a literary text but always forms part of the message itself. No literary work can be fully decoded without the contribution of socio-historical (variational) linguistics.

In this paper language is interpreted as a key to the world of Aristophanic comedy. The aim is to retrace Athenian socio-cultural attitudes and classifications through their reflection in comic language. A linguistic analysis of various levels of comic discourse leads to the reconstruction of three circles of Athenian identity. The discussion is based on two theoretical premises: (1) every ancient text is the intentional intellectual product of one (or rarely, several subsequent) author(s) and contains a set of conscious and subconscious sociocultural values and opinions, whose discovery could be expected of at least some members of the primary audience (and whose discovery is one of the main tasks of modern classical scholarship), and (2) in the absence of contrary evidence it is legitimate to assume that this set of sociocultural values and opinions was (*a*) in accordance with the sociocultural values and opinions of the historical author himself, and (*b*) shared to some degree (though not necessarily completely) by the primary audience so that its reconstruction allows conclusions not only about the values and opinions of the author but also about those of the society in which he lived and for which he wrote. The latter assumption is particularly justified in the case of a comic playwright such as Aristophanes, for Attic comedy was, as Henderson (1990) argues, a 'yearly unofficial review' of public life *on behalf of* the *demos*.[1]

2. COMIC LANGUAGE AND ATHENIAN IDENTITY

2.1. Comedy as an anti-genre

Like all literary genres—but perhaps more so than most of them—Attic comedy cannot be understood in a purely diachronic perspective. When Aristotle tries to sketch a history of comedy (or rather of the interacting elements of comedy: actors, masks, prologues, plots, invective) he cannot conceive of it being an

[1] Cf. [Xen.] *Ath. Pol.* 2.18 and Bremer (1993: 134–43) on Aristophanic passages which reflect the poet's sensitivity to the demands of his audience.

autonomous subject: it is always the counter-history to tragedy. Tragedy is a *μίμησις σπουδαίων*, comedy a *μίμησις φαυλοτέρων*, tragedy belongs with epic, comedy with iambic poetry (*Poet.* 1448^b25–1449^b9).

There is something like an Aristotelian echo in the formulation of Taplin (1986: 164) that 'fifth-century tragedy and comedy help to define each other by their opposition and their reluctance to overlap'. Aristophanic comedy itself does not conceal to what a degree it is an anti-genre. In unmistakable allusion to the serious sister, *κωμῳδία* loses her proper name and becomes *τρυγῳδία*, almost-*τραγῳδία* (cf. Pickard-Cambridge 1962: 186; Taplin 1983: 332–3). In *Acharnians* (500) Dikaiopolis in the guise of the tragic Telephos exclaims the famous words:

> τὸ γὰρ δίκαιον οἶδε καὶ τρυγῳδία
>
> Even comedy is acquainted with justice[2]

—and, with *καί*, leaves no doubt that he is thinking of tragedy as his model (Foley 1988: 40).

Of course comic elements do infiltrate tragedy here and there, especially in Euripides (though also earlier: cf. Sommerstein's contribution in this volume). And yet it is comedy that makes a living from imitations of tragedy, not vice versa. Paratragedy is omnipresent, paracomedy at best exceptional.[3] Metatheatrical exclamations like that of Trygaios high up in the air on his dung-beetle Pegasos in *Peace* (174):

> ὦ μηχανοποιὲ πρόσεχε τὸν νοῦν . . .

Mr Crane Operator, pay attention . . .

or that of Euripides in *Acharnians* (409):

> ἀλλ' ἐκκυκλήσομαι . . .

Very well, I'll have myself wheeled out . . .

are funny because they violate the dramatic illusion and make something happen that must never happen in the paradigmatic world of tragedy.[4]

[2] For passages from the extant plays of Aristophanes, I quote the translations by Sommerstein in his complete edition (Warminster, 1980–2001).

[3] Taplin (1986: 171) points out that 'paracomedy' is theoretically possible but not desirable for tragedy; cf., however, Sommerstein's contribution and the Introduction at pp. 13–14.

[*See p. 114 for n. 4*]

Is there a similar 'reluctance to overlap' between comic and tragic language? Paratragic passages must certainly be excepted: parody presupposes imitation and overlap in order to evoke the original whose harmony of form and content is to be disrupted (cf. Rau 1967: 11). But what about the *basic* language of comedy—that fundamental linguistic layer which would not have attracted special attention from an average Athenian spectator, struck him as uncommon, or provoked an emotive reaction in him, but which creates the necessary contrast to other, marked, styles (such as vulgar language, sophistic language, paratragic language, foreign language, lyric language)?[5] The question is best answered by reference to some 'hard' linguistic facts of phonology, morphology, syntax, and word-formation.

2.2. Comic language as *Kunstsprache*

On the most general level there is much overlap between the languages of tragedy and comedy. What Goldhill (1997: 128) writes about tragic language is also true for the language of comedy: it is 'public, democratic, male talk' and 'in all senses of the term political'. But the parallelism reaches farther. Even though the language of comedy is rarely defined as such, it is, like tragic language, a *Kunstsprache*, an artificial language.[6] The most obvious proof is the metre: Aristotle may be right in saying that the iambic trimeter is closest to the rhythm of speech (*Poet.* 1449^{a}24–8), but no Athenian would have conducted a daily conversation in trimeters.

From a linguistic point of view 'polymorphy' is equally revealing. Polymorphy is defined as the coexistence of two or more semantically and stylistically equivalent forms that are formally

[4] Cf. Taplin (1986: 168–70). Chapman (1983: 4–22) gives a rather too inclusive list of Aristophanic passages where the dramatic illusion is broken.

[5] Dover (1987: 224) distinguishes 'normal language' and 'the spoken language, which rarely enters into serious poetry'. If this is a distinction between standard (literary prose) language and substandard (colloquial) language, an ending -μεσθα, for instance, does not belong to either of Dover's categories, whereas it does belong to my 'basic language' since its use in comic dialogue is completely conventionalized. With -μεσθα statistic frequency is a reliable criterium, but very often it is difficult to ascertain if a linguistic element was stylistically unmarked.

[6] On the tragic *Kunstsprache* see Björck (1950).

dissimilar and therefore exchangeable according to metrical, rhythmical, or euphonic needs (Björck 1950: 84–5). In phonological and morphological matters Attic prose and Attic inscriptions are the best comparanda and may stand for 'real-life' language. When both tragedy and comedy fundamentally disagree with the evidence from these texts their forms are likely to be artificial.

The ending of the first person plural in the middle voice is always -*μεθα* in Attic prose, never -*μεσθα*. The latter cannot have been a living form in spoken Attic Greek at the end of the fifth century. In tragedy *and* comedy both forms are found. The tolerance for -*μεσθα* seems a little greater in lyric passages and in the earlier plays of Aristophanes (in *Acharnians* -*μεσθα* is as frequent as -*μεθα*), but on the whole -*μεσθα* is neither stylistically nor chronologically confined to certain contexts. In Aristophanes 76 cases of -*μεσθα* stand against 177 of -*μεθα* (Lautensach 1896: 26–8; neither -*μεθα* nor -*μεσθα* is attested in the Attic inscriptions).

In the dative plural of *a*-stems and *o*-stems, -*οις* and -*αις* are the regular endings in comedy. Even in the earliest plays of Aristophanes they are twice as frequent as -*οισι(ν)* and -*αισι(ν)*.[7] In *Acharnians*, *Knights*, and *Clouds* I have counted, from the text of the electronic *Thesaurus Linguae Graecae*, 271 instances of -*οις* and 122 of -*αις*, as against 104 of -*οισι(ν)* and 39 of -*αισι(ν)*. The shorter forms prevail also if we except 88 cases of -*οις* and 36 of -*αις* which are prevocalic (and could therefore be interpreted as -*οισ'* and -*αισ'*), but the existence of -*οισι(ν)* and -*αισι(ν)* is undeniable. In the Attic inscriptions the longer forms disappear around 420 BC and since official inscriptions tend to be conservative, it is likely that -*οισι(ν)* and -*αισι(ν)* had disappeared from spoken Attic much earlier (cf. Dover 1987: 34; López Eire 1993: 49; Threatte 1996: 25–32, 96–101).

In the case of -*οισι* and -*μεσθα* the artificial character of comic language is qualitative. It is less conspicuous when it is 'only' quantitative. Substantive subordinate clauses ('*that*-clauses') are introduced by either *ὅτι* or *ὡς* in Attic Greek. In tragedy and Ionic

[7] It is impossible to know whether Aristophanes wrote -*ησι* (-*ασι*) or -*αισι*; the rarity (except after -*ι*-) of -*αισι* in the inscriptions of the fifth century might at first sight suggest the former (cf. Threatte 1996: 99–100), but we should then have to assume, quite implausibly, that an extensive orthographical revision of the text took place at some stage.

prose (Herodotus) ὡς is much more frequent than ὅτι. In Aristophanic comedy ὅτι and ὡς roughly balance each other. In the unprestigious speeches of Aristophanes' contemporary Lysias ὅτι is far more common than ὡς.[8] The best explanation for this situation is that spoken Attic around 400 BC knew both ὅτι and ὡς in substantive clauses, but preferred ὅτι. Tragedy, against everyday usage and perhaps under Ionic influence, made ὡς its favourite. The distribution in comedy, then, was less artificial than in tragedy but did not reproduce faithfully the statistical predominance of ὅτι in spoken language.

One might want to excuse the artificiality of certain linguistic features in comedy as required by the metre. However, such an explanation misses the point as the two qualitative examples show. In Middle and New Comedy both -μεσθα and -οισι(ν)/-αισι(ν) are gradually vanishing although metrical considerations continue to play a role in the composition of comedy.[9] These cases indicate that a poet like Aristophanes *could* have reduced the amount of artificiality in his language if he had wanted to. But obviously the consensus was that comedy, too, had the right to employ a *Kunstsprache*.

2.3. Comic language vs. tragic language

Nevertheless, the gap between the basic languages of tragedy and comedy is wide. Again a few examples must suffice. In metrically unambiguous contexts, Aristophanes always uses the standard Attic form of the preposition εἰς, never ἐς—except for parodic purposes as in the paratragic lines of Euripides(-Perseus) who wants to rescue his Relative(-Andromeda) from the grim Scythian archer in *Thesmophoriazusae* (1121–2):

τί δ' οὐκ ἐᾷς λύσαντά μ' αὐτήν, ὦ Σκύθα,
πεσεῖν ἐς εὐνὴν καὶ γαμήλιον λέχος;

[8] Monteil (1963: 399) gives the following figures for ὡς : ὅτι: Herodotus 271 : 110, Aeschylus 28 : 8, Sophocles 56 : 35, Euripides 95 : 12, Aristophanes 85 : 79, Lysias 135 : 293.

[9] Apart from the fossilized θεοῖσιν ἐχθρός (Men. *Pk.* 268), Gomme–Sandbach (1973: 735) list only six examples of -οισι/-αισι in Menander (and some of them are conjectural): *Sam.* 516, *Theoph.* 25, frr. 425, 451, 764, 860. Lautensach (1896) counted 9 -μεσθα : 62 -μεθα in Middle and New Comedy; new finds may have changed the absolute numbers but hardly the relative frequency.

Why, Scythian, wilt thou not let me release her to fall upon the bed and nuptial couch?

Here the comic poet also pokes fun at the omission of definite articles, which had been a necessary ingredient of non-poetic Greek syntax for centuries (cf. Wackernagel 1928: 147–50); elsewhere he may laugh at the use of poetic plurals (cf. Bers 1984: 57–9) or the replacement of usual word-formations by exquisite variants. Aristophanes' Euripides combines these features when he gives the following order to his slave (*Ach.* 432):

ὦ παῖ, δὸς αὐτῷ Τηλέφου ῥακώματα.

Give him the ragments, boy, of Telephus.

Conversely, comedy admits linguistic features that are banned from tragedy. For instance Aristophanic comedy avoids the simplex verb *βαίνω*. Compound forms such as *καταβαίνω* or *πρόβαινω* are used, but *βαδίζω* is how comic characters simply 'go' (except if they are Spartans or lyric poets).[10] In classical Attic prose (simplex) *βαίνω* coexists with *βαδίζω*, which suggests that comedy followed a 'sub-literary' colloquial usage (or non-usage). This is not to say, of course, that the Aristophanic norm would admit every colloquialism: thus *ναίχι*, which is frequent in vase-inscriptions, is only used by the vulgar Scythian archer in *Thesmophoriazusae* (1183–4, 1196, 1218).[11]

Often comedy and prose join each other more closely in disagreeing from tragic usage. Certain particle combinations (*μέν γε*, *ὥσπερ γε*, *δήπου*, causal *ἅτε*, etc.) are rare or absent in tragedy but common in comedy and prose (Denniston 1954: lxxiv–lxxvi). Deictic -*ί* in pronouns and adverbs such as *ὁδί*, *οὑτοσί*, and *ἐνθαδί* is completely absent from tragedy[12] and Thucydidean prose, while

[10] In Aristophanes there are 97 examples of *βαίνω* with a preverb and 86 of *βαδίζω* (only once with a preverb). The simplex *βαίνω* appears, apart from the imperative *βαῖνε* (*Ach.* 198 and *Thesm.* 956 lyr.), in *ἔβα* at *Lys.* 106 (Laconian), *Nub.* 30 (= Eur. fr. 1011), *Av.* 944 (= Pind. fr. 105b), *βαίην* (*Av.* 1396: in Kinesias' dithyrambic style), *βεβηκώς* (*Eq.* 1039: a mock-oracle), and *βέβηκε* (*Eccl.* 913: a parodic wailing-song). The success of *βαδίζω* is relatively short-lived and it is restricted already by the time of Menander: Shipp (1979: 122–4). The predilection for simplex verbs in poetic style is discussed by Wackernagel (1928: 186–91), none of whose examples occurs in an unmarked context in Aristophanes.

[11] Cf. Fraenkel (1977: 52).

[12] With the unique exception of Eur. fr. 572.1 Nauck if the manuscripts are trustworthy.

there are literally hundreds of examples in Aristophanic comedy. This -ί must have been a characteristic of spoken Attic and it therefore appears—though not as frequently as in Aristophanes—also in oratory and in the Platonic dialogues (cf. Dover 1997: 63–4, with statistics). In final clauses, *ὡς* (*ἄν*) is by far the most common conjunction in tragedy. Comedy agrees with Attic prose in virtually ignoring this option and using *ἵνα* (or much more rarely *ὅπως* (*ἄν*)) instead. As with the substantivizing conjunction *ὡς*, tragedy may stand under Ionic influence, for final *ὡς* (*ἄν*) is not quite as rare in Herodotus as it is in Attic oratory and prose.[13]

Thus, comic and tragic language share some common ground insofar as they are both literary *Kunstsprachen*, but *within* that framework we do find a 'reluctance to overlap'. If spoken everyday Attic is the central reference-point in the linguistic universe of Attic drama, we may use the terminology of Bakhtin (1981: 271–2; cf. Duranti 1997: 76) and diagnose a struggle between a 'centrifugal' (tragic) language and a 'centripetal' (comic) language. For an observer who places himself in the centre of this universe, tragic language is therefore more remarkable and worthy of comment—as for instance for a certain Ariphrades who 'ridiculed the tragedians for using expressions which no one would ever say in conversation' (Arist. *Poet.* 1458^{b}31–59^{a}2, transl. S. Halliwell), or for Plato, in whose terminology speaking *τραγικῶς* means speaking in an unnaturally grand and obscure metaphoric style (*Rep.* 413 B; cf. Goldhill 1997: 127).

But we can also look at it the other way round. Since both comedy and tragedy make use of a *Kunstsprache* and since comedy defines itself through its opposition to tragedy, it makes just as much sense to take the tragic *Kunstsprache* as reference-point, at least for the reduced universe of Attic drama. It is then the language of comedy which becomes centrifugal. Its greater 'realism' (cf. Colvin 1999: 31–3) is not just negatively marked through the absence of tragic fancies but positively constructs an alternative to tragedy's flight from naturalism.

[13] Weber (1884–5) gives the following figures for *ἵνα* : *ὡς* (*ἄν*) : *ὅπως* (*ἄν*) (cf. Goodwin 1889: 398; Monteil 1963: 402; Amiguès 1977: 99): Aeschylus 2 : 34 : 16, Sophocles 14 : 57 : 33, Euripides 71 : 209 : 26, Aristophanes 183 : 17 : 42, Thucydides 52 : 2 : 114, Herodotus 107 : 27 : 18, Plato 368 : 1 : 48, Ten Orators 579 : 4 : 54, Demosthenes 253 : 0 : 18.

2.4. Linguistic realism for a 'popular' drama

Dramatic realism appears to have been a hotly debated topic in the literary world of Athens at the end of the fifth century. In Aristophanes' *Frogs*, the first major work of Greek literary criticism to have been preserved, two dramatic concepts are compared. Euripides is proud to have taught the Athenians, among other things (*Ran.* 958–9):

> . . . περινοεῖν ἅπαντα, . . .
> οἰκεῖα πράγματ' εἰσάγων, οἷς χρώμεθ', οἷς ξύνεσμεν.

. . . [how to think] all round everything by bringing *everyday* matters on stage, things we're used to, things we're familiar with.

Aeschylus replies with the claim that his plays have served as models and that he staged heroic characters such as Patroklos or Teukros (*Ran.* 1041–2):

> . . . ἵν' ἐπαίροιμ' ἄνδρα πολίτην
> ἀντεκτείνειν αὑτὸν τούτοις . . .

. . . in the hope of inspiring every man in the citizen body to measure up to their standard.

In nuce these are programmatic declarations in favour of a realistic and an idealistic drama respectively. That Aristophanes' comic portrayal of Aeschylus' and Euripides' artistic ideologies is not freely invented can be demonstrated with the actual linguistic situation in the works of the two tragedians. Especially in his phraseology Euripides borrowed from colloquial usage much more liberally than Aeschylus (Stevens 1976). Euripides' tragedy thereby moved both towards linguistic realism and towards comedy. With his new style Euripides apparently met a demand. Even *Frogs*, where Aeschylus ultimately triumphs over his younger rival, is explicit about the latter's success. This is why the search for umpires in the contest between Aeschylus and Euripides was so difficult (*Ran.* 807–10):

> (Οἰ.) οὔτε γὰρ Ἀθηναίοισι συνέβαιν' Αἰσχύλος
> (Ξα.) πολλοὺς ἴσως ἐνόμιζε τοὺς τοιχωρύχους.
> (Οἰ.) λῆρόν τε τἄλλ' ἡγεῖτο τοῦ γνῶναι πέρι
> φύσεις ποητῶν . . .

(Servant) Aeschylus wouldn't agree to the Athenians as judges—
(Xanthias) Perhaps he thought too many of them were villains.
(Servant) —and he reckoned that all the others were rubbish when it came to deciding on the quality of poets.

The positive evaluation of tragic realism must have been around for some time. Aristophanes may, but need not, have known Gorgias' concept of positive *ἀπάτη* ('deception', hence 'illusion'?) in tragedy. No matter if Gorgias meant to defend the freedom of literature from the laws of empirical reality (T. G. Rosenmeyer 1955: 234; cf. Verdenius 1981: 124) or if he already thought of *ἀπάτη* as the result of successful *μίμησις* (Lucas 1968: 270; cf. Kerferd 1981: 81), his reflections certainly betray an awareness of the critical issue.[14] At least for the writer of the *Dissoi Logoi*, perhaps around 400 BC, *ἀπάτη* has become the technical term for realistic illusionism so that *ἀπάτη* and *μίμησις* converge (90.3.10 D.–K.; cf. Segal 1962: 130–1):

ἐν γὰρ τραγῳδοποιίᾳ καὶ ζωγραφίᾳ ὅστις πλεῖστα ἐξαπατῇ ὅμοια τοῖς ἀληθινοῖς ποιέων, οὗτος ἄριστος

In the composition of tragedy and in painting whoever deceives most by making things similar to reality, that one is best.

The paradigmatic change that literary criticism underwent during the last quarter of the fifth century, which was certainly supported by a general tendency to give primacy of rank to the communicative rather than the poetic use of language (Lanza 1979: 93), has its implications for the present context. At a time when realism became an aesthetic ideal in dramatic theory, comedy could step out of the shadow of tragedy. No doubt

[14] Gorgias 82 B 23 D.–K. (= Plut. *Mor.* 348 C): *ἤνθησε δ' ἡ τραγῳδία καὶ διεβοήθη, θαυμαστὸν ἀκρόαμα καὶ θέαμα τῶν τότ' ἀνθρώπων γενομένη καὶ παρασχοῦσα τοῖς μύθοις καὶ τοῖς πάθεσιν ἀπάτην, ὡς Γοργίας φησίν, ἣν ὅ τ' ἀπατήσας δικαιότερος τοῦ μὴ ἀπατήσαντος καὶ ὁ ἀπατηθεὶς σοφώτερος τοῦ μὴ ἀπατηθέντος. ὁ μὲν γὰρ ἀπατήσας δικαιότερος ὅτι τοῦθ' ὑποσχόμενος πεποίηκεν, ὁ δ' ἀπατηθεὶς σοφώτερος· εὐάλωτον γὰρ ὑφ' ἡδονῆς λόγων τὸ μὴ ἀναίσθητον* 'But tragedy blossomed forth and won great acclaim, becoming a wondrous entertainment for the ears and eyes of the men of that age, and, by the mythological character of its plots, and the vicissitudes which its characters undergo, it effected a deception wherein, as Gorgias remarks, "he who deceives is more honest than he who does not deceive, and he who is deceived is wiser than he who is not deceived." For he who deceives is more honest, because he has done what he promised to do; and he who is deceived is wiser, because the mind which is not insensible to fine perceptions is easily enthralled by the delights of language.' (transl. F. C. Babbitt); cf. Gorg. *Hel.* 10.

comic language had always been closer to everyday speech than tragic language, but what had been a shortcoming as long as people agreed that literary artificiality (or 'idealization') was desirable suddenly turned into an asset. With its 'centrifugal' tendency against the gravitational pull of the tragic *Kunstsprache* and with its more 'realistic' character comic language could now support the claim that comedy, not tragedy, was the kind of drama the public demanded—not only for lowly pleasure as the drama of the mob but with sound aesthetic arguments as the drama of the people. With due attention to the verbal side of the coin, Aristophanes self-consciously announces his 'new' comedy's new role in the *polis* (*Nub.* 537–44):

> (*Xo.*) . . . ἥτις πρῶτα μὲν
> οὐδὲν ἦλθε ῥαψαμένη σκύτινον καθειμένον
> ἐρυθρὸν ἐξ ἄκρου, παχύ, τοῖς παιδίοις ἵν' ᾖ γέλως·
> οὐδ' ἔσκωψεν τοὺς φαλακρούς, οὐδὲ κόρδαχ' εἵλκυσεν·
> οὐδὲ πρεσβύτης ὁ λέγων τἄπη τῇ βακτηρίᾳ
> τύπτει τὸν παρόντ', ἀφανίζων πονηρὰ σκώμματα·
> οὐδ' εἰσῇξε δᾷδας ἔχουσ' οὐδ' "ἰοὺ ἰού" βοᾷ·
> ἀλλ' αὑτῇ καὶ τοῖς ἔπεσιν πιστεύουσ' ἐλήλυθεν.

(Chorus) First of all, she hasn't come with a dangling bit of stitched leather, red at the end and thick, to give the children a laugh; nor has she made fun of men who are bald, nor danced a cordax; nor does an old man, the one with the leading part, conceal bad jokes by hitting whoever is around with his stick; nor does this comedy rush on stage with torches, nor cry 'help, help'; no, she has come trusting in herself and in her script.[15]

2.5. Parochialism and the comic profession of 'Atticness'

Linguistic realism had its price. Although the comic audience would laugh at article-less ῥακώματα, the anti-naturalistic tendencies of tragic language bestowed a certain poetic dignity on the genre. Even more seriously a realistic reproduction of colloquial Attic meant forsaking the prestige that was attached to the cultural *koine* of fifth-century Athens: an Attic imbued with Ionicisms,

[15] On similar 'self-conscious' passages in Aristophanes (*Ach.* 655–6, *Eq.* 510, *Vesp.* 1043, *Ran.* 686–7) see Bremer (1993: 127–34).

which tragedy and Attic prose actively promoted. Bers (1984: 7–9) has pointed out that it is often difficult to ascertain where Attic Greek stands under Ionic influence, but some of the most famous innovations may well have originated in Ionic prose (López Eire 1993: 44–57; 1996*a*: 19–42): the spread of adjectives in -ικός, derided by Aristophanes,[16] the use of *nomina actionis* in -σις with a concrete meaning (as in οἴκησις 'house'), or the periphrasis of verbal forms by *nomina actionis* + auxiliary verb (as in ἀγῶνα ποιεῖσθαι for ἀγωνίζεσθαι).

Some of the features discussed earlier may also have had an Ionic ring in Attic ears. I have already pointed out that final ὡς (ἄν) may have been stronger in Ionic and that ὡς as a conjunction in substantive clauses perhaps spread from Ionia. We are sure that the prepositional form ἐς was the Ionic equivalent to Attic εἰς and the long dative plurals in -οισι(ν)/-αισι(ν) were—at least from a synchronic point of view—Ionicisms, too. In tragedy there is an extensive group of words that are 'unknown in Comedy or Prose but normal in Ionic' (Rutherford 1881: 1–31; e.g. ξυνός, ἀντιοῦμαι, εὐφρόνη) and for the sake of polymorphy tragedy even adopted Ionic vocalism in words such as ξεῖνος or γούνατα (cf. Björck 1950: 158–63).[17]

The most remarkable aspect of this 'Ionicization' of cultivated Attic Greek is the fact that it also affected phonology, a highly automatized level of language. There are only a few features by which Attic differs phonologically from East Ionic (which was *the* Ionic prestige variety thanks to its rich literary tradition). Four of the more prominent features are (1) the lack of compensatory lengthening after the fall of digamma in words like Attic κόρη and ξένος (= Ionic κούρη and ξεῖνος < *κόρϝη and *ξένϝος), (2) the preservation (or reintroduction) of long α after ε, ι, ρ, the so-called *alpha purum* (where Ionic has η: Attic σοφία, πράττω = Ionic σοφίη, πρήσσω), (3) the assimilation of a consonantal group ρσ to yield ρρ e.g. in Attic ἄρρην or θάρρος (= Ionic ἄρσην, θάρσος), and (4) the development of a geminate ττ instead of Ionic σσ from the original groups **κy* and **χy* (and mostly also from **τy* and **θy*), as in Attic φυλάττω, κρείττων, or γλῶττα (= Ionic φυλάσσω, κρέσσων, γλῶσσα).

[16] Cf. *Eq.* 1378–80, *Vesp.* 1132–1280, Peppler (1910: 436–7), and Dover (1987: 229; 1997: 118–19).

[17] On lexical and morphological (ἴτωσαν for ἰόντων) Ionicisms in tragedy see also Meillet (1965: 218–21) and Horrocks (1997: 20).

Tragedy accepts the Attic forms for (1) and (2), the lack of compensatory lengthening and the *alpha purum*, and it uses the Ionic variants of (1) only as polymorphic by-forms. With (3) and (4), however, it does not follow the Attic way and adopts *ρσ* and *σσ* instead of the Attic geminates *ρρ* and *ττ*. The same Ionicizing preference is found in early Attic prose, notably in Thucydides, but not in the Attic inscriptions. Cases for *ρσ/ρρ* are comparatively rare, but *σσ/ττ* is a common group where the choice would perceptibly influence the appearance of a text.

The only plausible explanation for the use of Ionicizing *σσ* in Attic prose and tragedy appears to be that *ττ* had the stigma of parochialism (Allen 1987: 13; Horrocks 1997: 27). In fact the region where *ττ* is common does not extend very far beyond the boundaries of Attica: only Boeotia and Euboea share the Attic development of dental stops (cf. Buck 1955: 69–70).[18] It is difficult to know how much the Ionic elegance affected upper-class *spoken* Attic in the fifth century. López Eire (1993: 51) wonders if Hippias' wife was called *Μυρσίνη* (not *Μυρρίνη*) out of aristocratic taste and Cassio (1981: 92) plausibly suggests that *ὑποθηλυτέρα* in the famous Aristophanic fragment 706, in which a speaker[19] rejects a *διάλεκτος ἀστεία ὑποθηλυτέρα*, an 'urbane, rather feminine style of speech', may allude to a certain Ionic softness in cultivated speech. Moreover, the consonantism *σσ* and *ρσ* was going to become the regular one in Koine Greek, which is essentially an internationalized outgrowth of Attic.

Whatever the situation may have been in cultivated conversation, the dramatic evidence is unambiguous—and not limited to phonology. A similar point may be made for syntax with the use of the dual. As often with syntactic features, the difference between tragedy and comedy is here quantitative rather than qualitative. The dual had been lost early in Ionic but was very much alive in fifth-century Attic. In the Attic inscriptions it is used consistently until 409 BC (Meisterhans–Schwyzer 1900: 199–201; cf. for the attested forms Threatte 1996: 18–20, 91–5, 54), but in the prose of Thucydides it is very weakly represented. Tragedy actually becomes more dual-friendly over time, another symptom of increasing linguistic realism. But even in a rather late play of

[18] And similarly Crete, but in classical times Crete was not the place to look for linguistic or other fashions.

[19] Possibly the poet himself: Bremer (1993: 145).

Euripides', the *Phoenician Women*, the dual appears only in about 25 per cent of the cases in which the context would have allowed its use. The figure sharply contrasts with about 57 per cent in the Aristophanic corpus (Cuny 1906; cf. Hasse 1891). Like the ττ consonantism, the dual was ultimately going to disappear so that historically speaking comedy is again on the losing side.

If tragedy shied away from using the dual and forms such as θάλαττα or πράττω because of their parochial stigma although the plays were written to be performed by Attic actors on an Attic stage, the different attitude of comedy deserves attention. By its linguistic realism, which implied a separation from traditional literary standards and ideals, comedy consciously opted for parochialism and professed 'Atticness'. That this was a conscious choice can be gathered from the fact that Aristophanes did introduce Ionicizing forms into solemn hymns and some elaborate lyric passages, as for instance the hoopoe's invocation of the birds in *Av.* 238–9 and, with an echo of Alcman, 250–1:

> ὅσα (sc. φῦλα/γένη) θ' ὑμῶν κατὰ κήπους ἐπὶ κισσοῦ
> κλάδεσι νομὸν ἔχει . . .,

And all of you who find their food in gardens on the ivy branches,

> ὧν τ' ἐπὶ πόντιον οἶδμα θαλάσσης
> φῦλα μετ' ἀλκυόνεσσι ποτῆται

And you whose tribes fly with the halcyons over the swell of the open sea.[20]

But again things must be seen in a wider context. Just as its linguistic realism had made of comedy a superior dramatic genre

[20] Some further examples in hymns: *Nub.* 568 θαλάσσης, *Thesm.* 988 κισσοφόρε, *Thesm.* 999 κισσός, *Ran.* 328 and 340/1 τινάσσων; in a paratragic monody: *Thesm.* 1052 λεύσσειν; in the lyrics of the anonymous poet: *Av.* 908 μελιγλώσσων; in a 'paraepic' passage: *Pax* 1286 θωρήσσοντο; in paratragic contexts or with reference to tragedy (including tragic lyrics): *Ran.* 827 γλῶσσ' ἀνελισσομένη, *Ran.* 892 γλώσσης, *Ran.* 898 γλῶσσα, *Ran.* 992 λεύσσεις, *Ran.* 1172 κηρύσσω, *Thesm.* 889 θάσσεις, *Ran.* 1309 θαλάσσης, *Ran.* 1314 εἱειειειλίσσετε, *Ran.* 1349 εἱειειειλίσσουσα; cf. *Thesm.* 681 λύσσῃ (lyr.) in a song full of tragic elements and perhaps also Ar. fr. 765 ἀκύμων θάλασσα. In Ar. fr. 638 γλῶσσα is probably corrupt and in *Thesm.* 1192 the consonantism is a feature of the Scythian's broken Attic. Proper names and non-Greek words stand apart (*Eq.* 1088 Ἐρυθρᾶς θαλάσσης, *Ran.* 1057 and 1212 Παρνασσῶν/-όν, Ar. fr. 431 Μοσσυνικά, Ar. fr. 857 νάρκισσος). The regularity in the variation of σσ and ττ proves that the two forms are not just graphic variants (unless one cares to assume the unlikely scenario of a meticulous editor correcting all the Aristophanic texts): cf. Colvin (1999: 266) on *Pax* 47 αἰνίττεται.

when literary paradigms were inverted, parochialism could become a virtue. Old Comedy flourished during the Peloponnesian War, at a time when allies changed and the only certain value was Atticness. Parochialism now symbolized 'national' loyalty. There is a somewhat puzzling fragment of the grammarian Aelius Dionysius (fr. 298 Schwabe) which may imply that Pericles was the first Attic orator to adopt the *ττ* consonantism in public speeches (Allen 1987: 13 n. 5).[21] If the interpretation is correct, it is hard to believe that Pericles had euphonic reasons when others found the Ionic way more elegant. The nationalist leader rather gave a political signal—and comedy gives the same signal: having established itself as the true drama of the people, comedy now becomes the drama of the *Athenian* people.

3. COMIC LANGUAGE AND GREEK IDENTITY

3.1. Non-Athenians in Aristophanes' peace-plays

Up to this point my description of comic language has been generic. As far as we can judge from the fragments of Old Comedy, Aristophanes operated within an established linguistic

[21] Eustathius p. 813.43: *Αἴλιος δὲ Διονύσιος τοὺς κωμικοὺς μάλιστα ἐκκλίνειν πᾶν τὸ ἔχον σιγμὸν καὶ ἐξήχησιν καὶ ψόφον, ἃ τῇ τραγῳδίᾳ μάλιστ' ἂν ἁρμόττοι. διὸ καὶ διασύροντες τοὺς τραγικοὺς προσπαίζουσιν ἐν τῷ "ἔσωσας ἡμᾶς ἐκ τῶν σῖγμα τῶν Εὐριπίδου"* (= Pl. Com. fr. 29). *λέγει δὲ καὶ ὅτι Περικλέα φασὶ πρῶτον ἐκκλῖναι τὸν διὰ τοῦ σ σχηματισμὸν τοῦ στόματος, ὡς ἀπρεπῆ καὶ πλατύν, γυμναζόμενον ἀεὶ πρὸς τὸ κάτοπτρον.* 'Aelius Dionysius claims that the comedians clearly avoided every kind of hissing, unpleasant sound, or noise, which would be most appropriate for tragedy. Therefore, ridiculing the tragedians they make fun of them with the line "You saved us from the *sigmas* of Euripides". (Aelius Dionysius) also says that Pericles was allegedly the first (orator) to avoid the variant with *sigma* as being inappropriate and broad and that he used to practise in front of the mirror.' The passage may be connected with the question of *ττ/σσ* because of the following remarks, which are illustrated with *θάλαττα, πίττα, καρδιώττειν*, etc. The context in Eustathius also thematizes word-initial dialect variation as in *σήμερον/τήμερον* or *σεῦτλον/τεῦτλον* (cf. Alexis fr. 147.5–6, Euphro fr. 3.2). But what did Pericles (who must have grown up with *ττ*) practise in front of the mirror? And if *σχηματισμὸς τοῦ στόματος* were only referring to the mouth-positions in pronouncing [s] or [t] respectively, is the difference between the two big enough to justify so much concern?

framework. Aristophanes' originality lay in the claim that comedy should become an equal, if not superior, partner of tragedy at a time when attitudes towards dramatic realism were changing and when national values took precedence over poetic traditions. By implicitly supporting this claim, the linguistic appearance of comedy gained a new programmatic prominence. To a large degree, however, this could still be a subconscious process since it did not require any transformation of comic language.

On a different level, the comic authors had linguistic options which were not predetermined by the genre. Where there was greater artistic freedom, the playwrights had to make more conscious decisions. These, in return, allowed an intimate connection of form and content. As a consequence, their relevance to literary interpretation is more immediate. On the following pages we will look at how the individual Aristophanes actively moulded language to encode his personal vision of Athenian identity.

Every definition of identity has a negative part. By saying who I am, I also say who I am not. Those who saw themselves as Athenians could not see themselves as Spartans or Persians at the same time. The question arises, then, whether the proudly Athenian character of comedy and comic language left room for anything but a distinctly negative attitude towards the non-Athenian. Of course, Aristophanes' dialect passages spring to mind as a linguistic testing ground. Colvin (1999: 302–6) has recently argued that the traditional view whereby 'to Athenian ears all the other dialects (except for Ionic) sounded laughable and half-barbaric' (cf. Kaibel 1896: 991) does not explain why the foreign dialects are on the whole represented faithfully and without exaggeration, and why no Athenian interlocutor on stage is ever amused, perplexed, or exasperated by the dialect spoken by other Greeks. Colvin detects in the reproduction of foreign dialects the search for dramatic realism rather than the wish to laugh at the linguistic Other.

Given the surroundings in which Aristophanes' dialect parts occur, Colvin's view is compelling. Foreign dialect is prominent in *Acharnians*, where a Megarian and a Boeotian come to Dikaiopolis' peaceful market, and in *Lysistrata*, where the Spartans come to terms with the Athenians thanks to the initiative of the women on both sides. *Acharnians* and *Lysistrata* both belong to Aristophanes' peace-plays. Aristophanes may not have been a pacifist in the modern sense, but his frequent advocacy of peace in some form or other seems to be beyond reasonable doubt (Newiger 1980: 236). With de Ste. Croix (1972: 358) we may imagine him as a 'Cimonian' who dreamed of a restoration of the time when Athens and Sparta jointly dominated the Greek world (cf. *Pax* 1082 *κοινῇ τῆς Ἑλλάδος ἄρχειν*).[22] It would be perverse if Aristophanes wanted to promote such an attitude but at the same time opened gaps by deriding the enemy instead of building bridges in order to achieve his goal.

In this section I shall argue that both in *Acharnians* and in *Lysistrata* there are in fact linguistic strategies through which the non-Athenian is integrated into the Athenian discourse of comedy. As we will see, in *Lysistrata* it is precisely the use of foreign dialect which enables the integration. In *Acharnians* Aristophanes chooses an entirely different approach, which falls under the heading of discourse analysis. This branch of linguistic pragmatics broadly understands discourse as an interaction in society, which makes explicit or implicit statements about social or individual ideologies. Political discourse in particular tries to act upon an audience by means of persuasive power, and these means are often of a subtle linguistic nature (cf. van Dijk 1997*a*: 16–34).

3.2. *Acharnians*, discourse analysis, and the construction of a panhellenic WE

The one passage of *Acharnians* that deserves the label of 'political discourse' without reservation is Dikaiopolis' speech in the guise of the tragic Telephos. Its crucial importance for the interpretation of *Acharnians* as a whole has been underlined by MacDowell (1995: 66–7): 'That all this [= Dikaiopolis' speech] is meant to be taken seriously, as a convincing argument, is confirmed by what happens afterwards. Neither the chorus of Akharnians nor any other character contradicts what Dikaiopolis has said.'[23] Some

[22] De Ste. Croix's appendix is a necessary reaction against Gomme (1938), whose concept of a quasi-photographic neutral playwright looks Chekhovian, not Aristophanic. For further references supporting de Ste. Croix's position see Harvey (2000: 97, 119 n. 38).

[23] Cf. Foley (1988: 39–43). Carey (1993: 251–8) wants to separate the war in *Acharnians* from the Peloponnesian War, but is it possible during a real war to

have denounced Dikaiopolis' peace as selfish (Dover 1972: 87–8; Newiger 1980: 223; Foley 1988: 45–6), but since his course of action is imagined as being open to everybody, the later refusal to share the blessings of peace with other men (not women, for women do not have the option of acting on their own) is didactic rather than cruel and does not invalidate the righteousness of Dikaiopolis' words (cf. MacDowell 1995: 75–7).

By analysing the use of person-deixis in Dikaiopolis' speech, I propose to show how ideology and persuasive power are enacted in a very concrete manner. Person-deixis is an ideal test case because it plays a central role in creating linguistic 'subjectivity' (Benveniste 1966: 261–3). In fiction, for example, 'the choice of a first person narrator where the "I" is also a primary character in the story produces a personal relationship with the reader which inevitably tends to bias the reader in favour of the narrator/character' (Leech–Short 1981: 265). The persuasive function of person-deixis in modern political speeches has been shown by Chilton–Schäffner (1997: 216–19).

Dikaiopolis defends himself for having concluded a private peace-treaty with the enemy after bellicose elements threw him out of the people's assembly at Athens. He argues that, although he too hates the Spartans, he must blame the Athenians themselves for the current war. In his first words he acknowledges that he has become an outcast from Athenian society. There is a clear opposition between the *πτωχός* as I (represented by the enclitic pronoun *μοι*) on the one hand and the Athenian addressees (*ἄνδρες οἱ θεώμενοι, ἐν Ἀθηναίοις*) as YOU on the other (*Ach.* 497–9):

μή μοι φθονήσητ', ἄνδρες οἱ θεώμενοι,
εἰ πτωχὸς ὢν ἔπειτ' ἐν Ἀθηναίοις λέγειν
μέλλω περὶ τῆς πόλεως, τρυγῳδίαν ποιῶν.

Be not indignant with me, members of the audience, if, though a beggar, I speak before the Athenians about public affairs in a comedy.

Instantly, the picture becomes more complex. It has often been noted (cf. A. M. Bowie 1982: 29–32; Slater 1993: 407–8; Foley 1988: 33, 37) that the I of Dikaiopolis begins to combine an I_1 of Dikaiopolis and an I_2 of Aristophanes (as it had done before, in *Ach.* 378–82). This is an important device to make the speech

stage a play on war and peace that will not be automatically understood as referring to the real war?

acceptable both to the chorus and to the audience since the outlaw's I$_1$ is now inseparable from the I$_2$ of the officially elected poet.[24] In the interactional terminology of Goffman (1981; cf. Duranti 1997: 295–307), the fusion of the 'animator', i.e. 'the one who produces or gives a voice to the message that is being conveyed' (= Dikaiopolis), with the 'author', i.e. 'the one who is responsible for the selection of words and sentiments that are being expressed' (= Aristophanes), leads to a situation in which the role of the 'principal', i.e. 'the person whose position or beliefs are being represented', is taken up *jointly* by Dikaiopolis *and* Aristophanes.

At the same time a third group THEY$_1$ (*ξένοι*) enter. The identification of the newly mentioned *πόλις* with the *Ἀθηναῖοι* (YOU) a few lines earlier is straightforward, but the individual *Κλέων* is singled out (HE). Linguistically it is not clear whether *Κλέων* is actually a member of the YOU (*Ach.* 501–3):

> *ἐγὼ δὲ λέξω δεινὰ μέν, δίκαια δέ.*
> *οὐ γάρ με νῦν γε διαβαλεῖ Κλέων ὅτι*
> *ξένων παρόντων τὴν πόλιν κακῶς λέγω.*

And what I have to say will be shocking, but it will be right. This time Cleon will not allege that I am slandering the city in the presence of foreigners.

The next line brings the first move towards integration. The I (as 'Aristophanic' I$_2$ no longer outlawed) and the YOU become united as WE in the first-person plural form *ἐσμέν*. Also the identity of the THEY$_1$ (*ξένοι*) is specified: not all the non-Athenians are meant but only the *ξύμμαχοι* (*Ach.* 504–6):

> *αὐτοὶ γάρ ἐσμεν οὑπὶ Ληναίῳ τ᾽ ἀγών,*
> *κοὔπω ξένοι πάρεισιν· οὔτε γὰρ φόροι*
> *ἥκουσιν οὔτ᾽ ἐκ τῶν πόλεων οἱ ξύμμαχοι.*

For we are by ourselves and it's the Lenaean competition, and there are no foreigners yet; neither tribute money nor troops have arrived from the allied cities.

Dikaiopolis-Aristophanes then goes on to explain the composition of the WE in greater detail: WE comprises both *ἀστοί* and *μέτοικοι*.

[24] E. L. Bowie (1988: 184) suggests that the name 'Dikaiopolis' was modelled upon 'Eupolis', but even so the identification holds: the difference between the names implies that *another* comic poet is speaking—Aristophanes.

What had looked so far like an exclusively Athenian category imperceptibly acquires a first international aspect through this inclusion of the *μέτοικοι* as 'ratified participants' (*Ach.* 507–8):

> *ἀλλ' ἐσμὲν αὐτοὶ νῦν γε περιεπτισμένοι·*
> *τοὺς γὰρ μετοίκους ἄχυρα τῶν ἀστῶν λέγω.*

This time we are alone, ready hulled; for I reckon the immigrants as the civic bran.

After the I is firmly established in the WE (so that he can address the audience/YOU as *φίλοι*), a new outside group $THEY_2$ (*Λακεδαιμόνιοι*) is introduced (*Ach.* 509–14):

> *ἐγὼ δὲ μισῶ μὲν Λακεδαιμονίους σφόδρα . . .*
> *κἀμοὶ γάρ ἐστιν ἀμπέλια κεκομμένα.*
> *ἀτάρ, φίλοι γὰρ οἱ παρόντες ἐν λόγῳ,*
> *τί ταῦτα τοὺς Λάκωνας αἰτιώμεθα;*

Now I hate the Spartans intensely . . . I too have had vines cut down. But look—for there are only friends here listening—why do we blame it all on the Laconians?

The following lines look again at the WE. It is now subdivided into a *πόλις* fraction, easily identifiable as a continuation of the WE, and a fraction of people who are set apart as $THEY_3$, the *ἀνδράρια μοχθηρά*. It is not made explicit, but perhaps the audience are meant to include among the $THEY_3$ the one HE who had been separated from the *πόλις* earlier: *Κλέων*. Also, there are the *Μεγαρῆς*, in theory as $THEY_4$, but since they represent, like the Laconians, the enemy from outside and are neither *ξύμμαχοι* ($THEY_1$) nor *ἀνδράρια μοχθηρά* among the citizens ($THEY_3$), they can be included in the group $THEY_2$ (*Ach.* 515–19):

> *ἡμῶν γὰρ ἄνδρες, οὐχὶ τὴν πόλιν λέγω—*
> *μέμνησθε τοῦθ', ὅτι οὐχὶ τὴν πόλιν λέγω—*
> *ἀλλ' ἀνδράρια μοχθηρά, παρακεκομμένα,*
> *ἄτιμα καὶ παράσημα καὶ παράξενα,*
> *ἐσυκοφάντει Μεγαρέων τὰ χλανίσκια*

For it was men of ours—I do not say the city; remember that, I do not say the city—but some bent, ill-struck pieces of humanity, worthless counterfeit foreign stuff, who began denouncing the Megarians' little woollen cloaks.

Dikaiopolis adds a description of how the sycophants (THEY$_3$) heap provocation upon provocation until the THEY$_2$ (*Μεγαρῆς*) react—and thus, rather paradoxically, trigger their own integration. *All* the Greeks (*Ἕλληνες πάντες*) are united in their suffering from the *ἀνδράρια μοχθηρά*, who have stirred up the 'Avenging God' (*Περικλέης*). In other words, the WE and the THEY$_2$ (and implicitly also the THEY$_1$ who are, as *ξύμμαχοι*, involved in the war) have been melted together and Dikaiopolis' rhetoric has managed not to oppose Athenians (WE + THEY$_3$) and non-Athenians (THEY$_1$ + THEY$_2$), but good Greeks (WE + THEY$_1$ + THEY$_2$) and bad Greeks (THEY$_3$) (*Ach.* 526–31):

> *κᾆθ' οἱ Μεγαρῆς ὀδύναις πεφυσιγγωμένοι*
> *ἀντεξέκλεψαν Ἀσπασίας πόρνας δύο.*
> *κἀντεῦθεν ἀρχὴ τοῦ πολέμου κατερράγη*
> *Ἕλλησι πᾶσιν, ἐκ τριῶν λαικαστριῶν.*
> *ἐντεῦθεν ὀργῇ Περικλέης οὐλύμπιος*
> *ἤστραπτ', ἐβρόντα, ξυνεκύκα τὴν Ἑλλάδα.*

After that the Megarians, garlic-stung by the smart, stole two whores of Aspasia's in retaliation. And from that broke forth the origin of the war upon all the Greeks: from three prostitutes. Then in his wrath Olympian Pericles lightened and thundered and threw Greece into turmoil.

Through the skilful manipulation of person-deixis, Dikaiopolis (or Aristophanes) first establishes himself as the spokesman of the *polis* and subsequently does not allow his audience to construct different categories. If they want to find themselves at the end on the good side, as innocent sufferers, they have to accept their prime enemies as companions. The speech of an individual first widens into an Athenian discourse but ends up in the same panhellenic mood that will characterize a few years later the next peace-play, *Peace*.[25] Every Athenian, Aristophanes teaches, has (*a*) an identity as an individual, (*b*) an identity as an Athenian, and (*c*) an identity as a Greek. An Athenian national comedy therefore does not, or cannot, exclude a positive attitude towards the panhellenic idea.

[25] Cf. Dover (1972: 136–9), Newiger (1980: 227), and also Cassio (1985*a*: 142–5), despite his focus on the 'panionic' ideology of *Peace* (pp. 105–18). On the emergence of panhellenism see E. Hall (1989*a*: 8–9).

3.3. *Lysistrata*, sociolinguistics, and the cultural impact of language

3.3.1. Language and national identity

In *Lysistrata* the linguistic strategy of integration is different, but the outcome is the same. I will set out from an observation of modern sociolinguistic research (Fishman 1977; Giles–Bourhis–Taylor 1977). Linguistic differences often serve as symbols of social or ethnic identity even within one and the same language. Because 'ethnicity is most consciously and forcefully enacted when both contrast and opposition, boundaries and conflict, are consciously recognized' (Fishman 1977: 26), tensions or open conflicts between two ethnic (or social: cf. Hudson 1996: 206–20) groups commonly lead to two related linguistic results:

(1) Speakers of a dialectal or sociolectal variety A begin to stress the divergences of variety A from variety B with whose speakers they are in conflict: 'language saliency' is strengthened. An extreme case is the development of a 'shibboleth'. According to the Biblical Book of Judges (11: 5–6) the Ephraimites were found out by their enemies of Gilead when, upon being challenged to pronounce the word *shibboleth* 'ear of corn', they were unable to produce the Gileadite sibilant. Similar stories are reported from other times and places, for instance the 'Sicilian Vespers' (Calvet 1998: 23–4).

(2) Variety B itself becomes the focal point of all the negative associations which speakers of A have projected upon speakers of B. Speakers of A begin to depreciate B as an inferior variety and a vicious circle starts to spin. First the attitude towards the speakers of B influences the attitude towards their speech, but subsequently the speech reinforces the negative evaluation of the speakers of B by the speakers of A. The linguistic prejudices can be more or less strong and take various forms ranging from aesthetic judgments over the reproach of unintelligibility to the assumption of intentional affront.

Let me give some modern examples to illustrate phenomena (1) and (2).

(1*a*) The breakdown of the Socialist Republic of Yugoslavia a few years ago culminated in a war (in some respects not dissimilar to the Peloponnesian War) between the two largest and most powerful groups of population: Serbs and Croats. Serbs and Croats speak the same South-Slavonic language, which is commonly called Serbo-Croat outside the territory of the former Yugoslavia. Within this language—just as in ancient Greek—a complicated dialect situation exists (Ivić 1958; Corbett 1990: 128–30). Serbo-Croat is first divided into 'Štokavian', 'Čakavian', and 'Kajkavian' (after the respective words for 'what'), but the four standardized variants of Croatia, Bosnia, Serbia, and Montenegro are all based on Štokavian. Within Štokavian there is a distinction between 'Ekavian', 'Yekavian', and 'Ikavian' (after the reflex of the Old Slavonic vowel *jat'*, *ě*, in words like *dete/dijete/dite* 'child'). Roughly speaking the borders between 'Ekavian' and 'Yekavian' correspond to the borders between Serbia on the one side and Croatia and Bosnia on the other. The speakers of these dialects had long seen their respective languages as symbolic identity-markers, indexed by two different ways of writing: 'Orthodox' Serbian in a Cyrillic, 'Catholic' Croatian in a Latin alphabet. Apart from minor phonological divergences such as the one just mentioned, the differences were mainly lexical (e.g. Sb. *hleb* 'bread', *hiljada* 'thousand', *vlak* 'train' vs. Cr. *kruh*, *tisuća*, *voz*) and involved very few morphological (Sb. *studentkinja* vs. Cr. *studentica*) or syntactic features (Sb. *možeš da odeš* 'you may leave' vs. Cr. *možeš otići*); between the two groups, there was no communicative problem at all (Škiljan 1996: 307–14; Garde 1996: 129–40).

When the war broke out, many speakers on both sides started to think of their dialects as distinct languages. They artificially differentiated them as much as possible, for instance by stigmatizing lexical variants used by the other side.[26] Often this was actively supported from above by language policies (Škiljan 1996: 322–5). The symbolic opposition between the two linguistic varieties became so strong that people tried to build up a communicative opposition as well.

(1*b*) Linguistic differentiation does not necessarily presuppose a war. When the new Scottish Parliament was created, some Scottish nationalists suggested recording the proceedings not in

[26] Cf. the anecdote cited by Garde (1996: 137 n. 9): 'A Croatian father corrects his son: "I told you *hiljadu puta* ('a thousand times') that you mustn't say *hiljada*, but *tisuća*."'

standard ('English') English but in 'Lallans' (Lowland Scots), a distinct dialect with a long literary history beginning in Middle English and nowadays even with guidelines for written consistency (Aitken 1979; 1984). Here the parallel with ancient Greece is less sinister. During the eighteenth century literary Scots, which was used in poetry, ballads, and humorous tales, came to be called 'Doric' because of its rough and undefiled nature that was felt to be reminiscent of Doric poetry. Today the term 'Doric' designates the rural dialects of the north-east (Crystal 1995: 328–33).

(2*a*) The transfer of negative evaluations from speakers seen as opponents onto their language can be observed in Switzerland. Nobody in Switzerland would seriously think of promoting Swiss German ('Schweizerdeutsch') or one of its strongest dialects into the role of a written standard language. In this respect Standard German ('Hochdeutsch' or 'Schriftdeutsch') is the 'H-variety', the socially higher-classed option in the diglossic situation of German-speaking Switzerland. But since World War II, the position of Swiss German has been continually strengthened in many domains of daily life, for example in broadcasting and television, in primary schools, and sometimes even in conversation with non-native speakers of German. Thus, the situation again illustrates self-differentiation in a time of (subliminal) confrontation.

At the same time Germans have come to be regarded as arrogant and intrusive by many Swiss. These negative assessments are frequently transferred onto spoken (but not written) Standard German and find their expression for instance in mockery of 'German' German accents. World War II, during which the relationship between Switzerland and Germany was very strained though not openly hostile on a political level, has had a significant psychological impact. At the beginning of the century, it could happen that educated Swiss people spoke Standard German with each other, but this is now ruled out completely because of the new negative image of the 'opponent's' variety (cf. Schiffman 1991).

(2*b*) In a similar case from the English-speaking world, linguistic prejudices have often been disguised as scholarly observations and the linguistic depreciation has persevered over centuries. English attacks against the American language began at the end of the eighteenth century and it is quite obvious that the American

Revolution together with the preceding movements toward independence must have been the psychological trigger.[27] Friendlier times could dampen, but not silence, the dispute and America shot back quickly (cf. Mencken 1963). For instance, in 1833 the Englishman Thomas Hamilton observed in *Men and Manners in America* that 'the amount of bad grammar in circulation is very great; that of barbarisms enormous' (p. 127) and he complained that 'the privilege of barbarizing the King's English is assumed by all ranks and conditions of men. Such words as *slick*, *kedge* and *boss*, it is true, are rarely used by the better orders; but they assume unlimited liberty in the use of "expect," "reckon," "guess," and "calculate," and perpetrate conversational anomalies with the most remorseless impunity' (p. 129). In 1936 the American critic H. L. Mencken 'replied' in the *Yale Review* that the increasing adoption of American words and phrases in England is natural and inevitable because England has 'nothing to offer in competition with them—that is, nothing so apt or pungent, nothing so good'. And again, when Mencken (1963: 102) prophesies that 'the future of what was once the Anglo-Saxon tongue lies on this side of the water', an anonymous English reader in one of Oxford's University Libraries felt the need to add in the margin: 'God forbid. aaaaaaaaaghhh!!.. Spitter!'[28]

3.3.2. *Language and identity during the Peloponnesian War*

Back to Greece. Nobody tells us explicitly that the Peloponnesian War brought about the two linguistic consequences of self-differentiation and devaluation of the other's language. In a typological perspective, however, this is not unlikely given the socio-psychological or anthropological similarities with the situations just described. Both language and dialect were clearly felt to be indicators of national and tribal identity. We gather this, for

[27] On an isolated attack in 1735 against the word *bluff* see Mencken (1963: 3–4).

[28] Even mere spelling reforms can provoke similar reactions: in November 2000, the British Qualifications and Curriculum Authority wished to introduce the American (and in the former case etymologically preferable) spellings *fetus* and *sulfate* for *foetus* and *sulphate* into national school examinations to bring schools in line with international scientific convention, but after immediate violent reactions the School Standards minister was forced to intervene and halt the new guidelines (source: *The Independent*, Saturday, 25 November 2000).

instance, from the Athenians' famous promise to Sparta to remain faithful to Greece against the Persians: Greek identity is here based on genetic origins and on linguistic community, *ὁμογλωσσία* (Hdt. 8.144). The same idea that language mirrors ethnic identity and genetic relationships is found very often elsewhere too (Hdt. 2.2, 2.42, 2.105, 4.108, 4.117, 6.138, 7.70, Xanthus of Lydia, *FGrH* 765 F 15, Hes. fr. 9 M.–W.) and ultimately reflected even in the term *βάρβαρος* (E. Hall 1989*a*: 9–10). Furthermore, Morpurgo Davies (1987: 16–18) has shown that an abstract linguistic concept of 'Greek' must have existed by the end of the fifth century. Perhaps the most revealing, though often neglected, evidence for the importance of language as a symbol of identity is the fact that everybody, including women and slaves, could become initiated into the Eleusinian mysteries, provided he or she could make him- or herself understood in Greek (*φωνὴν συνετός*: Cels. ap. Orig. 3.59; cf. Hdt. 8.65).

As for the symbolic function of Greek *dialects*, we read in one of Thucydides' speeches how the rowers on Athenian ships, who were not genetically Athenians, were stimulated to fight for Athens because 'you have been taken for Athenians and admired throughout Hellas thanks to your knowledge of our language and your cultural assimilation' (Thuc. 7.63.3: *Ἀθηναῖοι νομιζόμενοι καὶ μὴ ὄντες ἡμῶν τῆς τε φωνῆς τῇ ἐπιστήμῃ καὶ τῶν τρόπων τῇ μιμήσει ἐθαυμάζεσθε κατὰ τὴν Ἑλλάδα*). In Eupolis' *Demes* a demagogue is denounced as speaking Attic only in order to be socially acceptable (fr. 99.25; cf. Ar. *Ran.* 678–81; Ehrenberg 1962: 160–1; Colvin 1999: 36). And during the Peloponnesian War, the two sides were so much associated with *linguistic* divisions that language acquired strategic importance. In attacking the Dorian Ampraciots, the Athenian general Demosthenes put the Messenians, Dorian allies of Athens, into the front lines; they were to deceive the enemy's outposts by addressing them in their Doric dialect (Thuc. 3.112.3–4; cf. Thuc. 4.3.3, 4.41.2). The Athenians, in turn, were terrified by the warlike Doric paean of their own Dorian allies in a battle near Syracuse: the enemy suddenly seemed to be everywhere (Thuc. 7.44.6).[29]

[29] Such passages argue against the views of Hainsworth (1967: 64–5) and J. M. Hall (1997: 170–7) that categories like 'Doric', 'Aeolic', or 'Ionic' had no common linguistic denominator for a speaker of Greek. Hainsworth neglects the fact that the existence of names for local dialects (e.g. Megarian, Corinthian, Laconian) does not exclude another more general classification (e.g. Doric, Aeolic, Ionic), and Hall's

To be sure, in order to find out precisely how much linguistic self-differentiation was going on during the Peloponnesian War, we should need much more material, especially for the language of Sparta. J. M. Hall (1997: 180) boldly suggests that the Laconian linguistic conservatism might be a 'conscious and deliberate process, specifically designed to maintain a distinct Lakonian identity and to identify the Spartans as the true Dorians of the Peloponnese'. In fact, Aristophanes' speakers of Doric very often[30] use the dialect word *λῶ* 'to wish', and never the Doric equivalent of Attic *βούλομαι*, which is attested as *δήλομαι* in a fourth-century inscription from the Tarentine colony (i.e. Laconian granddaughter colony) Herakleia in Lucania (*DGE* 62.146)—but obviously Aristophanes had, within the limits of linguistic realism, every interest in making the Laconians' speech sound as exotic as possible. The epigraphic divergences between Messenian and Laconian, which seemingly contradict Thucydides' view (4.3.3) that Messenians and Laconians are *ὁμόφωνοι*, have also been explained as a result of self-differentiation in the early fourth century when the Messenian helots fought for independence (Katičić 1959: 135–6). In this light the 'Ionicization' of Attic at the end of the fifth century acquires a new dimension too. It coincides in time with a war where the ethnic frontlines were clear and where it was exceptional that the Argives fought as 'Dorians against Dorians with the Athenians who are Ionians' (Thuc. 7.57.9; cf. 1.124.1, 4.61.2, 5.9.1, 6.6.2, 6.77.1, 7.57).[31] Was the high prestige of Ionic culture the only reason for 'reinventing Attic'? And is it not likely that the official adoption of the Ionic alphabet in Athens shortly after the war was a paralinguistic act of differentiation from the victorious Dorians?[32]

reasoning that terms like 'Doric' or 'Ionic' could not be linguistic in character because 'it seems barely credible that the Greeks were capable of using linguistic criteria to assign local dialects to dialect groups' is purely academic. Every adult speaker of Swiss German *is* capable of establishing general groups like 'Eastern Swiss German' for a whole range of dialects (which he or she might well be able to locate more precisely, e.g. 'St Gall', 'Thurgau', etc.), even though (*a*) he or she could not define the relevant isoglosses, and (*b*) there is no such thing as an 'Eastern Swiss' ethnic identity.

[30] *Lys.* 95, 981, 1105, 1162, 1163, 1188 (but 1080 *σέλει*); cf. *Ach.* 749, 766, 772, 776, 788, 814; Colvin (1999: 244).

[31] Cf. Ollier (1933: 78), Rawson (1969: 16), Alty (1982). The 'Ionian' identity of Athens is of course established much earlier: Solon fr. 4a West; Connor (1993: 198–201).

[32] Cf. D'Angour (1999: 119–25); similarly Roesch, in Taillardat–Roesch (1966:

Evidence for the depreciation of the enemy's language should not be expected from the Athenian women in *Lysistrata*. They must display solidarity, not hatred. But perhaps the *name* of the enemy serves as a linguistic substitute for their language. When one of Aristophanes' narrow-minded Athenians hears 'Sparta' or 'Laconian', the reaction is always the same—and always derided by the poet.[33] In *Wasps* Philokleon almost has a stroke when his son Bdelykleon wants him to wear a better type of shoes, called *Λακωνικαί* (*Vesp*. 1157–60):

> (*Βδ.*) *ἄγε νυν, ὑπολύου τὰς καταράτους ἐμβάδας,*
> *ταςδὶ δ' ἀνύσας ὑπόδυθι τὰς Λακωνικάς.*
> (*Φι.*) *ἐγὼ γὰρ ἂν τλαίην ὑποδύσασθαί ποτε*
> *ἐχθρῶν παρ' ἀνδρῶν δυσμενῆ καττύματα;*

(Bd.) Come now, take off those damned shoes, and hurry up and get into these Laconians.

(Ph.) What, how could I ever endure to put on 'the hateful soles that from our foemen come?'

Similarly an unnamed Attic patriot, in a fragment from Aristophanes' *Farmers*, exclaims (Ar. fr. 110):

> *. . . συκᾶς φυτεύω πάντα πλὴν Λακωνικῆς·*
> *τοῦτο γὰρ τὸ σῦκον ἐχθρόν ἐστι καὶ τυραννικόν.*
> *οὐ γὰρ ἦν ἂν μικρόν, εἰ μὴ μισόδημον ἦν σφόδρα.*

I plant all kinds of figs—apart from the Laconian: for this fig is an enemy, a tyrant. It would not be so small if it did not detest democracy.

And Euelpides' suggestion to name the birds' new state 'Sparta' is rejected by a horrified Peisetairos (*Av*. 812–15):

> (*Εὐ.*) *φέρ' ἴδω, τί δ' ἡμῖν ὄνομ' ἄρ' ἔσται τῇ πόλει;*
> *βούλεσθε τὸ μέγα τοῦτο τοὐκ Λακεδαίμονος*
> *Σπάρτην ὄνομα καλῶμεν αὐτήν;* (*Πε.*) *Ἡράκλεις·*
> *σπάρτην γὰρ ἂν θείμην ἐγὼ τἠμῇ πόλει;*
> *οὐδ' ἂν χαμεύνῃ. . . .*

78–87), argues that Boeotia, threatened by Sparta, officially adopted the Ionic alphabet in 395 or 394 in order to display its goodwill towards its new ally Athens.

[33] On the image of Sparta in comedy see Ollier (1933: 61–3, 71–2); Rawson (1969: 25–6); Harvey (1994).

(Eu.) Well, let's see, what shall we have as our city's name? Do you want us to call it by that great Lacedaemonian name—Sparta?

(Peis.) Heracles! Do you think I'd use Sparta as a name for my city? I wouldn't even use esparto cords for a bedstead. . . .

If we treat all these cultural and literary indications as cumulative evidence and add to them the sociolinguistic patterns that have been observed cross-culturally in more recent ethnic conflicts, it seems safe enough to suppose that the language of the Spartan arch-enemy must have provoked a highly negative psychological response in the average Athenian. In their historical context the dialect parts of *Lysistrata* are an emotional bomb.

3.3.3. From enemy language to poetry language

If Aristophanes meant the peaceful message of *Lysistrata* to become a success, he had to soothe and transform the feelings of his audience. In order to achieve this, he exploits another stereotype attached to Sparta and its language. Sparta had once been the capital of music and dance in Greece. According to the writer of an ancient treatise *On Music* ([Plut.] *Mor.* 1134B–C), two of the most important lines of lyric tradition originated in Sparta and such famous figures as Terpander and Thaletas were attracted by the festivals of Laconia (Hooker 1980: 71–81; M. L. West 1992: 334–5). The image of Sparta as the stronghold of the Muses lived on when the star of Spartan poetry declined. Two hundred years after the days of Alcman, whose poems were still well-known enough to be cited in comedy (*Av.* 250–1), Ion of Samos celebrated Sparta in an epigram on the victory of Lysander at Aigospotamoi in 405 BC both as 'citadel of Greece' (*Ἑλλάδος ἀκρόπολις*) *and* as 'fatherland of the beautiful choruses' (*καλλίχορος πατρίς*) (*CEG* 871.9–12, Delphi, *c.*400 BC). This is more than adulatory rhetoric: maiden choruses continued to be performed at the Hyacinthia even in post-classical times (Calame 1977: 308–10) and in fifth-century Athenian literature there are references to choral dances in Sparta which seem to be more than mere memories of a distant past (Eur. *Alc.* 449–51, *Hel.* 1465–70). One of these is the final song of *Lysistrata* (1302–13):

(*Χο.*^Λ) ὦ εἶα μάλ' ἔμβη,
ὦ εἶα κοῦφα πᾶλον, ὡς Σπάρταν ὑμνίωμες,
τᾷ σιῶν χοροὶ μέλοντι
καὶ ποδῶν κτύπος,
χᾇ τε πῶλοι ταὶ κόραι
πὰρ τὸν Εὐρώταν
ἀμπάλλοντι, πυκνὰ ποδοῖν
ἀγκονίωαί,
ταὶ δὲ κόμαι σείονται
ᾇπερ βακχᾶν θυρσαδδωᾶν καὶ παιδδωᾶν.

(Laconian chorus) Step it, hey! prance lightly, hey! that we may hymn Sparta, which delights in dances in honour of the gods and in the stamp of feet, and where beside the Eurotas the maidens prance like fillies, raising clouds of dust with their feet, and their hair bobs like the hair of bacchants who sport and ply the thyrsus.

Also, it is certainly more than Aristophanic fantasy when the Athenian ambassador, the representative of the Athenian people, tells his Spartan colleague how much he likes performances of Spartan dancers (*Lys.* 1245–6; cf. Cratin. fr. 173):

λαβὲ δῆτα τὰς φυσαλλίδας πρὸς τῶν θεῶν
ὡς ἥδομαί γ' ὑμᾶς ὁρῶν ὀρχουμένους.

Yes, I beg you, do take the pipes. I do enjoy watching you people dance.

Thus, in the Athenian cultural consciousness the Laconian dialect had both negative and positive connotations. It was not only the language of the enemy but also a language of songs and poetry. This dichotomy may have lived on for centuries in aesthetic evaluation, not unlike the negative attitude towards American speech in England. Pausanias at least was still surprised by the fact that 'the Spartan dialect did not spoil the charm of Alcman's songs, although it is usually so far away from sounding pleasant' (Paus. 3.15.2). Whereas Laconian as a spoken dialect evoked the abhorrent Other, Laconian as a sung dialect, as the Doric of choral lyrics, evoked the attractive Other—that Other which everyone desired to integrate, as the Athenian ambassador's request illustrates, and as Athens had professed by 'de-Othering' it and introducing it, in a somewhat tamed shape, into her own literary genre, the choruses of tragedy.[34]

[34] An attempt to take possession of the Doric or Spartan cultural past is also made by constructing, doubtless against the historical facts, an Athenian identity

Despite the emotional gap between the two aspects of the Spartans' language, both belong to the same people in *Lysistrata*. At the *beginning* of the play, when the women's conspiracy seems so dangerous for the *polis*, the Spartan dialect is only spoken. In this form it is the language of the enemy in a war which is going to be explained, towards the end, as a failure of spoken communication between the two sides (*Lys.* 1233–4):

(*Πρ.*^{A}) . . . ὅ τι μὲν ἂν λέγωσιν οὐκ ἀκούομεν,
ἃ δ' οὐ λέγουσι, ταῦθ' ὑπονενοήκαμεν

(Athenian ambassador) . . . we don't hear what they say, and suspect them of meaning things which they don't say.

In the world of music, on the other hand, even a real *faux pas* cannot destroy the re-established friendship (*Lys.* 1236–8):

(*Πρ.*^{A}) νυνὶ δ' ἅπαντ' ἤρεσκεν· ὥστ' εἰ μέν γέ τις
ᾄδοι Τελαμῶνος, Κλειταγόρας ᾄδειν δέον,
ἐπῃνέσαμεν ἂν καὶ πρὸς ἐπιωρκήσαμεν.

(Athenian ambassador) But *this* time everything pleased us; so that if, say, someone sang 'Telamon' when he should have been singing 'Cleitagora', we'd acclaim him and even swear blind that—.[35]

Hence, at the *end* of the play, when Athens and Sparta are saved, the Spartan dialect is only sung, without a hint of parody, as language of the Muses. While the plot of *Lysistrata* invites rational reflection about the integration of the enemy as a friend, Aristophanes' use of the enemy's dialect is a linguistic trick to support this integration on an emotional level. In 411 BC Aristophanes has recognized that a true peace, not one that pursues mainly economic goals like that of *Acharnians*, is possible only if the emotional boundaries are removed—and it is through the dramatic use of language that he conveys this new concept of peace to the people of Athens.

for Tyrtaeus and an Ionian identity for Alcman: Hinze (1934), Prato (1968: 1*–5*), Calame (1983: xiv–xvi).

[35] 'It is not clear why it was a mistake on this occasion to sing one instead of the other': Henderson (1987: 209).

4. COMIC LANGUAGE AND THE IDENTITY OF A CIVILIZED WORLD

4.1. Non-Greeks in Aristophanic comedy

The first circle of this paper has argued that the basic language of comedy establishes comedy as *the* Athenian popular and national drama during the last decades of the fifth century. The second circle has then illustrated how Aristophanic comedy at the same time develops language into a carrier of *polis*-transcending, panhellenic, ideas and linguistically integrates the non-Athenian Greek. In a third and final circle let us now ask how the treatment of language in comedy reflects attitudes towards the non-Greek.

Non-Greeks enter the comic stage only rarely and they do not have much to say. In Aristophanes' 11 complete plays there are three barbarians who open their mouths: in *Acharnians* a Persian ambassador, who briefly addresses the Athenian assembly, in *Birds* a Triballic god, who accompanies the gods' negotiators Poseidon and Herakles to the bird-city, and in *Thesmophoriazusae* a Scythian archer, who has the task of guarding Euripides' Relative when the latter has been arrested after his intrusion into the women's festival. The Persian and the Triballian say only a few words in broken Greek, but the Scythian talks at some length both to Euripides, who wants to free his Relative under various disguises, and to the captive himself.

Fifth-century Athens had a standing police force formed exclusively by men of the warlike Scythian people from the far North. This squadron was employed mainly to keep order in the assembly and to execute various other policing tasks under the orders of magistrates (but not independently like a modern police corps).[36] Their integration into Athenian society was very limited and they lived apart in barracks on the Areopagus. Moreover, the picture Aristophanes draws of his Scythian does not suggest that they were held in high esteem. Not surprisingly, then, these outsiders did not learn proper Attic and their bad Greek became a wonderful target for a comic poet.

[36] See, apart from *Thesmophoriazusae*, Ar. *Ach.* 54–5, *Lys.* 433–62, and *Eccl.* 143, as well as Plassart (1913: 192–4), Jacob (1928: 57–64), V. J. Hunter (1994: 147), and Bäbler (1998: 167–9).

4.2. The Scythian's Greek as 'foreigner talk'

Thesmophoriazusae presents the only extensive piece of ancient 'foreigner talk'. In sociolinguistics the term 'foreigner talk' designates two related phenomena. In the first place it refers to a more or less conventionalized 'simplified register' or language-variety which is used by members of a speech community to address people whose knowledge of the language of the community is felt to be less than normal (Ferguson–DeBose 1977: 100). If a native speaker is asked by a foreigner for the way to a restaurant and answers with something like 'You go corner of street, find eat there', he is using (primary) foreigner talk. Although C. A. Ferguson (1971: 102–3) suggests that this kind of foreigner talk may be a linguistic universal, we have no testimonies for such a register in ancient Greece or Rome.

What Aristophanes' *Thesmophoriazusae* presents is the other type of foreigner talk, so-called 'secondary foreigner talk' (Hinnenkamp 1982: 40–1; cf. C. A. Ferguson 1975: 2). Here a native speaker (Aristophanes) reproduces the broken language of a non-native speaker (the Scythian). Secondary foreigner talk in modern literature has been extensively studied, especially in the late 1970s and early 1980s (e.g. C. A. Ferguson 1975; Corder 1975; Valdman 1977; 1981: 47–9; cf. Hinnenkamp 1982: 196–7). The results of this research provide an adequate typological framework for a new discussion of Aristophanes' foreigner talk.

So far the most extensive treatments of the Scythian's Greek in *Thesmophoriazusae* are those by Friedrich (1918) and Brixhe (1988). Both Friedrich and Brixhe first draw up very useful inventories of the relevant linguistic features but then proceed to dubious conclusions. They mistakenly seek to extrapolate from the Scythian's barbarisms certain characteristics of an otherwise unattested lower-class Attic used by *native* speakers.

Let me give an example. The Scythian very often does not pronounce final -*ν*, sometimes omits final -*ς*, occasionally gets his vowel quantities wrong, does not aspirate the consonants *φ*, *θ*, *χ*, and seems to pronounce [i(:)] when proper Attic had [e:] (⟨ei⟩). Thus, he asks (*Thesm.* 1086, also with a wrong nominal gender):

πῶτε τὸ πωνή; . . .

Where dat voice from?

instead of *πόθεν ἡ φωνή*, or (*Thesm.* 1102–3):

> . . . *τί λέγι; τὴ Γοργόνο*[37] *πέρι*
> *τὸ γραμματέο σὺ τὴ κεπαλή;* . . .

What you say? You garryin' de 'ead of Gorgo de segretar'?

instead of *τί λέγεις; τὴν Γοργόνος φέρεις τοῦ γραμματέως σὺ τὴν κεφαλήν;*

Now, Brixhe (1988: 127–8) points out that from about 350 BC onward mistaken vowel-quantities (as with *πω-* instead of *πο-* in *πόθεν*) appear in Attic inscriptions, a fact which led Teodorsson (1978: 94–8) to the (bold) conclusion that by this time a large group of native speakers of Attic had confounded long and short vowels. Assuming that Aristophanes reproduced in *Thesmophoriazusae* not just features of a foreigner's broken language but sociolectal variants within native Attic, Brixhe suggests to set Teodorsson's date even higher, right into the fifth century (even though Teodorsson 1974: 252 had rightly dismissed the Scythian's Greek as irrelevant for his argument). Similar reasonings make Brixhe and Friedrich postulate also extremely early dates for the loss of final *-ν* and *-ς* and for Attic iotacism in the pronunciation of ⟨*ει*⟩.

The methodological flaw lies in the connection of two unrelated phenomena. An English author who wishes to represent the broken English of Italian or French people makes them drop the initial [h-] in words like *have* or *help*. Since initial aspiration is also dropped in Cockney English (as in various traditional dialects of England), the resulting forms *'ave* or *'elp* might as well represent a native sociolect. However, there is no causal link between the two things and it would not be legitimate to conclude from the Italian's or Frenchman's *'ave* and *'elp* that there *must* be a group of native speakers who do not pronounce initial [h-]. In other words, it is very possible that some Athenians were iotacizing before 400 BC (cf. Duhoux 1987; Teodorsson 1987), but the Scythian's Greek in *Thesmophoriazusae* does by no means strengthen such a claim.

Instead we must treat Aristophanes' foreigner talk, like modern secondary foreigner talk, as a literary phenomenon. There are many overlaps in the strategies of how language is simplified by

[37] *Γοργόνος* (MS) is metrically impossible. *Γοργόνο* without final *-ς* is more 'regular' for the Scythian's broken Attic than Bothe's *Γόργος*; the Scythian does not care how an *o*-stem *Γόργος* should be declined after he has just heard *Γοργόνος*.

foreigners in literature. Typical features of modern foreigner-talk registers include:

(1) in phonology: articulatory simplifications (in English for instance the addition of a vowel to final consonants),

(2) in morphology: the reduction of inflection, often by selection of one or two all-purpose forms,

(3) in syntax: short sentences and parataxis rather than hypotaxis, analytic paraphrases of certain grammatical constructions, and the omission of function words such as articles, prepositions, and auxiliaries,

(4) in the lexicon: paraphrases for difficult lexical items ('boss of city' for 'mayor'), a special and often reduced list of quantifiers ('plenty', 'much', etc.), and sometimes particular foreign or foreign-sounding items (cf. English 'savvy') (Ferguson–DeBose 1977: 104; cf. Meisel 1977: 90–1; Hinnenkamp 1982: 15–31).

When we check the Scythian's language against this list, it emerges that only his phonology and morphology are extensively simplified. The main features of phonology (loss of final *-ν* and occasionally final *-ς*, confusion of vowel quantities, lack of consonant aspiration, iotacistic [i(:)] for [e:]) have already been mentioned. Nominal morphology is simplified by the application of an all-purpose form in *-ο* for the oblique cases of consonant stems, for instance with *γέροντο* and *σανίδο* (*Thesm.* 1123–4):

εἲ σπόδρ' ἐπιτυμεῖς τὴ γέροντο πύγισο,
τὴ σανίδο τρήσας ἐξόπιστο πρώκτισον

If you wan' all dat much, [den] bugger de ol' man, [. . .] bore a 'ole in de board an' fuck her from be'ind (= *εἲ σφόδρ' ἐπιθυμεῖς, τὸν γέροντα πύγισον, τὴν σανίδα τρήσας ἐξόπισθε πρώκτισον*).

Similarly, a form in *-ι* can stand for all present singular forms of the verb: thus, *λέγι* and *πέρι* replace *λέγεις* and *φέρεις*, and *δῶσι* and *τρέξι* represent *δώσω* and *θρέξω* (*Thesm.* 1196, 1222, 1225). With an iotacizing pronunciation of [e:] (graphic ⟨*ει*⟩) and the loss of final *-ν* this form might stand for an infinitive (*-ειν*). The infinitive has a similar role in numerous simplified registers of modern languages, for instance in *Gastarbeiterdeutsch*, in Turkish foreigner talk, in West African Pidgin English, or in simplified Italian (Clyne 1968: 132–4; Ferguson–DeBose 1977:

104; Valdman 1981: 48; Hinnenkamp 1982: 19, 155). Already in the medieval Mediterranean pidgin language 'Lingua Franca' or 'Sabir' the infinitive replaced finite verb forms (Schuchardt 1909), and in the twelfth century Giraldus Cambrensis wrote about a conversation with an uneducated anchorite who knew just enough Latin for the most essential purposes but used it 'per infinitivum nec casus servabat' (Brewer 1861: 90–1).

The Scythian's syntax and lexicon are much less simplified. Occasionally a paratactic structure may replace a hypotactic construction, but there are good hypotactic clauses as well. In the example just given (*Thesm.* 1123–4) there is a correct εἰ-clause followed by two imperatives, and it is stylistic quibbling if we criticize that the first imperative should better be replaced by an infinitive πυγίσαι. The Scythian is perfectly at ease with the whole range of Greek vocabulary, especially its vulgar domains. Even more remarkably, he never omits function-words like prepositions and the article. In contrast Hinnenkamp (1982: 52–3) has shown that the article is nearly always omitted in German secondary foreigner talk.

4.3. The sociocultural implications of foreigner talk

It appears, then, that the Aristophanic foreigner is no more primitive than many a foreigner in modern literature. The Scythian's bad Greek is sometimes understood as reflecting the ethnocentric attitude of the Greeks towards the barbarians. MacDowell (1995: 271) comments that 'many Athenians probably thought patronizingly that a man must be stupid if he could not speak Greek properly'. While primary foreigner talk may be meant to facilitate the communication with non-native speakers, secondary foreigner talk in literature generally reflects a feeling of superiority of the author and his audience or readership (Hinnenkamp 1982: 172–85; cf. Valdman 1977: 127–8; Meisel 1977: 98).[38] However, our comparison of ancient and modern material shows that the society of fifth-century Athens was not in this respect any different from the average modern society.

[38] For an exception see Nichols (1980: 405).

Of course this is not to say that the basic image of the Scythian was not that of an uncultivated savage (Long 1986: 106–7; E. Hall 1989*b*: 52). All I want to stress is that the comic exploitation of linguistic shortcomings is not by itself a compelling argument. There may have been other images of 'the Scythian'. Modern readers and listeners, too, can find the imitation of foreigners' speech funny without necessarily thinking that there is something intrinsically wrong with the foreigners' culture. In fact, for Herodotus (4.46) the Scythians are visualized as the quintessential 'Other' (Hartog 1988), but they are *not* counted among the ἔθνεα ἀμαθέστατα of the Black Sea region. Moreover, in the semi-mythical figure of Anacharsis classical Athens did have an alternative image of the Scythian as a potentially 'wise' savage—although the myth did *not* make Anacharsis a perfect speaker of Greek (cf. Kindstrand 1981: 7; Werner 1983: 594).

And yet, there is one linguistic point which does suggests that the Scythians were socioculturally disqualified. In fifth-century ideological discourse there was clearly a primary opposition between 'Greek' and 'barbarian' (E. Hall 1989*a*). But did the Greeks really think of all barbarians as one indistinct mass? It is hard to imagine that anybody would have written a tragedy *Scythians* along the lines of Aeschylus' *Persians*, or that any Greek would have thought of learning Scythian and going into exile in Scythia, as Themistocles did in Persia (Thuc. 1.138.1–2). Support for a more differentiated view comes from Aristophanes' foreigner talk. According to Valdman (1981: 49), who discusses foreigner-talk variation in the French comic strips *Tintin* by Hergé and in Richard Adams's novel *Watership Down*, 'the lower the status of a group of foreigners, the more stereotypic the foreigner talk used to portray their approximation to the target language'. Hence, if one barbarian is made to speak better Greek than another barbarian, the Greeks probably thought of him as more civilized and 'closer' to themselves. And indeed, Aristophanes' foreigners do not all speak with the same accent.

The Persian ambassador Pseudartabas utters only one sentence in broken Greek (*Ach.* 104):

οὐ λῆψι χρυσό, χαυνόπρωκτ' Ἰαοναυ

You not vill get goldo, you open-arsed Iaonian.

The iotacism in λήψει (with a wrong quantity) and the loss (or nasalization?) of final -ν in χρυσόν are reminiscent of the Scythian's Greek, but unlike the Scythian the Persian is able to pronounce aspirates and—more importantly—his sentence shows a good mastery of Greek morphology[39] and syntax, to say nothing of his impressive lexicon (χαυνόπρωκτος!). Furthermore, the Persian's higher position is reflected in the fact that he is allowed to say a sentence in his own language (*Ach.* 100–1):

> (*Ψε.*) *ιαρταμαν εξαρξαν απισονα σατρα.*
> (*Πρ.*) *ξυνήκαθ' ὃ λέγει; (Δι.) μὰ τὸν Ἀπόλλω 'γὼ μὲν οὔ.*

(Pseudartabas) Iartaman exarxa[n] apisona satra.
(Ambassador) Did you understand what he says?
(Dikaiopolis) By Apollo, *I* didn't.

It does not even matter whether the ambassador's sentence is actual Old Persian or not (although that, too, is a culturally important question and should not be brushed aside too lightly). What counts is that the Persian's utterance leads to a dramatic situation in which the *Greeks* have to struggle because *they* need to understand him. At that moment the linguistic power-relationship between the barbarian and his Greek interlocutors is inverted. The Scythian in *Thesmophoriazusae*, on the other hand, always remains linguistically inferior, however much physical power he may have over his Greek prisoner. Thus the level of intellectual and cultural foreignness correlates with the amount of linguistic proficiency.

To be sure, neither the Persian nor the Scythian is integrated into the Greek world of comedy. However, through their respective languages Aristophanes assigns them different degrees of social acceptability. The anonymous (third-century?) author of the first 'Letter of Anacharsis' (*Epistolographi Graeci*, p. 102 Hercher = p. 37 Malherbe) complains, in the name of Anacharsis, that the Scythians are derided in Athens because of their imperfect command of Greek, whereas the Persians are taken seriously although their linguistic competence is equally poor. The situation which Pseudo-Anacharsis describes is exactly the same as that which we can infer from the linguistic analysis of Aristo-

[39] If *αυ* at the end of the line is not taken as a 'vocative-ending' but, with the scholiast (ὡς βάρβαρος δὲ τὸ αυ ἔφη, Δωρικὸν ὂν ἀντὶ τοῦ ἑλληνιζομένου 'being a barbarian he added the *αυ*, which is Doric rather than Common Greek'), as emphatic *αὖ* (as in some Laconian passages of *Lysistrata*: Colvin 1999: 234).

phanes' foreigner talk. There could hardly be a better proof for the validity of sociocultural reconstructions on the basis of linguistic material.

5. CONCLUSION

The interpretation of language variation in comedy has revealed an implicational scale of identity and otherness in the Athenian imagination. The basic language of comedy seeks to be, against the conventions of 'higher' literature, a popular *Athenian* language in the narrowest sense. But by skilfully manipulating the linguistic form of a political discourse on war and peace in *Acharnians* and by transforming, in *Lysistrata*, the linguistic Other into a language of poetic tradition, Aristophanes endows Athens with a wider Greek identity which supports, rather than contradicts, the panhellenic vision of his plays. Beyond that identity, there is an outside world composed of foreign elements: all of them foreign in the sense of non-Greek, but some of them more foreign, more 'barbaric', than others. Comedy—or at least Aristophanic comedy—does not attempt to integrate these elements, but hidden behind the clouds of condescending laughter there are the vague contours of a third and last Athenian identity: that of Athens as the centre of the entire civilized world.

Greek comedy is not just a literary genre. It is also a vast set of sociocultural attitudes encoded in language. To read the linguistic choices of comedy is a task for the linguist, the literary scholar, and the cultural historian alike.

7

Comic Elements in Tragic Language: The Case of Aeschylus' *Oresteia*

ALAN H. SOMMERSTEIN

Past explorations of the relationship between Aeschylean tragedy and the comic have mainly been channelled in three directions—and none of the three channels has been very much frequented in recent years.[1] In the first place, though quite a long time ago now, there was a tradition of attempting to seek in Aeschylus' earlier plays, or what were thought to be his earlier plays, supporting evidence for Aristotle's assertion that tragedy started 'from petty plots and ludicrous diction . . . [and] acquired grandeur at a late stage' (*Poet.* 1449^{a}19–21). This tradition was struck a hard blow by the discovery that *Suppliants*, once regarded as typical of very early tragedy, actually belonged to the 460s,[2] and the apparent discovery that the much-admired Achilles trilogy may have been written very early in Aeschylus' career—though one would be more ready to believe those who confidently assert that artistic evidence establishes a date for it close to 490, or even before,[3] if they took on board what is an inevitable consequence of that thesis, namely that this trilogy did not win first prize when it was performed (since Aeschylus' first victory only came in 484). Secondly, the *Suppliants* papyrus (*P. Oxy.* 2256 fr. 3) stimulated an attempt in the sixties, principally associated with the name of John Herington (especially Herington 1963), to turn Aristotle's claim almost on its head, and to argue that it was Aeschylus' *latest* work that betrayed strong comic influence; the case for this was

[1] I am most grateful to all participants of the Corpus Christi Classical Seminar who took part in the discussion, especially Ian Ruffell and Martin West.

[2] Garvie (1969) provides *inter alia* a detailed post-mortem on this tradition.

[3] Such as Döhle (1967), Kossatz-Deissmann (1981: 106–14), Shapiro (1994: 18–20), Garzya (1995: 46–7).

mainly based on plot structure and ethos rather than diction, and it was necessary to assume, against such little evidence as we have, that in plot structure and ethos the Athenian comedy of the 460s (dominated by Magnes) was not too different from that of the 430s (dominated by Cratinus). And thirdly, the category of 'comic relief', invented to justify certain scenes in the tragedies of Shakespeare and his contemporaries that offended against what were thought to be fundamental aesthetic canons, was from time to time applied to Aeschylus' plebeian characters, especially those in the *Oresteia*—the Watchman, the Herald, the Nurse, and the Servant.

I do not wish to reopen any of these channels. I do not believe that Aristotle's statement about the 'late' development of tragedy refers to any distinction perceived by him between earlier and later works of Aeschylus; indeed the very word which he uses to describe this development, ἀπεσεμνύνθη, with its strong echo of the *Frogs*,[4] suggests that Aristotle, like Aristophanes, perceived the major break as coming not within Aeschylus' career but *at its outset* by comparison with his predecessors,[5] and that 'late' only means 'significantly later than the first appearance of the genre'—just as when Aristotle says 'even the well-known myths are well known only to a few' (*Poet.* $1451^{b}25$–6), by 'few' he means 'significantly less than 100 per cent'. I do believe that Herington was right to see some analogies in structure between certain late Aeschylean tragedies, especially their endings, and the Old Comedy of a generation later, but that may merely indicate that comedy, not for the last time, had been trying to remodel itself to

[4] Cf. Ar. *Ran.* 833 ἀποσεμνυνεῖται πρῶτον, 1004–5 πρῶτος . . . πυργώσας ῥήματα σεμνὰ καὶ κοσμήσας τραγικὸν λῆρον.

[5] It is common ground between 'Aeschylus' and 'Euripides' in the *Frogs* debate that Aeschylus' work can be compared as a whole with that of a predecessor like Phrynichus (*Ran.* 909–10, 1299–1300) and that the Achilles plays are a typical example of his technique (*Ran.* 911–13, 924–37, 1041, 1264–5). Note that Aristotle couples the 'late' advance of tragedy to 'grandeur' with a change from the ⟨trochaic⟩ tetrameter to the iambic ⟨trimeter⟩ as the typical non-lyric metre of tragedy (*Poet.* $1449^{a}21$–4), and any such change almost certainly predated all, or almost all, the Aeschylean plays whose texts were available to him: the evidence of the Aeschylean fragments, which contain at most *two* trochaic tetrameters (Aesch. frr. 60, 296) attributable to tragedies rather than satyr-plays, indicates that *Persians* cannot be regarded as typical in this respect of Aeschylus' style in any period for which we have any knowledge of it—and even *Persians* has only 113 tetrameters compared with 429 trimeters. Cf. E. Hall (1996: 120): 'Aeschylus may . . . well have selected the metre at will for exclusively aesthetic reasons' (also ibid. 158).

some extent on the basis of tragedy. And while I shall be concentrating mainly on the *Oresteia*, I shall not be focusing particularly on the low-life characters: the comic features of language that I shall be identifying are by no means to be found solely, or even predominantly, on their lips. Indeed of the 30 or so instances of such language that I shall discuss,[6] only two are uttered by characters of low status.

I define a comic feature of language, for this purpose, as a feature that is common in comedy (and/or in other low-register forms of verse, such as iambus) but very rare or unknown in tragedy. One advantage of concentrating on language is that while it would be foolish to pretend that we know much about the structure or ethos of comedies being produced in Aeschylus' last years, it is reasonable to suppose that the typical linguistic register of comedy at that time was at any rate no higher than that of comedy in Aristophanes' time. Aristophanes' own claim that his drama was more intellectual and sophisticated than that of his rivals[7]—about which we might well be sceptical if it rested on his own word alone—is supported by the casual, disparaging comment of Cratinus fr. 342,[8] and more broadly by the fact that Aristophanes is the only comic dramatist of his time known to have praised himself for this particular merit (Sommerstein 1992); and his characterization of Magnes in *Knights* 520–2 suggests that Magnes was remembered as being strong on sound effects, innovative costumes, and the like, but weak on the verbal side of comedy (*τοῦ σκώπτειν*).

There is no untragic vocabulary to be found in the early part of *Agamemnon*. The Watchman uses a vivid phrase or two ('this watch has thrown me a triple-six' 33, 'a great ox has stepped on my tongue' 36–7) but these phrases are made up of words common in all registers of the language; the Herald may complain of having been plagued with lice in the camp before Troy (562),

[6] See the table on pp. 167–8. The third column of the table gives the number (or in some cases the details) of occurrences of the word (or of the root underlined in the previous column) in Aristophanes (or, where Aristophanic instances are lacking, in other comedy); the fourth, those in tragedy outside the *Oresteia*; the fifth either specifies whether the passage was spoken by, to, or about the Erinyes, or refers to a mention of them in its neighbourhood (see pp. 163–4). Information given in the table is not necessarily repeated in the text or footnotes.

[7] Ar. *Nub.* 518–62; *Vesp.* 55–66, 650, 1043–59; *Pax* 734–61.

[8] Where a 'smart spectator' is spoken of as *ὑπολεπτολόγος, γνωμιδιώκτης, εὐριπιδαριστοφανίζων*.

but the language in which he does so is impeccably reticent (ἐσθημάτων τιθέντες ἔνθηρον τρίχα); and Klytaimestra herself maintains the dignity of her language as flawlessly as she maintains her pretence of being a loving and loyal wife.

The first sign of something different comes, significantly, just after the murder. As Klytaimestra stands, bloody sword[9] in hand, over the corpses of her husband and Kassandra, she describes in quasi-erotic terms (cf. Moles 1979) the pleasure she felt on being showered with his blood (1389–92)—and we can be sure that we are not being anachronistic or prurient in calling it quasi-erotic, because that is how Sophocles read the lines, as we know from his adaptation of them in his description of the last embrace of Haimon and Antigone (*Ant.* 1238–9). And in this passage, Klytaimestra speaks of the dying Agamemnon as ἐκφυσιῶν ὀξεῖαν αἵματος σφαγήν, 'puffing out a rapid spurt of blood'. Now it must be admitted that φυσιάω is attested only once in comedy (Epicharmus fr. 10.2 D.-K.). But it belongs to a semantic class (that of verbs denoting bodily noises) that is thoroughly at home there, and its distribution in tragedy contrasts markedly with that of its synonym φυσάω: only four occurrences in all of the verb and its derivatives, two of them in this passage and its Sophoclean imitation, the other two both in *Eumenides* and both with reference to the Erinyes, once in their own mouths (248) and once in that of the Pythia (53). In view of the many gruesome descriptions of the dying in tragedy, should we not expect this lexeme to be rather more frequent there if it were truly part of the tragic linguistic register?

This linguistic impropriety is one of many signs in Klytaimestra's speech over the corpses (1372–1406) that she is setting utterly at defiance all the norms of proper behaviour for any human being and especially for a woman: she said at the outset that she 'w[ould] not be ashamed' to say the exact opposite of everything she had said up to that point (1372–3), and the whole speech indicates that she is immune to all shame (αἰδώς) whatsoever.[10] No wonder the chorus think she is mad (1407–9, 1426–8). But her third speech in this scene (1431–47) is more shameless still. She proclaims her own adultery to the world

[9] See Sommerstein (1989*b*), Prag (1991) (*contra*, Davies 1987).

[10] Cf. Cairns (1993: 205–6), who does not, however, discuss the linguistic evidence of Klytaimestra's ἀναίδεια.

(1435–6) and denounces at great length the extramarital sexual activities of her husband, which in most male Greeks' view—with the sole exception of his insult to her in bringing Kassandra to her home—were none of her business. And in the course of doing so she uses two highly untragic vocabulary items. One is the notorious *ἱστοτριβής* (1443), referring to Kassandra. It will be necessary to take some time over this word, in view of some of the truly desperate attempts that have been made to keep Aeschylus at this point within the commonly assumed canons of tragic diction. M. L. West (1990*a*: ad loc.), with a reference to *Iliad* 1.31,[11] notes *coniugis nauticae nocturno muneri diurnum additur*: but for one thing one could not do loom-weaving on board an ancient ship, for another, of the two words which on this view would refer to Kassandra's sexual duties, *κοινόλεκτρος* (1441) and *ξύνευνος* (1442), neither has anything in its own immediate context to suggest that she is being portrayed as a *nautical* consort, and for a third, and most importantly, it is absurd to make Klytaimestra climax this passage, which is dripping throughout with her jealousy of the women who replaced her abroad and the one who nearly supplanted her at home, by referring to the ordinary work of a maidservant which, far from being any threat to the mistress of the house, actually emphasizes her superiority inasmuch as she does not have to do it herself! Lloyd-Jones (1978: 58–9), building on a suggestion by Latte, sees an allusion to the practice in at least one Greek state (we do not know which) of punishing women for some offence (probably, but not certainly, unchastity) by making them sit on top of a *ἱστός* (more likely a loom, as Lloyd-Jones thinks, than a pole, as suggested by O'Daly 1985: 13: the object, according to Hesychius α 2576, was to humiliate, not to torment). This neatly enables us to have our cake and eat it, by allowing *ἱστοτριβής* to mean 'whore' or the like while keeping Aeschylus free from 'an obscenity . . . unparalleled in tragic diction' (O'Daly 1985: 13); but it depends on our accepting that a word referring to a very specific punishment, and not one used at Athens, would be instantly intelligible to Aeschylus' Athenian audience. This audience, too, was one accustomed to comedy (not to mention satyr-drama), and even if it wasn't yet quite as alive to the ludicrous

[11] Where Agamemnon brutally tells Chryses that he will never get his daughter back till old age has overtaken her in Agamemnon's palace *ἱστὸν ἐποιχομένην καὶ ἐμὸν λέχος ἀντιόωσαν*.

possibilities of ambiguity or near-ambiguity as it was fifty years later when the actor Hegelochos said γαλῆν ὁρῶ instead of γαλήν' ὁρῶ[12] and was never allowed to forget it, ambiguity was certainly something that Aeschylus himself knew a thing or two about. Are we really meant to suppose that he *accidentally* made Klytaimestra refer to Kassandra, in a sexually charged context, by a word which could so easily be taken to mean πόρνην ἥτις τὸ πέος τρίψοι (Ar. *Vesp.* 739; cf. also Ar. *Ach.* 1149, *Vesp.* 1344)—and that neither he nor anyone else noticed it in rehearsal and changed the word? Unless we emend,[13] we have no alternative but to accept the obscenity. It may be alien to tragedy, but it is far from alien to this particular tragic character. The whole point about Klytaimestra, especially in this scene, is that she breaks all the rules; and this word, prominently placed at the beginning of a line before a pause, is the culmination of her rule-breaking. What is more, by using it she contrives to perpetrate a maximal insult to Kassandra and Agamemnon at once. If, as the comic parallels suggest, ἱστοτριβής would be taken as meaning approximately 'one who gives hand jobs', then on the one hand the princess and prophetess Kassandra (to whom Klytaimestra was so elaborately sympathetic in 1035–46) is being downgraded to the level of the meanest slave in a Peiraeus brothel, and on the other hand it is being insinuated that Agamemnon had been suffering from erectile dysfunction and had needed manual assistance to overcome it. All this, let it be remembered, is being said as we and the chorus gaze at the bodies of Kassandra and Agamemnon, the latter enveloped in a multi-coloured robe that reaches to his feet (cf. *Cho.* 998)—to a fifth-century Athenian much more like a feminine than a masculine garment; and the message is probably reinforced when Kassandra is called Agamemnon's φιλήτωρ (1446), a noun of masculine and agentive formation that implies that she rather than Agamemnon was the active partner in their relationship.[14]

After this, as O'Daly (1985: 14–15) rightly saw, παροψώνημα

[12] Making Eur. *Or.* 279 ('After the stormy waves I see calm weather again') into 'After the stormy waves I see a weasel again': cf. Ar. *Ran.* 303–4, Sannyrion fr. 8, Strattis fr. 1, 63.

[13] Diggle (1968: 2–3) proposed κοιτοτριβής: but after κοινόλεκτρος and ξύνευνος this would be a trifle monotonous.

[14] Until fairly recently the same effect could have been created in English by speaking of her as his 'lover'; but the sexual revolution of the last half-century has done away with the old convention whereby this noun, when singular in number and sexual in reference, invariably denoted a male.

(1447) will have similar connotations; indeed it neatly unites the spheres of sex and ichthyophagy, whose close relationship in Greek and especially Athenian thought James Davidson (1993, 1997) has documented so well. The noun ὄψον is very rare in tragedy (probably only Eur. fr. 467.2, from *The Cretan Women*, since Aesch. fr. 309 is likely to be satyric), and ὀψωνεῖν is not attested there at all; while in comedy παροψίς and παροψωνεῖν are capable of having sexual overtones, meaning either, in modern idiom, 'something on the side' (Ar. fr. 191, in reference to the lover of a married woman; so also perhaps, but not certainly, Ar. *Eccl.* 226) or 'foreplay' (Plato Com. fr. 43). Lloyd-Jones (1979: ad loc.) thought that Klytaimestra was saying that 'the pleasure of having killed her husband's concubine [w]ould heighten her own sexual satisfaction'; but ἐπήγαγεν and παροψώνημα indicate that she is speaking of something that has been 'acquired' and 'brought ⟨home⟩ in addition', in other words that the phrase εὐνῆς (or should it be εὐνῇ?) παροψώνημα τῆς ἐμῆς χλιδῆς is a description (yet another!) of Kassandra whom Agamemnon acquired at Troy and brought home as an ἐπακτὸς γυνή (cf. Soph. *Ajax* 1296 ἐπακτὸν ἄνδρ'), that τῆς ἐμῆς χλιδῆς refers to the pleasure Klytaimestra can give rather than to the pleasure she can get, and that Agamemnon is the subject of ἐπήγαγεν. O'Daly says that this 'change of subject . . . would be harsh, and unintelligible to an audience without some explanatory word, e.g. a pronoun'; he forgets that Agamemnon is present on stage and therefore gesture will suffice to explain that he is meant. There is probably a hint at a three-in-a-bed arrangement—picked up, perhaps, by Sophocles in the words of that transformed Klytaimestra, Deianeira, at *Trach.* 539–40,[15] a passage that Easterling (1982: ad loc.) calls 'metaphorical' but which is perhaps better thought of as rhetorically and emotionally hyperbolical.

When Aigisthos arrives on the scene (1577 ff.), he gives a plausible but highly slanted account of his father's quarrel with Atreus, which is expressed with proper tragic dignity, despite its increasingly horrendous subject-matter, until 1599, when he unnecessarily mentions that Thyestes *vomited out* the flesh of his slaughtered children (ἀπὸ σφαγὰς ἐρῶν), incongruously combining a tmesis that is more epic than tragic (let alone comic) with a verb which, like its synonym ἐμεῖν, tragedy systematically avoids, and

[15] καὶ νῦν δύ' οὖσαι μίμνομεν μιᾶς ὑπὸ | χλαίνης ὑπαγκάλισμα.

whose use is all the more improper given that the speaker is claiming a throne and that the man of whose degradation he speaks is his own father. This slip gives us a first clue to the coarseness of the man, well before we see his tyrannical reaction to the Elders' defiance, which nearly leads to their massacre.

The next signs of vulgarism come when Orestes and the Erinyes are juxtaposed for the first time—that is, when Orestes tells Electra and the chorus of *Choephoroi* of the threats of the Erinyes' wrath that accompanied Apollo's command to him to avenge his father. One of the menaced evils is a skin disease (279–82) whose effects include λευκὰς . . . κόρσας: κόρση is not otherwise found in tragedy—though a derivative, ἀποκορσοῦσθαι, is cited from Aeschylus' *Hypsipyle* (fr. 248)—and we know that τύπτειν ἐπὶ κόρρης (cf. Pherecrates fr. 165) was a phrase that could be censured, or apologized for, as unfit for polite conversation (Pl. *Grg.* 486 c). Apollo's warnings culminate in a picture of the delinquent's dying despised and friendless 'wretchedly pickled (ταριχευθέντα) by a death that wastes him all over' (296)—a phrase that compares a man to cheap preserved fish. Words from the root ταριχ- occur twice in the tragic corpus, in Sophocles' *Triptolemos* (fr. 606) and in one of his *Phineus* plays (fr. 712), but in both cases there is independent reason to believe that the plays may be satyric: at any rate *Triptolemos* contained a mention of *garum* sauce (fr. 606 again) paralleled in the tragic corpus only in Aeschylus' satyr-play *Proteus* (fr. 211) and falls, besides, with its theme of the origin and spread of agriculture, squarely in the tradition of satyr-plays about 'marvellous inventions and creations' (Seaford 1984: 36–7), nor does it seem very likely that a character in a tragedy could say that someone's 'eyes are as shut as a tavern[16] door' (Soph. fr. 711, from one of the *Phineus* plays).

An allusion to a comic linguistic technique of quite another kind occurs when Orestes, in explaining his plan of campaign, says that he and Pylades, when they come to the palace, will speak like Phokians from Parnassos (563–4). As is well known (Colvin 1999), it is typical of comedy, in all periods we know about, for non-Athenians to be represented as speaking in their native dialects;

[16] καπηλεῖον occurs only here in the tragic corpus: other derivatives from the same root do appear in tragedy (Aesch. *Sept.* 545, fr. 322; Eur. *Hipp.* 953), but only in the generic senses '(be a) petty trader' or '(be a) dishonest advertiser', not in the specific sense '(be a) tavern-keeper' known from comedy (e.g. Ar. *Thesm.* 347, *Eccl.* 154, *Plut.* 435), oratory (Isoc. 7.49, 15.287) and other texts.

similarly, barbarians in Old Comedy can speak broken Greek or foreign-sounding gibberish.[17] It is possible, though the state of the text makes it hard to be sure, that the Egyptians and/or their herald were treated in this way in *Suppliants* (825ff.). In *Choephoroi*, as has often been noted, nothing of this kind actually happens—but the arrival of Orestes and Pylades at the palace *is* presented in a partly comic mode just the same. Orestes, rather than address the chorus as arrivals from a distance in tragedy normally do, goes straight to the door and knocks at it, a practice, as Taplin (1977*b*: 340) notes, 'hardly used again in surviving tragedy', calling *παῖ παῖ* in regular comic style—and possibly producing, in 654, a trimeter without any recognizable caesura[18]—though in the same breath using some decidedly elevated vocabulary, morphology, and phraseology (*ἐν δόμοις* 654, *ἐκπέραμα δωμάτων* 655, *Αἰγίσθου διαί* 656); and whereas in tragedy visitors are normally met by the master or mistress of the house, here more realistically, as usually in comedy (and as in one richly comic scene in Euripides' *Helen* [435–82]), the door is answered by a servant, whose first words *εἶέν, ἀκούω* reappear only in Ar. *Pax* 663 and contain a metrical abnormality that has no clear tragic parallel except in proper names (see M. L. West 1977: 100; 1982: 82).

The typically comic stress on physical and bodily phenomena resurfaces in the speech of the Nurse when she makes explicit mention of the baby Orestes' tiresome habit of yielding without warning to *λιψουρία* (756)—a compound that strikingly wraps together in one word a highly untragic reference to urination with a verbal root (that of *λέλιμμαι*) so elevated that it is hardly known otherwise except from Hellenistic epic (e.g. Apoll. Rhod. 4.813) and two passages of *Seven against Thebes* (355, 380). The following sentence, *νέα δὲ νηδὺς αὐταρκὴς τέκνων*, is presumably a veiled reference to the evacuation of solid waste: Garvie (1986) thinks otherwise, but wrappings that were merely wet would hardly require the services of a *κναφεύς* (760). To speak openly of faeces would be too much even for Aeschylus—even the perfectly decent noun *κόπρος*, which gave Homer no trouble

[17] Plautus' *Poenulus* makes it tempting to believe that they sometimes did so in New Comedy too, though no Greek textual evidence survives.

[18] *τίς ἐστιν ὦ παῖ παῖ μάλ' αὖ τίς* (Schwerdt: *μάλ' αὖθις* cod. unicus) *ἐν δόμοις;* The line will have a caesura only if (1) Schwerdt's emendation is right *and* (2) West (1990*a*) is right in taking *παῖ μάλ' αὖ* as grammatically independent of, and separated by a pause from, what precedes.

(e.g. *Iliad* 24.640, spoken by Priam), is avoided in tragedy, and this may be part of the reason why the herald of Eurystheus, whose name Kopreus was well established in tradition (e.g. *Iliad* 15.639), is left anonymous in the text of Euripides' *Herakleidai*.

The greatest concentration of comic vocabulary in the *Oresteia* is to be found in two lines of *Eumenides* (52–3), and it is led up to in a way that may provide some clue to the place of this feature in the design of the trilogy. After her dignified and orderly opening prayer, the Pythia has gone into the temple at Delphi and returned terrified on her hands and knees. She describes, or tries to describe, what she has seen. On the one hand, a suppliant at the navel-stone, with bloody hands and a sword: a sufficiently horrifying sight, yet she speaks of it very coherently, in a single sentence (indeed a single clause) more than five lines in length (40–5). Then she turns to the beings who are besetting him, and words fail her. She first calls them 'women' (47); then she decides that it would be closer to the truth to say 'Gorgons' (48), but a moment later that they are not really like Gorgons either (49). She has seen something similar in a painting of the Harpies snatching away Phineus' food (50–1), but these beings cannot even be Harpies, for they have no wings (51). In her five and a half lines about Orestes she had said everything that could be said about him by someone who had not seen him before; now after speaking for six and a half lines about his besetters (to the middle of 52), she has told us nothing specific about them except that they are female and black (i.e. clothed in dark garments[19]—though a dark complexion is not necessarily to be ruled out either). And it is at this point, when she is totally at a loss for words, that she turns to comic language to say what tragic convention would not allow her to say: these beings are utterly *βδελύκτροποι* 'nauseating in their ways', and in particular they 'belch out gases that one cannot bear to be near' (*ῥέγκουσι δ' οὐ πλατοῖσι φυσιάμασιν*). She cannot, in fact, describe at all what they look like; only what they *smell* like. Comedy delights in describing smells (Thiercy 1993) just as it delights in belches, farts, and other digestive noises. By contrast, in Sophocles' *Philoktetes*, where we are given an unusually harrowing presentation of Philoktetes' sufferings both visually and aurally, and it is repeatedly made clear (7, 39, 696, 783–4, 1378) that his wound is open and discharging a noxious fluid, the loathsome smell of it,

[19] Cf. 370, *Cho.* 1049.

which according to (Proclus' summary of) the *Kypria* was the reason for his being abandoned on Lemnos, is referred to only twice, both times by Philoktetes himself, both times at strategic moments. The first mention (891–2) directly precedes, and may even be understood as provoking, Neoptolemos' sudden revulsion (895) at his mission of deception, which *he* now perceives to stink;[20] the second (1032) comes near the climax of Philoktetes' denunciation of Odysseus, when he tauntingly recalls the justifications originally offered for his abandonment ('how comes it that you don't find me lame or smelly any more?'); both are very mild in expression compared with what is said here.[21]

When taxed by the ghost of Klytaimestra with their sleepy inaction, the Erinyes (by now probably visible to the audience)[22] whine and growl, pant and bark, like dogs in their slumber (117–31). Again there is nothing like this in tragedy, whereas animal choruses were characteristic of comedy (Sifakis 1971) as far back as we can go (titles ascribed to Magnes include *Frogs*, *Birds*, and *Gall-Flies*).

The Erinyes wake up and find Orestes gone, and presently Apollo appears, bow in hand, to drive them out of his temple—threatening (184) to make them 'vomit' the blood they have drunk. His roll–call of the horrendous executions and mutilations among which they are at home (186–92) mostly stays within tragic convention, but *μύζω* 'moan' (189) is a verb of typically comic formation, derived from an onomatopoeic interjection, which appears otherwise in tragedy only at 118; and a moment later he says that the proper place for the Erinyes to dwell is the den of 'a blood-slurping lion' (*λέοντος . . . αἱματορρόφου*), using a verb which in comedy is normally applied to the consumption of thick soup, and which otherwise appears in tragedy only in 264 and in Soph. *Trach.* 1055 and fr. 743—of which the first certainly, the last probably,[23] refer to the Erinyes' own vampiric activities, while in

[20] Cf. 900–3 where Philoktetes asks anxiously whether 'the distastefulness (*δυσχέρεια*) of my affliction' is deterring Neoptolemos from taking him on board ship, and receives the unexpected response 'Everything is *δυσχέρεια* when a man deserts his own nature and does what does not befit him'.

[21] The expressions used are respectively *κακῇ ὀσμῇ* and *δυσώδης*.

[22] See A. L. Brown (1982: 26–8), Sommerstein (1989*a*: 92–3).

[23] Since it describes Teiso, probably an earlier or abbreviated form of the name of the Erinys T(e)isiphone ([Apoll.] 1.1.4; Verg. *G.* 3.552, *Aen.* 6.555, 6.571, 10.761).

the *Trachiniai* passage Herakles is describing how his body and blood are being eaten up by what, in a virtual quotation from *Agamemnon* (1382 + 1580), he has just called Ἐρινύων ὑφαντὸν ἀμφίβληστρον (1052).

The Erinyes then engage Apollo in reasonably civilized dialogue, and leave Delphi on the trail of Klytaimestra's blood. Catching up with Orestes at Athens, they speak in the now familiar style: the long chase has left them puffing and panting (φυσιᾷ σπλάγχνον, 248–9), but now they have found Orestes they will 'slurp' the blood from his living body (264). Only they call the blood 'a red clotted liquid' (265), and ἐρυθρός is another non-tragic word (except in references to the 'Red Sea'). Why is tragedy, which has so often to speak of blood, so unwilling to use the ordinary Greek word for 'red'? The explanation is found in the word's pattern of use in comedy. The adjective ἐρυθρός occurs four times in Aristophanes. Two of these (*Eq.* 188, *Av.* 145) refer to the 'Red Sea'; the other two (*Ach.* 787, *Nub.* 539) refer to the male generative organ. We may take it that ἐρυθρός, like e.g. μέγα καὶ παχύ,[24] had acquired ribald connotations that it could not shed except when it was part of a proper name.

This is almost the end of the trail. There is a moment when Athena, confronted with the hideous sight of the Erinyes, is about to speak of them in terms that might have been slightly improper, but she checks herself (413–14) on the ground that it is wrong to speak offensively of one who has done nothing wrong. Thereafter she and the Erinyes each address the other respectfully (cf. 435), and in the ensuing choral song (490–565) the Erinyes advance so far in dignity that many of their utterances are later taken over almost verbatim by Athena herself. They maintain this level in the trial scene, and it is Apollo who loses control when he furiously calls them ὦ παντομισῆ κνώδαλα (644)—which is not how one addresses rational beings in tragedy, only in comedy and satyr-drama;[25] later (730), in an echo of 184, he predicts that when they lose the case they will 'vomit' their poison to no avail. And that is the last time the Erinyes either are spoken of, or speak, in this low-register language: even the threats and laments of 778–891 are uttered in diction entirely appropriate to tragic lyric.

[24] Ar. *Ach.* 787, *Pax* 1351 (= 1359 Olson), *Lys.* 23–4, *Eccl.* 1048.

[25] In the latter genre cf. θῆρες in Soph. fr. 314.221 and Eur. *Cyc.* 624 (both addressed to the satyrs, who *are* of partly bestial form).

But one untragic word has been heard meanwhile—and heard from Athena. In her speech establishing the Council of the Areopagos, Athena underlines her warning against changes to its laws by either recalling or inventing a proverb: 'You'll never get a drink if you pollute a clear spring of water with mud (*βορβόρῳ*)' (694–5). If one needs to talk about mud in tragedy one can call it *πηλός* (e.g. *Ag.* 495): *βόρβορος* is a comic word, evidently being used to drive home a political point with earthy force to what Athena calls 'my citizens of the future' (707–8)—except that Aeschylus has taken great care to ensure that it shall be entirely unclear just what political point is in fact being driven home (Sommerstein 1989*a*: 31–2, 215–19).

What patterns can we perceive in this collection of data? In the first place, the use of comic language in the *Oresteia* is limited in time: it begins almost precisely at the moment of Agamemnon's murder, and ends during the time when the first Council of the Areopagos is voting to decide the fate of Orestes—that is, just at the same stage at which a whole raft of themes and images that have figured all through the trilogy with sinister overtones are turned on their heads and start being associated with happiness and prosperity.[26] In other words, far from being light relief of any sort, comic language is used in the *Oresteia* to heighten the blackness and bleakness of the vicious cycle of retaliatory violence, and disappears at the point where that cycle is broken.

Secondly, it cannot be a coincidence that almost all the instances of comic language in the *Oresteia* occur in passages that *have to do with the Erinyes*—passages spoken by them, passages spoken to or about them, passages in whose immediate context[27] they are mentioned. The Erinyes, of course, are the embodiments of the vicious cycle of violence of which I have spoken. I have discussed altogether 31 instances of the use of comic language in the trilogy.[28] Of these, ten are on the lips of the Erinyes; seven are addressed to them (two by the ghost of Klytaimestra, five by Apollo—none by Orestes or Athena); three occur in the Pythia's description of the Erinyes, and five in other

[26] Sommerstein (1989*a*), index s.v. 'themes of play and trilogy: . . . ominous themes transformed into auspicious ones'; Sommerstein (1996: 241, 251, 254).

[27] As indicated in the text below, 'in the immediate context' means either (1) within the same speech or (2) within a distance of five lines.

[28] Counting as separate instances the two occurrences of *παῖ παῖ* in *Cho.* 653–4 and the seven quasi-canine utterances in *Eum.* 117–31.

speeches in which they are explicitly mentioned (*Ag.* 1431–47, cf. 1433; *Ag.* 1577–1611, cf. 1580; *Cho.* 269–305, cf. 282); three more appear at the moment when Orestes comes to the door of his father's palace, directly after a choral song whose last word was Ἐρινύς (*Cho.* 652). That leaves only three of the 31 without any close connection with the Erinyes (*Ag.* 1389, *Cho.* 756, and *Eum.* 694). But the overwhelming majority of the comic language in the *Oresteia* does have such a connection—and more than half of it (18 instances out of 31) occurs between ll. 52 and 265 of *Eumenides*, only 6 per cent of the text of the trilogy, but covering the crucial period from the time when the Erinyes are first seen by sane eyes (the Pythia's) to the time when Orestes appeals to Athena for assistance against them. And as we have seen, the Pythia's words themselves suggest that comic language and the Erinyes go naturally together—that this is the only kind of language in which they can be properly described. Their hideous, terrifying appearance is commented on more than once by Athena (*Eum.* 410–12, 990) as well as by Orestes (*Cho.* 1048–62), and may well have been reminiscent of the monsters and ogres whom we know to have featured prominently in early comedy (Sommerstein forthcoming *a*); their incongruous costume (dark grey belted mini-dresses, to judge by some slightly later vase-paintings)[29] is both untragic and, by contemporary standards, unfeminine. In a word (a word with two ranges of meaning), they are αἰσχραί, and it is not therefore surprising that the language associated with them is sometimes αἰσχρόν too by the standards of tragedy. It looks, too, as though Sophocles may have perceived the link between the Erinyes and untragic language, for as we have seen, it is reflected in his own usage of the root of ῥοφεῖν.

Thirdly, there is a strong tendency to couple distinctively comic with distinctively tragic language—often in a sentence, sometimes in a phrase, occasionally in a single word like λιψουρία—so that the low-register material comes as a sudden and startling lapse from the normal level of diction. This is itself a comic technique; a notable example comes in Aristophanes' *Lysistrata* (706–17) where the heroine and the chorus conduct a dialogue which is entirely in tragic metre with the exception of l. 715, and entirely in tragic diction with the exception of one word in that line, βινητιῶμεν. The effect in the *Oresteia* is as though the αἰσχρότης were

[29] Cf. Prag (1985: 48–9, 144–6, pll. 30–2).

breaking through in spite of all efforts to contain it, revealing the reality of ugly deeds that can only be described in an ugly way; and the only way to get rid of the ugly language is to get rid of the ugly deeds, as Athena eventually succeeds in doing. And even as she does so, she perpetrates one last linguistic ugliness herself (*Eum.* 694): for as she will imply later, to overturn the system she has instituted will mean the return of a state of things that cannot be spoken of in polite language, of tit-for-tat killings leading swiftly to the ruin of Athens (*Eum.* 976–83, cf. 858–63).

I wish to draw two further corollaries from this analysis. One has still to do with the *Oresteia*; the other is of more general application.

The first corollary arises from the fact that the use of what I have called 'ugly language' sets in only after the killing of Agamemnon. This strongly suggests that we are being encouraged to regard this murder as being on a different level from the past atrocities of which we have heard previously—on the one hand the sacrifice of Iphigeneia, on the other the fate of Thyestes' children. I do not mean that we are meant to perceive it as *morally* more heinous. I doubt if even ancient Greeks really thought that it was that much worse for a wife to kill her husband than for a father to kill his daughter or for two children to be killed, dismembered, and served as a meal to their father, particularly given that the earlier victims had been wholly innocent whereas Agamemnon was not; and Aeschylus seems to have agreed with me, for in the second and third plays he never allows Klytaimestra or her defenders even to mention these past crimes—she speaks of the relatively trivial matter of Agamemnon's sexual infidelities (*Cho.* 918) but not of the sacrifice of Iphigeneia of which she had had so much to say in the latter part of the first play.[30] Clearly he wants to balance her murder against Agamemnon's, preparing for the split vote of the Athenian jury: to allow her to raise these matters from the past would upset the balance. But from the *dramatic* point of view, there is an enormous difference between them and the death of Agamemnon and Kassandra. The former we only heard *about*, long after the events:[31] the latter we have first imagined in advance

[30] The sacrifice is alluded to only by her opponents—Electra (*Cho.* 242) and, obscurely, Apollo (*Eum.* 631–2; cf. Sommerstein 1989*a*: 202).

[31] And by the time that the Thyestean feast is first alluded to (1090ff.), Agamemnon has already passed, and Kassandra has been invited to pass, through the door that we know leads only to death.

through the visions and speeches of Kassandra, then actually heard happen, then we have seen its outcome for ourselves in all its perversity and degradation. And we should remember, too, that while we knew all along (and should have known even without Kassandra's help) that Agamemnon was going to be killed, and that his wife would at least have a hand in the murder, no one had previously made her the *sole* killer (see Sommerstein 1996: 190–7), and no one had ever before been able to display the murder scene to an audience. It is fitting that that unprecedented sight should be accompanied by the first appearance in the trilogy of language that is itself perverse and degraded by the criteria of tragedy.

Secondly, the wider point. If Aeschylus can use language like this in the tragedies of the *Oresteia*, 31 times, we are on very dangerous ground if we assume he cannot have used it in other tragedies too. And if Sophocles can imitate it in an appropriate context, as we have seen him do, in a play like *Antigone*, why, again, should he not have done so elsewhere? It will be perceived that I am hinting at the problem of criteria for distinguishing between tragedy and satyr-drama. It has sometimes been argued that Aeschylus' *Ostologoi* must have been a satyr-drama because Odysseus speaks of an 'evil-smelling chamber-pot (οὐράνη)' being thrown at him (fr. 180); but if Aeschylus can make a character in a tragedy speak of λιψουρία I see no reason why he should not have made another character in another tragedy speak of an οὐράνη, even a smelly one. And in that case Sophocles, taking over the passage almost word for word in *Syndeipnoi* (fr. 565), will have been recycling an Aeschylean idea in another tragedy, just as he recycled ideas from the *Oresteia* in *Trachiniai* or *Antigone*. But that must be a subject for another paper.[32]

[32] Sommerstein (forthcoming *b*); the question of linguistic (and other) criteria for distinguishing between tragedy and satyr-drama will also be discussed in several other contributions to the same volume (by A. López Eire, J. Redondo Sánchez, R. M. Rosen, and P. Voelke).

TABLE 7.1. *Comic features in the language of the* Oresteia

Passage	Word/phrase	Ar.	Tragedy (outside *Oresteia*)	Erinyes
Ag. 1389	(ἐκ)φυσιάω	(Epich. fr. 10.2 D.-K.)	Soph. *Ant.* 1238	—
Ag. 1443	ἱστοτριβής	τρίβω *Ach.* 1149, *Vesp.* 739, 1344; ἱστός (Strabo 8.6.20)	none	cf. 1433
Ag. 1447	παροψώνημα	× 5; cf. παροψίς fr. 191	none	cf. 1433
Ag. 1599	ἀπεράω	(Pherecrates fr. 138)	none	cf. 1580
Cho. 280	κόρση	(Pherecrates fr. 165)	(ἀποκορσωσαμέναις Aesch. *Hypsipyle* fr. 248)	cf. 283
Cho. 296	ταριχεύω	× 9	Soph. *Triptolemos* fr. 606, Phineus *A* or *B* fr. 712	cf. 283
Cho. 653–4	παῖ παῖ (*bis*)	× 14	none	cf. 652
Cho. 657	εἶέν, ἀκούω	*Pax* 663	none	cf. 652
Cho. 756	λιψουρία	× 11	οὐράνη Aesch. *Ostologoi* fr. 180, Soph. *Syndeipnoi* fr. 565	—
Eum. 52	βδελύκτροποι	× 26	ἀβδέλυκτ' Aesch. *Myrmidons* fr. 137	described
Eum. 53	ῥέγκω	× 4	[Eur.] *Rhesos* 785 (of horses)	described
Eum. 53	φυσίαμα		see above (*Ag.* 1389)	described
Eum. 117–31	canine noises (7)	μυμυ *Eq.* 10, *Thesm.* 231; αὖ αὖ *Vesp.* 902	none	uttered by
Eum. 118	μύζω	*Thesm.* 231	none	spoken to
Eum. 124	ὤζω	*Vesp.* 1527	none	spoken to
Eum. 184	ἐμέω	× 9	none	spoken to
Eum. 189	μύζω		see above (*Eum.* 118)	spoken to

TABLE 7.1. (*cont.*):

Passage	Word/phrase	Ar.	Tragedy (outside *Oresteia*)	Erinyes
Eum. 193	αἱματορρόφου	× 12	Soph. *Trach.* 1055; Soph. fr. 743 (prob. of the Erinys Teiso = Teisiphone)	spoken to
Eum. 248	φυσιάω		see above (*Ag.* 1389)	spoken by
Eum. 264	ῥοφέω		see above (*Eum.* 193)	spoken by
Eum. 265	ἐρυθρός	*Eq.* 188, *Av.* 145 (Red Sea); *Ach.* 787, *Nub.* 539 (phallus)	Aesch. fr. 192 (Red Sea)	spoken by
Eum. 644	κνώδαλον	*Vesp.* 4, *Lys.* 477	only of beasts	spoken to
Eum. 694	βόρβορος	× 6	none	—
Eum. 730	ἐμέω		see above (*Eum.* 184)	spoken to

8

Μάγειρος ποιητής: Language and Character in Antiphanes

GREGORY W. DOBROV

1. INTRODUCTION

Having had recently the occasion to get back to Plautus, *Pseudolus* in fact, I was enjoying a literary respite from the perils of academic life—like Dionysus aboard his trireme in *Frogs* 52–4—when I was 'struck at the heart by a certain desire' to understand better the pedigree of Plautus' clever slave. Where *did* this remarkable stage figure come from? Plautus may have promoted him, but he surely did not invent him.[1] Then, where and when was the fellow born? Athens, somewhere between Cratinus and Menander perhaps? Indeed, but where exactly might we find traces of his existence before Menander? Alas, unlike Dionysus I do not have the option of visiting a dead poets' society to resolve my literary difficulties. Fortunately, Pseudolus' soliloquy (ll. 395–405) offers a clue:

quid nunc acturu's, postquam erili filio
largitu's dictis dapsilis? ubi sunt ea?
quoi neque paratast gutta certi consilii[2]
neque exordiri primum unde occipias habes,
neque ad detexundam telam certos terminos.
sed quasi poeta, tabulas cum cepit sibi
quaerit quod nusquamst gentium, reperit tamen,
facit illud veri simile, quod mendacium est,
nunc ego poeta fiam: viginti minas,
quae nusquam nunc sunt gentium, inveniam tamen

[1] Lowe (1999: 14–15) underscores the authority of *Plautinisches im Plautus* on this matter. 'That Plautus liked to enhance the role of the scheming slave,' he notes, 'has been generally accepted since Fraenkel.'

[2] Following Ussing I delete line 398. See Willcock (1987: ad loc.).

What are you going to do now? After regaling the young master with sumptuous words. . . . Where are they now? You haven't a drop of a definite plan. You don't have a place to start nor a definite goal for weaving your plot. But *just as a poet*, when he takes tablets in hand, seeking what exists nowhere on earth, yet finding it, makes a lie seem the very truth, now I'll become a poet myself. Those twenty minae which now are nowhere on earth, I'll find all the same.

A fine insight into the craft of the *servus callidus*! (Let no one say that poetry is not a lucrative profession.) The implicit riddle here, 'who takes X [a reed?] in hand to seek and find what exists nowhere on earth?' is reinforced later when Pseudolus warns Simo that he will answer him 'in Delphic utterance' (ll. 479–80). Concealing from the latter the truth of his son's activities, Pseudolus makes good his threat by switching to Greek!

Now 'poetic' invention (script and plot) as well as verbal play with power and meaning (riddles) are emblematic of the *servus callidus* role. Chrysalus of *Bacchides*, Palaestro of *Miles Gloriosus*, Toxilus of *Persa*, Milphio of *Poenulus*, Terence's two Parmenos (*Eunuchus*, *Hecura*) come to mind. One thinks back, in this connection, to Menander's Daos (*Aspis*) and, especially, to Aristophanes' Karion (*Wealth*), the earliest clear example of the clever slave (as a type) who is both manipulative and 'poetic' in the literal sense. The purpose of these stage figures, according to one authority, is:

to provide humour . . . (and) to supervise or assist in trickery and impersonation. They entertain us, they win our interest, but they do not gain our sympathy. Perhaps by way of compensation they have . . . a third dimension of comic or farcical delight, of rhythmical and linguistic agility, of tasty and expressive liveliness. . . . [Remarkably] they carry us through their outrageous undertakings to an exultant and laughable conclusion. (Duckworth 1952: 250)

This comic conjunction of poetry and riddles calls to mind certain titles of Middle Comedy such as Eubulus' *Sphingokarion*, the *Milesians* and *Cauldron* of Alexis,[3] and, above all, the many and often substantial fragments of Antiphanes. The main speakers in these texts, however, are cooks that participate in the early-to-

[3] It is worth noting here the connection between Alexis' *Cauldron* and Plautus' *Aulularia* as well as the possible relationship between the same Greek poet's *Pseudomenos* and the *Pseudolus*. See Arnott (1996*b*: 730 and 361–5).

mid fourth-century 'fad' in which lowly figures are made to express themselves in high tragic-dithyrambic style. This trend was, without doubt, an innovation of the period, one that overlaps with an explicit and implicit deployment of riddles. I shall propose that the invention of the poetic *μάγειρος* of Middle Comedy marks the conception of a stage figure that later develops, 'grows up to be' the *servus callidus*, the clever *ἡγεμὼν θεράπων*—to use T. B. L. Webster's phrase—of New Comedy and the *palliata*.

Athenaeus, who should know, observes that 'the entire tribe of cooks is *ἀλαζονικόν*.'[4] Now a new sort of comic cook made his dramatic entrance in the 380s as the 'star' of the elderly Aristophanes' *Aiolosikon*. The idea was developed in the work of his successors Antiphanes, Anaxandrides, Eubulus, *et al.* While this culinary *ἀλαζονεία* looks back to that of the Old Comedy,[5] there can be little doubt that, in an important sense, the Middle Comedy *μάγειρος* offers something new: a tricky and aggressive *τεχνίτης* whose behaviour and function, despite a nominally free status, overlap with those of slaves (at least phenomenologically, on the comic stage).[6] I should like to examine here the *ἀλαζονεία* of the *μάγειρος* in Middle Comedy with special attention to his language. In particular, I shall examine the striking intersection between dithyrambic language and the riddle, or *γρῖφος*, characteristic of his speech.

'The cook,' observes Nesselrath (1990: 257), 'makes his [dramatic] entrance [in Middle Comedy] not only as a culinary specialist, but as a word-wizard (*Sprachzauberer*) as well.' Consider the following example in trochaic tetrameters from the *Aphrodisios* of Antiphanes (fr. 55):

[4] Athenaeus 7.290B: *ἀλαζονικὸν δ' ἐστὶ πᾶν τὸ τῶν μαγείρων φῦλον*. Here *ἀλαζονικόν* denotes the qualities of an *ἀλαζών*: impostor, interloper, quack—a *terminus technicus* of comedy.

[5] Old Comedy was no stranger to cooks and cooking. The culinary thematics of *Knights* are well known. Dikaiopolis in *Acharnians* and Heracles in *Birds* are cooks, in a manner of speaking. Plato Comicus' *Phaon* (fr. 189) cleverly combines literary criticism and the culinary art. Yet, until Middle Comedy, we do not find in a single prominent character the fusion of three salient features: (1) lowly social status, (2) the skill of a professional *mageiros*, and (3) manipulative speech in an exalted 'poetic' style. Again Aristophanes' Karion is an apparent first in this category (*Wealth*).

[6] See Arnott (1996*b*: 22) on the connection between *ἀλαζονεία* and technical skill.

(A.) *πότερ' ὅταν μέλλω λέγειν σοι τὴν χύτραν, ⟨χύτραν⟩ λέγω*
ἢ τροχοῦ ῥύμαισι τευκτὸν κοιλοσώματον κύτος,
πλαστὸν ἐκ γαίης, ἐν ἄλλῃ μητρὸς ὀπτηθὲν στέγῃ,
νεογενοῦς ποίμνης δ' ἐν αὐτῇ πνικτὰ γαλακτοθρέμμονα,
τακερόχρωτ' εἴδη κύουσαν; (B.) *Ἡράκλεις, ἀποκτενεῖς*
ἆρά μ', εἰ μὴ γνωρίμως μοι πάνυ φράσεις κρεῶν χύτραν.
(A.) *εὖ λέγεις. ξουθῆς μελίσσης νάμασιν δὲ συμμιγῆ*
μηκάδων αἰγῶν ἀπόρρουν θρόμβον, ἐγκαθειμένον
εἰς πλατὺ στέγαστρον ἁγνῆς παρθένου Δηοῦς κόρης,
λεπτοσυνθέτοις τρυφῶντα μυρίοις καλύμμασιν,
ἢ σαφῶς πλακοῦντα φράζω σοι; (B.) *πλακοῦντα βούλομαι.*
(A.) *Βρομιάδος δ' ἱδρῶτα πηγῆς;* (B.) *οἶνον εἰπὲ συντεμών.*
(A.) *λιβάδα νυμφαίαν δροσώδη;* (B.) *παραλιπὼν ὕδωρ φάθι.*
(A.) *κασιόπνουν δ' αὖραν δι' αἴθρας;* (B.) *σμύρναν εἰπέ, μὴ μακράν,*
μηδὲ τοιοῦτ' ἄλλο μηδέν, μηδὲ τοὔμπαλιν λέγων,
ὅτι δοκεῖ τοῦτ' ἔργον εἶναι μεῖζον, ὥς φασίν τινες,
αὐτὸ μὲν μηδέν, παρ' αὐτὸ δ' ἄλλα συστρέφειν πυκνά.

(A.) When I want to say pot to you, am I to say pot, or the hollow-bodied vessel formed by the whirl of the wheel, fashioned of clay, baked in another house of Mother Earth, and bearing in its womb the tender-fleshed forms, milk-nursed and stewing, of the new-born flock?

(B.) Heavens! You'll be the death of me, surely, if you don't say to me, quite intelligibly, a pot of meat!

(A.) Correct answer! Shall I say, then, the creamy flood that flows from bleating she-goats, mingled with fountains from the tawny bee, and nested in a flat covering of the maiden daughter of chaste Demeter, luxuriating in countless delicately-compounded wrappings, or shall I say plainly to you, a flat-cake?

(B.) I prefer flat-cake.

(A.) And shall I say the sweat from the Bromiad spring?

(B.) Cut it short and say wine.

(A.) The dewy stream of the Nymphs, redolent breath of cassia coursing through the air?

(B.) Just say myrrh for short saying nothing else like that, nor repeating questions again in your talk. For it seems to me rather pompous, as some say, never to name the thing itself, but to twist together in a thick mass other things beside the point.

Here, dithyrambic periphrasis and ornament are employed in a formal series of five riddles put by a cook to his employer (a rustic?) (Nesselrath 1990: 257–8). The latter solves the riddles successfully, but concludes with a sharp criticism of the game. In other words, the boss does not appreciate being challenged by a cook who sounds like Timotheus[7] while 'never saying the thing itself but twisting together in a thick mass other things beside the point.'

In its verbal virtuosity and challenge to authority this striking, indeed illicit, congress of forms—dithyramb and riddle[8]—looks forward to the *servus callidus*, a stage figure that develops far beyond the *μάγειρος* to 'star' status in New Comedy and its Roman adaptations. Owing to the 'Athenaeus accident', as we shall see, the relevant data have quite a bit to do with food. I submit, however, that the early prominence of the cook as a gastro-lyric riddler (indeed he has a patent on the dithyrambic riddle in Middle Comedy) is not merely an artefact of the selection, but a significant development that bore fruit in Menander and the *fabula palliata*. We start with something small, an *ἀλαζών* and low-status technician who seeks recognition and influence through a projection from craft (cooking) to craftiness (words, wit). From this germ develops the general endowment of 'low-status' characters (slaves) with the creative power to 'poetically' manipulate and direct the very play of which they are a part (e.g. Plautus' *Pseudolus*). Thus, Arnott (1996*b*: 22) notes that the cooks of Middle Comedy exhibit '*alazoneia* combining arrogance, self-confidence, irritability and above all a claim to expertise in matters both culinary and extra-curricular.'[9] In other words, we discern the outlines of a distinct, if stylized, character-type, with linguistic characterization into the bargain.[10]

A defining characteristic of the *servus callidus* in later comedy is his pretension to a sort of equality, indeed superiority, with respect to his master or 'boss'. I discern the roots of this social paradox (so evident in Menander and Plautus) in the language of Middle Comedy, namely, in the experiment with dithyrambic riddles attested in the fragments. This experiment is not an isolated and relatively short-lived literary cul-de-sac, but rather

[7] The sort of periphrasis exemplified by the phrases 'blood (or sweat) of Bacchus' or 'tears (dew) of the Nymphs' were a trademark of Timotheus. See *PMG* fr. 780: *αἷμα Βακχίου νεορρύτοισιν | δακρύοισι Νυμφᾶν.*

[8] The *griphos*—literary or symposiastic—has no *necessary* connection with the poetry and performance of the dithyramb per se. Tragedy and comedy contain a fair amount of riddles and riddling games. For surveys of the *griphos* form, see Schultz (1912) and Ohlert (1912).

[9] In the case of Alexis' *Cauldron* (fr. 129) the 'extracurricular expertise' in question is demonstrated through the use of medical and scientific terminology.

[10] See Alexis fr. 129, especially lines 6, 15 with Arnott (1996*b*: ad loc.).

the first formal step in an evolution that finally produced the crafty ἡγεμὼν θεράπων, the leading slave role. Such slaves presume to equality with their superiors by daring to set riddles in symposiastic play, as it were. At the same time, they would demonstrate a daring virtuosity in words and thought of the sort associated with the poetic avant-garde of the New Dithyramb.[11] In other words, the cooks of Middle Comedy should be recognized as pioneers of social pretension and poetic innovation in their genre. While the role of the cook, strictly speaking, appears to diminish in New Comedy and Plautus, this contribution endures in transposed form.

2. THE ROLES OF COOKS AND SLAVES

In his study of typical comic roles Nesselrath is quite clear: formally speaking, Old Comedy had no μάγειρος type and few noteworthy slave roles.[12] As the epigone of the Old Comic βωμολόχος, the slave is rather slow to develop in Middle Comedy, despite the promise of fifth-century plays such as *Knights* and *Frogs*. On the other hand, the new ἀλαζών on the block appears to be the cook, a stage figure whom we first detect in the 380s and whose social status and dramatic function were somewhat more fluid. In the fourth century cooks were free men hired in the agora to work in private homes on particular occasions. The dramatic profile, so to speak, of a Middle Comic μάγειρος is that of a low-status braggart who associates with slaves.[13]

An interesting social shift suggested by the fragments of

[11] See Dobrov–Urios-Aparisi (1995: 151–4). Zimmermann (1992*b*: 41) identifies the cultivation of variety (ποικιλία) as central in musical innovation of this 'avant garde'.

[12] With the possible exception of Xanthias in *Frogs*, that is, in the outermost field of the 'old' period; see Nesselrath (1990: 283–309). This is not to deny, however, the function of cooking on the part of characters such as Dikaiopolis, Trygaios, Peisetairos, or Heracles.

[13] Not normally a 'live-in' employee, the work of a *mageiros* variously combined the duties of butcher, cook, and caterer; see Arnott (1996*b*: 393) and cf. Athenaeus' comment at 14.661 D (Alexis fr. 134): 'Alexis in his *Cauldron* makes clear that the cook's profession was the pursuit of free men: "for this cook reveals in himself a citizen (πολίτης) not without blemish".'

Posidippus[14] and other sources is the wider use of slave μάγειροι after the Macedonian conquests.[15] In the light of this possibility, I would argue that the craft/craftiness of the *servus callidus* has roots in a stage figure that was originally a free hireling. As the real-life boundary between cooks and slaves softened, however, so did the boundary separating them in the theatre. The name of Eubulus' *Sphingokarion* suggests that this character was both a riddling cook and a slave (see R. L. Hunter 1983: 199–200). Karion, the cook in Menander's *Epitrepontes*, appears to be a slave, though there is sufficient ambiguity to keep us wondering. On the other hand, the proposed 'translation' of Alexis' *Cauldron* into Plautus' *Aulularia* would require Plautus to have changed the status of Congrio, the cook and central character, from free hireling to slave (see Arnott 1996*b*: 859–64). Thus, it is important to allow that the special ἀλαζονεία of the 'free' μάγειρος of the Middle period intersects with 'slave' ἀλαζονεία from at least the beginning of Menander's career through the adaptations of Plautus.

Concerning the introduction of the μάγειρος figure, Dohm (1964) has emphasized the early integration of the cook into the comic plot (*contra*, Nesselrath 1990: 297). The extent of this integration is hard to assess as we know little about the plots of Middle Comedy. What is striking, however, is the rift between the language of the clever cook and his boss. In Middle Comedy, as we see in the *Aphrodisios* fragment above, the plain-speaking master is contrasted with his riddling and puzzlingly poetic μάγειρος. The verbal dexterity of the latter is explicitly bound up with pride in his τέχνη and its status. Thus in the *Areopagite* of Demetrius a cook characterizes cooking as a 'smoky tyranny', a profession in which he has achieved far more than any actor in his respect.[16] 'Our craft has an aura of sanctity about it (ἱεροπρεπής)!' exclaims Sikon defensively at *Dyskolos* 646. When Parmenon (*Samia* 283–5) worries that the cook will 'cut everyone up into

[14] e.g. Posidippus frr. 2 and 25. In fr. 2 a cook speaks of serving his master. In fr. 25 a *mageiros* explains the conditions of his purchase (in answer to the question 'have you been set free?').

[15] 'It is notable,' writes Arnott (1996*b*: 393) in this connection, 'that names of slave *mageiroi* first appear on Athenian manumission inscriptions c. 330 (*IG* II^2. 1555.21–2, 1570.36, 90, cf. M. N. Tod, *Ann. BSA* 8 [1901/2] 208 and *Epigraphica* 12 [1950] 8).'

[16] Demetrius Comicus II, fr. 1, ll. 1–3: 'No actor has achieved anything comparable in his craft to what I have in mine. This craft is a smoky tyranny!'

little pieces with his tongue', he hears the arrogant reply, 'how could you ever understand? You're not an artist!'.[17] Thus the cook is an artistically refined tyrant who enjoys divine sanction! 'I hereby enroll the cook in the sophists' guild!' exclaims a character in the *Milesians* of Alexis. Examples of this theme could be multiplied (see Handley 1965: 244, Arnott 1996: 393).

'Cooks are experts,' notes Handley (1965*b*: 199), 'and like other experts ancient and modern, they can be amusing when they exaggerate their own skill and importance and otherwise impose on any non-experts who happen to be at their mercy, whether as fellow dramatic characters or members of a theatrical audience; most of them, as seen by Comedy, have a dash of sophistry and pretentiousness.'[18] A curious feature, however, of the Middle Comic *μάγειρος* is his association with the *γρῖφος* (riddle) as a very specialized form of sophistry. The very name of Eubulus' *Sphingokarion* brings us to the fascinating section of Athenaeus' tenth book known as *περὶ γρίφων*.

3. THE *ΓΡΙΦΟΣ* AND COMEDY

Athenaeus introduces his long list of riddles from Middle and New Comedy with a definition from a peripatetic monograph on the subject: 'A riddle is a problem put in jest, requiring, by searching the mind, the answer to the problem to be given *for a prize or penalty*.' (Clearchus of Soloi, quoted in Athenaeus 10.448 C). Now, riddles in one form or another appear first in Hesiod (fr. 266) and had been featured in Greek poetry for some time thereafter, including tragedy.[19] Aristophanes, too, offers the occasional riddle.[20] The period of Middle Comedy, however, saw a riddling fad of sorts attested in the tenth book of *Deipnosophistae*.

It is important to note, however, that the *γρῖφος* is introduced by

[17] Thus Slavitt–Bovie's (1998) interpretive rendering of the exclamation *ἄθλιε, ἰδιῶτα* (ll. 285–6).

[18] For bibliography on cooks in comedy see Arnott (1996*b*: 116) and Nesselrath (1990: 297–309).

[19] Some examples from drama: Aeschylus fr. 116, Sophocles fr. 395, Euripides fr. 83 N. and other passages (Aeschylus also had the satyr-play *Sphinx*).

[20] e.g. Ar. *Vesp.* 21: riddling slaves, no less.

Athenaeus primarily as an *agonistic* form of discourse, that is, one in which there is something at stake, something to gain or lose (τιμῆς ἢ ἐπιζημίου χάριν εἰρημένον). The stakes ranged, historically, from simple approval to a matter of life and death. In the light of the deployment of riddles by clever 'low-class' cooks or slaves in creative tension with their 'boss' or other figures of higher social standing, it is important to remember that the γρῖφος, in fourth-century Athens, was closely associated with the symposium. The many Middle-Comedy riddles in περὶ γρίφων fit so well into Athenaeus' discussion precisely because of their intrinsically symposiastic and culinary focus.

For this connection between the riddle and the symposium consider the following passage from Antiphanes' *Man of Knoithe*:[21]

> ἐγὼ πρότερον μὲν τοὺς κελεύοντας λέγειν
> γρίφους παρὰ πότον ᾠόμην ληρεῖν σαφῶς
> λέγοντας οὐδέν· ὁπότε προστάξειέ τις
> εἰπεῖν ἐφεξῆς ὅ τι φέρων τις μὴ φέρει,
> ἐγέλων νομίζων λῆρον, οὐκ ἂν γενόμενον
> οὐδέποτέ γ', οἶμαι, πρᾶγμα παντελῶς λέγειν,
> ἐνέδρας δ' ἕνεκα. νυνὶ δὲ τοῦτ' ἔγνωχ' ὅτι
> ἀληθὲς ἦν·

Before this I used to think that people who required us to tell riddles during a drinking-bout were plainly drivelling and talking nonsense: whenever a man enjoined us to guess in succession 'what somebody brought which he did not bring', I used to laugh, thinking he was talking drivel of a thing which could never by any possibility happen, just to catch us. Today, however, I have come to realize that it is true after all . . .

The speaker then applies the symposium metaphor to himself and other Athenian στρατηγοί bribed by Philip as well as to the Macedonian ruler's λογοποιία. The riddle here, τί φέρων τις μὴ φέρει; 'what somebody brought which he did not bring', is based on the phrase φέρειν ἔρανον, 'to participate in, contribute to, a meal'.[22]

We note that the dynamic of 'social riddling' as an intellectual after-dinner diversion requires interaction *among peers*. I use the

[21] Antiphanes fr. 122.1–8, from Κνοιθιδεύς or Γάστρων (*Pot-Belly*).

[22] ἔρανον φέρειν usually meant little more than 'enjoy a meal'. Although all participants in an ἔρανος were, in theory, required to 'contribute' to it, clearly the principle was not always enforced or respected.

term 'intellectual' *pace* Plato, who in the *Republic* (479 B) is evidently annoyed by 'riddlers at symposia' as vain exploiters of ambiguity whose games had little to do with knowledge. Whether they enjoyed the respect of the philosopher or not, the participants in the serial exchange of γρῖφοι (perhaps taking turns going from left to right) were citizen males and their guests. Ezio Pellizer (1990: 179) emphasizes, in this connection, 'the rules of an elaborate system of [sympotic] communication, which shows some distinctive modes of statement and response.' He goes on to note that this λόγος συμποτικός 'at some point in the gathering comes to assume the role of a contest, a demonstration which each member is expected to make of his ability and his technical and executive capacities'. One would hardly find a slave or lowly τεχνίτης here since participation in the dialogue—setting and solving riddles—was an extension of participation in the symposium. Only social equals were allowed to participate in this *agon*, this demonstration of wit and παιδεία. As we might expect of gentlemanly competition, the actual prizes and penalties were trivial: a kiss, a scone.[23]

In a broader mytho-historical context, the γρῖφος was a power play in which a mortal victim played with a god for σωτηρία of some sort. As students of ancient riddles have pointed out, the γρῖφος is rooted in the lying fable, the αἶνος, hence it is a specific form of αἴνιγμα (see Ohlert 1912, Schultz 1912). The ambiguity of Delphi, in its folkloric and literary manifestations,[24] as well as the tryanny of the Sphinx are famous. Herodotus (1.67), for example, narrates the σωτηρία of Sparta by Lichas, a resourceful commissioner who solved a particularly obscure riddling oracle.[25] Like Oedipus, Lichas eventually gets into trouble and is banished, suggesting that an *agon* between contestants of unequal standing can never be fair. Similarly, a comic cook or slave who challenges

[23] Antiphanes fr. 75, Clearchus fr. 63 (Wehrli), Pollux 6.107.

[24] Fontenrose (1978) explores the significant difference in quality between folkloric, literary, and historical responses.

[25] The context of the given digression on Sparta is, of course, the story of Croesus notorious for his failure at the game of ambiguity (cf. Plato's ἐπαμφοτερίζειν). Instructed to find the bones of Orestes to ensure success against Tegea (and in future conflicts), the Spartans were told to obtain the bones of Orestes. By way of instructions the Pythia set a riddle: 'In Arcady there lies a level plain, | where under strong constraint two winds are blowing; | Smiting is there and countersmiting, and woe on woe; | This earth, this, giver of life holds Agamemnon's son. | Bring him home and you will prevail over Tegea.'

his boss with riddles is formally marked as playing a dangerous game in that he arrogates manipulative power and status to himself.

True to his Peripatetic calling, Clearchus of Soloi derives a taxonomy of seven types of riddle based on what might be called the 'focal unit', progressing from riddles 'dependent on' a single letter, to those based on a syllable, to those based on a word, etc. (Athenaeus 10.448 C–E). It is doubtful that this approach (of which we have only the barest sketch) offers sufficient explanatory power to comprehend the wide range of riddles in Greek antiquity. Although ambiguity, by definition (pun intended), is too elusive a subject for Peripatetic taxonomy, it must be admitted that modern scholarship, too, likes a list.[26] A more immediately important formal aspect of the *γρῖφος*, however, is that it depart from common speech, more precisely, it must be poetry, both to frame it as a special challenge (a power play) and to justify its obscurity.

For a lowly stage figure like the *μάγειρος*, arrogating a certain status as social equal and setter-of-riddles is easy enough, especially if his boss is weak in character or intellect. But there arises a formal problem: riddles were commonly in hexameters and elegiacs, as we see from the literary oracle tradition (see Fontenrose 1978: 320). How might the special linguistic or poetic requirement be fulfilled within the context of the common (non-dactylic) metres of drama? Specifically, how is the clever underling to mark his riddling as poetically distinct from the 'default' iambics or trochees of comedy? An obvious solution might involve the metre or vocabulary of epic. Skipping forward to some time after the dithyrambizing comic fad had passed,[27] we find in Straton fr. 1 (*Phoinikides*) a tricky cook using Homeric diction to affect oracular authority.[28] As was common in Middle Comedy, Straton pits his obscurantist *μάγειρος* against a rustic employer. It

[26] 'Ambiguity itself,' writes William Empson (in *Seven Types of Ambiguity* cited in Pucci 1987: 236), 'can mean an indecision as to what you mean, an intention to mean several things, a probability that one or other or both of two things has been meant, and the fact that a statement has several meanings.'

[27] The *Life of Straton* in the *Suda* places him with poets of the Middle Comedy. The mention in fr. 1.43 of Philitas (of Cos) would suggest a floruit closer to that of Menander.

[28] Citing Athenaeus' amplified version (in Kassel–Austin 1989 the text of Athenaeus and that of the Cairo Papyrus are presented separately).

is interesting for our purposes to note that this cook used to be a slave and has joined the given household a free man:[29]

> *σφίγγ' ἄρρεν', οὐ μάγειρον, εἰς τὴν οἰκίαν*
> *εἴληφ'. ἁπλῶς γὰρ οὐδὲ ἕν, μὰ τοὺς θεούς,*
> *ὧν ἂν λέγῃ συνίημι· καινὰ ῥήματα*
> *πεπορισμένος πάρεστιν. ὡς εἰσῆλθε γάρ,*
> *εὐθύς μ' ἐπηρώτησε προσβλέψας μέγα·*
> *"πόσους κέκληκας μέροπας ἐπὶ δεῖπνον; λέγε."*
>
> (fr. 1.1–6)

I have taken into my house a male Sphinx, not a cook. Really I understand absolutely not one thing, by the gods, of all that he says. He has come with a stock of strange expressions. For the moment he entered, he looked at me and loudly asked, 'How many *μέροπες* have you invited to dinner? Tell me.'

The Sphinx metaphor points up this clever fellow's tyranny over his employer who is subjected to a barrage of epic terms: *δαιτυμών*, *θύειν ἐρυσί-*[vel: *ῥηξί-*]*χθονα*, *θύειν βοῦν δ' εὐρυμέτωπον*, *μῆλα θυσιάζειν*, etc. The rustic is frustrated:

> *"⟨μάγειρε,⟩ τούτων οὐδέν, οὐδὲ βούλομαι.*
> *ἀγροικότερός εἰμ', ὥσθ' ἁπλῶς μοι διαλέγου."*
> *" "Ομηρον οὐκ οἶσθας λέγοντα;" "καὶ μάλα*
> *ἐξῆν ὃ βούλοιτ', ὦ μάγειρ', αὐτῷ λέγειν.*
> *ἀλλὰ τί πρὸς ἡμᾶς τοῦτο, πρὸς τῆς Ἑστίας;"*
> *"κατ' ἐκεῖνον ἤδη πρόσεχε καὶ τὰ λοιπά μοι."*
> *" Ὁμηρικῶς γὰρ διανοεῖ μ' ἀπολλύναι;"*
> *"οὕτω λαλεῖν εἴωθα." "μὴ τοίνυν λάλει*
> *οὕτω παρ' ἔμοιγ' ὤν."*
>
> (fr. 1.23–32)

(A.) 'I don't understand you at all, cook. I don't know any of these things and I don't want to. I am too much the rustic. So talk to me simply.'

(B.) 'Don't you know that Homer used these words?'

(A.) 'He might have used whatever he wanted to, cook, for all I care. But what has that to do with us, by Hestia?'

(B.) 'Do thou now, as [Homer] would say, give heed to what I still have to tell.'

(A.) 'So, you really mean to kill me in Homeric fashion?'

[29] *P. Cairo* 65445 (third century) contains ll. 4–50. Athenaeus alone provides ll. 1–4. The papyrus alone furnishes lines 48–50; in Athenaeus but not in the papyrus are ll. 9–10, 12, 16, 22, 26–30.

(B.) 'That's my way of talking.'

(A.) 'Well, don't talk in that way when you are in my house.'

The poor rustic employer must finally resort to a lexicon, 'one of Philitas' [of Cos] books' (v. 43–4) in order to understand the poetry of the uncompromising *μάγειρος* who, he concludes, 'must be the ex-slave of some sort of rhapsode or other, an offender from childhood who was subsequently filled with Homeric vocabulary.'[30]

In *Riddle* (*Πρόβλημα*) Antiphanes experiments with metrical verisimilitude: a wily servant rather startlingly interupts the iambic flow with actual hexameter riddles. As in the case of 'lexical disruption' in Straton fr. 1 and the Middle Comic dithyrambic fad, this passage (fr. 192) seeks to amuse through disruption of lexicon and syntax as well as metre:

> (A.) *ἰχθύσιν ἀμφίβληστρον ἀνὴρ πολλοῖς περιβάλλειν*
> *οἰηθεὶς μεγάλῃ δαπάνῃ μίαν εἵλκυσε πέρκην·*
> *καὶ ταύτην ψευσθεὶς ἄλλην κεστρεὺς ἴσον αὐτῇ*
> *ἦγεν. βουλομένη δ' ἕπεται πέρκη μελανούρῳ.*
> (B.) *κεστρεύς, ἀνήρ, μελάνουρος, οὐκ οἶδ' ὅ τι λέγεις·*
> *οὐδὲν λέγεις γάρ.* (A.) *ἀλλ' ἐγὼ σαφῶς φράσω.*
> *ἔστι τις ὃς τὰ μὲν ὄντα διδοὺς οὐκ οἶδε δεδωκὼς*
> *οἷσι δέδωκ' οὐδ' αὐτὸς ἔχων ὧν οὐδὲν ἐδεῖτο.*
> (B.) *διδούς τις οὐκ ἔδωκεν οὐδ' ἔχων ἔχει;*
> *οὐκ οἶδα τούτων οὐδέν.* (A.) *οὐκοῦν ταῦτα καὶ*
> *ὁ γρῖφος ἔλεγεν. ὅσα γὰρ οἶσθ' οὐκ οἶσθα νῦν*
> *οὐδ' ὅσα δέδωκας οὐδ' ὅσ' ἀντ' αὐτῶν ἔχεις.*
> *τοιοῦτο τοῦτ' ἦν.* (B.) *τοιγαροῦν κἀγώ τινα*
> *εἰπεῖν πρὸς ὑμᾶς βούλομαι γρῖφον.* (A.) *λέγε.*
> (B.) *πίννη καὶ τρίγλη φωνὰς ἰχθῦ δύ' ἔχουσαι*
> *πόλλ' ἐλάλουν, περὶ ὧν δὲ πρὸς ὃν τ' ᾤοντο λέγειν τι,*
> *οὐκ ἐλάλουν· οὐδὲν γὰρ ἐμάνθανεν, ὥστε πρὸς ὃν μὲν*
> *ἦν αὐταῖς ὁ λόγος, πρὸς δ' αὐτὰς πολλὰ λαλούσας*
> *αὐτὰς ἀμφοτέρας ἡ Δημήτηρ ἐπιτρίψαι.*

(A.) A man who expected to wrap his net round many fish pulled in a single perch at great expense; disappointed in her, the grey mullet brought him another like her. For a perch willingly follows a bream.

(B.) Grey mullet, man, bream! I don't know what you mean. You are really talking nonsense.

(A.) Well, I'll tell you plainly. Many a man who gives his goods knows

[30] These lines (48–50) are preserved only in the Cairo papyrus.

not that he has given them, to whom he has given them, nor even that he now has what he did not lack at all.

(B.) What? Someone gave what he did not give, and has what he does not have? I can't make head or tail of that.

(A.) Well, that's what the riddle said. All that you know, you don't know at this moment, nor all that you have given, nor all that you have in place of it. It meant something like that.

(B.) Well, then I should like in my turn to put a riddle to you.

(A.) Go ahead.

(B.) A pinna and a red mullet, two fishes with voices, were talking a lot, but concerning what and to whom they thought they were saying something, they talked not at all. For the one addressed couldn't understand a word, so that, while their talk was addressed to him, they were talking a lot to themselves and may Demeter destroy both!

We applaud the master in this situation who turns the epic weapon on his subordinate to make a good point.

The innovation of Middle Comedy, however, was to seek the formal poetic quality for its riddling cooks and slaves in the dithyramb *as a general style*, which for Anaxandrides, Alexis, Antiphanes, Eubulus, *et al.* was a prestigious discourse admired for its technique. That is, it was admired or criticized for a number of specific features. Here we need to emphasize especially the cook's self-consciousness as an expert who needs words to match his physical ability. 'Come now, Dromon,' says the master in Dionysius fr. 3, 'Whatever cunning, clever, or subtle trick you know in your profession, bring it to light for the benefit of your teacher. Today I demand an exhibition of your skill.' Professional pride, that is, the social arrogance of the *μάγειρος* finds expression in 'verbal wizardry' for which, in the spirit of the times, the dithyramb was an ideal vehicle.[31]

4. *ΜΑΓΕΙΡΙΚΗ ΤΕΧΝΗ/ΠΟΙΗΤΙΚΗ ΤΕΧΝΗ*

A challenge in assessing the language of Middle Comedy is what might be called Meineke's paradox: the apparent contradiction in the ancient critical tradition concerning the language of Middle

[31] The *δεῖπνον* had been the subject of dithyramb, after all (e.g. Philoxenus).

Comedy.[32] The Anonymous on Comedy[33] notes that 'The poets of Middle Comedy did not use the poetic style. They employed the familiar language so that their merits are rhetorical; poetic qualities are rare in their [work]. They all expend study on their plots.' This lack of *ποιητικὸς χαρακτήρ*, and a corresponding *συνήθης λαλιά* (speech in realistic conformity to character) and *λογικαὶ ἀρεταί* (pure and clear vocabulary)[34] contrast with an influential scholarly assessment concerning a passage in Aristophanes' *Wealth*. Penia utters the phrase at l. 515, *ἢ γῆς ἀρότροις ῥήξας δάπεδον καρπὸν Δηοῦς θερίσασθαι* 'or fracturing the plain with plows to reap the fruit of Demeter'. 'This passage,' notes a scholiast 'reeks of Middle Comedy.' Which is it then? Absence of *ποιητικὸς χαρακτήρ* or dithyrambic colour?

The answer is 'both'. Much of Middle Comedy conforms to the prosy, quotidian characterization given by the Anonymous. There are, at the same time, strikingly obscure poetic passages indebted to the new dithyramb and later tragedy affected by the 'new' poetic style. There are, in the extant fragments, significant traces of the dithyramb in 37 plays by twelve different poets. Of these 26 are found in works by the Big Four:[35]

Antiphanes: fr. 1, 51, 55, 91, 110, 170, 172, 179;
Anaxandrides: fr. 6, 31, 42;
Alexis: fr. 5, 93, 124, 153;
Eubulus: fr. 34, 36, 41, 43, 56, 64, 75, 102, 106, 108, 111.

The evidence for this dithyrambic fad suggests clearly that the high-flown language was deployed in limited contexts and by a specific type of speaker: servants, slaves, and especially cooks appear to be the exclusive exponents of the style whose poetics is significantly bound up with that of the *γρῖφος*.[36] Perhaps a clear

[32] Meineke (1839: i.21) offers a series of passages parallel to this and, understandably, sides with the Scholiast.

[33] Koster (1975) iii, 9.44–10.45. Amidst much of questionable value is this, 'the most valuable testimonium of ancient literary history concerning the three periods of [Greek] comedy' (Nesselrath 1990: 51). See also Dobrov (1995*a*: 78–81).

[34] Dion. Hal. *De imit.* 2.2 suggests that these *ἀρεταί* include the following: (the quality of being) *βραχεῖς* 'short', *μεγαλοπρεπεῖς* 'majestic', *δεινοί* 'clever', *ἠθικοί* 'ethical' (see also the *Letter to C. Pompeius*, end of §3).

[35] Nesselrath (1990: 254–6) gives a nuanced discussion of the literary and linguistic implications of this distribution. All in all, there are 43 individual fragments in which dithyrambic elements are found. Twenty-six of these are very short (1 or 2 verses) or exhibit a mere sprinkling that stands out from its context.

[36] Nesselrath (1990: 265): 'Rätselspaß, absurdes Bravourstück und sprachliches

point of origin is to be found in Ar. *Plut.* 290–321, where Karion, the tricky slave of Chremylos, calls the chorus of rustics to perform variations on the riddling dithyramb *Cyclops* by Philoxenus of Cythera.[37] The intersection between the list of dithyrambic fragments above with Athenaeus' series of comic riddles yields passages spoken by one sort of speaker, namely, the cook.[38] Thus in Middle Comedy the *μάγειρος* is prolifically dithyrambic, the most frequent riddler, and the only one who *specializes* in combining the two skills.

How did comedy read the dithyramb, what aspects of the genre did comedy admire? Consider this passage from Antiphanes' *Tritagonistes*, in which we encounter Philoxenus again:[39]

> πολύ γ' ἐστὶ πάντων τῶν ποιητῶν διάφορος
> ὁ Φιλόξενος. πρώτιστα μὲν γὰρ ὀνόμασιν
> ἰδίοισι καὶ καινοῖσι χρῆται πανταχοῦ·
> ἔπειτα ⟨τὰ⟩ μέλη μεταβολαῖς καὶ χρώμασιν
> ὡς εὖ κέκραται. θεὸς ἐν ἀνθρώποισιν ἦν
> ἐκεῖνος, εἰδὼς τὴν ἀληθῶς μουσικήν·
> οἱ νῦν δὲ κισσόπλεκτα καὶ κρηναῖα καὶ
> ἀνθεσιπότατα μέλεα μελέοις ὀνόμασι
> ποιοῦσιν ἐμπλέκοντες ἀλλότρια μέλη

Far superior to all other poets is Philoxenus. For, first and foremost, he uses novel and special words everywhere. And then how nicely his lyrics (μέλη) are tempered with modulation and ornamentation! He was a god among men, he knew true poetry. Poets of today compose ivy-twisted, fountainy, flower-flitting songs—useless (μέλεα) things with useless words which they weave into strange songs (ἀλλότρια μέλη).

Despite the possibility that the speaker may be the butt of humour (the third-rate actor of the title?), we note a special emphasis on clever and new vocabulary and an admiration for Philoxenus' *μέλη*. This praise of the modulation and ornamentation of his lyric

Medium gerade der frechesten und sozial am weitesten unten stehenden Bühnencharaktere—diese drei Funktionen haben das Dithyrambisieren in der Mittleren Komödie offenbar zu einem wichtigen Mittel der Komik werden lassen.'

[37] See Dobrov–Urios-Aparisi (1995: 167–71). Athenaeus (1.6 E ff.) reports that Philoxenus' composition was an autobiographical allegory of sorts in which a (real) love triangle was represented in mythical terms.

[38] e.g. Antiphanes fr. 51, 55, Xenarchus fr. 1, Anaxandrides fr. 6.

[39] Antiphanes fr. 207. Athenaeus names Philoxenus of Cythera in the given context, though it should be noted that the latter is sometimes confused with Philoxenus of Leucas, author of the dithyramb *Deipnon*.

appears to stand in contrast with the actual practice of Middle Comic *mimesis* where the melic and metrical aspects of the dithyramb do not play a prominent role. The following lines make it clear, however, that our speaker's comment sports a bit of self-contradictory humour that uses typical dithyrambic coinages to criticize poets who trade in the same. Mention of *μέλος* in l. 4 would appear to be motivated primarily by the desire to set up the puns (*μέλος* ~ *μέλεος*) in ll. 8 and 9.

So for a start, vocabulary was the thing. We can see from another Antiphanes passage (fr. 205, *Traumatias*) that details of the poetic lexicon were taken seriously. In this symposiastic exchange we see careful attention to the order of a few letters in the first syllables (*ἀερσίγυιος* vs. *ἀρκεσίγυιος*?)[40] even as the participants prepare to trade 'tangles of words'.

(A.) *μὴ μεστὰς ἀεὶ*
ἕλκωμεν, ἀλλὰ καὶ λογισμὸς εἰς μέσον
παταξάτω τις, καί τι καὶ μελίσκιον,
στροφὴ λόγων παρελθέτω τις. ἡδύ τοι
ἔστιν μεταβολὴ παντὸς ἔργου πλὴν ἑνὸς
⟨ ⟩ *παραδίδου δ' ἑξῆς ἐμοὶ*
τὸν ἀρκεσίγυιον, ὡς ἔφασκ' Εὐριπίδης.
(B.) *Εὐριπίδης γὰρ τοῦτ' ἔφασκεν;* (A.) *ἀλλὰ τίς;*
(B.) *Φιλόξενος δήπουθεν.* (A.) *οὐθὲν διαφέρει,*
ὦ τᾶν· ἐλέγχεις μ' ἕνεκα συλλαβῆς μιᾶς

(A.) Let us not be forever draining full cups, but let's also strike up some reasoning power in our midst and a little song; let a tangle (*στροφή*) of words issue forth! A change from every task, save one, is a pleasant thing . . . ⟨ ⟩ Then hand over to me directly the 'limb-strengthener' (*ἀρκεσίγυιος*), to quote Euripides.

(B.) Euripides said that?

(A.) Well then, who?

(B.) Philoxenus, of course.

(A.) No difference, my friend; you're picking on me for a single syllable!

We are at once reminded of the symposiastic *agon* and how easily the dithyrambic lexicon may be applied thereto. It is no coincidence that Athenaeus' speaker here, Ulpian, initiates the *περὶ γρίφων* shortly after this quotation.

Now, there was considerable interest in dithyrambic metre and

[40] Thus Kock; see Nesselrath (1990: 248 n. 17).

music on the part of Old Comic poets such as Aristophanes and Pherecrates,[41] an interest expressed on the levels of *analysis* (Pherecrates fr. 155) and *mimesis* (*Thesmophoriazusae* 101–29). Middle Comedy, on the other hand, is almost exclusively focused on smaller linguistic units, ignoring the aesthetics of music and performance. The rarity of passages like Antiphanes fr. 192 with its hexameter 'grafts' suggests that attention to extra-linguistic aspects of the dithyramb was not very welcome in essentially *κατὰ στίχον* comic versification. The poets of the Middle Comedy, without apparent exception, followed the technique later applied to epic by Straton in *Phoinikides*, that is, *mimesis* on the level of the word and phrase.[42]

Thus it is accurate to characterize the process of representing the dithyramb in Middle Comedy essentially as a 'lexicalization', that is, a reduction to small linguistic elements. This reduction might be expressed in terms of a few salient *differentiae* that distinguish the speech of clever servants:

1. Extravagant new compounds, mostly adjectives, in which only one morpheme is operative, e.g. *στερεοπαγής* for *στερεός*. Similarly *λευκαυγής*, *παλαιγενής*, *κοιλοσώματος* in the simple sense of 'white', 'old', and 'hollow' respectively.

2. Coordination instead of subordination: this proceeds from the emphasis on vocabulary and other 'first' elements of style. There is a preference for, and multiplication of, specific modifiers, individual words as well as small clauses, e.g. tautological relative clauses and asyndetic adjectival series. As an example of the latter we have seen 'tender-fleshed, milk-nursed, stewing' in Antiphanes fr. 55.

3. An inclination to periphrasis and absurdly allusive metaphors such as the 'dogs of Hephaestus' of Alexis fr. 153; a seeking after mystification and periphrastic complexity on the semantic level, as Richard Seaford (1977/8: 88–9) noted some time ago in *Maia* regarding the 'hyporcheme' of Pratinas.

This 'lexicalization' and lack of technical interest in music of

[41] Ar. *Ach.* 16, *Nub.* 963–72, *Pax* 829, *Av.* 1373–1409: the Kinesias scene. See Dobrov–Urios-Aparisi (1995: 145–67).

[42] Curiously, however, the trimeter does stiffen up to a remarkable degree when comedy reaches for the high style: Porson's Law observed, resolution avoided, caesura present. Hunter (1983) on Eubulus fr. 75 and Antiphanes fr. 216 notes that 'In Antiph. 217 there is no resolved syllable in twenty trimeters and only one minor infringement of Porson's law.'

the dithyramb is symptomatic of the striking *absence* of 'intertextuality' and parody in the Middle Comic dithyrambic passages.[43] Specific phrases, themes, or poets are not mentioned for purposes of mockery or criticism; rather the dithyrambic style, as a general *modus dicendi*, is engaged for special effect, much as current pseudo-King-James English is 'distinguished' by a few (often bogus) *differentiae* such as 'thou' and 'saith'. The point of this comparison is to emphasize that in Middle Comedy dithyrambic discourse has been reduced to a 'shorthand' version identified by the few selective features (*differentiae*) listed above. When a comic ἀλαζών seeks to exalt himself and his performance, he employs this shorthand and his κωμῳδία becomes 'high drama' or τραγῳδία of sorts. It would appear that, in terms of the comic stage, an ἀλαζών who appropriates the 'high' poetic style thereby assimilates his performance to the prestige and importance of tragedy.

Despite superficial similarities to late tragic lyric, however, I would argue that there is a significant difference: Middle Comic poets made their cooks speak the dithyramb in an effort to impart to their character certain qualities which were not relevant to a tragic chorus, but rather associated in the fourth century with the dithyramb as avant-garde art. The qualities include (1) the technical prowess of a celebrity virtuoso and soloist, (2) the pursuit of aesthetic effect at the expense of traditional elements (social matrix and cult song of the old dithyramb), (3) the triumph of form over content.[44]

What I am suggesting is that, in using dithyrambic language, the μάγειρος promotes *himself* as a virtuoso: not only cook as ἀρχιτέκτων τῆς ἡδονῆς (to quote Alexis' cook in *Milesians*) but Neoteric Word Wizard. 'The preparation of food is an important comic ritual,' notes R. L. Hunter (1983: 167, on Eubulus' *Orthanes*), 'and so the common association of dithyrambic language and carousing in Comedy should not cause surprise.' What is important is that the μάγειρος brought with him *new* rituals which he wrote and managed. Like the new dithyramb in which innovations and aesthetics had suppressed the social and cultic

[43] Noted and discussed in Nesselrath (1990: 241–63) and Dobrov–Urios-Aparisi (1995: 164–73).

[44] For the social and aesthetic aspects of the New Dithyramb see Zimmermann (1992*b*: 118–36).

connections of the old style, our new stage figure represents a departure from comic tradition in his profession, social hubris, and artistic pretension. Moreover, he frequently appropriates the symposiastic ritual of competing with γρῖφοι as part of his hubristic posture. This is progress from an *agon* of the *polis* to the *agon* of the clever new poet-individual. Citing the testimony of fourth-century choregic monuments Zimmermann characterizes this 'progress' as the displacement of a *Kultlied* by a *musikalisches Ereignis*.[45]

I am suggesting that, in addition to exalting himself as a player of an intellectual *agon* with his social betters, the new ἀλαζών, the poetic μάγειρος, challenges tradition with the resources of his genre. In place of poetic styles traditionally featured in comedy, we have the new and difficult dithyramb; instead of the tangential craftsman or servant, we have an aggressive τεχνίτης whose integration into the plot and promotion of comic ego (individuality) appear to be strengthening. The μάγειρος, as it were, wants us to think of him as an artist, not unlike a composer of the new dithyramb whose originality and virtuosity replaced the social and cultic basis of the traditional dithyramb. Moreover, as Sutton, Zimmermann, and others have pointed out, towards the end of the fifth century the dithyramb assimilated ever more to the mimetic dynamic of tragedy.[46] We recall that Timotheus of Miletus, Philoxenus of Cythera, Melanippides of Melos, and other masters of the genre, though known in the *polis* (and some active there), were not Athenians; similarly our μάγειρος ποιητής is a (social) 'outsider' operating, wheeling and dealing, in the heart of the *oikos*.

I remind you of Pseudolus, with whom I began. Somewhere rather far back in his family tree, as I hope I have been able to persuade you, is the poetic, symposiast-riddler μάγειρος of Middle Comedy. In a humble Roman street, distracted by the noise of vendors and the competition of tight-rope walkers, it may have been easy not to notice the clever slave characterize his role as that of a 'poet' and manipulative speech as 'Delphic utterance'. In the context of an Athenian festival of the first half of the fourth

[45] Zimmermann (1992*b*: 142), with special emphasis on the role of the aulos and virtuoso performance.

[46] Zimmermann (1992*b*: 133–6), Sutton (1983: 37–8), Dobrov–Urios-Aparisi (1995: 167–8).

century, on the other hand, the idea of a clever underling as a competitor in gentlemanly sport at a symposium has rather clear and strong associations. A cook who arrogates the prowess and prestige of a dithyrambic poet is little short of astonishing. And the evidence of the many fragments justifies our astonishment! I leave you with a final fragment to make my point, calculating that, like Antiphanes' rustic *κύριος* here, you may be tired of reading and ready for refreshment. So what's for dinner, you ask? The dithyrambic cook of Antiphanes fr. 1 (*Agroikos*) offers a description that rivals the hyperbole of a good 'menu blurb':

(A.) *καὶ πρῶτα μὲν*
αἴρω ποθεινὴν μᾶζαν, ἣν φερέσβιος
Δηὼ βροτοῖσι χάρμα δωρεῖται φίλον·
ἔπειτα πνικτὰ τακερὰ μηκάδων μέλη,
χλόην καταμπέχοντα σάρκα νεογενῆ.
(B.) *τί λέγεις;* (A.) *τραγῳδίαν περαίνω Σοφοκλέους*

(A.) And first of all, I exalt the yearned-for *maza* which life-bestowing Deo lavishes as a felicity upon mortals; then the smothered, tender limbs of kids' flesh newly born, vested in verdant foliage.
(B.) What are you talking about?
(A.) Just running through a bit of Sophoclean tragedy!

What, indeed, we might ask, is he talking about? The point of the last line is twofold: first, the cook is no simple hireling, but rather a performer in the best tragic tradition; second, he delights in insulting his boss before a sophisticated audience with a joke over the rustic's head. Like cartoon characters that attribute a tatter of popular lyric to Shakespeare, so here we have dithyramb sold as Sophocles![47]

What *is* this cook talking about? Are these the words of the old, now classic tragedian? No, this is the poetry of a new comic type, an arrogant riddler who delights in outwitting his social betters. New speech for a new character who might take as his motto the words of dithyrambist Timotheus (fr. 796 *PMG*):

οὐκ ἀείδω τὰ παλαιά,
καινὰ γὰρ ἀμὰ κρείσσω·
νέος ὁ Ζεὺς βασιλεύει,
τὸ πάλαι δ' ἦν Κρόνος ἄρχων·
ἀπίτω Μοῦσα παλαιά.

[47] How odd that some—not Radt!—implausibly accepted these lines as the tragedian's or his son's (Kock).

I do not sing the old
for new things are better.
New (young) Zeus who now reigns,
but of old Kronos was ruler.
Depart, Muse of the old!

9

Some Orthographical Variants in the Papyri of Later Greek Comedy

W. GEOFFREY ARNOTT

While editing and translating Menander for the Loeb Classical Library, I sought to note down as carefully as I could the normal and variant spellings of those words which in Attica, at the time of Menander and his contemporaries, were commonly or occasionally spelt in two or more different ways. The findings that emerged as the result of this long chore may be of some use to future editors of Menander and of other early Hellenistic writers who used the contemporary Attic dialect, although those findings cannot be taken to prescribe or sometimes even to describe an author's own deliberate orthographical practice. Comic poets such as Menander may not have been consistent in their choices, and the papyri, which range in date from the third century BC down to at least the fifth century AD, may at times reflect the spellings accepted at the time of the copying scribes rather than those of the original authors. Nevertheless, at several points when the relevant evidence of papyri is weighed against the general practices of Ptolemaic or Imperial copyists and the engravers of Attic inscriptions, there are hints of a more definite code of practice than one would perhaps have anticipated. Of course problems remain, for which the available evidence can offer no solutions. One difficulty, for example, is the relation of metrical constraints to the conventions of contemporary speech in Menander's time, an area of study where scholarly work would be desirable, if only more evidence on which it could be based had survived (cf. Handley 1970: 138). Here fr. com. adesp. 1000.27 provides an exemplary illustration of the difficulties. One of its two scribes, writing in the second century BC, opens an iambic trimeter with *φέρ' ἐάν*, 'Now, if . . .'. Writers of that time apparently preferred ἐάν to ἄν in this use,[1] yet here φέρ' ἐάν involves word-division after the first short of an anapaest in a way that later Greek comic poets tolerated but did not love.[2] The original author here could have written either φέρ' ἐάν or φέρ' ἄν.

A further difficulty is faced by researchers when they attempt, for purposes of comparison, to cite the texts of book fragments of later Greek comedy exactly as they appear in the mediaeval manuscripts of authors such as Athenaeus. Here even the best editors tend not to cite apparently minor orthographical variants either consistently or at all. For this reason I have here sought to check readings in the Marcianus codex (A) of the original version of Athenaeus and in manuscripts C and E of its Epitome from photographs in my possession.

In this paper the line-numberings are generally those given in my Loeb edition of Menander (Arnott 1979, 1996*a*, 2000), differing from those of Sandbach's Oxford text (1972, 2nd edn. 1990) especially in *Theophoroumene*, *Kolax*, *Misoumenos,* and *Phasma*; in *Epitrepontes* the line numbers for the new fragments of Acts III and IV are those adopted by Sisti and Martina in their editions (Sisti 1991, Martina 1996); book fragments of Menander and other comic poets, together with unattributed book and papyrus fragments, take their numbers from the Kassel–Austin edition, details of which are listed in the bibliography.

ἀεί/αἰεί

αἰεί is the Ionic and early Attic form; inscriptions show that from the mid-fifth down to the mid-fourth century BC both *αἰεί* and *ἀεί* coexisted, with *ἀεί* becoming dominant in the early fourth century and virtually displacing the other form by 350.

Papyri of later Greek comedy virtually always spell the word *ἀεί*: 18 times at least[3] with first syllable short: Men. *Asp*. 65, *Dys*.

[1] See below, and cf. Mayser–Schmoll (1970: 128).

[2] Cf. Arnott (1957), Handley (1965*b*: 63–6), Coccia (1960), and Sardiello (1983*b*).

[3] Although I have taken great care to include in this study not only what remains of Menander but also (1) those unattributed papyri which have been plausibly identified as New Comedy, (2) book fragments of New Comedy poets such as Anaxippus, Diodorus, Diphilus, Philemon, and Posidippus, and (3) of comic poets such as Alexis, who straddle the periods of Middle and New Comedy, those book fragments which can be plausibly dated to the later period, it is possible that I have missed a few instances here and elsewhere. Future publications of papyri will doubtless increase many of the figures given here.

145, 286, 426, 664, 679, 717, 969, *Epit.* 791, *Theoph.* 49, *Pk.* 142, 152, 537, *Sam.* 273, 728, Posidippus fr. 6.13 (*P. Heidelberg* 183), fr. com. adesp. 1000.15, 1057.8; 9 times with *α* anceps: Men. *Dys.* 573, *Mis.* 100, *Pk.* 744, *Sam.* 115, 737, *Sik.* 315, 413, fr. com. adesp. 1093.50 and 136; twice with *α* long: Men. *Kith.* 77, *Fab. Inc.* 1.14 (ἤρα μὲν ἀεί, but Menander could have written ἀεὶ μὲν ἤρα). Papyri have αιει at *Epit.* 706 (× –, *P. Michigan*), fr. com. adesp. 1120.3 (– –), and possibly also 1120.4 (× –: α[.]ει). αιει is B's reading at *Dys.* 904 (scanning – –, hardly explicable here as the use of an old form for poetic heightening:[4] more likely a careless anticipation of the word's final *iota*). At *Sam.* 723 also B's scribe originally wrote αιει, but then scored out the first *iota* (C αει). B's αιε[at *Dys.* 31 (⏑ –, line end) could originally have been a third erroneous αιει, or αιε written in mistake for αει, as in the same papyrus at *Asp.* 173 (× –).[5]

For other problems with intervocalic *iota*, see the sections below on κα(ί)ω, κλα(ί)ω, and υἱός.

ἄν/ἐάν (+ subjunctive: 'if')

In later comedy unchallenged instances of ἄν (scanned as one long) outnumber those of ἐάν by a considerable margin: ἄν × 51 (plus ἄνπερ fr. com. adesp. 1129.5, and κἄν Men. *Dys.* 809, *Pk.* 393), ἐάν × 31. The figures for ἄν might be increased by the inclusion of cases where (1) the spelling before a following μή is assimilated to αμ (*Asp.* 234); (2) αν is corrupted to an unmetrical εαν (*Georg.* 44, *Sam.* 440, 471; cf. also *Epit.* 818, where *P. Oxy.* 3532 correctly has αν, *P. Michigan* has εαν); and finally (3), in a lacuna there is space only for α]ν (*Pk.* 364). The figures for ἐάν also may be raised slightly by the addition of *Dys.* 407 (where αν is B's corruption for ἐάν) and fr. com. adesp. 1056.17 (where the spelling is assimilated to εαμ before ποτε.). At *Sam.* 341, however, B's εαν is probably a corruption, substituting a synonym for C's οταν. The figures of comic papyri here contrast significantly with those of other

[4] Such heightening is not detectable until v. 932 (see Handley's commentary [1965*b*] on 946–53; cf. also R. L. Hunter 1983: 9–20 and Nesselrath 1990: 265–6), although Mayser–Schmoll (1970: 84) note that rare occurrences of αἰεί in Ptolemaic papyri may be explained as literary reminiscences.

[5] Cf. Kühner–Blass (1890–2: 1.134, 136–7, 2.302 n. 2), Lademann (1915: 8–9), LSJ (1940: s.v. ἀεί), Schwyzer (1939: 236, 266, 619 n. 4), Mayser–Schmoll (1970: 84), Threatte (1980: 275–7).

Ptolemaic papyri and of Attic inscriptions, where *ἐάν* is the regular form, although *ἄν* does occur.[6]

A number of passages pose the problem highlighted in my opening paragraph, with papyri offering *εαν* after a short syllable, thus dividing the anapaest after the first short. At *Dys.* 176 B has -*ησατεεαν*, and at 205 -*ομεαν*; in both places editors correct to -*ήσατ' ἄν* and -*ομ' ἄν*; accordingly at fr. com. adesp. 1000.27 we ought also perhaps to improve the readings of the two papyri (*φερεανυν* with *υ* corrected from *ο*, and *φερεοαν̣ ̣ν*) not to *φέρ' ἐὰν ὁ νῦν* with Blass, but to *φέρ' ἂν ὁ νῦν*. Yet in all three places we cannot be certain to what extent comic poets might have tolerated an anapaest so split after a short syllable with elision, and in the last one there is the additional difficulty that we are there dealing not with professional scribes but with a pair of recluses whose spelling and accuracy leave much to be desired (Thompson 1988: 212–65).

αὖθις/αὖτις

Comic papyri divide here. The Attic form *αὖθις* appears in Men. *Epit.* 1110 (C), *Sik.* 64 (S) and fr. com. adesp. 1000.30; the Ionic and Koine spelling *αὖτις* at *Epit.* 579 (C); at *Sam* 626 *αὖθις* B, *αυτις* C, while 637 *αυτις* C, *ουτος* (!) B. Before the last World War, when C prevailed as the main evidence for Menandrean orthography, and when papyri of other Attic authors yielded evidence of the *αὖτις* spelling (e.g. Soph. *Ichneutai* 233 *αυτι*[*ς*, 235; cf. L at *OC* 234), it was assumed that *αὖτις* was also acceptable in Athens by the side of *αὖθις*.[7] However, since *αὖτις* is never found on Attic inscriptions (Threatte 1980: 386, 393, 404–5), and is rejected as un-Attic by ancient grammarians such as Helladius (in Photius *Bibl.* 535[a]: *τὸ μὲν αὖτις Ἰωνικόν, τὸ δὲ αὖθις Ἀττικόν*), it appears more sensible to explain its occurrences in later comic papyri as scribal introductions of a Koine form. What perhaps needs to be stressed is that the third-century BC Sorbonne papyrus of *Sik.* has *αυθις*.

ἄχρι(ς)/μέχρι(ς)

Atticist grammarians such as Phrynichus maintain that *μέχρις καὶ ἄχρις σὺν τῷ σ ἀδόκιμα· μέχρι καὶ ἄχρι λέγε* (*Ecl.* 6 Rutherford,

[6] Lademann (1915: 112), Mayser–Schmoll (1970: 128), Threatte (1996: 672–4), cf. Threatte (1980: 620–3).

[7] Cf. Wilamowitz (1907: 872) and Pearson (1917) on the *Ichneutai* passages.

Fischer; cf. also Helladius in Phot. *Bibl.* 535[ab], Moeris α 74 Hansen, Philetaerus 69 Dain, Thomas Magister 13.11 Ritschl),[8] and this ordinance is borne out by Attic inscriptions up to the first half of the second century AD and by papyri of the Ptolemaic period, which show only forms in -χρι. Comic papyri and manuscripts of Attic authors generally have the true Attic forms in -ι before consonants (ἄχρι fr. com. adesp. 1056.3; μέχρι Men. *Dys.* 33, 274, *Mis.* 8, *Sam.* 666, *Sik.* 270, fr. com. adesp. 1000.32; cf. Men. fr. 337.3) and rarely too before vowels (ἄχρι Hegesippus fr. 1.26; μέχρι Diphilus fr. 3.4, Machon fr. 2.8). At *Sam.* 394 B and C uniquely give αχρις αν. Book fragments of comedy often show a mixed tradition: e.g. Men. fr. 748.1 (μέχρι ἄν SM, μέχρις ἄν A of Stobaeus 3.29.17), Phoenicides fr. 3.3 (μέχρι ἂν A, μέχρις ἂν CE of Athenaeus 10.415 A). This tangled set of leads is best explained by the assumption that Menander himself normally used -ι not -ις, with some scribes later adjusting the spelling to what was normal in their own times.[9]

γί(γ)νομαι

Ionic's γίνομαι, ἐγινόμην usurps the place of Attic γίγνομαι, ἐγιγνόμην in Attica from the third century BC, and is the normal form in Ptolemaic papyri from 277 BC onwards (with spellings in -ιγν- then confined to copies of earlier Attic literary texts).[10] We do not know which of the two forms Menander preferred nor even whether a poet of his time was consistent in his orthography. Comic papyri of later Greek comedy almost universally offer the -ιν- spelling (× 32 at least). To these may be added 6 or 7 passages where the scribe writes γειν-, a spelling common from the second century BC on (*P. Michigan* at *Epit.* 706, Z at *Koneiaz.* 20, B at *Sam* 223, fr. com. adesp. 1008.7 and 18, *P. Oxy.* 4095.4 certainly;

[8] Some ancient grammarians, however, seem more ready to accept the forms with *sigma*: e.g. Ammonius 91 (p. 23) Nickau, [Herodian] 1.511.19–20 Lentz, Hesychius α 8923 Latte, Photius α 3457 Theodoridis, *Suda* α 4718, and the anon. συναγωγὴ λέξεων χρησίμων 475.6 Bekker = 176.8 Bachmann. Cf. in general Kühner–Blass (1890–2: 1.207–8, 2.302 n. 2, 581), Meisterhans–Schwyzer (1900: 212, 219), Durham (1913: 17, 48–9), Lademann (1915: 86–7), Mayser (1938: 243), Schwyzer (1939: 405), Schwyzer–Debrunner (1950: 549–50), C. Austin (1970) on Men. *Sam.* 394, Mayser–Schmoll (1970: 215), Threatte (1980: 386, 669–71).

[9] This assumption has been supported by scholars who supplement broken texts (e.g. *Mis.* 8: Turner, *Sam.* 159: Oguse, West, fr. com. adesp. 1091.3: Lloyd-Jones) and correct the transmission (e.g. *Sam.* 394: Headlam).

[10] Cf. Kühner (1841), Kühner–Blass (1890–2: 2.391), Thumb (1901: 206–7), Lademann (1915: 55–6, 113), Mayser–Schmoll (1970: 156), Threatte (1996: 561–5).

probably *P. Oxy.* 409 at *Kol.* A11, if the text there is rightly read as γε[.]νεται), together with two passages where the tradition is divided between -ιν- and -ειν- (*Asp.* 158 FB, *Sam.* 594 CB). The four certain instances of Attic -ιγν- are S (third century BC!) at *Sik.* 27, B at *Sam.* 212 and 490, and C at *Sam.* 223, while at *Sam.* 65 B writes γιγνομαι with an ε added above the first ι and the second γ struck out. At *Sam.* 43 B has ...]νομην with room only for εγι], and at fr. com. adesp. 1084.38 *P. Ant.* 15 has ..]νωμ', with space only for γε] (Maas) or γι]. At *Asp.* 521 there is no means of knowing whether B originally had γιγ]ν or γι]ν, although the evidence from the other passages discussed above supports the latter spelling. Cf. also γι(γ)νώσκω below.

γι(γ)νώσκω

This verb, like γί(γ)νομαι, normally has the Ionic and Koine spelling with γιν- in papyri of the Ptolemaic period,[11] and of its 12 occurrences in comic papyri 11 give simply γιν-, while the two papyri of the other (Men. *Epit.* 696) divide between γιν- (C) and γειν- (*P. Michigan*).

η as augment of verbs whose stem begins with a consonant

Three such verbs[12] (βούλομαι, δύναμαι, μέλλω) in Attic formed the augment regularly with ἐ- down to *c.*350 BC, when in Attic inscriptions ἠ- seems first to have come in as an alternative to, and by 330 BC to have totally replaced, ἐ-.[13] The ἐ- form is dominant in the papyri of later Greek comedy; those places where the form chosen is dictated by the metre are indicated by * in the following lists:

[11] Cf. Kühner (1841), Kühner–Blass (1890–2: 2.391–2), Lademann (1915: 56), Mayser–Schmoll (1970: 156), Threatte (1996: 561–5).

[12] I leave out (ἐ)θέλω, where ἐθέλω → ἤθελον, θέλω → ἔθελον; cf. Schwyzer (1939: 654), claiming that the duality of the augment form with this verb influenced the augment form with *eta* of the three verbs discussed in this section. So also Debrunner (1954: 85–6 and 108), noting that this suggestion was first made by Buttmann (1819: 323–4).

[13] Threatte (1996: 474). Ancient grammarians give contradictory judgments about the η- augments, claiming that they are Attic (Moeris η 5 Hansen, [Herodian] 2.326.4, 354.14 and *passim* Lentz), Ionic (anon. in Cramer 1835: 374.32–3), or a barbarism (anon. περὶ βαρβαρισμοῦ in Valckenaer 1739: 195). They were much favoured in second-sophistic Greek (W. Schmid 1896: 590). See also Kühner–Blass (1890–2: 2.9), Debrunner (1954: 101–4, 108–9), and my commentary on Alexis fr. 263.1 (Arnott 1996*b*: 733).

ἐβουλ-: Men. *Georg.* 83, *Dis Ex.* 58, *Dys.* 708, 784*, *Epit.* 166*, 1123*, *Mis.* 631*, *Pk.* 190, *Sam.* 529*, 563* (BC), 640 (BC), *Sik.* 133*, 202, *Fab. Inc.* 1.61, 62.

ἠβουλ-: fr. com. adesp. 1147.31; cf. Alexis fr. 263.1 (CE of Epitome of Ath.), Machon fr. 144 Gow (A of Ath.).

ἐδυν-: *Dys.* 686*, *Pk.* 709*, *Sam.* 16*, fr. com. adesp. 1091.6*.

ἠδυν-: cf. Philippides fr. 16* (A + CE of Ath.).

ἐμελλ-: *Asp.* 134 (BF), 136* (B), *Dys.* 216*, 673, *Epit.* 251*, *Mis.* 454, *Pk.* 1002*, fr. com. adesp. 1017.63*. At *Epit.* 682 *P. Michigan* has [.]μ̣ελλ̣[where the metre requires [ε].

(ἐ)θέλω, ἤθελον, ἠθέλησα

ἐθέλω and θέλω stand side by side in fifth-century Attic; θέλω is used by tragedy, ἐθέλω normally by Old Comedy (except in phrases such as εἰ/ἂν θεὸς/-οὶ θέλει/-ῃ/-ουσι/-ωσι, or in tragic parody). Prose writers vary, although in the fourth century there is a tendency to use θέλω in the phrases cited above and after a long vowel or diphthong.[14] There are perhaps too few examples in later comedy for firm rules to be formulated; the phrase cited above is recorded only twice for Menander (*Georg.* 44–5, fr. 43.1, but cf. the related *Mis.* 555) and once for Alexis (fr. 249.1), and decisions whether to use θέλω or ἐθέλω may have been generally influenced by either an increasing popularity of the θέλω form or metrical convenience, but occasionally perhaps by the fact that in Menander's time the form with initial ε had a more formal and polite ring.[15]

ἐθέλω: *Dys.* 269, 854 (both polite), *P. Oxy.* 4021 fr. 3.14 (unplaced fr. of *Epit.*).

θέλω: *Asp.* 413, *Georg.* 45 ([.]ε̣λ̣ω̣σ̣ι G with space for only one letter), *Mis.* 555, fr. com. adesp. 1000.29, 1092.6, 1127.19; cf. e.g. Diphilus fr. 98.2, Nicolaus fr. 1.34, Philemon fr. 97.8, Phoenicides fr. 4.3, fr. com. adesp. 247.7, 882.

ἠθελ-: *Dys.* 767, *Sik.* 76; cf. Criton fr. 3.4.

Uncertain are *Heros* 53 (]ελοιμ' ω[), *Kol.* fr. 13a.7 Arnott (]θελε[ ), and fr. com. adesp. 1090.7 (]θελησκ[). I ignore fr. com.

[14] Cf. Rutherford (1881: 415–16), Kühner–Blass (1890–2: 1.187–8, 2.408–9), Lademann (1915: 127), LSJ (1940: s.v. ἐθέλω), Debrunner (1954: 87–101, 104–8, 109), Schwyzer–Debrunner (1950: 491), Threatte (1980: 426; 1996: 637–8), MacDowell (1990*b*: 82–4).

[15] Cf. Wilamowitz (1895: 11–12), Arnott (1964: 117; 1995: 151).

adesp. 1095.8, where (in anapaestic tetrameters probably from Old or Middle Comedy) the reading δεθελει may be divided as either δ' ἐθέλει or δὲ θέλει.

εἶπα/εἶπον

Comic papyri give (and metre requires) both εἶπα (Men. *Dis Ex.* 83 [ε]ιπα, *Pk.* 318, supported by Philemon fr. 133.1) and εἶπον (*Asp.* 65, B's correction at *Dys.* 256) as 1st person singular, and εἶπας (*Epit.* 815, *Pk.* 309 [ε]ιπας) as 2nd. This reflects contemporary Attic practice, although in Menander's time εἶπον may still have been considered more correct as 1st person singular, with εἶπα perhaps considered a vulgarism.[16]

εὑρίσκω and εὐ- compounds: augments and perfect forms

In earlier Attic εὑρίσκω and verbs beginning εὐ- were augmented and given perfect forms with ηὑ- and ηὐ- respectively, but by the end of the fourth century BC ευ had generally replaced diphthongal ηυ wherever the latter had previously occurred, with the consequence that the augmented and perfect forms of the verbs changed to εὑ- and εὐ-. Occasionally, however, in papyri of the Ptolemaic period the older forms seem to have been retained as a more literary spelling.[17] This picture is reflected in both comic papyri and book fragments: εὑρίσκω and its compounds (ἐξ-, ἐφ-) are always augmented or given a perfect form with ευ- (papyri: ×23 certainly, probably also fr. com. adesp. 1001.13, where the scribe's ευρμα was emended by Herzog to εὗρον, by Blass to εὑρών; book fragments: ×17 certainly, probably also Athenion fr. 1.20, where A at Ath. 14.660 E has ἐξευρημένοι, CE ἐξηυ-).

Verbs beginning εὐ- are mostly augmented or given their perfect form with εὐ- (εὐτυχῶ: Men. *Pk.* 994, 1007, *Fab. Inc.* 1.49; εὔχομαι: *Sik.* 413), less commonly with ηὐ- (ηυτρεπιζον B at *Dys.* 940, ηυχομη[ν] S at *Sik.* 48).

[16] Cf. my commentary (Arnott 1996*b*) on Alexis fr. 2.3, where I note other parallels in later comedy (Athenion fr. 1.38, Euangelus fr. 1.1, Philemon fr. 133) and satyric drama (Eur. *Cycl.* 101), but further examples in Solon fr. 34.6 West, Theodectes fr. 6.8, fr. trag. adesp. 655.6, Xen. *Mem.* 2.2.8 and [Dem.] 47.41 may be held to run counter to this view. See also Rutherford (1881: 215–21), Kühner–Blass (1890–2: 2.422–3), Wackernagel (1916: 112 [= 272] n. 2), Mayser (1938: 135), Schwyzer (1939: 744, 755), Threatte (1996: 549–50).

[17] See e.g. Kühner–Blass (1890–2: 2.10–11), Mayser (1938: 101), Schwyzer (1959: 127, 655, 709 n. 2), Mayser–Schmoll (1970: 108), Threatte (1980: 384–5; 1996: 482–3, 499, 564).

κα(ί)ω, κλα(ί)ω

A tendency in the fourth and third centuries BC to drop intervocalic *iota* in spelling was probably influenced by pronunciation, but records of these two verbs in comic papyri (as in other papyri and inscriptions) are still too few for statistical analysis.[18] Yet whatever the spelling, the relevant syllable is always long or anceps.

κα(ί)ω: at Men. *Asp.* 76 B has κλαιειν in error, copied presumably from an earlier καιειν rather than καειν.[19] Alexis fr. 153.15 has κάεται (ACE Ath. 9.379 A), Philemon iun. fr. 1.4 κατακάει (ACE Ath. 7.291 D), Baton fr. 4.2 καίεται (A Ath. 14.662 C), while the manuscripts of Stob. 3.6.13 citing Phoenicides fr. 4.13 divide between ἔκαε (LM[d]) and ἔκαιε (A).

κλα(ί)ω: -αι- at *Asp.* 227 (B), *Sam* 406 (C), fr. com. adesp. 1125.5 (on *Asp.* 76 see above); more frequently -α- at *Asp.* 385, *Dys.* 674, *Epit.* 487, *Mis.* 696, *Pk.* 174, 189, 758 ([κ]λάεις suppl. Headlam), *Sam.* 73, 245 (BC), 406 (B's correction), fr. com. adesp. 1014.44, *P. Oxy.* 1239.5 = Austin (1973) fr. 249.5. Philemon fr. 77.5 is cited by the manuscripts of [Plut.] *Mor.* 105 E with κλάῃς, of Stob. 4.44.1 with κλαίῃς.

Cf. also the entries on ἀ(ι)εί and υἱός.

κλείω/κέκλει(σ)μαι/κέκλημαι

(1) In the present/future/imperfect/aorist active/middle and the perfect active, the old Attic spelling κλῄω was replaced by κλείω between the end of the fifth and the middle of the fourth century BC; thus (-)κλείω is the normal form in the manuscripts of Aristophanes (× 12: but *Av.* 1262 -κεκλῄκαμεν PVΦS, *Eccl.* 355 -κλῄσασ' S, -κλείσας RG), the book fragments of Middle- and New-Comedy poets (× 7, including Menander fr. 163.3), together with C at Men. *Pk.* 377. At *Dys.* 427 B has κλισασ', corrected to κλει- by ed. pr.

(2) κέκλεισμαι with an intrusive *sigma* appears as the perfect middle/passive form in mediaeval manuscripts of Aristophanes and comic fragments: e.g. Ar. *Vesp.* 198 (RV), *Lys.* 423 (B: -κλισμαι R), *Plut.* 206 (RU), Alexis fr. 106.2 (A of Pollux), Men.

[18] Cf. Kühner–Blass (1890–2: 1.133–4, 2.452, 459–60), Schwyzer (1939: 236), Mayser–Schmoll (1970: 83–5), Threatte (1996: 503).

[19] Corrected by Kassel (καίειν or κάειν); cf. Austin (1969), (1970), and Gomme–Sandbach (1973), all ad loc.

fr. 410.3, 851.2 (see below). Whether this variant was introduced in later Attic by analogy with forms like *σέσεισμαι*, *πέπεισμαι*, *ἔσπεισμαι*, and *πεφεισμένος*, or was a late post-classical form known to and accepted by Byzantine copyists, remains uncertain.[20] Since the Menander papyri give *κεκλειμενη* *Pk.* 1076, *εγκεκλειμ[ενη]* (suppl. Norsa and Vitelli) *Theoph.* 22, *εγκεκλει[* *Fab. Inc.* 1.9, it seems reasonable to suppose that B's *εγκεκλισαι* at *Asp.* 345 and *P. Oxy.* 2825's *κατακεκλημεν[* at *Phasma* 85 should both be corrected to -*κεκλει*- (Austin and Arnott, respectively). Similarly the manuscripts of Menander book fragments, which twice yield -*κεκλεισμ*- (410.3, cited by Harpocration *κ* 85 Keaney; 851.2, by Stob. *Ecl.* 4.43.1) are corrected to -*κεκλειμ*- by Körte and Herwerden respectively.

μέχρι(ς)

See under *ἄχρι(ς)*.

μηδείς/μηθείς/οὐδείς/οὐθείς, etc.

Evidence from Athenian inscriptions and from papyri of the Ptolemaic period shows that the combination of *delta* and rough breathing in Attic Greek led—presumably by assimilation[21]—to an orthographical change from *δ* to *θ* in *οὐδαμῶς*, *οὐδείς*, and *μηδείς* at the beginning of the fourth century BC. The spelling with *θ* then dominated Attic and Koine Greek right down to the first century AD, after which it disappeared and the spelling with *δ* resumed its original place. In Attic inscriptions of Menander's period (*c.*320–*c.*290 BC) the use of *θ* is universal, while non-literary papyri spell with *θ* 87 per cent of the time. These facts make it likely that Menander and his rivals normally used the form with *θ*, although it would be unwise to assume total or deliberate consistency.[22] The figures for comic papyri, however, are as follows:

spellings with *δ*: *μηδαμῶς* ×10, *μηδείς* ×28 (including C's supralineal correction at *Pk.* 319 and Z's correction at *Koneiaz.* 18), *οὐδαμῶς* ×1 (*Epit.* 561), *οὐδείς* ×92 (including misformula-

[20] Cf. e.g. Kühner–Blass (1890–2: 2.460–1), LSJ (1940: s.v. *κλείω* (A)), Mayser–Schmoll (1970: 51), Threatte (1980: 370), Arnott (1996*b*: 289) on Alexis fr. 106.2.

[21] Thus it affected those forms of *οὐδείς/μηδείς* where the *εἷς* component had a rough breathing, but never those (e.g. *οὐδεμία*) in which it did not.

[22] See Kühner–Blass (1890–2: 1.633–4), Thumb (1901: 148 n. 7), Durham (1913: 18, 81), Lademann (1915: 60–1, 113–14), Schwyzer (1939: 408, 617), Mayser–Schmoll (1970: 148–9), Threatte (1980: 472–6).

tions such as *ουδ'εις* and *ουδε εις*: e.g. B at *Dys.* 534 and *Sam.* 372 respectively);

spellings with *θ*: *μηθαμοῦ* × 1 (Apollodorus fr. 14.5 = *P. Berlin* 9772), *μηθαμῶς*? × 2 (*Phasma* 87, and B's supralineal correction at *Sam.* 573),[23] *μηθείς* × 17 (excluding *Koneiaz.* 18 before correction), *οὐθαμῶς* never, *οὐθείς* × 56.

These figures (63% with δ, 37% with θ) probably reflect the fact that many of the comic papyri date from the imperial period; those of the third century BC on the other hand clearly prefer the spelling with θ (e.g. S at *Sik.* 115, 239, fr. com. adesp. 1014.11, 41, 56, 1017.59, 82, 86, 1064.9, 1072.7, 1081.4, 1093.83, 105, 171, 377, 1147.184). A complication is added by the number of cases where two or more papyri preserve the same passage and differ over their choice of dental; the following list shows B writing θ where F or C write δ: *Asp.* 158, 429, *Sam.* 615, 631, 643, 653, 671.

-(*ν*) *endings to adverbs*

In most cases the -*ν* in Attic is basic to the word, but with several adverbs the *nu* came falsely to be considered as paragogic, and was dropped often for metrical convenience in verse, but occasionally also during the fourth and third centuries in Attic prose inscriptions. Each word is best dealt with separately, since they receive varying treatment; Ptolemaic papyri, for instance, always write *παντάπασιν* with *nu* and *πέρυσι* without, while *πάλιν* is usual but *πάλι* also is found even before a vowel.[24]

ἄνωθεν: always with *ν*: *Dys.* 627, 632, 672, 940, *Epit.* 240, *Sam.* 233, fr. com. adesp. 1084.30, Philemon fr. 82.6.

αὐτόθεν: apparently always with *ν*: *Dys.* 99 ([*αὐτ*]*όθεν* suppl. ed. pr.), 263, *Kolax* D217 (*αὐτ*[*ό*]*θ*[*εν* suppl. Arnott), *Sik.*12. At Men. fr. 60.2 (cited by Athenaeus 15.700B) Bentley's conjecture *ἀλλ' ἀποσείειν αὐτόθεν* for ms. A's *αλλὰ ποδιειν αυτόν* is consummate.

ἐντεῦθεν: always with *ν*: *Dys.* 87, 447 (*ἐντ*]*εῦθεν* suppl. ed. pr.), 913, *Kith.* 99, *Pk.* 374, fr. com. adesp. 1101.10 (*ἐντεῦθε*[*ν*]).

ἔμπροσθε(*ν*): -*θεν* before vowel at *Pk.* 804 (C after correction); -*θε*

23 Here C has *μαινεται*, B has *μαινομαι* with a correcting *η θαμως* written above; it is a one-word reply in which both *μαίνεται* and *μηθαμῶς* make acceptable sense, with the latter perhaps more forceful in the context. See esp. Gomme–Sandbach (1973: 609).

24 Cf. Kühner–Blass (1890–2: 2.308–11), Lademann (1915: 83), Schwyzer (1939: 405–6, 627–8), Mayser–Schmoll (1970: 213–14), Threatte (1996: 385–6, 395–6).

before consonant at *Asp.* 55, *Sam.* 233 (-θε C, -θεν unmetrically B), Hegesippus fr. 1.20 (-θε C at Ath. 7.290 B, -θεν unmetrically A), Nicomachus fr. 1.14.

ἐξόπισθ': Philemon fr. 115.1, and conjectured by Meineke at Men. fr. 662, where Schol. T on Hom. *Il.* 13.289–91 writes ἐξόπισθεν, but there neither conjecture nor attribution to Menander is wholly convincing.

ἔξωθεν: with ν at *Dys.* 245, *Sam.* 252, 416; at *Mis.* 562, however, B has εξωθενεπιθεωρε[, which does not scan (ἔξωθ' Merkelbach).

ἐπάνωθ[εν]: so supplemented by Lefebvre at *Epit.* 634.

ἐπίπροσθε: only at *Epit.* 813 (*P. Oxy.* 3532, here misread by Turner, and *P. Michigan*), without ν before a consonant at penthemimeral caesura.

ὄπισθε(ν): with ν before vowel at *Kolax* B38 (ο[π]-) and fr. 268; ὄπισθ' before vowel at *Kolax* B46, ὄπισθε before consonant at *Georg.* fr. 9c.6.

πάλιν: always with ν where checkable, with a favourite seat at the end of an iambic trimeter; the word occurs ×61 in Menander papyri, ×21 in unassigned papyri, ×12 in Menandrean book fragments. Here I include *Epit.* 754 (my decipherment of C, but πανυ̣ is read by Guéraud, Koenen, Gagos), and passages where only part of the word survives (*Epit.* 289, *Mis.* 505, 559, *Pk.* 364, *Sik.* 259, fr. com. adesp. 1008.5, 1014.145, 1032.4). Excluded are *Theoph.* fr. 3.1 (cited by Ath. 11.504 A: unscanning πάλι in A deleted by Cobet) and *Mis.* fr. 7.1 (cited by [Justin] *De monarchia* 5: ⟨πάλιν⟩ plausibly added by Bentley at line end to complete an otherwise defective trimeter).[25]

παντάπασι(ν): with ν at *Georg.* 68, *Dys.* 894 (παντά[πασι]ν suppl. ed. pr.), *Pk.* 358 (παν[τά]πασιν suppl. ed. pr.), all before vowels; without ν at Men. fr. 764.3 (Stob. 3.42.6, all manuscripts) before a consonant. In non-literary Ptolemaic papyri παντάπασιν always has the final ν (Mayser–Schmoll 1970: 213–14).

25 πάλι is found without final ν occasionally in Hellenistic and later Greek poetry, presumably for its metrical convenience: Asclepiades 16.6, Hedylus 6.1, Meleager 71.1 Gow–Page (πάλιν unmetrically ms., corr. Reiske), Callimachus *Epigr.* 33.2 Gow–Page = 10.2 Pfeiffer, Herodas 2.52 (but πάλιν 5.47, 7.6, 7.98), [Scymnus] *periegesis* 585 Müller (πάλιν unmetrically ms., corr. Meineke); cf. Phrynichus *Ecl.* 247 Fischer = 249 Rutherford: πάλι· οὕτω λέγουσιν οἱ νῦν ῥήτορες καὶ ποιηταί, δέον μετὰ τοῦ ν πάλιν, ὡς οἱ ἀρχαῖοι λέγουσιν. πάλι occurs rarely too in non-literary Ptolemaic papyri and once in a late Roman metrical inscription. See Rutherford (1881: 347–8), de Gregori (1901: 177 and n. 8), Headlam–Knox (1922) on Herodas 2.52, Schwyzer (1939: 619), Mayser–Schmoll (1970: 213), Threatte (1996: 395–6).

παντόθεν: only at Men. fr. 733.1, with final *ν*.

πέρυσι(ν): papyri of later Greek comedy give -*ν* before vowels (*Epit.* 862, *Sik.* 126, fr. com. adesp. 1088.3), and -*ι* before consonants (*Epit.* 476, *Kolax* B49 [before *πτ*- at penthemimeral caesura]). At *Kolax* B34 *P. Oxy.* 409 has an inconclusive *περυσι*[. . .]*ε̣ι̣*[. Non-literary Ptolemaic papyri always have *πέρυσι*, even before a vowel (Mayser–Schmoll 1970: 213–14).

πρόσθε(ν): before a vowel always with *ν* (*Theoph.* 26, *Sam.* 710, Men. fr. 840.3); before a consonant sometimes with *ν* (*Dys.* 906, *Sam.* 168, 214, C at 357), sometimes without *ν* (*Dys.* 920, *Mis.* 468, 796, *Pk.* 299, *Sam.* 405, B at 357). The situation at *Sam.* 357 confirms scribal responsibility at times for such orthographical decisions. At *Mis.* 608 it is possible to supplement either *πρ*[*όσθ*]*ε*[*ν τὴν* (Sandbach) or *πρ*[*όσθ*]*ε τὴν*. Cf. also *ἔμπροσθε(ν)* and *ἐπίπροσθε* above.

οἶδας/οἶσθα/οἶσθας

All three forms of the 2nd person singular of *οἶδα* are attested in the manuscripts of Athenian comedy: the Attic form *οἶσθα* most commonly at all times, *οἶσθας* as a metrically convenient alternative to *οἶσθ'* before a vowel (cf. Aelius Dionysius s.v., p. 131 Erbse), and *οἶδας* at the end of the period, presumably as an Ionic form accepted in the Koine.[26]

οἶσθα: Men. *Asp.* 72, 374, *Dys.* 115, 798 (B *οισθας* with final *ς* crossed out, before *τ* at penthemimeral caesura), *Epit.* 541, 871, 1127, *Theoph.* 20, *Sam.* 715, *P. Oxy.* 2533 = C. Austin (1973) fr. 251.6, probably Men. fr. 649 (*οἶσθ' ὡς* Schol. R Ar. *Thesm.* 870, *Suda ψ* 62 Adler, *οἶδ' ὅτι* Greg. Cor. *De dial. Att.* 2 p. 15 Schäfer), fr. com. adesp. 1056.19, 1098.6, 1116.3 ([*ο*]*ἶ̣σθα*); always in Aristophanes, and generally in book fragments of later comedy.

οἶσθας: *Epit.* 481 (before *π*, making a spondee in the first half of an iambic metron), Men. fr. 246.5, fr. com. adesp. 1017.65, Alexis fr. 15.11, Straton fr. 1.26, probably also Philemon fr. 45.5 (see below) and Posidippus fr. 29.2 (Pierson's plausible correction of *οἶσθα* A at Ath. 9.377 B); cf. Herodas 2.55.

οἶδας: not in the comic papyri or the book fragments of

[26] See Kühner–Blass (1890–2: 1.409–10, s.v. *ΕΙΔΩ*), Headlam–Knox (1922) on Herodas 2.55, LSJ (1940: s.v. **εἴδω* B pf. *οἶδα*), Schwyzer (1939: 662), Jacques's critical apparatus (1976) on Men. *Dys.* 798, Stevens (1976: 59–60), Arnott (1996*b*) on Alexis fr. 15.11.

Menander, but transmitted at Philemon fr. 45.3 (A at Ath. 4.175 D: v. 3 *οἶδας*, v. 4 *οἶσθα*, v. 5 ?*οἶσθας* Meineke for A's unmetrical *οἶσθ'*: a deliberate insertion of all three forms together, or just scribal carelessness?) and Phoenicides fr. 3.2 (ACE at Ath. 10.415 E).

At *Koneiaz.* 11 Körte supplied [*οἶσθ*]*α δήπου*; at *Mis.* 651 Turner restored to [*οἶσ*]*θας* ⟨*σ*⟩*ὺ*.

ὁρῶ in the perfect: *ἑόρακα* and *ἑώρακα*

ἑόρακα is the correct and only form in earlier Attic, but a spelling *ἑω-* begins to intrude in the manuscripts of prose and verse authors writing in the fourth century BC and later. How far this was due to the authors themselves, and how far to later copyists (from the third century BC onwards *ἑω-* becomes the norm and *ἑο-* quite rare), is disputed, but poetic scansion oddly confirms that in later comedy *ἑο-* is virtually universal, while in the speeches of Demosthenes *ἑω-* sometimes appears to be required in passages which would otherwise yield an un-Demosthenic run of short syllables (e.g. Dem. 22.14 *πάντες ἑοράκατε*, 45.64 *Φορμίωνα δὲ πάλιν ἑώρακεν* [so the manuscripts], *proem.* 46.1 *ἅπαντες ἑοράκατε*).[27] The instances from later comedy are as follows:

ἑο- where *ο* is metrically short and written in papyri and other manuscripts: Men. *Epit.* 383, 860 (*εο*[*ρ*]*ακα* C), *Mis.* 5 (*P. Oxy.* 3368), *Pk.* 520 (first hand of L: here C's and L's corrected spelling *ἑω-* would be part of an anapaest split after its first short, while *ἑο-* is part of a more acceptable tribrach), *Sam.* 61, fr. com. adesp. 1093.358 (*εορα*[*κ*]*α*), 1096.60 ([*ε*]*ορακεναι*) and 71, 1147.34, 45.

ἑω- written but *ἑο-* demanded metrically: *Dys.* 409, 669, *Mis.* 5 (manuscripts of Plut. *Mor.* 525 A), *Pk.* 520 (C, second hand of L: see above), Baton fr. 5.11 (Ath. 3.103 B, 7.278 F, ACE both times), Damoxenus fr. 3.10 (Ath. 1.15 B CE), Posidippus fr. 23.1 (Ath. 4.154 F A, unnoticed by modern editors).

ἑω- written and metrically required: Men fr. 187.2 (Photius *α* 1425: bS^{z}).

At *Kolax* C193 *ἑ*[*όρ*]*ακας* is Hunt's metrically required supplement.

27 See Kühner–Blass (1890–2: 2.503–4), Mayser (1938: 189), LSJ (1940: s.v. *ὁράω*), Threatte (1996: 488) (*προεωραμένος*). At Dem. 45.64 Blass went so far as to delete *πάλιν* in order to reduce the sequence of shorts.

οὕτω(ς)

In Attic Greek οὕτως is normal before vowels, οὕτω before consonants, right down to the end of the third century BC, but there may be just enough instances of οὕτως before consonants (while οὕτω is very rare before vowels) to prevent any automatic standardization in our texts.[28]

οὕτω before a consonant: ×30 in Menander and unattributed comic papyri, ×9 in book fragments of Menander; to these may possibly be added *Perinth.* 7 ([οὕτ]ω suppl. Leo). Cf. also Alexis fr. 160.7 and possibly Philemon fr. 101.6 (-ως Clem. Alex. *Strom.* 7.25.4, -ω Theodoretus, *Graec. aff. cur.* 6.16).

οὕτως before a vowel: ×35 in Menander and unattributed papyri, including *Epit.* 266 (where the final letter is illegible before ευ-) and *Sam.* 653 (-τως C: -τος B), ×6 in Menandrean book fragments (including fr. 479.1, where the words cited by Gregory of Nazianzus *or.* 2.1 do not scan).

οὕτως before a consonant: *Dys.* 135 (at penthemimeral caesura and with change of speaker), fr. com. adesp. 1060.3, Menander fr. 351.6 (A at Ath. 4.132E). At book fr. 131.3 (cited by Stob. 4.28.18) ms. S has -τω, MA -τως.

οὐδαμῶς/οὐθαμῶς/οὐδείς/οὐθείς

See under μηδαμῶς/μηθαμῶς/μηδείς/μηθείς.

πάπ(π)ας/παπ(π)ίας

Modern editors are divided about the spelling. Schwyzer (1939: 315) prefers πάππας and παππίας on the ground that Indo-Germanic sources seem to prefer gemination with childish and pet names, but on papyri and (to a lesser extent) mediaeval manuscripts the male forms are more often spelled πάπας/παπίας, while corresponding female forms (μάμμη/μαμμία) always present double *mu*. It is true that at times (e.g. *Pax* 120, 128) the mediaeval manuscripts of Aristophanes disagree among themselves, presenting both spellings (-π-, -ππ-) for the same passage, but the papyrus of Aesch. *Diktyoulkoi* fr. 47a v. 14 Radt has the

[28] Kühner–Blass (1890–2: 1.296–7), LSJ (1940: s.v. οὕτως), Schwyzer (1939: 404), Mayser–Schmoll (1970: 214); cf. also Friis Johansen–Whittle (1980) on Aesch. *Supp.* 338, M. L. West (1990*a*: xlix). Körte–Thierfelder's claim ad loc. (1959: on their fr. 154.3) that 'Menander οὕτως numquam ante consonantes ponit' can now be challenged.

-π- form.[29] Later comic papyri also give πάπας and παπίας, with the first syllable always long or (here indicated by ×) anceps:

πάπας: *Dys.* 194, 204 ([πα]πας B, with no space for a doubled π), 494 × (παπα[B), *Epit.* 705 ×, *Mis.* 614 (so *P. Berlin* 13281: παπ[*P. Oxy.* 2656), 649, 969.

παπίας: *Dys.* 856, 930; cf. Ephippus fr. 21.1 (παπία A at Ath. 8.358 F).

At *Epit.* 806 *P. Michigan* has παπ[, clearly a vocative, but in the four-letter gap that follows Koenen and Gagos's ἐμοί (after πάπ') is only one of several possibilities. At Philemon fr. 43.2 (cited by Ath. 8.340 E) A has πα, the Epitome manuscripts and Eustathius πάππα.

Comic papyri also give μαμμη at *Sam.* 243 (BC), and μαμμια at fr. com. adesp. 1091.5.

πλείων and its various forms

In Attic fifth-century drama the spelling with *iota* is normal for all genders, numbers and cases, excepting neuter nominative and accusative singular, where tragedy always has πλεῖον, but Aristophanes varies between πλεῖον (*Nub.* 1295, *Eccl.* 1132), πλέον (*Nub.* 1288 × 2, *Eccl.* 1063, 1094, *Plut.* 531) and most commonly the contracted form πλεῖν (× 17, including *Ach.* 858 and *Plut.* 1184). In fourth-century prose -ει- is regular before ω and ου in contracted forms (πλείω, πλείους), but πλέον appears commoner than πλεῖον. Attic inscriptions never omit the ι before ω and ου, but πλέον is always the neuter form until the late second century BC, while oblique cases divide between ε and ει before ο chronologically, with the former orthography occurring before, and the latter after, *c.*300 BC. Documentary papyri of the Ptolemaic period show ει predominating over ε before ο, ου, and ω generally from the third to the first centuries BC, except that πλέον is almost universal in the third century BC, but πλεῖον in the second and first centuries BC. Derivatives such as πλεονεκτεῖν, however, always spell with ε.[30]

[29] Compare and contrast Björck (1950: 51), Handley (1965) on *Dys.* 193–4, MacDowell (1971) on Ar. *Vesp.* 297, Olson (1998) on Ar. *Pax* 120.

[30] See especially Kock (1893: 214–15), Kühner–Blass (1890–2: 1.216, 571), Lademann (1915: 124), Schwyzer (1939: 127, 236, 249, 538), Mayser–Schmoll (1970: 57), Threatte (1980: 321–2, 394–5, 732; 1996: 311–12), M. L. West (1990*a*: l), commentators on specific passages (e.g. Aesch. *Ag.* 1299, Fraenkel; Soph. *Trach.* 944, Jebb, Easterling; Alexis fr. 160.3, 257.3, Arnott).

The papyri of Menander and later comedy reveal all three forms of the neuter nom./acc. singular:

πλεῖον: fr. com. adesp. 1088.7, 1093.100 (assimilated to *πλειομ* before *π*); cf. all manuscripts at Men. fr. 708.3, 766.5, Athenion fr. 1.16, 26. At Philemon fr. 106.5 Gesner's *πλεῖον*, correcting SMA's unmetrical *πλέον* in Stobaeus' quotation (4.35.1), would deserve more support if the authenticity of the line were not itself suspect (see Kassel–Austin 1989: 285, ad loc.). At *Dys.* 528 B's *πλειον* is part of an unsolved crux; at *Dys.* 741 the supplement [*πλείον*'] is the only one that suits both space and sense; at Men. fr. 835.6 *πλεῖον* is given by SMA at Stob. 4.29.30, but the same manuscripts give a different text without *πλεῖον* at Stob. 4.29.6 (where the fragment is repeated).

πλέον: *Epit.* 591, *Kolax* E231, *Sam.* 531, fr. com. adesp. 1014.4; cf. *Georg.* fr. 5.4, *Heros* 16 (C here supplemented from Choeroboscus, *Scholia in Theodosii Canones* 1.293.30 Hilgard), *Heros* fr. 2.1, *Kolax* fr. 2.3, book fragments 372.1, 708.1 (*πλέον* M^{d}Br at Stob. 3.3.23: *πλέω* as acc. pl. neut. A), 737.1, fr. com. adesp. 120.2.

πλεῖν: *Epit.* 419.

All other cases/genders/numbers in these papyri have *ει* before *ο*, *ου*, and *ω*: certainly *Asp.* 84, *Epit.* 795 × 2, *Sam.* 230, Posidippus fr. 6.6 (*P. Heidelberg* 183), fr. com. adesp. 1093.129; possibly *Epit.* 658 Martina (Wilamowitz's [*πλεί*]*ω* suits both sense and space). Book fragments of later comedy usually give *ει* before *ο*, *ου*, and *ω* (Men. fr. 91.2, 208.5, 219.7, 819.2, 877.6, Alexis fr. 264.4, Damoxenus fr. 3.11, Diphilus fr. 4.3, 5.1, Philippides fr. 6.4, Posidippus fr. 30.1, fr. com. adesp. 898.3). Hence at Men. fr. 230.2 the editorial correction *πλείω* of V's *πλέω* and of L's *πλείων* in Aelian's quotation (*NA* 13.4) merits acceptance.

Two derivatives are recorded in papyri of later comedy: *πλεονεκτεῖν* (*Asp.* 173) and *πλεονεξία* (*Mis.* 801, cf. Men. fr. 722.1).

-ρρ-/-ρσ-

The use of -*ρρ*- where Ionic and some other dialects retained -*ρσ*- was a shibboleth of correct Attic in fourth-century writers, although earlier in Athens the tragedians and prose writers like Antiphon, Gorgias, and Thucydides favoured -*ρσ*-. Comedy in the fifth and fourth centuries, however, seems generally to have preferred -ρρ-, even for some non-Attic place names (e.g. *Χερρονήσου* Ar. *Eq.* 262), apart from (1) a few originally non-Greek words such as *βύρσα* (e.g. Ar. *Eq.* 104, *Vesp.* 38) and their derivatives (*βυρσοδέψην* Ar. *Eq.* 44, *Nub.* 581, *βυρσοδεψεῖ Plut.* 167), (2) a limited number of formations in Attic correctly made, declined, or conjugated that result in a -ρσ- sequence (e.g. *κάθαρσις*, *τέτταρσι*), and (3) a few non-Attic personal names whose spelling was enshrined in myth (e.g. *Περσεύς*: Ar. *Thesm.* 1011, 1101, 1134); in all these cases the orthography of later Greek comedy seems to correspond with that of Attic inscriptions.[31] The information from the papyri and book fragments of later Greek comedy, however, is limited by the restricted range of its vocabulary here:

ἀνεπικόρριστος: fr. com. adesp. 277.

**ἀρραβών*: fr. com. adesp. 284.

ἀρρενοῦσθαι: fr. com. adesp. 567.

ἄρρην: so Straton fr. 1.1 = Philemon fr. 114.1 (ACE at Ath. 9.382 B and 14.659 B) and fr. com. adesp. 1085.12, but at Alexis fr. 247.6 ACE at Ath. 13.562 A unite with *ἄρσην*, which may perhaps be defended as an echo of higher poetic style in a notably flowery passage, although Dindorf's conjecture *ἄρρην* is now sometimes preferred. *ἄρσενες* is also the reading of the manuscripts at *monost.* 720 Jäkel.

Ἀρρηφόρος: Menander's title is so spelled, in (1) all the citations which name the play (Men. fr. 64, 65, 66, 71, 72, 73) except one (at fr. 65: Zenobius Ath. I.2 = vulg. VI.5 has *Ἀρηφ-*), and (2) a papyrus list of Menandrean titles (l. 14 of *P. Oxy.* 2462 = Men. test. 41 K.–A.).

**ἀρρύθμως*: Alexis fr. 265.2 (*ἀρρ-* mss. of *Suda* α 1930, *ἀρύ-* C and *ἀρι-* E at Ath. 1.21c).

δερριδόγομφοι: fr. com. adesp. 307.

**ἔρραν'*: Archedicus fr. 2.5.

**ἔρριψας*: Euphron fr. 1.25.

**ἐρρωγότας*: fr. com. adesp. 597.

εὐθαρσέστερον is the transmitted reading at Diphilus fr. 110 (SMA at Stob. 3.32.12), and although the stem verb *θαρρῶ* is

[31] See especially Kühner–Blass (1890–2: 1.147), Wackernagel (1888: 127–35 = 1953–79: 1.630–8; 1907: 12–25 = 1953–79: 2.1043–56), Lademann (1915: 11, 120–2, 129), Schwyzer (1939: 81, 86–7, 115, 127, 284–5, 322), Mayser–Schmoll (1970: 194–6), Threatte (1980: 534–7).

always spelt with -ρρ- in later comedy (Men. *Dys*. 692, *Kolax* B19 (×2 ?), *Sam*. 419, 539, 677, *Sik*. 13, fr. com. adesp. 1017.47; cf. Alexis fr. 115.7, 234.5, Dionysius fr. 3.5), this adjective and related compounds (εὔθαρσής: Xen. *Hell*. 7.1.9, *Ages*. 11.10, *Eq. mag*. 4.11, Diod. Sic. 11.35.4, Plut. *Mor*. 69 A,[32] Philo 20.188, 32.70; -ῶς Arist. *Eth. Nic*. 1115^a21, Philo 34.122; -θάρσεια App. *B. Civ*. 3.13.91; -θαρσία [Pl.] *Def*. 412 A) seem to preserve the -ρσ- sequence in the manuscript tradition of Attic and later writers from the fourth century BC onwards.

μυρρίνη: so Men. *Georg*. 36 (μυρρ[ίνην suppl. ed. pr.), probably also fr. 44.1 (*ΜΥΡΡ.ΥΝΑΣ* ms. A of Donatus on Ter. *An*. 726, corr. Clericus to μυρρίνας); cf. Alexis fr. 103.25, Chrysippus fr. 1.2. At Diphilus fr. 17.10 μυρίνην (scanning ⏑⏑–) is correctly written by A at Ath. 4.132 C ~ unmetrical -υρρι- CE.

Μυρρίνη: character name in Men. *Georg*. 41, *Dys*. 709 (Μυρ]ρίνη B, suppl. ed. pr.), *Heros* 72, *Pk*. 402 (μυρρην[.]ν C: suppl. and corr. ed. pr.); name of a real-life *hetaira* (cf. Ath. 13.590 C) in Timocles fr. 27.3.

*παρρησία: Nicolaus fr. 1.11, 1.15.

Πυρρίας: character-name in *Dys*. 71, *Perinth*. 8 (Πυρ]ρίας suppl. Wilamowitz), *Sik*. 120, 125, 147.

Φερρέφαττα: Epicrates fr. 8.3 (introduced in a pseudo-Doric oath: φερεφ- L, φαρεφ- V at Ael. *NA* 12.10: corr. Meineke).

Χερρονησίτης: Ephippus fr. 3.5 (χερρο- A at Ath. 9.370 C and CE at Ath. 2.65 C, χερο- CE at Ath. 9.370 C).

It will be noticed that the above list, for the sake of completeness, includes also those cases where -ρρ- does not correspond to Ionic forms in -ρσ-, but appears in loanwords (e.g. ἀρραβών from Semitic) or in processes of assimilation that are common to all dialects. In my list such cases are marked with an asterisk (*).

σήμερον/τήμερον

σήμερον is Ionic and Koine, τήμερον Attic. Ptolemaic documentary papyri offer the spelling σήμερον, but papyri of New Comedy favour the Attic form, although some book fragments have σήμερον:[33]

[32] Notably with παραθαρρύνοντας so written in the same sentence.

[33] Cf. Kühner–Blass (1890–2: 2.306), LSJ (1940: s.v. σήμερον), Schwyzer (1939: 308, 319, 621), Mayser–Schmoll (1970: 127).

τήμερον: Men. *Dys*. 372, 424, 571, *Karch*. 45, *Sam*. 172, 570, fr. 881, fr. com. adesp. 1014.20 and 23 (τὴν/(?)τῆς τήμερον ending vv. 20 and 23, with ἡμέραν in v. 21: cf. Dem. 4.40 τῆς τήμερον ἡμέρας), probably 1105.126 (τήμ̣[ερον suppl. ed. pr.). At fr. com. adesp. 1012.4 τήμερ̣[ον is Schröder's tentative supplement. Cf. also Epinicus fr. 2.2.

σήμερον: at fr. com. adesp. 1001.13 the papyrus gives εντησημερον (corrected to ἐν τῇ τήμερον, however, by Bücheler and Kock, the more convincingly because the scribe here was a youth and probably quoting inaccurately from memory, cf. Arnott 2000: 473–4).

-σσ-/-ττ-

The use of -ττ- in place of Ionic's (and other dialects') -σσ- was as much a touchstone of correct Attic as was the use of -ρρ- discussed above, in prose from the time of Lysias, in comedy already from the fifth century BC. The papyri and book fragments of later Greek comedy generally reflect a practice that is perhaps best illustrated by Attic inscriptions from the fourth century BC right down to the Roman period, where the spelling with -ττ- is 'virtually universal' (Threatte 1980: 537) in all except a few words of non-Attic origin.[34] The manuscripts of all the passages in the (probably incomplete) list below have -ττ-, except where otherwise indicated:

ἀθάλαττος: Men. fr. 351.9 (-σσ- A at Ath. 4.132 E, corrected to -ττ- by Bentley).

ἀντιπράττω: Alexis fr. 266.8.

ἀντιτάττω: Men. fr. 10.2 (-ττ- all manuscripts of Stob. 4.2.3 ~ -σσ- *Comp. Men. et Phil*. 2.106 Jäkel).

ἀπαλλάττω: Diphilus fr. 74.1, 134.

ἀποσάττω: Philemon fr. 71.1.

ἁρμόττω: Men. fr. 317.1, fr. com. adesp. 1000.2. The non-Attic form, however, is ἁρμόζω.

[34] Cf. in general Kühner–Blass (1890–2: 1.152–3, 268 §5), Wackernagel (1907: 12–25 = 1953–79: 2.1043–56), Lademann (1915: 57–60, 122), Schwyzer (1939: 75, 81, 86, 115, 121, 231, 316–20), Mayser–Schmoll (1970: 196–8), Threatte (1980: 537–41). On ἀθάλαττος see also Bruhn (1910: 65), Durham (1913: 39), Klaus (1936: 9), on ἀττικουργής Bruhn (1910: 65), Durham (1913: 47), Klaus (1936: 32), on νεοττίον Durham (1913: 80), on περιπλάττω Durham (1913: 87), on περιττός Klaus (1936: 114), on φρυάττομαι Bruhn (1910: 25), Durham (1913: 101).

Ἀττική/Ἀττικός: Men. *Dys.* 1, 604.

ἀττικίζω: Posidippus fr. 30.2.

ἀττικουργής: Men. fr. 528.

βασίλισσα: so Philemon fr. 15.1 (*βασίλισσαις ἤ* A Ath. 13.595 C, corrected to *βασίλισσ' ἔσῃ* by Bentley). A Macedonian loan-word.

βδελύττομαι: Men. fr. 362.6.

βρύττος: fr. com. adesp. 296.

γλῶττα: *Kolax* fr. 1.5, fr. com. adesp. 457.2, 832; at fr. com. adesp. 710 the manuscripts (Plut. *Mor.* 51 DE) spell with -*σσ*-.

γλωττοδεψῶ: fr. com. adesp. 176.

διαφυλάττω: *Sik.* 359.

διᾴττω: fr. com. adesp. 548.

διττός: Men. fr. 888.2 (the ascription is doubtful).

δρυμάττω: fr. com. adesp. 782.

ἐκπλήττω: *Epit.* 127 (*ἐκπλήτ[τομαι*, suppl. Cobet).

ἐλαττῶ: Apollodorus fr. 7.3.

ἐλάττων: *Dys.* 679, *Kolax* fr. 2.4, *Phasma* 47 Arnott, Men. fr. 708.3, Philemon fr. 145.2, fr. com. adesp. 843, 909.9.

ἐπιγλωττῶμαι: fr. com. adesp. 762.

ἐπικαττύω: fr. com. adesp. 599.

ἐπιτάττω: *Asp.* 466 (-*ταττετε* B, corrected to -*τάττεται* by Austin), Men. fr. 219.6 (-*ττ*- MSS at Plut. *Mor.* 100 E ~ -*σσ*- MSS at 471 B), Philemon fr. 11.1.

ἥττων: *Pk.* 471 (×2), 722, *Sam.* 82, 397, fr. com. adesp. 1017.1, 1093.105, Philemon fr. 31.6, 108.5, fr. com. adesp. 78.3, 719.2.

θάλαττα: sometimes spelt in the manuscripts with -*ττ*- (Men. *Theoph.* 32, *Kith.* 46, *Leukadia* 2, Men. fr. 378.1, Philemon fr. 28.1), sometimes with -*σσ*- (Men. fr. 27 = A at Ath. 7.303 C, 598.3 = MSS of Plut. *Vit. Alex.* 17.6, Alexis fr. 214.1 = SMA at Stob. 4.17.2, Euphron fr. 10.2 = CE at Ath. 1.7d, fr. com. adesp. 206 = Eustath. on Hom. *Od.* 1472.4). The -*σσ*- readings are normally corrected to -*ττ*- by editors.

θᾶττον: Alexis fr. 205.2, Diphilus fr. 79.1.

Θεττάλη: Menander's title is spelt with -*ττ*- by (1) the citers of book fragments 170–5, (2) Steph. Byz. p. 311.1 Meineke and Schol. E to Ar. *Nub.* 749 in references to the play. Cf. Anaxandrides' title *Θετταλοί*, so spelt in the one citation from it (fr. 17, Antiatticist p. 106.10 Bekker).

ἴσσα (!): Men. fr. 233 (-*σσ*- Phot. *ι* 204 = *Suda ι* 605). Presumably an onomatopoeic formation, spelt also with -*σσ*- at

Plato Com. fr. 68 (Antiatticist p. 100.26 Bekker); cf. ἰσσαῖ at Herodas 3.93, and Headlam's note (1922: ad loc.).

καταγλωττισμός: fr. com. adesp. 761.

κρείττων: Men. *Dys.* 771 (κριττω[ν B, suppl. Bingen, Kassel), 811, 957, *Epit.* 329, 1068, *Theoph.* fr. 1.13 and 18, *Karch.* fr. 4, *Sam.* 575 (κριττων B), Men. fr. 713.2, 727 (-ττ- SMABr at Stob. 3.12.5 ~ -σσ- Macarius Chrys.), 787.1, 841.1, 843.1, fr. com. adesp. 1020.2 (-σσ- the papyrus, but 'si revera comici poetae est, κρεῖττον scripsit': Kassel–Austin 1995: 323, ad loc.), Alexis fr. 205.1, 265.3, Diodorus fr. 3.3, Diphilus fr. 93.1, Hegesippus fr. 2.5, Nicomachus fr. 1.17, 1.23, Philemon fr. 120.2, 171, Philonides fr. 2 (-ττ- Stob. 3.33.7 SM and *monost.* 409 Jäkel ~ -σσ- corp. Par.), Posidippus fr. 19.2. At fr. com. adesp. 1094.2 Siegmann's suggestion κ]ρεί⟨σ⟩σονας is uncertain. At Apollodorus fr. 6.2 κρεῖσσον is transmitted (Stob. 4.53.14 SA) but corrected to -ττ- by Meineke.

ματτύη(ς): Alexis fr. 208.2, Machon fr. 1.1, Philemon fr. 8.1, 11.2, 71.2, fr. com. adesp. 125.1.

μάττω: Men. *Dys.* 549.

μέλιττα: Apollodorus fr. 14.7, Epinicus fr. 1.7 (-σσ- ACE Ath. 10.432 B).

Μεσσηνία: Menander's title is spelt with -σσ- by (1) the citers of Men. fragments 229–33 (apart from Photius α 2129 at 229 and s.v. ψύλλα at 232, where the manuscripts give μεση-), (2) Demetrius *Eloc.* 153, and (3) the Mytilene mosaic, portraying Μεσσηνίας μέ(ρος) ε′. Menander clearly retained here the -σσ- spelling for a word denoting the title figure's non-Attic origin. Criton's homonymous title has the same spelling in the one fragment cited (2).

μεταπλάττω: Diphilus fr. 84.2.

νεοττιά: *Pk.* 528.

νεοττίον: Men. fr. 40.2 (νεοττόν all manuscripts of Phot. s.v. νεοττός and *Suda* ν 214, except νεοττῶν V of *Suda*: corrected to νεοττίον by Meineke).

νηττάριον: Men. fr. 652.

Ὀδυσσεύς: *Kolax* E229, with the -σσ- spelling retained for a non-Athenian hero.

παλίγγλωσσος: so fr. com. adesp. 762 (-σσ- all manuscripts of Poll. 2.109).

περιπλάττω: Men. fr. 809.2.

περιττός: Alexis fr. 261.1, Simylus fr. 2.2.

πιττοκοπῶ: Alexis fr. 266.1.

πλάττω: Men. fr. 110.2, 777.1, fr. com. adesp. 1047.1.

πολύγλωσσος: fr. com. adesp. 762 (all manuscripts, Poll. 2.109).

πράττω: Men. *Asp.* 188, 204, 373, *Georg.* 1 (πράττων written in G as last word in an iambic trimeter: see Gomme–Sandbach 1973 and Arnott 1979, ad loc.), 43, *Dis Ex.* 90 (*P. Oxy.* 4407, ×2: πρ]ἀττ[ων. ὅ] τι πράττῃς, suppl. Handley), *Dys.* 135, 272, 280, 736 (πρατ' B, corrected to πρατ τ' by ed. pr.), 746, 816, *Epit.* 574, 656, 1098, 1099, *Theoph.* fr. 1.8 (misprinted in the Loeb) and 16, *Kolax* B27, D223, *Mis.* fr. 5.2, *Pk.* 333, 508, *Sam.* 116, 220, 224, 299, 380, 392, 607, Men. fr. 11.3, 125.3, 224.1, 372.7, 602.3 (-σσ- in *P. Oxy.* 3433 and manuscripts of [Plut.] *Mor.* 103 c, corrected to -ττ- by Meineke, but just possibly an echo of tragic language),[35] 641.2, 717.1, 757, 845.7, fr. com. adesp. 1014.16, 1094.16 (πρατ τ[), 1096.65 (πραττο....[), 1103.23; cf. Alexis fr. 267.6, Apollodorus fr. 9.1, 13.8, Damoxenus fr. 3.8, Diphilus fr. 103.2, Philemon fr. 56.1, 137.1, fr. com. adesp. 894.2, 909.5. At Philemon fr. 59.1 (Stob. 4.19.22) and fr. com. adesp. 140.2 (Clem. Alex. *Strom.* 6.71.6) the manuscripts spell with -σσ-.

προσπατταλεύω: Men. fr. 508.1, Hegesippus fr. 1.25.

προστάττω: Men. fr. 176.7, fr. com. adesp. 1004.5.

ῥαβάττω: fr. com. adesp. 535.

συμπράττω: Men. fr. 766.4.

συναποκηρύττω: *Sam.* 509.

συντάττω: *Dys.* 175.

ταράττω: *Dys.* 820, *Sam.* 672, fr. com. adesp. 1063.6 and 52 (ταραττομ[). At *Epit.* 931 it is uncertain whether *P. Oxy.* 1236 reads συν ταραττεις or συνταραττεις; at fr. com. adesp. 1085.16 there is no means of knowing whether the papyrus should be supplemented simply with τα]ράττομαι or a compound of that verb.

τάττω: fr. com. adesp. 1061.4 (ταττω[).

τετταράκοντα: Men. *Asp.* 84, *Kolax* E242 (τεττερακον[τα *P. Oxy.* 2655, corr. and suppl. Turner).

τέτταρες: *Asp.* 351, *Dys.* 390, 402, *Epit.* 134, *Pk.* 343, *Sik.* 355 (τετταρας S, corrected to τετραετές by Lloyd-Jones), Men. fr. 40.1, 66.4 (Ath. 10.442 D: -ττ- A ~ -σσ- CE and Eustath. 1505.1), 151.3, 258.1, 877.7, fr. com. adesp. 1033.2 (τέτταρ[α]ς), Philemon fr. 111.1.

[35] So Körte (cf. Kassel–Austin ad loc.), but the rhythms hereabouts are comic, and neither style nor diction seems particularly tragic, even though the speaker claims to be speaking 'more like a tragedian' (τραγικώτερον), v. 8.

φρυάττομαι: Men. fr. 582.

φυλάττω: *Dys.* 81, 799, 960, *Kolax* D204, D211 (*φυ[λ]άττεται*), *Sam.* 302 (C: *φυλλά-* B), *Phasma* 45 Arnott, Men. fr. 90.3, 712.2, fr. com. adesp. 1082.8, 1084.23, 1085.31 and 32. At Men. *Epit.* 410 Croiset's supplement *φ̣[υλάττειν]* is exemplary.

στιφρός/στριφνός

Moeris (*σ* 10 Hansen) writes *στιφρόν, Ἀττικοί· στριφνόν, Ἕλληνες*; cf. the Oxyrhynchus glossary of *λέξεις Ἀττικαί* (*P. Oxy.* 1803), giving *στιφρόν, ὃ οἱ πολλοὶ στριφνόν*, and citing Men. book fragment 343 as evidence, although in its quotation the scribe corrupts *στιφράς* to *στεφρας*. Although the adjective is rare in later Greek comedy, the Attic form appears to prevail. Men. *Epit.* 385 has *στιφ[ρο]ς* in *P. Oxy.* 4022, but *στριφνος* in C; Crobylus fr. 7.1 has *στιφράν*, and Timocles fr. 24.3 the derivative *στιφρότης*.[36]

σώ(ι)ζω, ἔσω(ι)σα, σέσω(ι)σα, etc.

This verb and its compounds form their tenses from two different stems: *σῴζω* with an *iota*, and *σαόω* without. This led to considerable confusion among writers and scribes, and considerable variation in practice at different periods. For present paradigms in classical and early Hellenistic Athens *σῴζω* retained the *iota*, only to lose it from around 100 BC onwards. The approved spelling in the perfect active and perfect and aorist passive seems generally to be without the *iota*, although examples with it persist in papyri and elsewhere. For the aorist active in Athens both *ἔσωσα* and *ἔσῳσα* are found, although on inscriptions only the form with *iota* is attested right down to Roman times, when there was a switch to *ἔσωσα* without *iota*.[37]

Papyri of later comedy and book fragments generally reflect these facts; *σωιζω* is recorded in third-century BC papyri (S of Men. *Sik.*, fr. com. adesp. 1032, 1092), *σῴζω* in the manuscripts of book fragments, *σωζω* in later papyri; (-)*σωισ-* occurs twice in third-century BC papyri (S of Men. *Sik.*, fr. com. adesp. 1147), (-)*σωσ-* once (fr. com. adesp. 1093), while later papyri and manu-

[36] Cf. Durham (1913: 93), Bruhn (1910: 40), Klaus (1936: 131), Schwyzer (1939: 127).

[37] Cf. Kühner–Blass (1890–2: 2.544–5), Mayser (1938: 120, 150), Schwyzer (1939: 736, 752 n. 2, 785), Mayser–Schmoll (1970: 112), M. L. West (1990: xliv), Threatte (1996: 506–8, 528, 652).

scripts of book fragments lack the *iota*. Perfects active and passive and aorists passive have no *iota*, except once in S of Men. *Sik.*:

(1) (-)σωιζ-/(-)σωζ-,

(*a*) with *iota*: Men. *Sik.* 182, 370, 371, 372, Men. fr. 156.4, 188.1, 372.5 (Stob. 1.16.1a, σῳ̣ζον F ~ ζῶον P after correction), 665.2, fr. com. adesp. 1032.13, 1092.28 (σωιζ̣[*P. Hibeh* 181); cf. Alexis fr. 269.2, Philemon fr. 28.8, 106.5, Philemon iun. fr. 7.2, Philippides fr. 7.2, Sosipater fr. 1.13, fr. com. adesp. 26 (the play title]ασωιζομ[on didascalic inscription *IG* II^2 2323.194), 900.3;

(*b*) without *iota*: Men. *Epit.* 408, 418, 714, 907, 1090, *Heros* 48, *Kolax* B22, *Pk.* 171, *Sam.* 164, Men. fr. 68.2, 859; cf. Hipparchus fr. 2.4, Philemon fr. 18.

(2) (-)σωισ-/(-)σωσ-, mainly aorist active, but also future active and perfects middle/passive in the passages indicated,

(*a*) with *iota*: Men. *Sik.* 253, fr. com. adesp. 1147.38;

(*b*) without *iota*: Men. *Asp.* 16, *Dis Ex.* 13, *Dys.* 203, 378, *Epit.* 343, 397 (ἀ]π̣[ο]σῶσαι, suppl. Lefebvre), 1021, 1096, *Perinth.* 5 (διασώσαι̣[τ' suppl. van Herwerden), Men. fr. 64.9 (σέσωσθ'), 246.3 and 6 (σεσωσμένον and σεσῶσθαι: ms. A at Ath. 11.474 B), fr. com. adesp. 1007.28, 29 (σ]ώσουσιν) and 41, 1093.359 (third century BC!); cf. Apollodorus fr. 14.12 (*P. Berlin* 9772), Diphilus fr. 74.4, Eubulus fr. 26.1, Euphron fr. 4.2, Philemon fr. 178.4, Posidippus fr. 13.7, Timocles fr. 1.1. At Men. *Asp.* 15 B's σασαν is probably an error for σ⟨ώσ⟩ασαν (Austin).

(3) σέσωικ-/σέσωκ-,

(*a*) with *iota*: Men. *Sik.* 379;

(*b*) without *iota*: Men. *Asp.* 493 (σεσοωκως *P. Robinson* with ο crossed out), *Dys.* 726, *Epit.* 351, 1108; cf. Archedicus fr. 2.12.

In perfects middle and passive and aorists passive, before θ and μ all attested comic instances have ω, not ῳ/ωι.

υἱός/ὑός

From about 350 BC onwards in Athens the word was normally second declension and then spelt ὑός, but the earlier Attic spelling υἱός returned into favour at the time of the Roman empire. Hence Theognostus p. 49.31–2 Cramer, υἱός καὶ γυιός· ταῦτα δὲ Ἀττικοὶ ἄνευ τοῦ ι γράφουσιν; cf. [Herodian] 1.112.6–7, 2.281.29–30 Lentz.[38] These facts persuaded Rutherford (1881: 141–3) to

[38] Kühner–Blass (1890–2: 1.506–8), Lademann (1915: 37–40, 113–14), Mayser

suggest that forms without the *iota* should be generally restored in Attic prose and comedy, at least when the first syllable need not be scanned long. Yet the comic papyri throw up a few mavericks, even though they more commonly spell the word without an *iota*, while the manuscripts of book fragments always spell υἱός:

ὑός: Men. *Asp.* 134 (BF), 335, *Dys.* 16, 22, 88, 731, *Kolax* A3, *Pk.* 1025, *Sam.* 135, 347 (*P. Bingen* 23 ~ υι- BC), 352 and 387 B (υι- C), 510, 702, *Sik.* 129, *Fab. Inc.* 1.45, fr. com. adesp. 1064.28.

υἱός: Men. *Georg.* 58, *Sam.* 347 (BC: υ- *P. Bingen* 23; see Gonis 2000: 127), 352 and 387 C (υ- B), 610, fr. com. adesp. 52.1 and 2 (*P. Sorbonne* 72), 1063.29, 1129.38.

All the book fragments of Menander (×9) and later comic poets (at least ×7) have υἱ-; all these (and all the papyri) decline the noun as second declension, except Alexis fr. 77.1 (υἱεῖς ms. A at Ath. 3.119F: see Kassel–Austin 1991: 61, ad loc.). The prose hypothesis of Menander's *Hiereia* (Kassel–Austin 1998: 137–9; Arnott 2000: 618–25) varies between υι- (ll. 51, 68, 90) and υ- (62, 73).

φῄς or φής?

The 2nd person singular of φημί is commonly spelt φῄς in both the manuscripts of Attic writers and in non-literary papyri of the third century BC. This irrational intrusion of an *iota* into the 2nd person singular of the present indicative active of a -μι verb elicited a divided response from ancient grammarians; thus *Et. Mag.* 791.49 (cf. [Herodian] 2.419.11–15 Lentz) recognized the irregularity but noted its general acceptance in the tradition, while Apollonius (according to the passage of [Herodian] already cited = Apollonius II p. VI.8–10 Uhlig) rejected it.[39] Comic papyri occasionally, but book fragments often, spell φῄς with the *iota*:

φῄς (φῆις): Men. *Dys.* 360, 456, 563 (all B); fr. com. adesp. 1032.21 (third century BC), 1053.7; cf. Amphis fr. 15.1, Antiphanes fr. 69.12, 200.1 (A at Ath. 6.257D ~ CE), Ephippus fr. 11.3 (A at Ath. 10.430F ~ CE), Heniochus fr. 4.3, Philemon fr. 45.4, Sosipater fr. 1.12.

(1938: 20–1), LSJ (1940: s.v. υἱός), Schwyzer (1939: 199, 348, 573–4), Threatte (1980: 338–42; 1996: 220–2, 735).

[39] Kühner–Blass (1890–2: 1.210–12), Mayser (1938: 125–6), LSJ (1940: s.v. φημί), Schwyzer (1939: 674–5).

φής: Men. *Asp.* 82, 270, *Dis Ex.* 64 (φ]ης *P. Oxy.* 4407), *Dys.* 50 (φησ' B), *Epit.* 471, 950, *Mis.* 436, 660, 677, 791, *Pk.* 325, 493, *Sam.* 480, 485, 524, 545, 557, *Fab. Inc.* 1.31, fr. com. adesp. 1000.20; cf. Antiphanes fr. 200.1 (CE), Ephippus fr. 11.3 (CE).

The above evidence leaves it uncertain whether we should supplement with φή[ις (Siegmann) or with φή[ς at line end in fr. com. adesp. 1093.267 (third century BC).

This orthographical survey deliberately ignores several areas of dispute that merit detailed discussion: e.g. the frequent omission of the *iota* in ποιῶ, especially before ει and η; the variation between -ει and -η in the 2nd person singular middle and passive of -ω verbs; the use of paragogic *nu* before consonants at the caesura; and the variation between -το and -τον in the neuter nominative and accusative singular of a series of pronouns (ὁ αὐτός, τηλικοῦτος, τοιοῦτος, τοσοῦτος). Their omission here is due mainly to limitations of space in this volume; some of these have been treated elsewhere (cf. Arnott 2001*a* and 2001*b*), and it is hoped that treatments of the others will follow.

10

Speech within Speech in Menander

RENÉ NÜNLIST

I. DEFINITION

Speech within speech, a regular literary device in Greek epic and dramatic poetry, occurs in Menander's comedies with great frequency and has many different functions. In order to explain which type of speeches falls within the scope of the present article, it may be useful to start with a definition. 'Speech within speech' (or, alternatively, 'quoted speech') means that a character reports a person's speech by actually quoting his or her words, for example:

(1) ὡς δ' ἐπαύσατο
κλᾶον, πρὸς αὑτήν φησιν "ὦ τάλαιν' ἐγώ,
πρῴην τοιοῦτον ὄντα Μοσχίων' ἐγὼ
αὐτὸν ἐτιθηνούμην ἀγαπῶσα . . ."[1]

When it [the baby] stopped crying, she [the nurse] said to herself 'Dear me, it's not so long ago that I nursed Moschion himself, and loved him just like you . . .' (Men. *Sam.* 244–7).

The character Demeas from Menander's play *Samia* quotes what the nurse said. This is to say—with respect to narrative texts—that a narrator who quotes the words of his characters (e.g. Homer quoting Achilles) does not fulfil the conditions of the definition.[2]

[1] Conventions of presentation: (*a*) All cited examples come from the speech of a character. In order to keep typographical matters simple, quotation marks in the Greek text are put *around the speech within speech only*. (*b*) Text examples are presented as a reading text, i.e. without app. crit., sublinear dots, etc. For details the reader is referred to the critical editions. (*c*) Unless attributed explicitly, translations are taken from the Loeb editions.

[2] It has been argued by participants of the Corpus Christi Classical Seminar that orally performed poetry like the Homeric epics are speech, and that for that reason

Equally excluded are passages where a character mentions another's speech without actually quoting (part of) it verbatim, i.e. reported speech. Furthermore, this paper does not treat quotations of written sources, literary quotations, or proverbs.[3]

II. SPEECH WITHIN SPEECH IN EARLY AND CLASSICAL GREEK POETRY

Speech (within speech) is a universal literary device which is not restricted to any specific genre, period, or literary tradition. Already the first Greek poet whose texts have been transmitted to posterity shows a remarkable fondness for speech in general and for quoted speech specifically (see Table 10.1). Homer's figures

TABLE 10.1. *Speeches in the Homeric epics*[a]

	Total number of speeches	% of entire text	number of quoted speeches	total number of lines	average length
Iliad	678	45	20	71	3.6
Odyssey[b]	557	66	118 (31)	1060 (266)	8.9 (8.6)

[a] The figures in this table are extracted from a computer data base which incorporates the lists of Fingerle (1939).
[b] Figures in brackets designate the *Odyssey* without books 9–12 (ἀπόλογοι).

for quoted speech differ considerably between the *Iliad* and the *Odyssey*. This is largely due to the ἀπόλογοι, where Odysseus virtually takes over the narrating function from the narrator. No fewer than 87 of the *Odyssey*'s 118 quoted speeches come from

all the speeches of the *Iliad* and the *Odyssey* fall under 'speech within speech'. But the narrator who quotes the speech of his characters belongs to a different category, for he not only quotes, but (as mouthpiece of the implied author) actually generates his characters' speeches. Therefore, he is to be situated on a different narrative level.

[3] Written sources (inscriptions, letters, etc.): e.g. Aesch. *Sept.* 434, 647–8; literary quotations: e.g. Men. *Asp.* 407 ff.; proverbs: e.g. Men. *Asp.* 372–3.

books 9–12. But the remaining 31 still outdo the *Iliad*'s 20 quoted speeches, and on average they are substantially longer.[4]

Dry as these figures may appear at first, they nevertheless prove that speech within speech is already a regular and well-established feature in the Homeric epics. More specifically, two different types can be discerned from a narratological point of view: (i) factual quoted speech and (ii) imagined quoted speech.

Factual quoted speeches are those that the speaker knows were actually spoken in the past, as when Menelaos reports his encounter with Proteus:

> (2) ἀλλ᾽ ὅτε δή ῥ᾽ ἀνίαζ᾽ ὁ γέρων ὀλοφώϊα εἰδώς,
> καὶ τότε δή μ᾽ ἐπέεσσιν ἀνειρόμενος προσέειπε·
> "τίς νύ τοι, Ἀτρέος υἱέ, θεῶν συμφράσσατο βουλάς,
> ὄφρα μ᾽ ἕλοις ἀέκοντα λοχησάμενος; τέο σε χρή;"
> ὣς ἔφατ᾽, . . .

But when the Old Man versed in devious ways grew weary of all this, he spoke to me in words and questioned me: 'Which of the gods now, son of Atreus, has been advising you to capture me from ambush against my will. What do you want?' So he spoke . . . (*Od.* 4.460–4, transl. Lattimore)

Imagined quoted speeches are those which the speaker imagines will be spoken in the future (or, exceptionally, have been spoken in the past),[5] as when Diomedes opposes Nestor's advice to retreat:

> (3) Ἕκτωρ γάρ ποτε φήσει ἐνὶ Τρώεσσ᾽ ἀγορεύων,
> "Τυδεΐδης ὑπ᾽ ἐμεῖο φοβεόμενος ἵκετο νῆας."
> ὥς ποτ᾽ ἀπειλήσει· τότε μοι χάνοι εὐρεῖα χθών.

For some day Hektor will say openly before the Trojans: 'The son of Tydeus, running before me, fled to his vessels.' So he will vaunt; and then let the wide earth open beneath me. (*Il.* 8.148–50, transl. Lattimore)

The two texts nicely illustrate the difference and therefore the validity of the distinction: Ex. (3) tells the reader much more

[4] The longest quoted speeches are respectively 74 lines in the ἀπόλογοι (*Od.* 12.37–110), 46 lines in the rest of the *Odyssey* (*Od.* 4.492–537), and 11 lines in the *Iliad* (2.60–70).

[5] The decisive factor for the distinction between 'factual' and 'imagined' is whether the speaker presents it as such: thus in *Il.* 6.164–5 Glaukos cannot actually know what Anteia said to Proitos, but he nevertheless presents it as a factual quoted speech.

about the quoting speaker (Diomedes) than about the character quoted (Hektor), whereas ex. (2) is much more neutral in this respect. Imagined speech within speech functions primarily as a characterization of the quoting speaker.[6]

A special case of speech within speech is quoted dialogue. In Homeric poetry, this literary device occurs in the *Odyssey* only.[7] Quoted dialogue in Homer never involves more than two speakers.[8] In most cases one of the two is identical with the speaker of the embedding speech.[9]

The treatment of speeches in the Homeric epics is also important for a formal analysis, because epic poetry sets a rather rigid model of how to indicate the boundaries of speech and quoted speech. The most important features of this model are:

(*a*) Homeric speeches are framed by speech formulae, an introductory formula at the beginning and a capping formula at the end.[10] In oral poetry, introductory and capping formulae have the function of quotation marks in a printed text and are therefore vital to a proper understanding of the orally performed text. Exceptions are rare.[11] The rule of introducing and capping speeches also holds for quoted speeches (see exx. 2 and 3 above).[12]

[6] The fact that these speeches reflect more on the imagining speaker is the main reason why the term 'imagined' is to be preferred over 'hypothetical' (so e.g. Schneider 1996: 9–10, who also underestimates the difference between the two types). Imagined quoted speech is more frequent in the *Iliad*: 10 cases out of 20, no less than 5 of which are spoken by Hektor (6.460–1, 6.479, 7.89–90, 7.301–2, 22.107).

[7] Most but not all instances come from the ἀπόλογοι, e.g. *Od*. 4.370–425, 4.461–571.

[8] A borderline case is *Od*. 10.63–76, where Odysseus quotes Aiolos' family (collectively), himself and Aiolos alone.

[9] A dialogue of the type 'I said—He/She said—I said' is easier to follow, but cf. *Od*. 9.402–13, 15.424–54.

[10] Many of these formulae provide excellent material to prove Parry's point (see e.g. M. W. Edwards 1970).

[11] Perhaps the most surprising exception is the very first speech of the *Iliad* (1.17–21) which has neither. At first sight one could argue that λίσσετο (1.15) has the function of a speech introduction, but λίσσομαι in this function usually is a participle and is accompanied by a finite *verbum dicendi* (*Lexikon des frühgriechischen Epos*, s.v., B 1a; cf. also 1.374 where no speech follows). And l. 22 does not even pretend to contain a capping formula, which is a little less exceptional than a missing introduction (Führer 1967: 41).—Absent or problematic introductory formulae led to notorious Homeric ζητήματα, e.g. *Il*. 15.346–7 (cf. Janko 1992: ad loc.). Cf. also schol. A on *Il*. 9.224.

[12] *Il*. 7.299–303 is exceptional because the quoted speech ends together with the embedding speech without its own capping formula.

(*b*) Homeric speeches (including quoted speeches) do not begin or end in the middle of the line. Speech boundaries coincide with verse boundaries. Of 1,235 speeches and 138 quoted speeches only three are in breach of this stichic principle.[13]

This epic formalism is softened and modified in post-Homeric poetry, but the process is comparatively slow.[14] As for quoted speeches specifically, they are important again in fifth-century drama.[15]

The sheer number of quoted speeches in tragedy necessitates that one draws just a few general conclusions from the material, which is again presented in the form of a table (Table 10.2).[16]

TABLE 10.2. *Quoted speeches in tragedy*

	Total	in messenger speeches	in other non-lyric	in lyric	quoted dialogue
Aeschylus[a]	18	3	6[a]	9	0
Sophocles	24	9	15	0	3 (8)[b]
Euripides	139	84	34	21	10 (22)

[a] The figures include one quoted speech from *PV*; no opinion is thereby expressed on the play's authenticity.
[b] Read: 3 quoted dialogues with a total of 8 speeches.

The most obvious observation is the prominence of quoted speech in Euripides which holds even if one takes into account the fact that the total of his plays is more than double that of the other

[13] They all come from the *Iliad*, once at the beginning of a 'normal' speech (23.855), once at the end of a factual quoted speech (2.70; cf. also 15.82, which strictly speaking is not a speech) and once at the beginning of an imagined quoted speech (6.479). The first exception is well known, whereas the two others are much less commented on, probably because they come from quoted speeches 'only'.

[14] For details see Führer (1967). An important step in this process is the absence of a capping/transitional formula in the dialogue of Hipponax fr. 25 West (= 35 Degani). Sophocles, on the other hand, caps all his quoted speeches.

[15] Speech within speech as defined above is absent from Hesiod and all lyric poetry (in its broad sense): 'In direkte Rede eingeschaltete *direkte* Rede läßt sich . . . in der Lyrik . . . nicht belegen' (Führer 1967: 95). The 'Homeric hymns' contain one certain instance, *h.Merc.* 363–4, where the quoted speech ends together with the embedding speech (cf. n. 12). A possible instance is the difficult and controversial passage *h.Ven.* 284–5.

[16] This survey excludes the fragments for practical reasons and the *Rhesos* because of its doubtful authenticity and date. The *Cyclops* (not in the table) contains one quoted dialogue with two speeches (ll. 413–19).

two. He also has a strong tendency to make messengers quote other characters, whereas in Aeschylus and Sophocles a majority of quoted speeches comes from other parts of the play. This, of course, has to do with Euripides' general fondness for messenger speeches (de Jong 1991). Another development can be observed in the number of quoted dialogues (10 in Euripides, consisting of 22 speeches in total) which are absent from Aeschylus. Most of Euripides' quoted dialogues come from messenger speeches.[17] Sophocles' three quoted dialogues cannot be explained as being due to Euripidean influence because two of them come from the early *Ajax*. Unlike the named characters who quote dialogues (cf. above on Homer), most anonymous messengers do not themselves take a speaking part in the quoted dialogue.[18] As a further development, the 'Homeric' restriction to two speakers in quoted dialogue is once ignored by Sophocles.[19]

Aeschylus, who alone does not provide a quoted dialogue, sides with Euripides in incorporating quoted speeches also in lyric passages, a feature which is absent from Sophocles.[20] Aeschylus and Euripides both show a tendency to use quoted speech in those lyric passages which deal with events that happened before the opening of the play (in narratological terms: in external analepsis).[21] Concerning the distribution of quoted speeches over external and internal analepsis, Aeschylus favours the former, Sophocles' distribution is more or less even, whereas Euripides clearly prefers quoted speech in internal analepsis.[22] This again goes together with Euripides' favouring of messenger speeches,

[17] 7 out of 10. In Sophocles only 1 out of 3 quoted dialogues comes from a 'real' messenger speech (*Aj.* 764 ff.), but Tekmessa's report to the chorus resembles one (*Aj.* 288 ff.). The former passage in any case contradicts de Jong, who states that 'dialogues [are] a technique not found in Aeschylean or Sophoclean messenger-speeches' (1991: 132).

[18] Contrast (apart from the Homeric examples) e.g. Soph. *Aj.* 288 ff. (speaker Tekmessa) with 764 ff. (messenger) or Eur. *Hec.* 531 ff. (Talthybios) with *El.* 779 ff. (messenger). An exception is Eur. *Or.* 874 ff. (messenger quoting himself), a borderline case is Eur. *IT* 1358 ff. (messenger quotes what 'people' said).

[19] Soph. *Phil.* 363 ff. A messenger may end up quoting more than two characters in his report (e.g. Eur. *HF* 922 ff.), but that is not the same phenomenon.

[20] Führer (1967: 163). Sophocles is also the author of the single play that does not contain speech within speech: *Oedipus Rex*.

[21] External analepsis is a back reference to events that happened before the beginning of the main story/the play, internal analepsis to events that happened during the main story/the play (Genette 1980: 48–67 = 1972: 90–105).

[22] The figures are (external/internal analepsis): Aesch. 8/3, Soph. 10/11, Eur. 28/93.

which often contain a report of off-stage (or backstage) actions which have happened during the play. As for the distinction between factual and imagined quoted speech, all three tragedians prefer the former, Aeschylus much less so than Sophocles and Euripides.[23]

Before looking at the specific formalism of how speech within speech is demarcated, it may be useful to give a sketch of quoted speech in Aristophanes. In quantitative terms, he resembles his favourite target Euripides (the 11 extant plays contain 112 quoted speeches, the fragments 4), and he is equally fond of quoted dialogues (12, with a total of 27 speeches).[24] Aristophanes, too, toys with the boundaries of speech within speech (see below, exx. 13 and 14). However, there are also substantial differences between the two poets. Factual quoted speeches are much less important in Aristophanes, who clearly prefers imagined and above all generalizing quoted speeches (regularly spoken by unnamed characters), as when Bdelykleon illustrates the sudden hysteria about 'tyranny':

(4) ἢν μὲν ὠνῆταί τις ὀρφώς, μεμβράδας δὲ μὴ 'θέλῃ,
εὐθέως εἴρηχ' ὁ πωλῶν πλησίον τὰς μεμβράδας·
"οὗτος ὀψωνεῖν ἔοιχ' ἅνθρωπος ἐπὶ τυραννίδι."
ἢν δὲ γήτειον προσαιτῇ ταῖς ἀφύαις ἥδυσμά τι,
ἡ λαχανόπωλις παραβλέψασά φησιν θἀτέρῳ·
"εἰπέ μοι, γήτειον αἰτεῖς; πότερον ἐπὶ τυραννίδι;
ἢ νομίζεις τὰς Ἀθήνας σοὶ φέρειν ἡδύσματα;"

If someone buys perch and doesn't want sprats, straight away the man selling sprats nearby says: 'This man seems to be buying fish like a would-be dictator.' Or if he asks for a free onion to season his sardines a bit, the woman selling vegetables gives him a sidelong glance with one eye and says: 'Tell me, are you asking for an onion because you hope to be a dictator? Or do you think Athens owes you a tribute of seasoning?' (Ar. *Vesp*. 493–9, transl. Sommerstein).[25]

The connection of such quoted speeches to the main story (plot, characters, time structure) is often rather loose, whereas

[23] The figures are (factual/imagined quoted speeches): Aesch. 11/7, Soph. 21/3, Eur. 120/19 (1.5:1, 7:1, 6:1).

[24] These figures are roughly the same as those which can be derived from Bers's tables (1997: 120–8). A few points of disagreement are noted in the footnotes.

[25] This type of quoted market conversation remains popular in the jokes about expensive fishmongers: Alexis fr. 16, Diphilus fr. 67, cf. also Amphis fr. 30.

Euripides' factual speeches within speech are easier to pin down in this respect. A possible explanation for this difference is Aristophanes' virtual neglect of the unity of place (as it will later be called). As a consequence, unlike Euripides he does not frequently bring on stage characters who report what has happened elsewhere.[26] Another explanation may be found in the subject-matter of the plays themselves. In order to discuss the problems of 'today', tragedy places its actions in a mythical past, a procedure in many respects (e.g. plots with named and known characters etc.) more clearcut and straightforward than Aristophanes' 'present day' plots, which are now 'provincial' (in the sense of 'strictly Athenian'), now fantastic, now utopian, now self-reflecting.[27] This is the world where political enemies are ridiculed in different 'masks', where triremes can hold a conversation, where utopian dreams are dreamt, where the comments of the audience are anticipated, etc.[28]

As for the demarcation of speech within speech, the formalism becomes less rigid in post-Homeric poetry. On the basis of Aristophanes' comedies, Victor Bers (1997: 116–17) has developed a set of eight possible types of signals which can be extended to all dramatic poetry. It goes without saying that a single passage can make use of several of these types, which then reinforce each other.[29]

The first four types lie outside the quoted speech and belong to the speaker himself. For practical purposes they will be called 'external demarcation signals' in this paper.

[26] Only 15 of his 116 quoted speeches are from reports of off-stage action (internal analepsis), which make for 93 of Euripides'.

[27] It certainly makes a difference whether a character's name is Orestes or Pisthetairos, independent of the (highly disputed) question of the extent to which the tragic plots were known to the audience. Despite the recent emphasis on metatheatrical tragedies, comedy no doubt plays more openly with theatrical conventions (e.g. by breaking the dramatic illusion).

[28] Politics: *Eq.* 50–2, 67–8, *Vesp.* 556–7, *Pax* 211–19; triremes: *Eq.* 1300–15; dreams: *Av.* 1442–3, *Eccl.* 693–709; audience: *Pax* 44–8.

[29] That demarcation is mainly a problem for the reader is equally evident. In performance, speech within speech is indicated by delivery. Quintilian's notorious criticism (11.3.91 = Men. fr. 355: *cum mihi comoedi quoque pessime facere uideantur, quod, etiam si iuuenem agant, cum tamen in expositione aut senis sermo, ut in Hydriae prologo, aut mulieris, ut in Georgo, incidit, tremula uel effeminata uoce pronuntiant*) is a comparatively late source for what must have been common practice at all times. As for Quintilian's position, it is conceivable that he does not criticize the technique itself, but exaggerations in imitation, notably of old people (*tremula uel effeminata uoce*).

(i) Introduction by explicit 'quotatives'.[30]

(5) ἓν τοῦτο δ' <u>εἴρει</u>· "τὴν ἐμαυτοῦ σ' ἀξιῶ
ἥκων ἀπολυτροῦν . . ."

He's harping on this one theme: 'I'm here demanding that you release my daughter . . .' (Men. *Mis.* 297–8)

(ii) Back reference by such verbs.

(6) ἐν ὅσῳ δ' "ἀλλά σ' ὁ Ποσειδῶν . . ." <u>λέγων</u>
κατέμυσα, . . .

While I shut my eyes and said 'Poseidon blast you,' . . . (Men. *Dys.* 112–13)

(iii) Forward and backward reference by interrupting 'quotative'.

(7) "ἥκω τι" <u>φημί</u> "πρός σε, πάτερ, ἰδεῖν τί σε . . ."

'I've come', I said,[31] 'on business, to see you, sir, . . .' (Men. *Dys.* 107)[32]

(iv) The use of demonstrative pronouns like τάδε.

(8) καὶ στᾶσ' ἐπ' ἄκρου χώματος λέξον <u>τάδε</u>·
"Ἑλένη σ' ἀδελφὴ ταῖσδε δωρεῖται χοαῖς . . ."

Then stand on top of the mound and say, 'Helen your sister presents you with these libations . . .' (Eur. *Or.* 116–17, transl. West)[33]

Three types of signal form part of the quoted speech itself (in the following 'internal demarcation signals'):

(v) A vocative, or words functioning as a vocative.

(9) καὶ ταῦτα δὴ τὰ κοινὰ "<u>φίλτατον τέκνον</u>" | εἰποῦσα

and said the usual things, 'My darling baby' (Men. *Sam.* 242–3)

(vi) The transition is indicated by a pronoun or the personal ending of a verb.

[30] By 'quotatives' Bers means *verba dicendi* (1997: 6 with n. 10).

[31] On the historic present see below, p. 237.

[32] This type is exceptional in tragedy: Eur. *HF* 988, *Tro.* 1182. In Menander such intercalated quotatives need not stand in the first sentence of a longer quoted speech, e.g. *Pk.* 322. On the basis of the 'late' φήσ' Lamagna (1998: 296 n. 25) unnecessarily introduces a change of speaker in 321, overlooking parallels like *Epit.* 267.

[33] This type cannot exactly be illustrated from Menander. The closest parallel is ταῦτα δὴ τὰ κοινά in ex. (9).

(10) ἐκάθαιρέ μ' αὐτῇ, "σοὶ δὲ κἀμοὶ πρᾶγμα τί ἐστιν;" λέγων . . .

and flogged me with it, said 'What dealings do we have?' (Men. *Dys.* 114–15)[34]

(vii) The speaker quotes a character whose linguistic characteristics differ from his/her own (gender-related, dialect, etc.).[35]

(11) πρὸς αὑτήν φησιν "ὦ τάλαιν' ἐγώ, . . ."

She says to herself 'Dear me . . .' (Men. *Sam.* 245, the speaker is a man, the invocation is used by women only)

Bers' eighth signal lies at the border between 'inside' and 'outside' the quoted speech.

(viii) The coincidence with metrical boundaries.

(12) αἳ δ' ἐβόων ἅμα
"ἄλευρ', ὕδωρ, ἔλαιον ἀπόδος, ἄνθρακας."
καὐτὸς διδοὺς . . .

The women at the same time yelled 'Let's have flour—water—oil—charcoal!' I gave them . . . (Men. *Sam.* 226–8)[36]

All these demarcation signals (except for type iii) are already present in Homer, the difference being that type (i) is compulsory and type (ii) almost so. On the other hand, there is a clear tendency from the last third of the fifth century on to avoid the evident signals (i)–(iv) and to favour less obtrusive signals. This holds especially for the comic poets.[37]

The following passage is a good illustration for the decreasing formalism. It also justifies two additions to Bers's list.

[34] The word-order with introductory σοί, deferred interrogative τί, and postponed quotative (type ii) is impossible to render in English.

[35] The description is slightly adapted from Bers's, which includes gender only. For dialect cf. e.g. Ar. *Pax* 47–8, 214, fr. 556. A special case is Alcibiades' speech defect: Ar. *Vesp.* 45.

[36] The few instances in post-classical poetry—(12) is exceptional—seem to indicate that the signal has mostly lost its function, but Sophocles, for one, appears to have felt strongly about it: none of his 24 quoted speeches ends in the middle of the line. And in his quoted dialogues the transitional speech formula covers at least one line.

[37] One indication for this tendency is the gliding transition from reported speech to quoted speech (e.g. Ar. *Eq.* 667–8, *Lys.* 519–20), which is not found in tragedy. Cf. also the transition from quoted to reported speech (e.g. Ar. *Eq.* 674, *Vesp.* 572–3). The same device may also be used to incorporate a dialogue when only one of the two speakers is actually quoted (Ar. *Nub.* 1137–41, Men. *Pk.* 318–23).

(13) χὠ μὲν σκυθράζει, δεσπότης δ' ἀνιστορεῖ·
"Τί χρῆμ' ἀθυμεῖς;" "Ὦ ξέν', ὀρρωδῶ τινα
δόλον θυραῖον. ἔστι δ' ἔχθιστος βροτῶν
Ἀγαμέμνονος παῖς πολέμιός τ' ἐμοῖς δόμοις."
ὁ δ' εἶπε· "Φυγάδος δῆτα δειμαίνεις δόλον . . ."

Aegisthus scowled, and my master [the unrecognized Orestes] asked him: 'Why are you downcast?' 'Stranger', he said,[38] 'I fear deceit from abroad. The son of Agamemnon is my bitterest personal enemy and is a foe to my house.' But Orestes said: 'Do you really fear trickery of an exile . . .' (Eur. *El.* 830–4)

To be sure, the change of speaker in the middle of l. 831 can be explained in terms of type (v), the vocative, but the illocutionary force of the question, namely to elicit an answer, is at least as important. Similarly in l. 834, εἶπε is of course a signal of type (i), but the change of speaker is already suggested by ὁ δέ. These two additions to Bers's list are necessary because in a number of passages the speaker relies respectively on the illocutionary force or the anaphoric pronoun (*vel sim.*) alone:

(14) ἦν δέ μοι φίλος,
ὅσπερ με διεκόρησεν οὖσαν ἑπτέτιν.
οὗτος πόθῳ μου 'κνυεν ἐλθὼν τὴν θύραν·
κᾆτ' εὐθὺς ἔγνων· εἶτα καταβαίνω λάθρᾳ.
ὁ δ' ἀνὴρ ἐρωτᾷ· "Ποῖ σὺ καταβαίνεις;" "Ὅποι;
στρόφος μ' ἔχει τὴν γαστέρ', ὦνερ, κὠδύνη·
εἰς τὸν κοπρῶν' οὖν ἔρχομαι." "Βάδιζέ νυν."

Now I had this friend, who had devirginated me when I was seven years old. He was longing for me, and he came and started scratching on the door. Then I realized at once who it was, and then I start quietly going downstairs. My husband asks: 'Where are you off downstairs to?' 'Where to?' I say [added by translator] 'I've got a griping and pain in my tummy, husband, so I'm going to the bog.' 'Go on, then.' (Ar. *Thesm.* 479–85, transl. Sommerstein).[39]

Add therefore to the list above:

(iv*a*) Anaphoric or personal pronouns, nouns, or names, that signal a change of the grammatical subject (cf. type iv above),

[38] Translators understandably tend to avoid obscurity in passages like this by adding quotatives and personal names which do not figure in the text.

[39] Cf. also Ar. *Eq.* 1300–15 (Bers 1997: 121 fails to indicate the dialogic structure) and *Pax* 1142–8 (taken as a single speech by Bers 1997: 124), in lyric poetry also fr. adesp. 935.19 *PMG*.

most often in connection with an adversative or connective particle like δέ.[40]

(via) Speech acts with a special illocutionary force, notably questions (provoking a reply), exclamations, and oaths.[41]

Type (iva) need not introduce an actual reply, it can simply indicate the end of the quoted speech (Eur. *Med.* 1156, *Hipp.* 1243, etc.), a subject on which Bers says surprisingly little. The following types of capping formulae are to be found in dramatic texts:

(i′) Back reference by 'quotatives' (= type ii above).[42]

(iv′) Back reference by demonstrative pronouns like *τοιαῦτα, τοιάδε, τοσαῦτα*, etc. (cf. type iv above).

(15) "σὺ δ' εἶ πατ]ὴρ ⟨καὶ⟩ κύριος." ταυτὶ λέγει.

'You are her father and her guardian.' All this he said. (Men. *Mis.* 294)

(iva′) Anaphoric or personal pronouns etc. resulting in a change of the grammatical subject (see above, iva).

(via′) Speech acts with a special illocutionary force (n. 41).

In many cases, however, the text does not provide an explicit capping formula. The transition from quoted speech to embedding speech is not advertised in the text. Nevertheless, the imperceptibility of the transition is sometimes lessened by the following factors: The speaker leads back to the embedding speech by using a particle (connective like *καί* or adversative like *ἀλλά*, e.g. Ar. *Nub.* 73). The quoted speech is a complete sentence (especially in connection with metrical boundaries), notably a question (cf. type via′). Finally, the quoted speech may simply end together with the embedding speech.[43]

Because of the uneven fates of their literary production, a

[40] Occasionally, this type can indicate change of addressee and therefore change of speaker (Eur. *Phoen.* 1252, though not in a quoted dialogue).

[41] A question like *ποῖ σὺ καταβαίνεις;* in (14) well illustrates the potentially double function of type (via): it identifies itself as a quoted speech and at the same time prepares for a reply by a second quoted speaker, thereby indicating its own end (cf. type via′ below).

[42] Occasionally, the quotative can be replaced by a verb of perception whose grammatical subject is the addressee of the quoted speech (e.g. Eur. *El.* 783, *Phoen.* 1148).

[43] e.g. ex. (4). An extreme example is Ar. *Eccl.* 404, where Chremes' quotation of Neokleides' question is followed in mid-line by Blepyros' quotation of what he would have said in answer.

comparison of the other poets of Old Comedy with Aristophanes is unlikely to lead to far-reaching conclusions. All one can say with certainty is that, not surprisingly, the other poets make their characters quote speeches too,[44] and that there is a similar tendency to toy with the boundaries of quoted speech. A striking example of a quoted dialogue without demarcation signal is Crates fr. 16 K.–A., a description of the good old days when dishes prepared and cooked themselves (a *topos*, for parallels see Kassel–Austin ad loc.). A whole list of quoted instructions is followed by:

> (16) "ἰχθὺ βάδιζ'." "ἀλλ' οὐδέπω 'πὶ θάτερ' ὀπτός εἰμί."
> "οὔκουν μεταστρέψας σεαυτὸν ἁλὶ πάσεις ἀλείφων;"

'Get moving, fish!' 'But I'm not done yet on the other side.' 'Would you please turn then and season yourself with salt!' (Crates fr. 16.9–10 K.–A.)[45]

The fish's witty reply comes all the more unexpectedly because several dishes and utensils have already been instructed to prepare themselves without a reaction on their part (ll. 5–8). In addition, the passage well illustrates that fifth-century poets had full confidence in the performing abilities of their actors.[46]

Between the end of Euripides' and Aristophanes' careers and the beginning of Menander's, there is a gap of roughly 80 and 60 years respectively. It is impossible to say in detail what happened to speech within speech because the evidence is too scanty. The tragic fragments hardly contain a quoted speech at all, with the curious exception of a 'speech within speech within speech' in an undatable *adespoton*:

> (17) ἔγνω 'παφήσας εἶπέ τ' ἐκ θυμοῦ τάδε·
> "τίς μοι τόδ' †ἀντόμοιον† μισητὸν κρέας
> πέμπων; γέλωτα δή με ποιοῦνται κόροι
> θύοντες, ὕβρει "τυφλός· οὔ τι γνώσεται",
> οὕτω λέγοντες." . . .

[44] Quoted speeches in Old Comedy: Crates fr. 16 and 17; Cratinus fr. 195; Eupolis fr. 1 and 385; Hermippus fr. 2; Pherecrates fr. 56, 162, 163; Strattis fr. 48 and 63.

[45] Translations are my own in exx. (16)–(18).

[46] Differently Bers (1997: 117): 'Perhaps Aristophanes did not entirely trust his actors, men whose professional skills were probably inferior to those of their counterparts of the late fourth century (see Pickard-Cambridge 1988: 94).' On the function of the actors see below, pp. 252–3.

He [Oedipus] recognized (the meat), threw it away and angrily said: 'Who is sending me this . . . (?) hateful meat? My sons are making a fool of me with their sacrifice, wantonly saying "he's blind, he won't notice."' . . . (fr. trag. adesp. 458.7–11 Snell–Kannicht).[47]

The speaker of this fragment (Polyneices or Eteocles) quotes what (he thinks) his father Oedipus said, who imagines what his sons had said. One wonders how an actor delivered the 'tertiary' quotation in l. 10.

The fragments of Middle Comedy do contain a number of quoted speeches. A favourite topic seems to be to make a character quote participants at a *deipnon* or a *symposium*:

(18) τὸ ποτήριόν μοι τὸ μέγα προσφέρει λαβών.
ἐπεχεάμην ἄκρατον· "ἔγχει, παιδίον,
κυάθους θεῶν τε καὶ θεαινῶν μυρίους· . . ."

He took the large drinking-cup and held it out to me. I poured unmixed wine. 'Boy, pour countless ladles of gods and goddesses . . .' (Antiphanes fr. 81.1–3 K.–A.).[48]

Despite the evident interest of Athenaeus (the most important source for Middle Comedy) in these matters, the preponderance is unlikely to be only a coincidence of transmission, especially since the cook seems to be an invention of Middle Comedy that was further developed in New Comedy (Nesselrath 1990: 297–309). But admittedly similar quoted speeches can be found in Old and New Comedy too.[49] The least one can say about Middle Comedy is that speech within speech seems to be as regular a feature as in Aristophanes and Menander.

[47] In the background to this fragment stands the story that Oedipus cursed his sons because they once failed to send the usual portion of the sacrifice. Instead of the shoulder they sent a hip (*Thebais* fr. 3 Bernabé, Aesch. *Sept.* 785–91). According to the source (Schol. Soph. *OC* 1375 De Marco), the story was ridiculed by the poet, probably because he made them send beef instead of the lamb shoulder which they had already hashed.

[48] Cf. also Alexis fr. 208 (speaker a lecherous character, e.g. a parasite, see Arnott 1996*b*: ad loc.), Epicrates fr. 5 (speaker a slave), Euphanes fr. 1 (speaker unknown), Sophilus fr. 5 (speaker a pimp?, so R. L. Hunter 1983: 179), Theophilus fr. 4 (speaker unknown).

[49] Old Comedy: Pherecrates fr. 162 (speaker a host of a *deipnon*); cf. also Cratinus fr. 195 (speaker unknown); New Comedy: Archedicus fr. 2 (cook), Euphron fr. 1 (cook), Menander fr. 401 (speaker unknown), Nicon fr. 1 (slave), Philemon fr. 42 (cook and his employer), fr. 43 (speaker unknown), Philippides fr. 5 (speaker unknown). Cf. also fr. com. adesp. 745 (citizen) and 1018 (slave). Except for the two *adespota* all fragments listed in this and the previous note are transmitted by Athenaeus.

III. SPEECH WITHIN SPEECH IN MENANDER

Given what one knows about the comedies of Menander in general, it will surprise no one that his usage of speech within speech resembles Euripides' more than anybody else's. Apart from the number of quoted speeches, which could be paralleled from Aristophanes too, the following characteristics put him in line with Euripides: (i) Factual quoted speeches are strongly preferred over imagined and/or generalizing ones. (ii) Consequently, the quoted speaker in most cases is a named or identifiable character. (iii) Within the group of factual speeches, internal analepsis (usually in reports of off-stage action, i.e. 'messenger speeches' in the broad sense) is more frequent than external analepsis. In addition, Menander has even more quoted dialogues than Euripides—all the more so if one takes into account the fact that his transmitted oeuvre is substantially smaller. The strongest parallel with Aristophanes is the decreasing formalism in demarcating the boundaries of quoted speech. But this may also be a consequence of the genre Comedy in general[50] and/or a modernization (see below, p. 252).

In the exposition of his plays, Menander always has a prologue speaker give an outline of the plot, together with the events that led to it.[51] The prologue, therefore, is an obvious place for quoted speech in external analepsis, e.g. in the *Sikyonioi*,[52] where the speaker (almost certainly a god) explains how Philoumene and her servant Dromon were sold to the Sicyonian soldier Stratophanes (or his foster father):

(19) *καθῆτό τ' ἐπὶ τῆς ἀγκ[άλης*
ἔ]χων ὁ θεράπων τὴν τροφίμην. πωλ[ουμένοις
π]ροσῆλθεν ἡγεμών τις· ἠρώτα "πόσ[ου
ταῦτ' ἐστιν;" ἤκουσεν, συνεχώρησ', ἐπ[ρίατο.
παλίμβολος δὲ τῷ θεράποντι πλησίο[ν
τ]ῶν αὐτόθεν τις ἕτερος ἅμα πωλουμ[ένων

[50] See above p. 226 with n. 27; cf. also comedy's relative freedom in metrical conventions.

[51] On Menander's prologues see e.g. Holzberg (1974).

[52] The form of the title (sg. or pl.) is a notorious *zetema*, which is well summarized by Arnott (2000: 196–8).

"β]έλτιστε, θάρρει," φησίν, "ὁ Σικυώνιος
ἠ]γόρακεν ὑμᾶς, ἡγεμὼν χρηστὸς σφόδρα
κ]αὶ πλούσιος . . ."

'The slave [Dromon[53]] sat holding his young mistress [Philoumene] on one arm. [They were] for sale. An officer approached. He asked 'How much are they?' He was informed, agreed, and [bought] them. Near the slave another of the men on sale there (he'd been through this hoop before) said 'Sir, cheer up! This man from Sicyon who's bought you is a colonel, very fine and wealthy too . . .' (*Sik.* 8–15)

As far as quoted speech is concerned, the technique chosen here is actually rare in Menandrean prologues. Passage (19) is the only example (from an admittedly limited number of extant prologues) that contains quoted speeches. It should, however, be noted that Euripides, too, has comparatively few quoted speeches in his prologues.[54]

Another possible place for incorporating speech within speech in external analepsis is the opening scene before the prologue.[55] This can be illustrated with a scene, which—to judge from the number of papyri—was among Menander's most popular passages in antiquity: the opening of *Misoumenos*. Thrasonides, the hated man of the play's title, is wandering around in front of his house in the middle of the night in the pouring rain, when—as his slave Getas remarks (*Mis.* A15–16)—one would not even send a dog out. In a monologue, Thrasonides vents his love frustration to the Night, and later explains to Getas that its cause is the hatred of his mistress Krateia. (She, by the way, hates him, because she believes him to have killed her brother—wrongly of course.) Thrasonides desperately tries to overcome her hatred, for example by putting up this charade:

(20) τηρῶ τὸν Δία
ὕοντα πολλῷ νυκτὸς [οὔσ]ης, ἀστραπάς,
βροντάς, ἔχων αὐτὴν δὲ κατάκειμ'. (Ge.) εἶτα τί;

[53] Prologue speakers in New Comedy regularly designate characters in terms of kinship or profession instead of their personal names (Handley 1965*b*: 129), with the possible exception of the most important character of the play (Raffaelli 1984: 98 n. 21). The same avoidance of personal names holds for ancient *hypotheseis*, see van Rossum-Steenbeek (1998: 42–5) who convincingly argues that this practice is a consequence of the type characters.

[54] The examples are *Heracl.* 29–30, *IT* 17–24, *Ion* 29–36, *Phoen.* 17–20, 40.

[55] Expository material need not come from the first act alone. An example for quoted speech in external analepsis later in the play is passage (23).

(Thr.) κέκραγα "παιδίσκη".[56] "βαδίσαι γάρ", φημί, "δεῖ
ἤδη με πρὸς τὸν δεῖν'," ⟨ὑπ⟩είπας ὄνομά τι.[57]
πᾶσ' ἂν γυνὴ δὴ τ[ο]ῦ[τό γ'] εἴποι, "τοῦ Διός
ὕοντος, ὦ τάλαν; [πρὸς ἄνθρ]ωπόν τινα;"

(Thr.) I'm waiting for a heavy downpour after dark, with lightning and thunder—then I'm in bed with her! (Getas) What then? (Thr.) I call out 'Girl!'. I say 'I've got to go to see a man now', filling in some name. Then any woman would respond [like this]: 'In this rain! You poor thing! [To see a man]' (*Mis*. A50–6)

Despite the gaps in the papyrus, one can be sure that this is not what Krateia said, or Thrasonides would not have ended up in the pouring rain, swallowing the bitter pill of a misfired test. The factual quoted speech in l. A53 is remarkable because Thrasonides had evidently prepared the whole scheme in advance (cf. ex. 24 below). The entire passage is a good illustration of that effect which every single scholar writing on the subject attributes to speech within speech: vividness.[58] But it is also a good example for characterization through (quoted) speech. Notably Krateia's speech, which belongs to the group of imagined quoted speeches, throws a remarkable light on Thrasonides and his outlook.

The same can be said about the following passage from *Dis Exapaton*: One of the two young lovers, Sostratos, has just handed over to his father the money he had collected in Ephesos (and he will need again all too soon). What effect will it have on his supposedly luxurious girlfriend that Sostratos all of a sudden is a poor man? (One has to remember that he is also fighting against feelings of jealousy because he suspects her of having an affair with his friend Moschos.) After his father's exit Sostratos says in a monologue:

[56] Sandbach's punctuation indicates that he assumes παιδίσκη to be shouted to a maid (to bring Thrasonides his cloak *vel sim*.). A change of addressee (also suggested by the different paraverbal quality of κέκραγα and φημί) better accounts for γάρ: Pamphile reacted with surprise (or so Thrasonides makes Getas believe . . .), and he explained why he called the maid (similarly Lamagna 1998: 296–7, who however fails to mention that παιδίσκη need not denote a slave, e.g. *Asp*. 266).

[57] This is Arnott's correction of the unmetrical papyrus (similarly Austin and West: ⟨ἐπ⟩είπας, adopted in the OCT). Handley, on the other hand, reads "ἤδη με πρὸς τὸν δεινά ⟨μ'⟩"· "εἶπας ὄνομα τί;" ('What did you say his name was?'). This interpretation (which also affects the supplement in l. A56) is certainly not excluded by Menander's technique for quoted dialogues (cf. signal type vi*a*), but the repetition of μ(ε) may decide against it.

[58] Already Demosthenes (6.19) speaks about quoted speech in terms of ἐναργῆ παραδείγματ(α).

(21) *κα]ὶ μ[ὴν δο]κῶ μοι τὴν καλήν τε κἀγαθήν*
ἰδεῖν ἐρωμένην ἂν ἥδ[έ]ως, κενός
πιθανευομένην καὶ προσδοκῶσαν αὐτ[ί]κα—
φησὶν δ' ἐν αὑτῇ—πᾶν ὃ κομίζω χρυσίον.
πάνυ γάρ· "κομίζει τοῦ[το] καί, νὴ τοὺς θεούς,
[ἐλ]ευθερίως—τί[ς] μᾶλλον;—ἀξί[ω]ς τ' ἐμοῦ."
α[ὕ]τη δ' ἱ[κα]ν[ῶς], καλῶς ποοῦ[σ]ά [γ'], εὑρέθη
ο[ἵ]α⟨ν⟩ ποτ' ᾤ⟨ι⟩[μ]ην οὖσα.[59]

I really do think I could be glad to see my fine lady of a lover being persuasive now I'm empty-handed—and expecting at once (so she tells herself) all the gold that I'm bringing. Very much so: 'He's bringing it like a gentleman, on my oath, and just as I deserve.' But she was found out clearly enough—and well done too—as being the sort I used to think she was.' (*Dis Ex.* 91–8, transl. Handley)

Although Sostratos gives a rather unfavourable description of his girlfriend, there can be little doubt about who is being 'found out' here in the first place.

Characterization through (quoted) speech is by no means restricted to imagined quoted speeches. Menander is fond of an indirect method of introducing characters. He makes his characters describe and quote other characters before they appear on stage themselves. An excellent illustration of this technique is the slave Pyrrhias' dynamic entry in Act I of the *Dyskolos*. His attempt to get in touch with Knemon, whom he had approached on behalf of his master Sostratos, ended disastrously before it had begun. Pyrrhias explains what happened:

(22) *ἐγὼ μὲν εἰς τὸ χωρίον*
ἐμβὰς ἐπορευόμην πρὸς αὐτὸν καὶ πάνυ
πόρρωθεν, εἶναί τις φιλάνθρωπος σφόδρα
ἐπιδέξιός τε βουλόμενος προσεῖπα καί
"ἥκω τι" φημί "πρός σε, πάτερ, ἰδεῖν τί σε
σπεύδων ὑπὲρ σοῦ πρᾶγμ'". ⟨ὁ δ'⟩ εὐθύς, "ἀνόσιε
ἄνθρωπέ," φησιν, "εἰς τὸ χωρίον δέ μου
ἥκεις ⟨σύ;⟩ τί μαθών;" βῶλον αἴρεταί τινα·
ταύτην ἀφίησ' εἰς τὸ πρόσωπον αὐτό μου.
(Ch.) *ἐς κόρακας.* (Py.) *ἐν ὅσῳ δ' "ἀλλά σ' ὁ Ποσειδῶν . . ." λέγων*
κατέμυσα, χάρακα λαμβάνει πάλιν τινά·
ἐκάθαιρέ μ' αὐτῇ, "σοὶ δὲ κἀμοὶ πρᾶγμα τί
ἐστιν;" λέγων, "τὴν δημοσίαν οὐκ οἶσθ' ὁδόν;"
ὀξύτατον ἀναβοῶν τι.

[59] Text as in *P. Oxy.* 4407.

Then I stepped onto his land and walked towards him. I was still a good way from him, but I wanted to be a friendly and tactful sort of fellow, so I greeted him. 'I've come,' I said, 'on business, to see you, sir, on business, it's to your advantage.' Right away, 'Damned heathen,' he said, 'trespassing on my land? What's your game?' He picked a lump of earth up, which he threw smack in my face!

(Chaireas) Hell!

(Py.) While I shut my eyes and said 'Poseidon blast you,' he'd now grabbed a stake again and flogged me with it, said 'What dealings do we have? Don't you know the public road?' He bawled fortissimo. (*Dys.* 103–16)

Pyrrhias exemplifies in a colourful way Pan's earlier description of Knemon as being a grumpy old man who avoids social contacts as much as he can (*Dys.* 6–13). Through the quoted dialogue, Knemon enters the stage, so to speak, in Pyrrhias' report roughly 40 lines before his actual entry. The audience already gets an impression of what to expect. The same introductory technique can be found e.g. in the *Epitrepontes.*[60] Pyrrhias' paraverbal comment *ὀξύτατον ἀναβοῶν τι* is indicative of Knemon's intonation which Pyrrhias probably imitates in his report. Knemon's shouting will later be confirmed by Sostratos when he hears him approaching.[61] The passage is also remarkable for the frequency of the 'historic presents'[62] which are so prominent in messenger speeches. According to the standard explanation, using a historic present means that a speaker mentally goes back in time and recounts the events as he experienced them.[63] The effect of the historic present is—again—vividness (cf. [Longinus] 25), and its purpose is to highlight the passage, e.g. as being the climax of the entire scene. In Menander's narratives, the transition from past tense to historic present regularly coincides with the introduction of quoted speeches, so the two reinforce each other.[64]

[60] See (25) below. This passage is remarkable because it is the last in a series preparing for Charisios' first entry, which does not come earlier than towards the end of act IV (*Epit.* 908).

[61] *Dys.* 149: *ἀλλὰ κ[αὶ β]οᾷ*. Knemon's first word, *εἶτα* (153), suggests that he has been listing arguments on his way to the stage (I owe this observation to A. Rijksbaron of Amsterdam).

[62] *φημί* 107, *φησιν* 109, *αἴρεται* 110, *ἀφίησι* 110, *λαμβάνει* 114; contrast *προσεῖπα* 106, *κατέμυσα* 113, *ἐκάθαιρε* 114.

[63] de Jong (1991: 39–45), see also Kühner–Gerth (1898–1904: 1.132), Rijksbaron (1994: 22–5).

[64] In addition to (22) see (5), (11), (15), (19), (20), (23), (26), (27), and *Theoph.* 18, *Mis.* 133, 305, 439, *Pk.* 319, 322, *Sik.* 189, 224, fr. 280, 607. This is one of the

Another function of speech within speech is to give one's words authenticity by referring them to another person. The speaker limits his function to that of the reliable witness who reports what another has said. In daily life this happens all the time: it may also help in court, e.g. Daos' pleading in the arbitration scene that gave the *Epitrepontes* its title. The shepherd explains how he came to give the baby to the charcoal-burner Syriskos:

(23) *σκυθρωπὸν ὄντα με*
ἰδών, "τί σύννους" φησὶ "Δᾶος;" "τί γάρ;" ἐγώ,[65]
"περίεργός εἰμι," καὶ τὸ πρᾶγμ' αὐτῷ λέγω,
ὡς εὗρον, ὡς ἀνειλόμην. ὁ δὲ τότε μέν
εὐθὺς πρὶν εἰπεῖν πάντ' ἐδεῖθ', "οὕτω τί σοι
ἀγαθὸν γένοιτο Δᾶε" παρ' ἕκαστον λέγων,
"ἐμοὶ τὸ παιδίον δός. οὕτως εὐτυχής,
οὕτως ἐλεύθερος. γυναῖκά" φησι "γάρ
ἔχω, τεκούσῃ δ' ἀπέθανεν τὸ παιδίον",
ταύτην λέγων, ἣ νῦν ἔχει τὸ παιδίον.
ἐδέου Συρίσκε;[66]

He [Syriskos] saw me looking glum. 'Why's Daos fraught?' he asked. 'Why not? I've been too nosy,' I said, telling him the story, how I'd found the child and picked it up. Then right away, before my tale was done, he started pleading, adding a 'Bless you, Daos' to each phrase. He said, 'Give *me* the baby, as you hope for luck and freedom. I've a wife, you see, her baby died at birth.' He meant the woman who's got the child now (*pointing to Syriskos' wife*). Did you ask, Syriskos? (*Epit.* 260–70)

Daos' argumentation is efficient and persuasive, but it nevertheless misfires because Syriskos never thought of contradicting *this* point. Yes, he did beg and plead (*Epit.* 295–8), but the real question is 'To whom belong the trinkets which were exposed

few differences from Euripides, who prefers past tense quotatives in his messenger speeches: 16 historic presents vs. 8 imperfects and 47 aorists (de Jong 1991: 40). In his comparatively small number of factual quoted speeches, Aristophanes too favours past tense over historic present (*Pax* 76, *Lys.* 393, 396, *Thesm.* 483 = (14), 507, 513, *Eccl.* 399). Especially striking is the absence of present quotatives in the 'messenger speech' about the assembly in the *Knights* (624–82).

[65] In terms of demarcation, this *ἐγώ* shows that pronouns indicating a change of the grammatical subject (type iv*a*) can even be postponed in Menander (cf. intercalated quotatives: type iii).

[66] A *nota personae* in a recently deciphered papyrus (to be published in *P. Oxy.* vol. 68) confirms the name as Syriskos (not Syros). This adds weight to de Stefani's correction (adopted in the OCT) of the Cairo codex, which gives l. 270 to Smikrines, who is unlikely to know the charcoal-burner's name.

with the baby?' The same device of 'authentication by quotation' is known from tragedy too, where it is used even in speeches of deception.[67]

The correspondence between Euripides and Menander is largely due to their common observance of the unity of place. As a consequence, they frequently make characters report what happened backstage or off-stage (including speeches). Most of these messenger speeches present a subsequent narration, i.e. the events are reported on stage after they happened elsewhere.[68] But Menander also has a fine example of a backstage scene, which is—as it were—anticipated on stage. In the *Epitrepontes*, the harp-player Habrotonon envisages the following intrigue: she is to pretend to be the girl whom the young husband Charisios had raped several months before the opening of the play, on which occasion he had lost a ring:

(24) (Habr.) *θέασ', Ὀνήσιμε,*
ἂν συναρέσῃ σοι τοὐμὸν ἐνθύμημ' ἄρα.
ἐμὸν ποήσομαι τὸ πρᾶγμα τοῦτ' ἐγώ,
τὸν δακτύλιον λαβοῦσά τ' εἴσω τουτονί
εἴσειμι πρὸς ἐκεῖνον. (On.) *λέγ' ὃ λέγεις· ἄρτι γὰρ*
νοῶ. (Habr.) *κατιδών μ' ἔχουσαν ἀνακρινεῖ πόθεν*
εἴληφα. φήσω "Ταυροπολίοις παρθένος
ἔτ' οὖσα", τά τ' ἐκείνῃ γενόμενα πάντ' ἐμά
ποουμένη· τὰ πλεῖστα δ' αὐτῶν οἶδ' ἐγώ.
(On.) *ἄριστά γ' ἀνθρώπων.* (Habr.) *ἐὰν οἰκεῖον ᾖ*
αὐτῷ τὸ πρᾶγμ⟨α δ'⟩, εὐθὺς ἥξει φερόμενος
ἐπὶ τὸν ἔλεγχον καὶ μεθύων γε νῦν ἐρεῖ
πρότερος ἅπαντα καὶ προπετῶς· ἃ δ' ἂν λέγῃ
προσομολογήσω τοῦ διαμαρτεῖν μηδὲ ἕν
προτέρα λέγουσα. (On.) *ὑπέρευγε νὴ τὸν Ἥλιον.*
(Habr.) *τὰ κοινὰ ταυτὶ δ' ἀκκιοῦμαι τῷ λόγῳ*
τοῦ μὴ διαμαρτεῖν· "ὡς ἀναιδὴς ἦσθα καὶ
ἰταμός τις". (On.) *εὖγε.* (Habr.) *"κατέβαλες δέ μ' ὡς σφόδρα·*
ἱμάτια δ' οἷ' ἀπώλεσ' ἡ τάλαιν' ἐγώ"
φήσω. πρὸ τούτου δ' ἔνδον αὐτὸ βούλομαι
λαβοῦσα κλαῦσαι καὶ φιλῆσαι καὶ πόθεν
ἔλαβεν ἐρωτᾶν τὴν ἔχουσαν. (On.) *Ἡράκλεις.*

[67] Aesch. *Cho.* 680–7, Soph. *Phil.* 364 ff. Orestes and Neoptolemos present speeches as factual that in reality are imagined (or invented).

[68] Cf. exx. (22), (25), (26), and (27).

(Habr.) τὸ πέρας δὲ πάντων, "παιδίον τοίνυν" ἐρῶ
"ἔστ]ι̣ γεγονός σοι", καὶ τὸ νῦν εὑρημένον
δείξω.

(Hab.) Onesimos, I've just had an idea. See what you think. I'll pretend this happened to *me*, and I'll go in to Charisios, wearing the ring.

(On.) Go on. I'm beginning to see . . .

(Hab.) When he sees me wearing it, he'll ask me where I got it, and I'll say, 'At the Tauropolia, when I was still a virgin.' And I'll tell the girl's story as my own—I know most of it, anyway.

(On.) Clever girl!

(Hab.) If he's the man responsible, he'll rush right in and give himself away. He's a bit tipsy now, and he'll blurt out the whole story before I even ask. I'll go along with everything he says, and avoid any mistakes by letting *him* mention details first.

(On.) Super!

(Hab.) I'll side-step any slips by flattery, and the usual platitudes. 'Ooh, you were a brute! In such a hurry, too!'

(On.) Great!

(Hab.) 'You threw me down so roughly', I'll say, 'and tore my poor dress to pieces.' And before I do all this, I'll go in and cry over the baby and kiss it and ask the woman where she got it.

(On.) You're a genius!

(Hab.) And to crown it all, I'll say, 'So you've got yourself a baby son', and show him the child that's just been found. (*Epit.* 511–35, transl. Miller)

Habrotonon not only explains what her procedure is going to look like, she actually acts out parts of the scene which she is to play shortly inside the house. The speeches she quotes in the name of the raped girl allow Habrotonon to give proof of her histrionic abilities which make it likely that she will succeed in fooling Charisios. Onesimos with his interrupting cheers, on the other hand, has the function, so to speak, of the 'audience within the play'.[69] In cases like ex. (24) one could speak of a 'rehearsal scene'. This type is especially apt for plays containing an intrigue.[70] It is, therefore, all the more surprising that the closest parallel from tragedy comes from Aeschylus and not from Euripides.[71] The effect of a rehearsal scene is not only to make the audience

[69] The 'audience within the play' is a feature which was further developed in modern theater, e.g. in Shakespeare's *Midsummer Night's Dream*.

[70] Cf. *Asp*. 343–4; rehearsal scenes are not restricted to the intrigue, e.g. *Epit*. 929–31.

[71] 'Closest' in the sense that it contains a quoted speech: Aesch. *Cho*. 569–70.

participate in a scene which otherwise they will not be able to see, but also to arouse their attention. For unlike the subsequent messenger speech, the rehearsal scene may turn out differently than anticipated, or it may not be translated into action at all.[72]

The setting of New Comedy is the typical street scene in front of the two or three houses which are inhabited by middle-class citizens 'like you and me'. The conventions of the genre allow for some departure from strict realism, e.g. when neighbours seem not to know each other or when a conversation with a rather delicate subject-matter is held in the street. The latter can be illustrated from the opening of Act IV of the *Epitrepontes*. In this scene, Smikrines tries to persuade his daughter Pamphile to leave her husband Charisios, who is staying next door[73] in the company of a *hetaira* because he suspects his wife of infidelity. But Pamphile defends her husband against Smikrines' accusations. Recent papyrus discoveries have confirmed that this conversation is serious in tone and subject-matter.[74] To have Charisios eavesdrop *on stage* (i.e. visible to the audience) would completely destroy the effect of the scene.[75] Of course, Menander can bring him on stage afterwards and make him explain in a monologue what he has just heard etc. (this is in fact what happens in ll. 908 ff.). One may even hypothesize that this is what the audience expects because they still await Charisios' first entry. But Menander's solution is neater and subtler. First Charisios' slave Onesimos enters:

(25) ὑπομαίνεθ' οὗτος, νὴ τὸν Ἀπόλλω, μαίνεται·
μεμάνητ' ἀληθῶς· μαίνεται νὴ τοὺς θεούς.
τὸν δεσπότην λέγω Χαρίσιον. χολὴ
μέλαινα προσπέπτωκεν ἤ τοιοῦτό [τι.
τί γὰρ ἄν τις εἰκάσειεν ἄλλο γεγονέναι;
πρὸς ταῖς θύραις γὰρ ἔνδον ἀρτί[ως πολὺν

[72] The contrast between Onesimos' hesitation (*Epit*. 412–14, 419–29, 448–50) and Habrotonon's enterprise (468 ff.) is an important aspect of the play and gives Onesimos' cheers in ex. (24) an additional meaning.

[73] In the house of his friend Chairestratos. This absence is Menander's dramaturgical 'excuse' for making the scene play in the street. Otherwise Charisios cannot witness it as an eavesdropper (Blume 1998: 61).

[74] See the edition by Martina (1997), who also prints the previously unpublished Michigan fragments.

[75] Contrast *Pk*. 779 ff., where the recognition dialogue between Glykera and her father is eavesdropped on by Moschion. The 'paratragodic' tone of the dialogue and Moschion's asides do not fail to have a comic effect.

χρόνον διακύπτων ἐνδ[ιέτριψ(ε) –⏑–
ὁ πατὴρ δὲ τῆς νύμφης τι περὶ [τοῦ πράγματος
ἐλάλει πρὸς ἐκείνην, ὡς ἔοιχ', ὁ δ' οἷα μέν
ἤλλαττε χρώματ', ἄνδρες, οὐδ' εἰπεῖν καλόν.
"ὦ γλυκυτάτη" δὲ "τῶν λόγων οἵους λέγεις"
ἀνέκραγε, τήν κεφαλήν τ' ἀνεπάταξε σφόδρα
αὑτοῦ. πάλιν δὲ διαλιπών, "οἵαν λαβών
γυναῖχ' ὁ μέλεος ἠτύχηκα." τὸ δὲ πέρας,
ὡς πάντα διακούσας ἀπῆλθ' εἴσω ποτέ,
βρυχηθμὸς ἔνδον, τιλμός, ἔκστασις συχνή.
"ἐγὼ" γὰρ "ἀλιτήριος" πυκνὸν πάνυ
ἔλεγεν "τοιοῦτον ἔργον ἐξειργασμένος
αὐτὸς γεγονώς τε παιδίου νόθου πατήρ
οὐκ ἔσχον οὐδ' ἔδωκα συγγνώμης μέρος
οὐθὲν ἀτυχούσῃ ταὔτ' ἐκείνῃ, βάρβαρος
ἀνηλεής τε." λοιδορεῖτ' ἐρρωμένως
αὑτῷ βλέπει θ' ὕφαιμον ἠρεθισμένος.

The man's quite mad—yes, by Apollo, mad! He's really crazy. Yes, he's mad, by heaven! I mean Charisios, my master. He's got melancholia, or some such ailment! How else could one explain the circumstances? You see, just now indoors [he spent a long (?)] time peeping through that door! His wife's father was discussing [the affair] with her, apparently, and, gentlemen, I can't with decency describe how he kept changing colour. 'O my love, to speak such words,' he cried, and punched himself hard on his head. Pause, then resumption: 'What a wife I've married, and I'm in this wretched mess!' When finally he'd heard the whole tale out, he fled indoors. Then—wailing, tearing of hair, raging lunacy within. He went on saying, 'Look at me, the villain. I myself committed a crime like this, and am the father of a bastard child. Yet I felt not a scrap of mercy, showed none to that woman in the same sad fortune.[76] I'm a heartless brute.' Fiercely he damns himself, eyes bloodshot, overwrought.' (*Epit.* 878–900)

This slightly artificial construction (Onesimos reporting how he overheard an eavesdropping Charisios)[77] does away with a visibly eavesdropping Charisios and, furthermore, describes aspects which could not be enacted (e.g. facial expressions). And, more importantly, Onesimos' amusing report releases the 'uncomic' tension which the serious conversation between Pamphile and

[76] Charisios' belief is a consequence of Habrotonon's intrigue (cf. ex. 24). The bastard children will of course turn out to be one only, his and Pamphile's legitimate son.

[77] One is reminded of the subtitle of Friedrich Dürrenmatt's last prose text (1986): 'Vom Beobachten des Beobachters der Beobachter'.

her father might have caused. On the other hand, a similar self-description by Charisios himself would easily make him appear a hopeless wimp (another anti-climax after the sensible arguments of his wife), whereas Onesimos can make fun of Charisios in a report that the audience is free to take *cum grano salis*.[78]

Although it has so far not been explicitly stated, the examples show that Menander not only follows Euripides, but actually outdoes him as far as liberty of demarcation, length, and number of quoted speeches per embedding speech are concerned. Another difference is the specific paraverbal remarks about how the quoted speech was spoken, which no doubt points to a matching delivery (cf. on ex. 22). An excellent illustration of this phenomenon comes from the Menandrean speech perhaps most famous in modern times. At the beginning of Act III of *Samia* Demeas explains in a long monologue how he came to discover that the father of the baby is actually his adopted son Moschion (and not he himself). During the hectic preparations for Moschion's wedding, Demeas happens to be in the vicinity of the kitchen:

(26) τοῦ δὲ Μοσχίωνος ἦν
τίτθη τις αὕτη, πρεσβυτέρα, γεγονυῖ' ἐμὴ
θεράπαιν', ἐλευθέρα δὲ νῦν. ἰδοῦσα δέ
τὸ παιδίον κεκραγὸς ἠμελημένον
ἐμέ τ' οὐδὲν εἰδυῖ' ἔνδον ὄντ', ἐν ἀσφαλεῖ
εἶναι νομίσασα τοῦ λαλεῖν, προσέρχεται
καὶ ταῦτα δὴ τὰ κοινὰ "φίλτατον τέκνον"
εἰποῦσα καὶ "μέγ' ἀγαθόν· ἡ μάμμη δὲ ποῦ;"
ἐφίλησε, περιήνεγκεν. ὡς δ' ἐπαύσατο
κλᾶον, πρὸς αὑτήν φησιν "ὦ τάλαιν' ἐγώ,
πρώην τοιοῦτον ὄντα Μοσχίων' ἐγώ
αὐτὸν ἐτιθηνούμην ἀγαπῶσα, νῦν δ' ἐπεί
παιδίον ἐκείνου γέγονεν ἤδη καὶ τόδε
(2 or 3 lines missing, 2 lines mutilated)
[ ] καὶ θεραπαινιδίῳ τινί
ἔξωθεν εἰστρέχοντι, "λούσατ', ὦ τάλαν,
τὸ παιδίον" φησίν, "τί τοῦτ'; ἐν τοῖς γάμοις

[78] The passage does not contain a historic present (except for βλέπει in l. 900, which comes after the quoted speeches). Unlike other 'messengers' who are drawn back in time by their vivid recollection (see on ex. 22), Onesimos appears to show off deliberately. Cf. also his address of the audience in l. 887 (ἄνδρες); for parallels see Bain (1977: 190–1).

τοῖς τοῦ πατρὸς τὸν μικρὸν οὐ θεραπεύετε;”
εὐθὺς δ' ἐκείνη “δύσμορ', ἡλίκον λαλεῖς”
φήσ'· “ἔνδον ἐστὶν αὐτός.” “οὐ δήπου γε· ποῦ;”
“ἐν τῷ ταμιείῳ”, καὶ παρεξήλλαξέ τι·
“αὐτὴ καλεῖ, τίτθη, σε” καὶ “βάδιζε καί
σπεῦδ'· οὐκ ἀκήκο' οὐδέν· εὐτυχέστατα.”
εἰποῦσ' ἐκείνη δ' “ὢ τάλαινα τῆς ἐμῆς
λαλιᾶς”, ἀπῆξεν ἐκποδών, οὐκ οἶδ' ὅποι.

This woman was our Moschion's old nurse, quite old. She then became my maid, but now she's free. She saw the child ignored and screaming, unaware that I was in the house. Thinking it safe to speak out loud, she went right up to it and said the usual things, 'My darling baby' and 'Great treasure—where's your mummy?' Then she kissed and danced it round. When it stopped crying, she said to herself 'Dear me, it's not so long ago that I nursed Moschion himself, and loved him just like you, and now that his own baby's born, already it as well . . .' . . . and then she told a maid who ran in from outside 'You bath the baby! Dear me, what's going on? Can't you look after the little mite on daddy's wedding day?' The girl immediately hissed 'Don't *shout*. Master's at home.' 'No! Where is he?' 'In the pantry!' And then, raising her voice, 'Mistress is asking for you, Nurse' and, quietly, 'Quick! He hasn't heard a word. We're in luck.' The Nurse said, 'My tongue will be the death of me', and off she went, I don't know where. (*Sam.* 236–61)[79]

Apart from its sheer length, the monologue is remarkable in several respects.[80] (i) Although a named speaker, Demeas quotes a dialogue, in which he himself does not take part. (ii) A man quotes the speeches of two women. *πρεσβυτέρα* in l. 237 may be an indication that the distinction was made by imitating an old and a young female voice. (iii) There is the shift from hushed dialogue (ll. 255–7) to deliberately formal instruction with the (unsuccessful) attempt at fooling Demeas (l. 258)[81] and back to hushed

[79] Lines 236–54 are taken from Arnott's translation, 255–61 from Miller's.

[80] Demeas' monologue covers almost 10 per cent of the entire play, approximately 80 of 896 or 897 lines (see Arnott 1999). It has been argued that Menander had comparatively little success in the dramatic contest (only 8 victories: test. 46) because people did not like his long monologues (Blume 1974: 79). This hypothesis is not easily reconciled with the evidence available from Menander and other comic poets (cf. e.g. 28, Diphilus fr. 42, Philemon fr. 82). Why should they indulge in a feature which was unlikely to win the favour of the jury and the audience?

[81] *παρεξήλλαξε* by itself does not indicate whether the maid is lowering (Arnott) or raising (Gomme–Sandbach, Miller) her voice. In context, the latter makes better sense as a charade in order to mislead Demeas. This leads to 'acting to the power of three': an actor plays Demeas who imitates the voice of a nervous female servant who plays a matter-of-fact servant.

dialogue again.[82] (iv) The demarcation signals become shorter and less explicit with the increasing excitement of the women. (v) It should also be noted that, from a dramaturgical point of view, the monologue is to a large extent superfluous. It is, of course, great fun, but its essence could have been said in a sentence or two. Taken together, these observations lead to the conclusion that speech within speech has become a part of his plays in which Menander indulged himself.

Further confirmation comes from the other speech which, because of its length, cannot possibly be presented in full in this paper. Originally over a hundred lines long, of which (parts of) 96 survive (*Sik.* 176–271), the messenger speech of the *Sikyonioi* is a report of a popular assembly. The frequent quotations of who said what make it come close to a reportage in a modern radio news show (except, of course, that there the speakers are quoted in their own voice). In the course of the assembly, a decision is taken about the fate of Philoumene, the girl who is to be recognized as an Athenian citizen. Right after the publication of the papyrus in 1964, scholars pointed out the similarity to the topic of the assembly in Euripides' *Orestes*, which is also reported in a messenger speech (Eur. *Or.* 866–956). This similarity is consolidated by the fact that the opening line of Menander's messenger speech echoes the opening line of Euripides'.[83] However, Sandbach's warning (Gomme–Sandbach 1973: 651) not to overestimate the connection is to be heeded. And as early as 1965, Eric Handley pointed to similarities in comparable reports about assemblies in Aristophanes' *Knights* and *Ekklesiazousai*.[84] As for speech within speech specifically, the messenger speech in *Sikyonioi* does not resemble that in *Orestes* more than other messenger speeches. A remarkable feature of Menander's messenger[85] is that he quotes what the crowd said during the debate, as will be

[82] The monologue thus consists of baby-talk, murmured monologue, shouted instructions, hushed dialogue, deliberately formal instruction, and hushed dialogue again, with intercalated 'narrator-text'.

[83] *Sik.* 176–7 ≈ *Or.* 866–7, and, in addition, *Sik.* 182, 188, 215 ≈ *Or.* 920, 871, 918, see Belardinelli (1994: ad locc.) and Katsouris (1975*c*: 29–54), whose conclusions, however, are somewhat simplistic.

[84] Handley (1965*a*: 61 n. 10) with reference to Ar. *Eq.* 624 ff. and *Eccl.* 395 ff. Cf. also Ephippus fr. 14 and, though without quoted speech, Plato Com. fr. 200 (see Fraenkel 1912: 34–6).

[85] His name and identity are the subject of a scholarly debate which can be ignored for the purpose of this paper (see e.g. Belardinelli 1994: 163–4).

illustrated with the final section of the speech. The scarcity of demarcation signals makes the correct interpretation of this passage extremely difficult, and no two scholars completely agree on it.[86] (The soldier Stratophanes proposes that Philoumene be put in the custody of the priestess of Demeter, until her father is found who can legally give her in marriage.)

> (27) "τῶν ἀντιπραττόντων δ' ἐμοὶ τῆς παρθένου
> μηθεὶς γενέσθω κύριος πρὶν ἂν φανῇ
> ἐκεῖνος." "ὀρθῶς καὶ δίκαι', ὀρθῶς", "ἄγε
> πρὸς τὴν ἱέρειαν, ἄγε λαβών." ὁ λευκόχρως
> ἐκεῖνος ἐξαίφνης τε παραπηδᾷ πάλιν
> καί φησι "ταυτὶ συμπέποιθ', ὡς οὑτοσί
> νῦν ἐξαπίνης εἴληφε διαθήκας ποθέν
> ἐστί τε πολίτης ὑμέτερος, τραγῳδίᾳ
> κενῇ τ' ἀγόμενος τὴν κόρην ἀφήσετ[αι;"
> "ἆρ' οὐκ ἀποκτενεῖς τὸν ἐξυρημένον;"
> "μὰ Δί', ἀλλά σ', ὅστις . . .— οὐ γάρ;" "οὐκ ἐκ τοῦ μέσου,
> λάσταυρε;" "πόλλ' ὑμῖν γένοιτο κἀγαθά·"
> ἐκεῖνος, "ἄγε, βάδιζ' ἀναστᾶσ'." ὁ θεράπων
> "ὑμῶν κελευόντων βαδιεῖται" φησί, καί
> "κελεύετ', ἄνδρες." "ναί, βάδιζ'." ἀνίστατο,
> ἐβάδιζε. μέχρι τούτου παρῆν· τ[ὰ δ' ὕστερα
> οὐκέτι λέγειν ἔχοιμ' ἄν, ἀλλ' ἀπέ[ρχομαι.

(Stratophanes) 'None of my opponents must take charge of her [Philoumene] before he's [her father] found!'

(ABC) 'That's right and fair, that's right!'

(D *or* Stratophanes) 'Now take her to the priestess, take her!' Instantly that white-faced lad [Moschion] jumped in once more and said 'Do you believe that suddenly he's found a will from somewhere, and is now your fellow citizen? That he will take the girl with this inane performance, then release her?'

(A) 'Won't you get rid of smoothface?'

(B *or* Moschion) 'No—get stuffed, whoever you are!'

(C *or* A) 'Out you go, you queer!'

(D *or* Moschion, sarcastically) 'Best wishes to you all!' He [Stratophanes, to Philoumene]: 'Up now, do come!' The slave [Dromon[87]]: 'She'll come, if you all tell her to,' and 'Sirs, tell her!'

[86] For that reason, the translation identifies the quoted speaker in round brackets, ABCD standing for unnamed members of the crowd.

[87] Unlike prologue speakers (cf. n. 53), the present messenger does not use personal names for reasons of consistency. As a casual witness of the assembly (ll. 176–89), he is not to know the names of the protagonists.

(ABC) 'Yes, come!' She rose and then began to move. I stayed till then. What happened after I couldn't now report, but off I went. (*Sik*. 255–71)

Difficulties of how the lines are to be assigned to the different speakers arise in ll. 257–8 and especially 264–6, whereas the distribution of the other lines is made perfectly clear by the messenger. This is unlikely to be a coincidence. Unambiguous indications of the speaker guarantee that those parts which are actually important for a proper understanding of the assembly scene are clear. The other parts may in fact be intended to give the impression of a tumultuous assembly which is about to dissolve into chaos. It may therefore be futile to decide whether ll. 264–6 are wild shouts from the crowd or a heated dialogue between an angry citizen and a frustrated Moschion.[88] Be that as it may, the messenger in any case quotes no less than five parties in the course of the entire speech: himself (l. 189), the slave Dromon, the crowd (collectively or as single voices), Moschion, and Stratophanes. It is evident that the designation of the speakers by means of distinctive delivery only reaches its limits here. Menander was well aware of that difficulty and identified the speaker whenever it appeared necessary.[89] Small details like these confirm that Menander was anything but a 'desk-playwright' and had an active sense of the practical problems of the stage and their solutions.

IV. SPEECH WITHIN SPEECH IN NEW COMEDY AND OTHER HELLENISTIC POETRY

In order to put the observations on Menander in a wider perspective, it may be worth looking at other contemporaneous and later poetry. As for New Comedy itself, the scarcity of non-Menandrean texts prevents a detailed comparison. There are, nevertheless, indications that quoted speech was not Menander's

[88] For the different views see Gomme–Sandbach (1973: ad loc.), Belardinelli (1994: ad loc.), N. Miller's translation (1987: 151) and Arnott (2000: 259 n. 25).

[89] Cf. ὁ λευκόχρως 258, ἐκεῖνος, ὁ θεράπων 267. The latter two remind one in their brevity of a single person quoting a dialogue scene from a play (e.g. a Hellenist in a lecture on stichomythia: 'Oedipus: . . . Tiresias: . . . Oedipus: . . .'). Cf. also *Phasma* 97–8.

personal prerogative. A number of pertinent fragments contain speech within speech.[90] More importantly, a general popularity of numerous quoted speeches with very few external demarcation signals is confirmed by Straton's ordinary citizen, who complains in a hilarious monologue about the pretentious and 'Homerizing' cook he has hired:[91]

(28) *σφίγγ' ἄρρεν', οὐ μάγειρον, εἰς τὴν οἰκίαν*
εἴληφ'. ἁπλῶς γὰρ οὐδὲ ἕν, μὰ τοὺς θεούς,
ὧν ἂν λέγῃ συνίημι· καινὰ ῥήματα
πεπορισμένος πάρεστιν. ὡς εἰσῆλθε γάρ,
εὐθύς μ' ἐπηρώτησε προσβλέψας μέγα·
"πόσους κέκληκας μέροπας ἐπὶ δεῖπνον; λέγε."
"ἐγὼ κέκληκα Μέροπας ἐπὶ δεῖπνον; χολᾷς.
τοὺς δὲ Μέροπας τούτους με γινώσκειν δοκεῖς;"
"οὐδ' ἄρα παρέσται δαιτυμὼν οὐθεὶς ὅλως;"
"ἥξει Φιλῖνος, Μοσχίων, Νικήρατος,
ὁ δεῖν', ὁ δεῖνα." κατ' ὄνομ' ἐπεπορευόμην·
οὐκ ἦν ἐν αὐτοῖς οὐδὲ εἷς μοι Δαιτυμών.
ὁ δ' ἠγανάκτησ' ὥσπερ ἠδικημένος
ὅτι οὐ κέκληκα Δαιτυμόνα. καινὸν σφόδρα.
"οὐδ' ἄρα θύεις ῥηξίχθον';" "οὐκ", ἔφην, "ἐγώ."
"βοῦν εὐρυμέτωπον;" "οὐ θύω βοῦν, ἄθλιε."
"μῆλα θυσιάζεις ἆρα;" "μὰ Δί', ἐγὼ μὲν οὔ."
"τὰ μῆλα πρόβατα." "μῆλα πρόβατ'; οὐκ οἶδ'", ἔφην,
"μάγειρε, τούτων οὐθέν, οὐδὲ βούλομαι.
ἀγροικότερός εἰμ', ὥσθ' ἁπλῶς μοι διαλέγου."
"τὰς οὐλοχύτας φέρε δεῦρο." "τοῦτο δ' ἐστὶ τί;"
"κριθαί." "τί οὖν, ἀπόπληκτε, περιπλοκὰς λέγεις;"
"πηγὸς πάρεστι;" "πηγός; οὐχὶ λαικάσει,
ἐρεῖς σαφέστερόν θ' ὃ βούλει μοι λέγειν;"
"ἀτάσθαλός γ' εἶ, πρέσβυ." φησίν. "ἅλα φέρε·
τοῦτ' ἔστι πηγός, τοῦτο δεῖξον." χέρνιβον
παρῆν· ἔθυεν, ἔλεγεν ἕτερα μυρία
τοιαῦθ' ἅ, μὰ τὴν Γῆν, οὐδὲ εἷς συνῆκεν ἄν,

[90] Archedicus fr. 2 and 3, Damoxenus fr. 2, Diodorus fr. 2, Diphilus fr. 42 and 67, Epinicus fr. 1 (?), Euphron fr. 1, Nicon fr. 1, Philemon fr. 42, 43, and 94, Philippides fr. 5 and 27, Theognetus fr. 1.

[91] Despite the *Suda*'s attribution to Middle Comedy (test. 1 K.–A.), Straton is more likely to be a poet of New Comedy (Nesselrath 1990: 62–3). Straton fr. 1 is one of the few texts to have survived as a book fragment as well as on papyrus. The latter proves that the former is heavily interpolated. For details see Kassel–Austin ad loc. and the literature cited there, also for the 'Homerizing' vocabulary of the cook. On Philitas' glossaries (l. 43) see Pfeiffer (1968: 90 ff.).

μίστυλλα, μοίρας, δίπτυχ', ὀβελούς· ὥστ' ἔδει
τὰ τοῦ Φιλίτα λαμβάνοντα βυβλία
σκοπεῖν ἕκαστον τί δύναται τῶν ῥημάτων.

It's the Sphinx's husband, not a cook that I've taken into my house: bless my soul, I simply do not understand a thing he says. He's come with a stock of brand-new words. When he came in he looked at me importantly and inquired: 'Tell me, how many Articulates have you invited to dinner?' 'Articulates? Invited to dinner? You're crazy! Do you suppose they are acquaintances of mine, these Articulates?' 'Then will there be no trencherman at all?' 'Philinus is coming, and Moschion, and Niceratus, and so-and-so, and what's-his-name.' I went through them by name, and I found no Trencherman among them. He was annoyed, as if someone had done him an injury, just because I hadn't invited Trencherman! Strange goings-on, to be sure! 'Then you are sacrificing no Earthbreaker?' 'Not I!' I replied. 'No broadbrowed ox?' 'I'm sacrificing no oxen, idiot!' 'Then you are immolating wethers?' 'Good lord, no, not I!' 'Wethers are sheep!' 'Wethers sheep? I know nothing about it, my dear cook, and I don't want to know anything. I'm just a simple fellow; talk to me in plain language.' 'Bring hither the groats!' 'What may they be?' 'The barley!' 'Then why talk in circles, madman?' 'Is there any brine?' 'Brine? Go to the devil! Tell me what you mean in plain language!' 'Thou art a wicked wight, old father,' he replied, 'bring me the salt—*that* is what brine is, shew me where that is!' The holy water was ready; he did sacrifice, spoke a myriad more words such as I swear no man on earth could have understood—slashes, lots, doubles, piercers—till you would have had to take the works of Philitas and look each word up to find its meaning . . . (Straton fr. 1.1–44 K.–A., transl. Page)

The 'ping-pong' in the middle of this long speech, which reminds one of *antilabe* in tragedy, is as good as free of external demarcation signals and relies above all on the illocutionary force (type vi*a*) of the short sentences. The exploration of the boundaries of (quoted) speech appears to be a central theme of these poets. It can be paralleled from other genres as well, e.g. from [Theocritus] 8: after a short exposition in ll. 1–4 (setting, characters), the narrator starts with a 'Homeric' presentation of the dialogue between Daphnis and Menalcas: introductory formula in l. 5, Menalcas' speech in ll. 6–7, capping/transitional formula in l. 8, Daphnis' speech in ll. 9–10. At this point the narrator seems to have sufficiently prepared the field for a proper understanding of the subsequent dialogue. He now withdraws and lets the characters 'speak for themselves' until l. 61 (resurfacing briefly in ll. 28–32), where he returns to introducing and capping each speech until the end. Perhaps even more significant are those texts in the *Corpus Theocriteum* which dispense altogether with the voice of the narrator, especially those with frequent change of speaker and numerous characters like *Idyll* 15.[92]

Another important source for the present topic is the 'dialogic' epigrams from the *Anthologia Palatina*, e.g. the following (probably fictitious) dedication:

(29) *τίν με, λεοντάγχ' ὦνα συοκτόνε, φήγινον ὄζον*
θῆκε—"τίς;" Ἀρχῖνος. "ποῖος;" ὁ Κρής. "δέχομαι."

For you, lion-strangling, boar-slaying lord, I, an oak club, was dedicated . . . 'By whom?' Archinus. 'From where?' He's a Cretan. 'I accept.' (Callim. *Epigr*. 34 Pf. = *Anth. Pal.* 6.351, transl. Gutzwiller)

Still more daring in style is the presentation of two conversations between a prostitute and a (potential) customer, one of which goes under the name of Philodemus:[93]

(30) *"χαῖρε σύ." "καὶ σύ γε χαῖρε." "τί δεῖ σε καλεῖν;" "σὲ δέ;" "μήπω*
τοῦτο φιλοσπούδει." "μηδὲ σύ." "μή τιν' ἔχεις;"
"αἰεὶ τὸν φιλέοντα." "θέλεις ἅμα σήμερον ἡμῖν
δειπνεῖν;" "εἰ σὺ θέλεις." "εὖ γε· πόσου παρέσῃ;"
"μηδέν μοι προδίδου." "τοῦτο ξένον." "ἀλλ' ὅσον ἄν σοι
κοιμηθέντι δοκῇ, τοῦτο δός." "οὐκ ἀδικεῖς.
ποῦ γίνῃ; πέμψω." "καταμάνθανε." "πηνίκα δ' ἥξεις;"
"ἣν σὺ θέλεις ὥρην." "εὐθὺ θέλω." "πρόαγε."

'Good day.' 'And good day to you.' 'What is your name?' 'And what is yours?' 'Don't be in a hurry about that yet.' 'Then don't you either.' 'Are you engaged?' 'To anyone who fancies me.' 'Will you dine with me today?' 'If it is your wish.' 'Good. And what will your company cost me?' 'Give me nothing in advance—' 'That's most unusual.' '. . . Only give me what you think right after you have slept with me.' 'You're very honest. Where will you be? I will send for you.' 'You can find out.' 'When will you arrive?' 'Whatever time you like.' 'The present moment is what I

[92] Lively dialogue between Gorgo and Praxagora in ll. 1–60, no less than 6 speakers in ll. 60b–149. A text like Theocritus 15 makes one wonder what kind of reception was intended for the *Corpus Theocriteum*. 'Recitation or even "performance" by more than one actor is certainly not an implausible complement to reception through reading' (R. L. Hunter 1999: 11). The part of the singer (100–44), by the way, contains a quoted speech (l. 127).

[93] *Anth. Pal.* 5.46 = Philodemus *ep.* 20 Sider; the other epigram is *Anth. Pal.* 5.101 (anonymous).

like.' 'Then lead the way.' (*Anth. Pal.* 5.46 = Philodemus *ep.* 20 Sider, transl. Page)

Taken together, these texts point in the direction of a gradual disappearance of external demarcation signals as a general tendency. Poets like Menander took part in this development in an important way, but it is unlikely that a single poet was influential alone. The interpretation as a general tendency is indirectly supported by a a pre-Menandrean prose text:

(31) *τὸ μὲν δὴ βιβλίον, ὦ Τερψίων, τουτί· ἐγραψάμην δὲ δὴ οὑτωσὶ τὸν λόγον, οὐκ ἐμοὶ Σωκράτη διηγούμενον ὡς διηγεῖτο, ἀλλὰ διαλεγόμενον οἷς ἔφη διαλεχθῆναι. ἔφη δὲ τῷ τε γεωμέτρῃ Θεοδώρῳ καὶ τῷ Θεαιτήτῳ. ἵνα οὖν ἐν τῇ γραφῇ μὴ παρέχοιεν πράγματα αἱ μεταξὺ τῶν λόγων διηγήσεις περὶ αὑτοῦ τε ὁπότε λέγοι ὁ Σωκράτης, οἷον "καὶ ἐγὼ ἔφην" ἢ "καὶ ἐγὼ εἶπον", ἢ αὖ περὶ τοῦ ἀποκρινομένου ὅτι "συνέφη" ἢ "οὐχ ὡμολόγει", τούτων ἕνεκα ὡς αὐτὸν αὐτοῖς διαλεγόμενον ἔγραψα, ἐξελὼν τὰ τοιαῦτα.*

(Eukleides speaking) Here is the book, Terpsion. Now this is the way I wrote the conversation: I did not represent Socrates relating it to me, as he did, but conversing with those with whom he told me he conversed. And he told me they were the geometrician Theodorus and Theaetetus. Now in order that the explanatory words between the speeches might not be annoying in the written account, such as 'and I said' or 'and I remarked,' whenever Socrates spoke, or 'he agreed' or 'he did not agree,' in the case of the interlocutor, I omitted all that sort of thing and represented Socrates himself as talking with them. (Pl. *Tht.* 143 B–C)

At first sight, this text seems irrelevant because it deals with the avoidance of speech within speech. Plato makes Eukleides write as it were a drama instead of a narrative text with an I-narrator.[94] It is, however, remarkable that he justifies this transformation by expressing fears that the quotatives could be annoying.[95] Plato/Eukleides consider a text without external demarcation signals as smoother. All in all, this is a slightly different question, but the

[94] An I-narrator Eukleides reporting what Socrates told him about the conversation with Theaetetus would lead to extensive quoted speeches.

[95] A considerably different function was given to these 'quotatives' in an adaptation of Plato's *Phaedo* for the stage by the Theater am Neumarkt in Zürich. Despite the transformation into a dramatic text, a number of 'X said's' were left in the text. On the one hand, they had the function of identifying the speaker because the different roles were played by two actors only. On the other hand, the 'breach of the dramatic illusion' also had something of a Brechtian *Verfremdungseffekt*.

passage proves that the function and effect of 'quotatives' were part of a general discussion from different points of view.

V. CONCLUSION

The present article shows summarily how the widespread literary device of speech within speech is used and further developed in early and classical Greek poetry until it reaches the most important representative of New Comedy, Menander. The focus of this survey is on (i) quantitative aspects, (ii) narratological distinctions (factual/imagined quoted speech; external/internal analepsis), and (iii) formalistic questions of demarcation. As it appears, Menander takes over a popular and full-fledged literary device, the possibilities of which he exploits and further develops for his own dramaturgical purposes. These developments concern notably the number and length of quoted speeches. (The purpose of the extensive quotations above is also to give an immediate impression of that quantity.) In addition, the system of demarcation signals becomes more and more sophisticated, in connection with a considerable increase of quoted dialogues. From comparisons with earlier, contemporaneous and later poetry it appears that this development is due more to a general tendency of 'modernization' than to the personal preference of a single author.

It is generally assumed that this 'modernization' has its roots in the growing influence of the actors in the fourth century. Long speeches with numerous quoted speeches are said to offer 'the actor an opportunity of displaying his virtuosity'.[96] This is no doubt true, but in my view one should not overestimate the difficulties of a successful delivery. Modern actors learn to master tasks of this kind during their education. Why should their counterparts in antiquity not be expected to have done likewise?[97] Actors in antiquity were used to playing several roles in a single play. In all likelihood, they reinforced the effect of different costumes and masks by a delivery which fitted each

[96] The phrase is Gomme–Sandbach's (1973: 570), the idea is ubiquitous: Flury (1968: 51–3), Lamagna (1998: 297–8), Arnott (2000: 259 n. 25), etc.

[97] On actors and their practising methods see Pickard-Cambridge (1988: esp. 167–71).

respective character. To do so in a single scene was (and is) less difficult than some scholars tend to believe. Nor should one exaggerate the difference between classical and post-classical acting. The growing importance of the actors in the fourth century (Pickard-Cambridge 1988: 94) should not blur the fact that fifth-century poets already expected a good deal of histrionic versatility from their actors. See above on ex. (16), and especially ex. (14) from Aristophanes' *Thesmophoriazousai*, where a male actor plays a male character (Euripides' in-law) who disguises as a woman and relates to the woman assembly an anecdote involving 'her' and 'her husband'.

An equally important consideration concerns Menander's exploitation of speech within speech for his dramaturgical purposes. Far from being a mere technical device to circumvent the restrictions of the genre (three-actor-rule, unity of place, masks), Menander uses speech within speech in its own right. Among the possible functions are: indirect introduction and characterization of new characters (exx. 22, 23, 25), characterization of the quoting character (exx. 20, 21, 25), comic effects (exx. 24, 25), vividness, etc. Furthermore, and perhaps more importantly, the 'narrative' device of speech within speech allows Menander to bring on stage scenes which could not be played there for more serious reasons than technicalities like the unity of place. Examples are the rehearsal scene (ex. 24), Charisios' anticlimactic eavesdropping (ex. 25), Demeas' overhearing in the pantry (ex. 26), or the tumultuous mass scene in the assembly (ex. 27). *If* speech within speech originally was a makeshift, Menander certainly made the best of it. One should perhaps not go as far as to turn the traditional explanation upside down and to claim that Menander forced his actors to learn how to deliver quoted speeches. But the respective needs and goals of dramaturge and actors are well cared for in the way Menander uses speech within speech in his plays.[98]

[98] It is a pleasure to thank Ela Harrison (Oxford/Stanford) for correcting my English.

VI. APPENDIX

Table 10.3 lists all instances of quoted speech in Menander. Given the nature of the transmission, it is very likely that a number of unrecognized instances lurk in the mutilated passages of Menander's oeuvre. 'Introduction' and 'Capping' list the demarcation signals (as described above, round brackets indicating minor variations) in the sequence they have in the text. 'Who?' names the speaker of the embedding speech, 'Whom?' the speaker of the quoted speech. A '+' in the column 'Dialogue' indicates that both speakers are actually quoted.

TABLE 10.3. *Quoted speech in Menander*

		Introduction	Capping	Who?	Whom?	Dialogue
Asp.	210	i, vi	vi′	Smikrines	Daos	
	343–4	i		Daos	Daos etc.	
	469	i		Smikrines?	Daos etc.	
DE	22	(i)		Sostratos	'Bacchis'[a]	
	23	vii, vi*a*		Sostratos	'Bacchis'	
	24	(i), vi		Sostratos	'Bacchis'	
	95–6	(i)		Sostratos	'Bacchis'	
Dys.	107–8	iii, vi, v	iv*a*′	Pyrrhias	Pyrrhias	+
	108–10	iv*a*, v, iii, vi	vi*a*′	Pyrrhias	Knemon	+
	112	vi	i′	Pyrrhias	Pyrrhias	+
	114–15	vi, iii, vi*a*	i′	Pyrrhias	Knemon	+
	538–9	iii, v		Sostratos	Gorgias	+
	539–41	vi*a*, (iv*a*)	vi*a*′, iv*a*′	Sostratos	Sostratos	+
	727–9	vi		Knemon	Gorgias	
Epit.	253–5	(i), vi*a*	vi*a*′, iv′	Daos	Daos	
	261	vi*a*, iii	vi*a*′	Daos	Syriskos	+
	261–2	vi*a*, (iv*a*)		Daos	Daos	+
	264–8	i, vi, v, iii	(iv′), i′	Daos	Syriskos	
	346[b]	vi, iii	iv′	Syriskos	Daos	
	424–5	i, vi*a*		Onesimos	Charisios	

Table 10.3. (*cont.*)

		Introduction	Capping	Who?	Whom?	Dialogue
Epit.	517–18	i		Habrotonon	Habrotonon	
	527–9	(i), (iv), vi, vi*a*	i′	Habrotonon	Habrotonon	
	533–4	iii, vi		Habrotonon	Habrotonon	
	888	v, vi*a*, vi		Onesimos	Charisios	
	890–1	(i), vi*a*		Onesimos	Charisios	
	894–9	iii		Onesimos	Charisios	
	913–18	v, vi	(iv′), i′	Onesimos	Daimonion	
	929–31	i, vi, v	vi*a*′	Charisios	Charisios	
Thph.	17–18	(iv*a*), iii	iv*a*′	Parmenon?	Girl	+
	19–23	iv*a*, vi*a*, vi, v		Parmenon?	? (male)	+
	fr. 1.1–5	i, v, vi	vi*a*′	Kraton	a God	+
	fr. 1.6–19	iii, vi		Kraton	Kraton	+
Kol.	50–4	i, v, vi		Gnathon?	Gnathon?	
	125–6	i, vi, v		pimp	Pheidias?	
Mis.	A53[c]	i, v		Thrasonides	Thrasonides	
	A53–4	iii	i′	Thrasonides	Thrasonides	
	A55–6	i		Thrasonides	a wife	
	132–3	(i), vi, v	vi*a*′	?	? (female)	+
	133–5	vi*a*, iii		?	? (male)	+
Pk.	319–23	iii		Daos	Myrrhine	

	547–50	i	(iv*a*′)	Moschion	Moschion	
Sam.	227	i, viii	(iv*a*′)	Demeas	women	
	242–3	(iv), v, iii	vi*a*′	Demeas	Nurse	
	245–?	i, v, vii		Demeas	Nurse	
	252–4	vi, vi*a*, iii	vi*a*′	Demeas	Nurse	+
	255–6	iv*a*, v, vi, iii		Demeas	Maid	+
	256	vi*a*	vi*a*′	Demeas	Nurse	+
	257–9	iii	i′	Demeas	Maid	+
	260–1	iv*a*, v, vii		Demeas	Nurse	
Sik.	9–10	i, iv*a*	(i′)	Prol. deity	Stratophanes	
	13–?	v, vi, iii		Prol. deity	Slave	
	189	v	i′	Messenger	Messenger	
	?–195			Messenger	Dromon	+
	197	iv*a*		Messenger	Crowd	+
	202	v, iii		Messenger	A	+
	203–4	vi*a*, vi	vi*a*′	Messenger	A	+
	204–7	iii		Messenger	Moschion	+
	223	v, vi*a*	vi*a*′	Messenger	Crowd	+
	224–6	(vi*a*), iii		Messenger	Stratophanes	+
	?–239			Messenger	Stratophanes	+
	239	vi*a*		Messenger	Crowd	+
	239–45	v, vi		Messenger	Stratophanes	+
	245	i, vi*a*	vi*a*′	Messenger	Crowd	+
	246–57	(vi*a*)		Messenger	Stratophanes	+

TABLE 10.3. (*cont.*)

		Introduction	Capping	Who?	Whom?	Dialogue
Sik.	257	vi*a*		Messenger	Crowd	+
	257–8	v, vi*a*	iv*a*′	Messenger	?[d]	+
	260–3	i, vi		Messenger	Moschion	+
	264	vi*a*, vi	vi*a*′	Messenger	?	+
	265	vi*a*, vi		Messenger	?	+
	265–6	vi*a*, v	vi*a*′	Messenger	?	+
	266	vi*a*		Messenger	?	+
	267	iv*a*, v, vi	iv*a*′	Messenger	Stratophanes	+
	268–9	iv*a*, vi, iii, v		Messenger	Dromon	+
	269	vi*a*, vi		Messenger	Crowd	+
Ph.	7?			a God		
	97	i	iv*a*′	?	? (female)	+
	98	iv*a*, vi		?	? ('you')	+
fr.	25.6	i		a gourmand	a gourmand	
	256.4	i		?	'one'	
	280.2		i′	?	a lover?	
	349.2		i′	?	arrogant people	
	401.2	ii		?	symposiasts	
	420.7	iii		a young lover	'one'	
	607.1	vi*a*, vi	vi*a*′	a parasite?	a parasite?	+

607.2	(via)		a parasite?	a soldier	+
607.2	via	via′	a parasite?	a parasite?	+
607.2–3	(via)		a parasite?	a soldier	+

[a] In Plautus' adaptation her name is 'Bacchis', in Menander perhaps 'Chrysis' (Handley 1968: 21).

[b] The table does not list quotations of what the dialogue partner just said (e.g. *Asp*. 273–4: (Chairestratos) *τοῦτο δ' οἴει; κατάβαλε.* (Smikrines) *"οἴει" λέγεις;* 'You think that? Drop it!' 'You say "think", do you?'). The present passage is different because of its distance from the quotation (*Epit*. 289).

[c] For the distribution of these lines see ex. (20).

[d] For the difficult attribution of this and the following entries see ex. (27).

References

ADAMI, F. (1901). 'De poetis scaenicis Graecis hymnorum sacrorum imitatoribus'. *Jahrbücher für classische Philologie*, Suppl. 26: 213–62.

ADAMS, J. N. (1984). 'Female Speech in Latin Comedy'. *Antichthon*, 18: 43–77.

ADKINS, A. W. H. (1970). 'Clouds, Mysteries, Socrates and Plato'. *Antichthon*, 4: 13–24.

AGOSTINIANI, L. (1988/9). 'I modi del contatto linguistico tra Greci e indigeni nella Sicilia antica'. *Kokalos*, 34/5: 167–208.

AHRENS, H. L. (1843). 'Epicharmi fragmenta', in id., *De graecae linguae dialectis: II. De dialecto Dorica*. Göttingen, 435–63.

AITKEN, A. J. (1979). 'Scottish Speech: A Historical View, with Special Reference to the Standard English of Scotland', in A. J. Aitken and T. McArthur (eds.), *Languages of Scotland*. Edinburgh, 85–118.

—— (1984). 'Scots and English in Scotland', in P. Trudgill (ed.), *Language in the British Isles*. Cambridge, 517–32.

ALBINI, U. (1984). 'Le commedie di Epicarmo'. *Sileno*, 10 (= *Studi in onore di Adelmo Barigazzi I*): 13–21.

ALLEN, W. S. (1968). 'Varia onomatopoetica'. *Lingua*, 21: 1–12.

—— (1987). *Vox Graeca: A Guide to the Pronunciation of Classical Greek*, 3rd edn. Cambridge.

ALONI, A., BARCHIESI, A., and CAVARZERE, A. (eds.) (2001). *Iambic Ideas*. Lanham, Md.

ALTY, J. (1982). 'Dorians and Ionians'. *JHS* 102: 1–14.

AMATI, C. (1901). 'Contributo alle ricerche sull'uso della lingua familiare in Euripide'. *SIFC* 9: 125–48.

AMIGUÈS, S. (1977). *Les Subordonnées finales par ὅπως en attique classique* (Études et commentaires, 89). Paris.

ANAGNOSTOPOULOS, G. P. (1925). '*Περὶ τῆς γλώσσης τῶν κωμῳδιῶν τοῦ Ἀριστοφάνους*'. *Athena*, 36: 1–60.

ANDERSON, A. R. (1913). 'Repudiative Questions in Greek Drama, and in Plautus and Terence'. *TAPhA* 44: 43–64.

ANDERSON, C. A. (1995). *Athena's Epithets: Their Structural Significance in Plays of Aristophanes* (Beiträge zur Altertumskunde, 67). Stuttgart and Leipzig.

ANDERSON, G. (1981). 'Ληκύθιον and αὐτολήκυθος'. *JHS* 101: 130–2.

ANDRISANO, A. (1984/5). 'Θέωρος "nome parlante" (Aristoph. *Vesp.* 42ss., etc.)'. *Museum Criticum*, 19/20: 71–85.

ARGENIO, R. (1964). 'Il comico Eubulo'. *Rivista di studi classici*, 12: 125–43.

ARNOTT, W. G. (1957). 'Split Anapaests with Special Reference to Some Passages of Alexis'. *CQ*, NS 7: 188–98.

—— (1964). 'The Confrontation of Sostratos and Gorgias'. *Phoenix*, 18: 110–25.

—— (1970). 'Towards an Edition of the Fragments of Alexis'. *PCPhS*, NS 16: 1–11.

—— (1979). *Menander*, vol. i. Cambridge, Mass.

—— (1986). 'Menander and Earlier Drama', in J. H. Betts, J. T. Hooker, and J. R. Green (eds.), *Studies in Honour of T. B. L. Webster*, 2 vols. Bristol (1986–8), i. 1–9.

—— (1993). 'Comic Openings', in N. W. Slater and B. Zimmermann (eds.), *Intertextualität in der griechisch-römischen Komödie* (Drama, 2; Stuttgart, 1993), 14–32.

—— (1995). 'Menander's Manipulation of Language for the Individualisation of Character', in De Martino–Sommerstein (1995), ii. 147–64.

—— (1996*a*). *Menander*, vol. ii. Cambridge, Mass.

—— (1996*b*). *Alexis: The Fragments. A Commentary*. Cambridge.

—— (1999). 'The Length of Menander's *Samia*'. *ZPE* 128: 45–8.

—— (2000). *Menander*, vol. iii. Cambridge, Mass.

—— (2001*a*). 'Some Orthographical Problems in the Papyri of Later Greek Comedy I: πο(ι)εῖν (Along with Compounds and Congeners)'. *ZPE* 134: 43–51.

—— (2001*b*). 'Some Orthographical Problems in the Papyri of Later Greek Comedy II: -ει or -η(ι) as the Ending of the Second Person Singular Middle and Passive in the Present and Other Tenses of Verbs in -ω'. *ZPE* 135: 36–40.

ARNSON SVARLIEN, D. (1990/1). 'Epicharmus and Pindar at Hieron's Court'. *Kokalos*, 36/7: 103–10.

ASTORGA, J. A. (1990). 'The Art of Diphilus: A Study of Verbal Humor in New Comedy'. Diss. Berkeley (*DA* 52/04: 1315; UMI order-no. 9126471).

AUSTIN, C. (1969, 1970). *Menandri Aspis et Samia*, 2 vols. Berlin.

—— (1973). *Comicorum Graecorum Fragmenta in papyris reperta*. Berlin.

AUSTIN, T. R. (1984). *Language Crafted: A Linguistic Theory of Poetic Syntax*. Bloomington, Ind.

BÄBLER, B. (1998). *Fleißige Thrakerinnen und wehrhafte Skythen: Nichtgriechen im klassischen Athen und ihre archäologische Hinterlassenschaft* (Beiträge zur Altertumskunde, 108). Stuttgart and Leipzig.

BACHMANN, P. (1961). *Ellipsen und Anakoluthe als Elemente der Umgangssprache in den* Acharnern *des Aristophanes*. Diss. Göttingen.

BAECHLE, N. W. (1993). 'Metrical Constraint and Poetic Style in the Greek Tragic Trimeter (Word Order)'. Diss. Yale (*DA* 55/05: 1253; UMI order-no. 9426189).

BAIN, D. (1977). *Actors and Audience: A Study of Asides and Related Conventions in Greek Drama*. Oxford.

—— (1981). 'Menander, *Samia* 580 and "Not- und Hilferufe" in Ptolemaic Egypt'. *ZPE* 44: 169–71; addendum *ZPE* 45 (1982), 270.

—— (1984). 'Female Speech in Menander'. *Antichthon*, 18: 24–42.

—— (1985). '*Ληκύθιον ἀπώλεσεν*: Some Reservations'. *CQ*, NS 35: 31–7.

—— (1991*a*). 'Six Greek Verbs of Sexual Congress (*βινῶ, κινῶ, πυγίζω, ληκῶ, οἴφω, λαικάζω*)'. *CQ*, NS 41: 51–77.

—— (1991*b*). '*Ἐπιβατεύω* in Aristophanes' *Frogs* (v. 48)'. *Eikasmos*, 2: 159–61.

BAKHTIN, M. M. (1981). *The Dialogic Imagination: Four Essays*, ed. M. Holquist, trans. C. Emerson and M. Holquist. Austin.

BALDWIN, B. (1981). 'The Use of *βινεῖν κινεῖν*'. *AJPh* 102: 79–80.

BANKS, T. R. (1973). 'A Study of the Imagery of Aristophanes' "Wasps" in its Dramatic Context'. Diss. Univ. of Minnesota (*DA* 34/07: 4223; UMI order-no. 7400683).

BARIGAZZI, A. (1955). 'Epicarmo e la figura di Ulisse *ἥσυχος*'. *RhM*, NF 98: 121–35.

BARON, S. H. (ed. and trans.) (1967). *The Travels of Olearius in 17th-Century Russia*. Stanford.

BARTOL, K. (1992). 'How was Iambic Poetry Performed? A Question of Ps.-Plutarch's Reliability (*Mus.* 1141A)'. *Euphrosyne*, 20: 269–76.

—— (1993). *Greek Elegy and Iambus: Studies in Ancient Literary Sources*. Poznań.

BASSET, L. (1997). '*Ἀλλ' ἐξόλοισθ' αὐτῷ κοάξ*: Réexamen des emplois d'*ἀλλά* à la lumière de l'énonciation dans les *Grenouilles* d'Aristophane', in Rijksbaron (1997), 75–99.

BAUCK, L. (1880). *De proverbiis aliisque locutionibus ex usu vitae petitis apud Aristophanem comicum*. Königsberg.

BECHTEL, F. (1923). *Die griechischen Dialekte*, ii: *Die westgriechischen Dialekte*. Berlin.

BECK, W. (1982). '*Ληκύθιον ἀπώλεσεν* (and Theocritus ii 156)'. *JHS* 102: 234.

BELARDINELLI, A. M. (1994). *Menandro* Sicioni*: Introduzione, testo e commento*. Bari.

BENVENISTE, É. (1966). *Problèmes de linguistique générale*. Paris.

BERK, L. (1964). *Epicharmus* (Diss. Utrecht). Groningen.

BERNABÉ, A. (1995). 'Una cosmogonía cómica: Aristófanes, Aves 685ss.', in López Férez (1995), 195–211.

BERNAYS, J. (1853). 'Epicharmos und der αὐξανόμενος λόγος'. *RhM* 8: 280–8 = id., *Gesammelte Abhandlungen*, ed. H. Usener, Berlin (1885), 109–17.

BERS, V. (1984). *Greek Poetic Syntax in the Classical Age*. New Haven.

—— (1997). *Speech in Speech: Studies in Incorporated* Oratio Recta *in Attic Drama and Oratory*. Lanham, Md.

BETA, S. (1992). 'Il linguaggio erotico di Cratino'. *QUCC* 40: 95–108.

BETTARINI, L. (1998). 'Dialetti e commedia: *Pap. Argent.* 2345^{r} (fr. *adesp.* 1035, 1–2 K.–A.)'. *AION(filol.)*, 20: 129–45.

BIRAUD, M. (1991). 'L'emploi exclamatif de οἷος dans les comédies d'Aristophane: syntaxe, sémantique, énonciation'. *Lalies*, 12: 145–52.

BJÖRCK, G. (1950). *Das Alpha impurum und die tragische Kunstsprache: Attische Wort- und Stilstudien* (Acta Societatis Litterarum Humaniorum Regiae Upsaliensis, 39.1). Uppsala.

BLASS, F. (1889). 'Das neue Wiener Fragment des Epicharmus'. *Neue Jahrbücher für Philologie und Paedagogik*, 139: 257–62.

BLASZCZAK, W. (1932). *Götteranrufung und Beteuerung: Untersuchungen zu volkstümlichen Ausdrucksformen in der griechischen Literatur*. Diss. Breslau.

BLUME, H.-D. (1974). *Menanders 'Samia': Eine Interpretation*. Darmstadt.

—— (1998). *Menander*. Darmstadt.

BLÜMNER, H. (1891). *Über Gleichnis und Metapher in der attischen Komödie*. Leipzig.

BLUNDELL, J. (1980). *Menander and the Monologue* (Hypomnemata, 59). Göttingen.

BONANNO, M. G. (1972). *Studi su Cratete comico*. Padua.

—— (1980). 'Nomi e soprannomi archilochei'. *MH* 37: 65–88.

—— (1983). 'Aristoph. fr. 198 K. (ὀνόματα καινά)'. *Museum Criticum*, 18: 61–70.

—— (1984/5). 'Δεξίνικος "nome parlante" (Aristoph. *Plut.* 800)'. *Museum Criticum*, 19/20: 99–101.

—— (1987). 'Metafore redivive e nomi parlanti (sui modi del Witz in Aristofane)', in S. Boldrini *et al.*, *Filologia e forme letterarie: Studi offerti a Francesco Della Corte*, 5 vols. Urbino, i. 213–28.

BORTHWICK, E. K. (1993). '*Autolekythos* and *lekythion* in Demosthenes and Aristophanes'. *LCM* 18: 34–7.

BOSCHERINI, S. (1959). 'ὀδύνης υἱός (Menandri, *Dysc.*, v. 88)'. *SIFC*, NS 31: 247–53.

BOSSI, F. (1990). *Studi su Archiloco*, 2nd edn. Bari.

BOWIE, A. M. (1982). 'The Parabasis in Aristophanes: Prolegomena, *Acharnians*'. *CQ*, NS 32: 27–40.

BOWIE, E. L. (1988). 'Who Is Dicaeopolis?'. *JHS* 108: 183–5.

—— (1990). '*Marginalia Obsceniora*: Some Problems in Aristophanes' *Wasps*', in Craik (1990), 31–8.

—— (1998). 'Le portrait de Socrate dans les *Nuées* d'Aristophane', in M. Trédé and P. Hoffmann (eds.), *Le Rire des anciens*. Paris, 53–66.

—— (2001). 'Early Greek Iambic Poetry: The Importance of Narrative', in Aloni *et al.* (2001), in press.

Brandenstein, W. (1964). 'Der persische Satz bei Aristophanes, Ἀχαρνῆς, Vers 100'. *Wiener Zeitschrift für die Kunde Süd- und Ostasiens*, 8: 43–58.

Bremer, J. M. (1993). 'Aristophanes on his own Poetry', in Bremer–Handley (1993), 125–72.

—— and Handley, E. W. (eds.) (1993). *Aristophane: sept exposés suivis de discussions* (Entretiens Hardt, 38). Vandœuvres-Geneva.

Brenk, F. E. (1987). '*Heteros tis eimi*: On the Language of Menander's Young Lovers'. *ICS* 12: 31–66.

Brescia, C. (1960). 'Lessico aggettivale del Dyscolos di Menandro', in *Menandrea* (1960), 113–24.

Brewer, J. S. (1861). *Giraldi Cambrensis Opera*, vol. i. London.

Brixhe, C. (1988). 'La langue de l'étranger non grec chez Aristophane', in R. Lonis (ed.), *L'Étranger dans le monde grec: Actes du colloque organisé par l'Institut d'Études Anciennes Nancy*. Nancy, 113–38.

Brown, A. L. (1982). 'Some Problems in the *Eumenides* of Aeschylus'. *JHS* 102: 26–32.

Brown, C. (1983). 'From Rags to Riches: Anacreon's Artemon'. *Phoenix*, 37: 1–15.

Brown, P. G. McC. (1987). 'Masks, Names and Characters in the New Comedy'. *Hermes*, 115: 181–202.

Bruhn, C. (1910). *Über den Wortschatz des Menander* (Diss. Kiel). Jena.

Brunius-Nilsson, E. (1955). *Δαιμόνιε: An Inquiry into a Mode of Apostrophe*. Uppsala.

Brzóstkowska, A. (1983). 'Degradacyjna rola terminologii ze świata niewolników w komediach Arystofanesa'. *Eos*, 71: 283–97.

Buck, C. D. (1955). *The Greek Dialects*. Chicago.

Bühler, W. (1999). *Zenobii Athoi proverbia V*. Göttingen.

Burckhardt, A. (1924). *Spuren der athenischen Volksrede in der alten Komödie*. Diss. Basel.

Burelli, L. (1973). 'Metafore monetali e provvedimenti finanziari in Aristofane'. *ASNP* 3: 767–86.

Burkert, W. (1972). *Lore and Science in Ancient Pythagoreanism*, trans. Edwin L. Minar, Jr. Cambridge, Mass.

—— (1994). 'Orpheus, Dionysos und die Euneiden in Athen: das Zeugnis von Euripides' *Hypsipyle*', in A. Bierl and P. von Möllendorff (eds.), *Orchestra: Drama, Mythos, Bühne*. Stuttgart and Leipzig, 44–9.

Buttmann, P. (1819). *Ausführliche griechische Sprachlehre*, vol. i. Berlin.

Byl, S. (1981). 'Le vocabulaire de la *mètis* dans les *Nuées* d'Aristophane'. *AC* 50: 112–20.

—— (1990). 'Le vocabulaire hippocratique dans les comédies d'Aristophane et particulièrement dans les deux dernières'. *RPh*, 3rd ser. 64: 151–62.

Cairns, D. L. (1993). *Aidos: The Psychology and Ethics of Honour and Shame in Ancient Greek Literature*. Oxford.

Calame, C. (1977). *Les Chœurs de jeunes filles en Grèce archaïque: I. Morphologie, fonction religieuse et sociale*. Rome.

—— (1983). *Alcman*. Rome.

Calder III, W. M. (1970). 'Aristophanes *Vespae* 68–69: An Unnoticed Obscenity'. *CPh* 65: 257.

—— (1971). 'Professor Calder Replies'. *CPh* 66: 262.

Calvet, L.-J. (1998). *Language Wars and Linguistic Politics*, trans. M. Petherham. Oxford.

Camacho Maxia, J. (1996). *Léxico marinero en Aristófanes*. Valencia.

Campagnolo, M. (1991/2). 'Le comique dans les fragments d'Euboulos selon la critique littéraire antique: analyse des fragments à la lumière du *Tractatus Coislinianus*'. *AIV* 150: 411–96.

Campbell, A. Y. (1943). 'The *οὐ μή* Constructions and Aristophanes, *Clouds* 295–7'. *CR* 57: 58–61.

Carey, C. (1986). 'Archilochus and Lykambes'. *CQ*, NS 36: 60–7.

—— (1993). 'The Purpose of Aristophanes' *Acharnians*'. *RhM*, NF 136: 245–63.

—— (1994). 'Comic Ridicule and Democracy', in R. Osborne and S. Hornblower (eds.), *Ritual, Finance, Politics: Athenian Democratic Accounts Presented to David Lewis*. Oxford, 69–83.

Carrière, J. C. (1979). *Le Carnaval et la politique: Une introduction à la comédie grecque suivie d'un choix de fragments* (Centre de recherches d'histoire ancienne, 26). Paris.

Cassio, A. C. (1981). 'Attico "volgare" e ioni in Atene alla fine del 5 secolo a.C.' *AION(filol.)*, 3: 79–93.

—— (1985*a*). *Commedia e partecipazione: La* Pace *di Aristofane*. Naples.

—— (1985*b*). 'Old Persian *marīka-*, Eupolis' *Marikas* and Aristophanes' *Knights*'. *CQ*, NS 35: 38–42.

—— (1985*c*). 'Two Studies on Epicharmus and his Influence'. *HSPh* 89: 37–51.

—— (1989). 'Lo sviluppo della prosa dorica e le tradizioni occidentali della retorica greca', in A. C. Cassio and D. Musti (eds.), *Tra Sicilia e Magna Grecia: Aspetti di interazione culturale nel IV sec. a. C. Atti del Convegno Napoli 19–20 marzo 1987 = AION(filol.)*, 11: 137–57.

—— (1993). 'Alcmane, il dialetto di Cirene e la filologia alessandrina'. *RFIC* 121: 24–36.

—— (1997). 'Futuri dorici, dialetto di Siracusa e testo antico dei lirici greci', in A. C. Cassio (ed.), *Katà Diálekton: Atti del III Colloquio internazionale di dialettologia greca Napoli-Ischia 25–28 settembre 1996 = AION(filol.)*, 19: 187–214.

—— (1998). '*γερωχία* e *ἀγερωχία*: comicità e dialetto nella Lisistrata di Aristofane'. *Seminari romani di cultura greca*, 1.1: 73–8.

—— (2000). 'Esametri orfici, dialetto attico e musica dell'Asia Minore', in A. C. Cassio, D. Musti, and L. E. Rossi (eds.), *Synaulía: Cultura musicale in Grecia e contatti mediterranei* (*AION(filol.*), Quaderni, 5). Naples, 97–110.

Cavallero, P. A. (1994). 'El humorismo en Menandro'. *Dioniso*, 64: 83–103.

Chantraine, H. (1962). 'Bemerkungen zum ältesten sizilischen und römischen Münzwesen'. *Jahrbücher für Numismatik und Geldgeschichte*, 12: 51–64.

Chantraine, P. (1962). 'Deux notes sur le vocabulaire comique d'Aristophane'. *REG* 75: 381–95.

Chapman, G. A. H. (1983). 'Some Notes on Dramatic Illusion in Aristophanes'. *AJPh* 104: 1–23.

Chiarini, G. (1983). '*Metafora* e *metonimia*: Per l'elaborazione di un modello interpretativo del teatro classico'. *Res publica litterarum (Univ. of Kansas)*, 6: 113–22.

Chilton, P., and Schäffner, C. (1997). 'Discourse and Politics', in van Dijk (1997*b*), 206–30.

Clyne, M. G. (1968). 'Zum Pidgin-Deutsch der Gastarbeiter'. *Zeitschrift für Mundartforschung*, 5: 130–9.

Coccia, M. (1960). 'Gli anapesti nei trimetri del *ΔΥΣΚΟΛΟΣ*', in *Menandrea* (1960), 159–64.

Collard, C. (1979). '*Βινεῖν* and Aristophanes, *Lysistrata* 934'. *LCM* 4: 213–14.

Colvin, S. (1995). 'Aristophanes: Dialect and Textual Criticism'. *Mnemosyne*, 4th ser. 48: 34–47.

—— (1999). *Dialect in Aristophanes and the Politics of Language in Ancient Greek Literature*. Oxford.

—— (2000). 'The Language of Non-Athenians in Old Comedy', in Harvey–Wilkins (2000), 285–98.

Connor, W. R. (1993). 'The Ionian Era of Athenian Civic Identity'. *Proceedings of the American Philosophical Society*, 137: 194–206.

Conti Bizzarro, F. (1998). 'Sull'impiego di forme inniche nella commedia greca', in García Novo–Rodríguez Alfageme (1998), 251–8.

Corbato, C. (1963). 'Il *Dyskolos* di Menandro, un saggio e una bibliografia'. *Dioniso*, 37: 157–221.

Corbett, G. (1990). 'Serbo-Croat', in B. Comrie (ed.), *The Major Languages of Eastern Europe*. London, 125–43.

CORDANO, F. (1992). *Le tessere pubbliche del tempio di Atena a Camarina*. Rome.

CORDER, S. P. (1975). 'The Language of Kehaar'. *Work in Progress: Department of Linguistics (University of Edinburgh)*, 8: 41–52.

—— and ROULET, E. (eds.) (1977). *Actes du 5ème colloque de linguistique appliquée de Neuchâtel 20–22 mai 1976: The Notions of Simplification, Interlanguages and Pidgins and their Relation to Second Language Pedagogy*. Neuchâtel.

CORSINI, E. (1993). 'Il prologo degli *Uccelli* di Aristofane', in Pretagostini (1993), ii. 679–88.

CRAIK, E. M. (ed.) (1990). *'Owls to Athens': Essays on Classical Subjects Presented to Sir Kenneth Dover*. Oxford.

CRAMER, J. A. (1835). *Anecdota Graeca e codd. manuscriptis bibliothecarum Oxoniensium*, vol. ii. Oxford (repr. Amsterdam, 1993).

CRÖNERT, W. (1922). 'Griechische literarische Papyri aus Straßburg, Freiburg und Berlin'. *Nachrichten von der Königlichen Gesellschaft der Wissenschaften zu Göttingen*, 1: 1–46.

CRYSTAL, D. (1995). *The Cambridge Encyclopedia of the English Language*. Cambridge.

CUNY, A. (1906). *Le Nombre duel en grec*. Paris.

D'ANGOUR, A. J. (1999). 'Archinus, Eucleides and the Reform of the Athenian Alphabet'. *BICS* 43: 109–30.

DANKER, F. W. (1960/1). 'The *υἱός* Phrases in the New Testament'. *NTS* 7: 94.

DAVIDSON, J. (1993). 'Fish, Sex and Revolution in Athens'. *CQ*, NS 43: 53–66.

—— (1997). *Courtesans and Fishcakes: The Consuming Passions of Classical Athens*. London.

DAVIES, M. (1987). 'Aeschylus' Clytemnestra: Sword or Axe?' *CQ*, NS 37: 65–75.

DEBRUNNER, A. (1954). 'Das Augment ἠ-', in A. Alt *et al.* (eds.), *Festschrift für Friedrich Zucker zum 70. Geburtstage*. Berlin, 83–110.

DE FALCO, V. (1930). 'Menandro'. *Athenaeum*, NS 8: 195–225.

—— (1949). 'Due note filologiche, II: Menandro, *Epitr.* 548–9 e *Peric.* 45–47'. *Emerita*, 17: 153–7.

DEGANI, E. (1987). 'Insulto ed escrologia'. *Dioniso*, 57: 31–47.

—— (1993). 'Aristofane e la tradizione dell'invettiva personale in Grecia', in Bremer–Handley (1993), 1–36.

DE GREGORI, L. (1901). 'Di Dioscuride e dei sui epigrammi'. *SIFC* 9: 149–93.

DELAUNOIS, M. (1986). 'Le comique dans les *Nuées* d'Aristophane'. *AC* 55: 86–112.

DEL CORNO, D. (1975). 'Alcuni aspetti del linguaggio di Menandro'. *SCO* 24: 13–48.

—— (1986). 'Scena e parola nelle "Rane" di Aristofane', in E. Corsini (ed.), *La polis e il suo teatro*. Padua, 205–14.

—— (1994). 'Lo stile di Menandro nella parola degli attori', in *Storia, poesia e pensiero nel mondo antico: Studi in onore di Marcello Gigante*. Naples, 173–80.

—— (1997). 'La caratterizzazione dei personaggi di Aristofane attraverso i fatti di lingua e di stile', in Thiercy–Menu (1997), 243–51.

DEMAND, N. (1971). 'Epicharmus and Gorgias'. *AJPh* 92: 453–63.

DE MARTINO, F., and SOMMERSTEIN, A. H. (eds.) (1995). *Lo spettacolo delle voci* (Le Rane, 14). Bari.

DENNISTON, J. D. (1927). 'Technical Terms in Aristophanes'. *CQ* 21: 113–21.

—— (1954). *The Greek Particles*, 2nd edn. Oxford.

DICKERSON, G. W. (1974). 'Aristophanes' *Ranae* 862: A Note on the Anatomy of Euripidean Tragedy'. *HSPh* 78: 177–88.

DICKEY, E. (1995). 'Forms of Address and Conversational Language in Aristophanes and Menander'. *Mnemosyne*, 4th ser. 48: 257–71.

—— (1996). *Greek Forms of Address: From Herodotus to Lucian*. Oxford.

DIELS, H., rev. KRANZ, W. (1951/2). *Die Fragmente der Vorsokratiker*, 6th edn. Berlin.

DIETERICH, A. (1893). 'Über eine Scene der aristophanischen *Wolken*'. *RhM*, NF 48: 275–83.

DIGGLE, J. (1968). 'Notes on the *Agamemnon* and *Persae* of Aeschylus'. *CR*, NS 18: 1–4.

DIJK, T. A. VAN (1997*a*). 'Discourse as Interaction in Society', in van Dijk (1997*b*), 1–37.

—— (ed.) (1997*b*). *Discourse as Social Interaction. Discourse Studies: A Multidisciplinary Introduction* (Discourse Studies, 2). London.

DIK, H. (1995). *Word Order in Ancient Greek: A Pragmatic Account of Word Order Variations in Herodotus*. Amsterdam.

DILLER, H. (1978). 'Zum Umgang des Aristophanes mit der Sprache—erläutert an den "Acharnern"'. *Hermes*, 106: 509–18.

DILLON, M. P. J. (1995). 'Gods, Tongues, and Dogs: The Use of Oaths in Aristophanic Comedy'. *G&R*, NS 42: 135–51.

DI MARCO, M. (1981). 'Aristoph. *Plut.* 800:. *Δεξίνικος*'. *Bollettino dei classici*, 2: 158–65.

—— (1987). '*Ἐρεβοδιφῶσιν*: paronimia e lusus osceno in Aristoph. *Nub.* 192 sg.'. *QUCC* 55: 55–8.

DITTMAR, W. (1933). *Sprachliche Untersuchungen zu Aristophanes und Menander* (Diss. Leipzig). Weida in Thüringen.

DOBROV, G. W. (1988). 'Winged Words/Graphic Birds: The Aristophanic Comedy of Language'. Diss. Cornell (*DA* 49/10: 3017; UMI order-no. 8900922).

DOBROV, G. W. (1995*a*). 'The Poet's Voice in the Evolution of Dramatic Dialogism', in Dobrov (1995*b*), 47–97.

—— (ed.) (1995*b*). *Beyond Aristophanes: Transition and Diversity in Greek Comedy* (American Classical Studies, 38). Atlanta, Ga.

—— (1997*a*). 'Language, Fiction, and Utopia', in Dobrov (1997*b*), 95–132.

—— (ed.) (1997*b*). *The City as Comedy: Society and Representation in Athenian Drama*. Chapel Hill.

—— and URIOS-APARISI, E. (1995). 'The Maculate Music: Gender, Genre and the *Chiron* of Pherecrates', in Dobrov (1995*b*), 139–74.

DÖHLE, B. (1967). 'Die Achilleis des Aischylos in ihrer Auswirkung auf die attische Vasenmalerei des 5. Jahrhunderts'. *Klio*, 49: 63–149.

DOHM, J. (1964). *Mageiros: Die Rolle des Kochs in der griechisch-römischen Komödie* (Zetemata, 32). Munich.

DOVER, K. J. (1957). 'Aristophanes 1938–1955'. *Lustrum*, 2: 52–112.

—— (1963). 'Notes on Aristophanes' *Acharnians*'. *Maia*, 15: 6–25; repr. Dover (1987), 288–306.

—— (1970). 'Lo stile di Aristofane'. *QUCC* 9: 7–23; English translation Dover (1987), 224–36.

—— (1971). 'Colloquial Formulae in Aristophanes', in W. Schmid (ed.), *Die Interpretation in der Altertumswissenschaft*. Bonn, 118–19.

—— (1972). *Aristophanic Comedy*. Berkeley and Los Angeles.

—— (1974). *Greek Popular Morality in the Time of Plato and Aristotle*. Oxford; repr. Indianapolis, 1994.

—— (1976). 'Linguaggio e caratteri aristofanei'. *RCCM* 18: 357–71; English translation Dover (1987), 237–48.

—— (1979). 'Il linguaggio del canto nelle culture primitive'. *Quaderni di Storia*, 9: 225–45; revised English translation Dover (1987), 1–15.

—— (1981). 'The Language of Classical Attic Documentary Inscriptions'. *TPhS* 1–14; repr. Dover (1987), 31–41.

—— (1985). 'Some Types of Abnormal Word-Order in Attic Comedy'. *CQ*, NS 35: 324–43; repr. Dover (1987), 43–66.

—— (1987). *Greek and the Greeks, Collected Papers I: Language, Poetry, Drama*. Oxford.

—— (1989). *Greek Homosexuality*, 2nd edn. Cambridge, Mass.

—— (1992). 'The Language of Criticism in Aristophanes' *Frogs*', in B. Zimmermann (ed.), *Antike Dramentheorien und ihre Rezeption* (Drama, 1). Stuttgart, 1–13.

—— (1993*a*) *Aristophanes: Frogs*. Oxford.

—— (1993*b*). 'The Chorus of Initiates in Aristophanes' *Frogs*', in Bremer–Handley (1993), 173–93.

—— (1997). *The Evolution of Greek Prose Style*. Oxford.

DUBOIS, L. (1989). *Inscriptions grecques dialectales de Sicile* (Collection de l'École Française de Rome, 119). Rome.

DUCKWORTH, G. E. (1952). *The Nature of Roman Comedy: A Study in Popular Entertainment*. Princeton.

DUHOUX, Y. (1987). 'Le vocalisme des inscriptions attiques: une question de méthodes'. *Verbum*, 10: 179–98.

—— (1997). 'Grec écrit et grec parlé: une étude contrastive des particules aux ve–ive siècles', in Rijksbaron (1997), 15–48.

DUNBAR, H., rev. MARZULLO, B. (1973). *A Complete Concordance to the Comedies and Fragments of Aristophanes*. Hildesheim and New York.

DURANTE, M. (1964/5). 'Il siculo e la sua documentazione'. *Kokalos*, 10/11: 417–43.

DURANTI, A. (1997). *Linguistic Anthropology*. Cambridge.

DURHAM, D. B. (1913). *The Vocabulary of Menander*. Princeton (repr. Amsterdam, 1969).

DÜRRENMATT, F. (1986). *Der Auftrag: Vom Beobachten des Beobachters der Beobachter*. Zurich.

DWORACKI, S. (1977). 'The Ending Formula in New Comedy'. *Symbolae Philologorum Posnaniensium*, 3: 35–40.

EASTERLING, P. E. (1982). *Sophocles: Trachiniae*. Cambridge.

EDWARDS, A. T. (1991). 'Aristophanes' Comic Poetics: *Τρύξ*, Scatology, *Σκῶμμα*'. *TAPhA* 121: 157–79.

EDWARDS, M. W. (1970). 'Homeric Speech Introductions'. *HSPh* 74: 1–36.

EHRENBERG, V. (1962). *The People of Aristophanes: A Sociology of Old Attic Comedy*, 3rd edn. New York.

ELLIOTT, R. T. (1914). *The Acharnians of Aristophanes*. Oxford.

EWBANK, J. B. (1980). 'Fable and Proverb in Aristophanes'. Diss. Univ. of North Carolina (*DA* 41/04: 1577; UMI order-no. 8022449).

FANTUZZI, M. (1978/9). 'Smikrines e Sostratos'. *Museum Criticum*, 13/14: 311–15.

FARIOLI, M. (1996). 'Note sul lessico, lo stile e la struttura delle commedie di Cratino'. *Aevum antiquum*, 9: 73–105.

FENERON, J. S. (1974). 'Some Elements of Menander's Style'. *BICS* 21: 81–95.

—— (1976). 'Some Elements of Menander's Style'. Diss. Stanford (*DA* 37: 954A; UMI order-no. 7618763).

FERGUSON, C. A. (1971). 'Absence of Copula and the Notion of Simplicity: A Study of Normal Speech, Baby Talk, Foreigner Talk, and Pidgins', in D. Hymes (ed.), *Pidginization and Creolization of Languages: Proceedings of a Conference held at the University of the West Indies, Mona, Jamaica, April 1968*. Cambridge, 141–50.

—— (1975). 'Toward a Characterization of English Foreigner Talk'. *Anthropological Linguistics*, 17: 1–14.

—— and DEBOSE, C. E. (1977). 'Simplified Registers, Broken Language, and Pidginization', in A. Valdman (ed.), *Pidgin and Creole Linguistics*. Bloomington, Ind., 99–125.

FERGUSON, J. (1979). '*Δῖνος* in Aristophanes and Euripides'. *CJ* 74: 356–9.

FERRANTE, D. (1965). 'Immagini etimologiche nei poeti greci dell'età ionico-attica'. *Rendiconti dell'Istituto Lombardo*, 99: 453–89.

FERRARI, M. L. (1996). 'Sequenze cumulative negli *Acarnesi* di Aristofane'. *SCO* 46: 347–64.

FERRERO, M. G. (1976). 'L'asindeto in Menandro'. *Dioniso*, 47: 82–106.

FINGERLE, A. (1939). 'Typik der homerischen Reden'. Diss. Munich (unpublished).

FISHMAN, J. A. (1977). 'Language and Ethnicity', in Giles (1977), 15–57.

FLOYD, E. D. (1986). 'Divergences from Standard Attic Greek: The Evidence from Aristophanes', in F. Marshall (ed.), *Proceedings of the Third Eastern States Conference on Linguistics*. Pittsburgh, 197–208.

FLURY, P. (1968). *Liebe und Liebessprache bei Menander, Plautus und Terenz*. Heidelberg.

FOLEY, H. P. (1988). 'Tragedy and Politics in Aristophanes' *Acharnians*'. *JHS* 108: 33–47.

FONTENROSE, J. (1978). *The Delphic Oracle: Its Responses and Operations, with a Catalogue of Responses*. Berkeley.

FRAENKEL, E. D. M. (1912). *De media et nova comoedia quaestiones selectae*. Diss. Göttingen.

—— (1960). *Elementi plautini in Plauto*, 2nd edn. Florence.

—— (1961). 'Eine Vergleichsform der attischen Umgangssprache'. *Glotta*, 39: 215; repr. in id., *Kleine Beiträge zur klassischen Philologie*, 2 vols. (Rome, 1964), i. 157.

—— (1962). *Beobachtungen zu Aristophanes*. Rome.

—— (1963). 'Attische Scheltreihen'. *Glotta*, 41: 285–6.

—— (1977). *Due seminari romani di Eduard Fraenkel:* Aiace *e* Filottete *di Sofocle*. Rome.

FRANCIS, E. D. (1973). 'Epicharmus fr. 177 Kaibel'. *CR*, NS 23: 1–3.

FRANÇOIS, G. (1977). 'L'encodage stylistique dans les *Cavaliers* d'Aristophane'. *LEC* 45: 3–30.

—— (1978). 'Épicharme et Cratès'. *AC* 47: 50–69.

FREYMAN, J. M. (1968). '*Καλός* in Aristophanes'. Diss. Univ. of Pennsylvania (*DA* 29/07: 2235; UMI order-no. 6900100).

FRIEDRICH, J. (1918). 'Das Attische im Munde von Ausländern bei Aristophanes'. *Philologus*, 75: 274–303.

—— (1921). 'Die altpersische Stelle in Aristophanes' *Acharnern*'. *IF* 39: 93–102.

FRIIS JOHANSEN, H., and WHITTLE, E. W. (1980). *Aeschylus, The Suppliants: Commentary*. Copenhagen.

FRISK, H. (1960–72). *Griechisches etymologisches Wörterbuch*. Heidelberg.

FRÖHDE, O. (1898). *Beiträge zur Technik der alten attischen Komödie*. Leipzig.

FÜHRER, R. (1967). *Formproblem-Untersuchungen zu den Reden in der frühgriechischen Lyrik*. Munich.

FUNAIOLI, M. P. (1984/5). '"Nomi parlanti" nella *Lysistrata*'. *Museum Criticum*, 19/20: 113–20.

GALANTE, L. (1914). *Caratteri della lingua di Menandro*. Pinerolo.

GALLI DE' PARATESI, N. (1969). *Le brutte parole: Semantica dell'eufemismo*, 3rd edn. Turin.

GARCÍA NOVO, E., and RODRÍGUEZ ALFAGEME, I. (eds.) (1998). *Dramaturgia y puesta en escena en el teatro griego/Drammaturgia e messa in scena nel teatro greco*. Madrid.

GARCÍA RAMÓN, J. L. (1977). 'Le prétendu infinitif "occidental" du type ἔχεν vis-à-vis du mycénien *e-ke-e*'. *Minos*, 16: 179–205.

GARDE, P. (1996). 'Langue et nation: le cas serbe, croate et bosniaque', in Sériot (1996), 123–47.

GARVIE, A. F. (1969). *Aeschylus' Supplices: Play and Trilogy*. Cambridge.

—— (1986). *Aeschylus: Choephori*. Oxford.

GARZYA, A. (1995). 'Sui frammenti dei Mirmidoni di Eschilo', in López Férez (1995), 41–56.

GENETTE, G. (1972). 'Discours du récit: Essai de méthode', in id., *Figures III*. Paris, 65–273.

—— (1980). *Narrative Discourse: An Essay in Method*. Ithaca, NY.

GEORGESCU, C. (1971). 'A Frequence Glossary of the Language of Menander'. *Anale Univ. Bucureşti (Limbi clasice si orientale)*, 20: 43–88.

GHEDINI, G. (1944). 'Nota grammaticale al PSI. 126'. *Aegyptus*, 24: 159–60.

GHIRON-BISTAGNE, P. (1989). 'Jongleries verbales sur les anthroponymes dans les comédies d'Aristophane'. *Cahiers du groupe interdisciplinaire du théâtre antique*, 5: 89–98.

GIANNINI, P., and PALLARA, E. (1983). 'I verbi composti con preposizione', in Prato (1983), 163–313.

GIGANTE, M. (1969). 'Il ritorno del medico straniero'. *PP* 24: 302–7.

GIL, L. (1970). 'Alexis y Menandro'. *Estudios Clásicos*, 14: 311–45.

—— and RODRÍGUEZ ALFAGEME, I. (1972). 'La figura del médico en la comedia ática'. *CFC* 3: 35–91.

GILES, H. (ed.) (1977). *Language, Ethnicity and Intergroup Relations* (European Monographs in Social Psychology, 13). London.

——, BOURHIS, R. Y., and TAYLOR, D. M. (1977). 'Towards a Theory of Language in Ethnic Group Relations', in Giles (1977), 307–48.

GLARE, P. G. W. (1996). *Revised Supplement* to LSJ (1940). Oxford.

GOFFMAN, E. (1981). *Forms of Talk*. Philadelphia and Oxford.

GOLDBERG, S. (1976). 'A Note on Aristophanes' φροντιστήριον'. *CPh* 71: 254–6.

GOLDHILL, S. (1991). *The Poet's Voice: Essays on Poetics and Greek Literature*. Cambridge.

—— (1997). 'The Language of Tragedy: Rhetoric and Communication', in P. E. Easterling (ed.), *The Cambridge Companion to Greek Tragedy*. Cambridge, 127–50.

GOMME, A. W. (1938). 'Aristophanes and Politics'. *CR* 52: 97–109.

—— and SANDBACH, F. H. (1973). *Menander: A Commentary*. Oxford.

GOMPERZ, T. (1889). 'Ein griechisches Komödienbruchstück in dorischer Mundart', *Mittheilungen aus der Sammlung der Papyrus Erzherzog Rainer*, 5. Vienna, 1–10; repr. in id., *Hellenika*, 2 vols. (Lepizig, 1912), i. 145–62.

GONIS, N. (2000). 'Two Literary Fragments from Antinoopolis: Menander, *Samia* 312–5, 341–50', in H. Melaerts (ed.), *Papyri in honorem Johannis Bingen Octogenarii*. Leuven, 125–8.

GONZÁLEZ MERINO, J. I. (1981/3). 'Las partículas en Menandro'. *Estudios Clásicos*, 25: 163–84.

GOODWIN, W. W. (1889). *Syntax of the Moods and Tenses of the Greek Verb*, rewritten and enlarged. London (repr. New York, 1965).

GRANDOLINI, S. (1976/7). 'Gli *hapax eiremena* nei frammenti papiracei dei comici greci'. *Annali della Facoltà di Lettere e Filosofia, Perugia*, 14: 445–53.

GRASSO, L. (1995). 'Il linguaggio dei vecchi nelle commedie di Menandro (imprecazioni ed esclamazioni)'. *Rudiae*, 7: 231–43.

GRIFFITH, J. G. (1970). '*Ληκύθιον ἀπώλεσεν*: A Postscript'. *HSPh* 74: 43–4.

GUIDO, R. (1983). '*Ὑποκριτική* e *γραφικὴ λέξις* (Ps. Demetr. *De Eloc*. IV 193)', in *Studi Adamesteanu* (1983), 127–35.

—— and FILIPPO, A. (1988). 'Responsione antistrofica di voci e suoni in Aristofane'. *Rudiae*, 1: 77–101.

GUSS, E. G. (1962). 'A Study of the Vocabulary of Aristophanes' *Plutus*'. Diss. Univ. of Pittsburgh (*DA* 23/06: 2125; UMI order-no. 6205127).

HAINSWORTH, J. B. (1967). 'Greek Views of Greek Dialectology'. *TPhS* 62–76.

HALDANE, J. A. (1965). 'A Scene in the *Thesmophoriazusae* (295–371)'. *Philologus*, 109: 39–46.

HALL, E. (1989*a*). *Inventing the Barbarian: Greek Self-Definition through Tragedy*. Oxford.

—— (1989*b*). 'The Archer Scene in Aristophanes' *Thesmophoriazusae*'. *Philologus*, 133: 38–54.

—— (1996). *Aeschylus: Persians*. Warminster.

HALL, J. M. (1997). *Ethnic Identity in Greek Antiquity*. Cambridge.

HALLIWELL, S. (1990). 'The Sounds of the Voice in Old Comedy', in Craik (1990), 69–79.

—— (1991). 'Comic Satire and Freedom of Speech in Classical Athens'. *JHS* 111: 48–70.

—— (1995). 'Forms of Address: Socratic Vocatives in Plato', in De Martino–Sommerstein (1995), ii. 89–121.

—— (1999). Review of Dickey (1996). *Classical Views*, 43: 110–18.

HAMP, E. P. (1970). 'Locative Singular in -ει'. *IF* 75: 105–6.

HÄNDEL, P., and MEID, W. (eds.) (1983). *Festschrift für Robert Muth zum 65. Geburtstag am 1. Januar 1981 dargebracht von Freunden und Kollegen* (Innsbrucker Beiträge zur Kulturwissenschaft, 22). Innsbruck.

HANDLEY, E. W. (1953). '*-sis* Nouns in Aristophanes'. *Eranos*, 51: 129–42.

—— (1956). 'Words for "Soul", "Heart" and "Mind" in Aristophanes'. *RhM*, NF 99: 205–25.

—— (1965*a*). 'Notes on the *Sikyonios* of Menander'. *BICS* 12: 38–62.

—— (1965*b*). *The* Dyskolos *of Menander*. London (repr. Bristol, 1992).

—— (1968). *Menander and Plautus: A Study in Comparison*. London.

—— (1970). 'The Conventions of the Comic Stage and their Exploitation by Menander', in Turner (1970), 3–26.

—— (1985). 'Comedy', in P. E. Easterling and B. M. W. Knox (eds.), *The Cambridge History of Classical Literature*, i: *Greek Literature*. Cambridge, 355–425.

HANSEN, O. (1956). 'Zum Persischen im Vers 100 der *Acharner* des Aristophanes', in M. Woltner and H. Bräuer (eds.), *Festschrift für Max Vasmer zum 70. Geburtstag*. Wiesbaden, 177–80.

HANSEN, P. A. (1983). *Carmina epigraphica Graeca saeculorum VIII–V a. Chr. n.* Berlin.

HARTOG, F. (1988). *The Mirror of Herodotus: The Representation of the Other in the Writing of History*, trans. J. Lloyd. Berkeley.

HARVEY, D. (1994). 'Lacomica: Aristophanes and the Spartans', in A. Powell and S. Hodkinson (eds.), *The Shadow of Sparta*. London, 35–58.

—— (2000). 'Phrynichos and his Muses', in Harvey–Wilkins (2000), 91–134.

—— and WILKINS, J. (eds.) (2000). *The Rivals of Aristophanes: Studies in Athenian Old Comedy*. London and Swansea.

HASSE, E. (1891). *Ueber den Dual bei den attischen Dramatikern*. Progr. Bartenstein.

HAURY, A. (1960). 'Le chant du rossignol ou Buffon mystifié par Aristophane'. *BAGB* 373–6.

HAWTREY, R. S. W. (1983). '*Παν*-Compounds in Plato'. *CQ*, NS 33: 56–65.

HEADLAM, W., and KNOX, A. D. (1922). *Herodas: The Mimes and Fragments*. Cambridge.

HEAP, A. M. (1992). 'Word Order in Menander'. *LCM* 17: 56–8.

HEATH, M. (1997). 'Aristophanes and the Discourse of Politics', in Dobrov (1997*b*), 230–49.

HENDERSON, J. (1972). 'The *Lekythos* and *Frogs* 1200–1248'. *HSPh* 76: 133–43.

—— (1973). 'A Note on Aristophanes, *Acharnians* 834–35'. *CPh* 68: 289–90.

—— (1974*a*). '*Κῳδάριον*: A Reply'. *Mnemosyne*, 4th ser. 27: 293–5.

—— (1974*b*). 'Sparring Partners: A Note on Aristophanes, *Ecclesiazusae* 964–965'. *AJPh* 95: 344–7.

—— (1987). *Aristophanes: Lysistrata*. Oxford.

—— (1990). 'The *Demos* and the Comic Competition', in J. J. Winckler and F. Zeitlin (eds.), *Nothing to Do with Dionysus? Athenian Drama in its Social Context*. Princeton, 271–313.

—— (1991). *The Maculate Muse: Obscene Language in Attic Comedy*, 2nd edn. New York.

—— (1998). 'Attic Old Comedy, Frank Speech, and Democracy', in D. Boedeker and K. A. Raaflaub (eds.), *Democracy, Empire, and the Arts in Fifth-Century Athens*. Cambridge, Mass., 255–73.

HERINGTON, C. J. (1963). 'The Influence of Old Comedy on Aeschylus' Later Trilogies'. *TAPhA* 94: 113–25.

—— (1967). 'Aeschylus in Sicily'. *JHS* 87: 74–85.

HEUBECK, A. (1970). 'Zu Menander, *Sikyonios* v. 364'. *ŽA* 20: 77.

HIERSCHE, R. (1970). *Grundzüge der griechischen Sprachgeschichte bis zur klassischen Zeit*. Wiesbaden.

HINNENKAMP, V. (1982). *Foreigner Talk und Tarzanisch: Eine vergleichende Studie über die Sprechweise gegenüber Ausländern am Beispiel des Deutschen und des Türkischen*. Hamburg.

HINZE, K. (1934). 'Zwei heimatberaubte spartanische Dichter'. *RhM*, NF 83: 39–52.

HOENIGSWALD, H. M. (1941). 'The Epicharmian Title *Λόγος καὶ Λογίνα*'. *Language*, 17: 247–9.

HOFFMANN, G. (1892). *Schimpfwörter der Griechen und Römer*. Programm Berlin.

HOFFMANN, O., and DEBRUNNER, A. (1969). *Geschichte der griechischen Sprache*, i: *Bis zum Ausgang der klassischen Zeit*, 4th edn. by A. Scherer (Sammlung Göschen, 111). Berlin.

HOLDEN, H. A. (1902). *Onomasticon Aristophaneum*. Cambridge (repr. Hildesheim, 1970).

HOLLOWAY, R. ROSS (1991). *The Archaeology of Ancient Sicily*. London.

HOLMES, L. M. (1990). 'Character Naming in Aristophanes (Greek Comedy)'. Diss. Harvard (*DA* 51: 4110A; UMI order-no. 9113168).

HOLZBERG, N. (1974). *Menander: Untersuchungen zur dramatischen Technik* (Erlanger Beiträge zur Sprach- und Kunstwissenschaft, 50). Nuremberg.

HOOKER, J. T. (1980). *The Ancient Spartans*. London.

HOPE, E. W. (1906). *The Language of Parody: A Study in the Diction of Aristophanes*. Diss. Baltimore.

HORN, W. (1970). *Gebet und Gebetsparodie in den Komödien des Aristophanes* (Erlanger Beiträge zur Sprach- und Kunstwissenschaft, 38). Nuremberg.

HOROWSKI, J. (1966). 'O niektórych wyrazach dźwiękonaśladowczych w komediach Arystofanesa'. *Eos*, 56: 227–37.

HORROCKS, G. (1997). *Greek: A History of the Language and its Speakers*. London.

HUART, P. (1973). *Γνώμη chez Thucydide et ses contemporains (Sophocle—Euripide—Antiphon—Andocide—Aristophane): Contribution à l'histoire des idées à Athènes dans la seconde moitié du Ve siècle av. J.-C.* (Études et commentaires, 81). Paris.

HUDSON, R. A. (1996). *Sociolinguistics*, 2nd edn. Cambridge.

HUGHES, G. (1991). *Swearing: A Social History of Foul Language, Oaths and Profanity in English*. Oxford.

HUMPERS, A. (1922). 'Le duel chez Ménandre'. *RPh*, 2nd ser. 46: 76–86.

HUNTER, R. L. (1983). *Eubulus: The Fragments*. Cambridge.

—— (1999). *Theocritus: A Selection*. Cambridge.

HUNTER, V. J. (1994). *Policing Athens: Social Control in the Attic Lawsuits, 420–320 B.C.* Princeton.

HURST, A. (1990). 'Ménandre et la tragédie', in E. Handley and A. Hurst (eds.), *Relire Ménandre*. Geneva, 93–122.

HUSQUINET, A. (1945). 'Syntaxe de Ménandre'. Thèse de licence, Liège.

IRELAND, S. (1981). 'Prologues [*sic*] Structure and Sentences in Menander'. *Hermes*, 109: 178–88.

IVIĆ, P. (1958). *Die serbokroatischen Dialekte: Ihre Struktur und Entwicklung*, i: *Allgemeines und die stokavische Dialektgruppe*. The Hague.

JACOB, O. (1928). *Les Esclaves publics à Athènes*. Liège and Paris.

JACOBI, O. (1857). *Comicae dictionis index*. Berlin.

JACQUES, J.-M. (1976). *Ménandre: Le Dyscolos*, 2nd edn. Paris.

JANKO, R. (1992) = G. S. Kirk (ed.), *The Iliad: A Commentary*, iv: *Books 13–16*. Cambridge.

JANSSENS, É. (1952). 'Les étrangers comme élément comique dans les comédies d'Aristophane', in *Mélanges Georges Smets*. Brussels, 455–60.

JOCELYN, H. D. (1980*a*). 'Attic βινεῖν and English *F*...'. *LCM* 5: 65–7.

—— (1980*b*). 'A Greek Indecency and its Students: λαικάζειν'. *PCPhS*, NS 26: 12–66.

JOHANNES, W. C. (1963). 'The People of Menander: A Study of Nouns

Designating Family, Occupation, Social and Servile Class'. Diss. Univ. of Michigan (*DA* 24/07: 2896; UMI order-no. 6400833).

JONG, I. J. F. DE (1991). *Narrative in Drama: The Art of the Euripidean Messenger Speech*. Leiden.

JUNGIUS, C. L. (1897). *De vocabulis antiquae comoediae Atticae quae apud solos comicos aut omnino inveniuntur aut peculiari notione praedita occurrunt*. Utrecht.

KAIBEL, G. (1896). 'Aristophanes (12)'. *RE* ii. 971–94.

—— (1899). *Comicorum Graecorum Fragmenta: I.1. Doriensium comoedia mimi phlyaces*. Berlin.

KAKRIDIS, J. T. (1970). 'Phrynicheisches in den Vögeln des Aristophanes'. *WS*, NF 4: 39–51.

KAKRIDIS, P. I. (1972). '*Κριτικὰ καὶ ἑρμενευτικὰ στὸν Ἀριστοφάνη*'. *Dodone*, 1: 109–24.

KAMEL, W. (1952). 'Epicharmus: His Achievement as a Forerunner of Greek Comedy'. *Bulletin of the Faculty of Arts, Cairo*, 14.1: 69–78.

KANN, S. (1909). *De iteratis apud poetas antiquae et mediae comoediae Atticae*. Diss. Giessen.

KAPP, E. (1928). '*Πισθέταιρος*'. *Philologus*, 84: 259–61.

KASSEL, R. (1999). 'Aus der Arbeit an den *Poetae Comici Graeci*, 9–12'. *ZPE* 128: 29–32.

—— and AUSTIN, C. (1983) = vol. iv; (1991) = vol. ii; (1984) = vol. iii/2; (1986) = vol. v; (1998) = vol. vi/2; (1989) = vol. vii; (1995) = vol. viii; (2001) = vol. i. *Poetae Comici Graeci*. Berlin.

KAT ELIASSEN, M. H. DE (1975). 'The Oaths in Menander's *Samia*'. *SO* 50: 55–60.

KATIČIĆ, R. (1959). 'Ein Problem des messenischen Dialektes'. *ŽA* 9: 133–6.

KATSOURIS, A. G. (1975*a*). *Linguistic and Stylistic Characterization: Tragedy and Menander* (*Dodone*, Suppl. 5). Ioannina.

—— (1975*b*). 'Word-Play in Greek Drama'. *Hellenica*, 28: 409–14.

—— (1975*c*). *Tragic Patterns in Menander*. Athens.

—— (1976). 'The Formulaic Ending of the Menandrean Plays'. *Dodone*, 5: 243–56.

—— (1995). *Menander Bibliography*. Thessaloniki.

KELLY, M. N. (1962*a*). 'L'emploi des prépositions dans la comédie moyenne et nouvelle d'Athènes'. *Phoenix*, 16: 29–40.

—— (1962*b*). 'La langue de Ménandre et la *κοινή*'. *Revue de l'Université Laval, Québec*, 17: 345–51.

KERFERD, G. B. (1981). *The Sophistic Movement*. Cambridge.

KINDSTRAND, J. F. (1981). *Anacharsis: The Legend and the Apophthegmata* (Studia Graeca Upsaliensia, 16). Uppsala.

KIRK, G. S., RAVEN, J. E., and SCHOFIELD, M. (1983). *The Presocratic Philosophers*, 2nd edn. Cambridge.

KLAUS, K. (1936). *Die Adjektiva bei Menander* (Klassisch-philologische Studien, 8). Leipzig.

KLEINKNECHT, H. (1937). *Die Gebetsparodie in der Antike* (Tübinger Beiträge zur Altertumswissenschaft, 28). Stuttgart.

—— (1939). 'Die Epiphanie des Demos in Aristophanes' *Rittern*'. *Hermes*, 74: 58–65.

KLOSS, G. (2001). *Erscheinungsformen komischen Sprechens bei Aristophanes*. Berlin.

KOCK, T. (1893). 'Zu den Fragmenten der attischen Komiker'. *RhM*, NF 48: 208–39.

KOMORNICKA, A. M. (1963). 'Quelques remarques sur l'originalité des figures poétiques chez Aristophane'. *Eos*, 53: 266–85.

—— (1964). *Métaphores, personnifications et comparaisons dans l'œuvre d'Aristophane* (Archiwum Filologiczne, 10). Wroclaw.

—— (1967). 'Quelques remarques sur la parodie dans les comédies d'Aristophane'. *QUCC* 3: 51–74.

—— (1981). 'Sur le langage érotique de l'ancienne comédie attique'. *QUCC*, NS 9: 55–83.

—— (1996). 'Les toasts portés au cours des banquets athéniens: à partir de fragments de la comédie grecque', in C. Klodt (ed.), *Satura lanx: Festschrift W. A. Krenkel* (Spudasmata, 62). Hildesheim, 169–78.

KÖRTE, A. (1911). 'Bericht über die Literatur zur griechischen Komödie aus den Jahren 1902–1909'. *Bursians Jahresbericht*, 152: 218–312.

—— (1929). 'ὑπόχρυσος—ἐπίχρυσος'. *Hermes*, 64: 267–70.

—— (1931). 'Menandros' Kunst: Sprache'. *RE* xv/1. 751–3.

KOSSATZ-DEISSMANN, A. (1981). 'Achilleus'. *LIMC* i. 37–200.

KOSTER, W. J. W. (1975). *Scholia in Aristophanem*, IA: *Prolegomena de Comoedia*. Groningen.

KRAUS, W. (1971). 'Forschungsbericht: Griechische Komödie'. *Anzeiger für die Altertumswissenschaft*, 24: 161–80.

—— (1973). 'Forschungsbericht: Griechische Komödie'. *Anzeiger für die Altertumswissenschaft*, 26: 31–56.

KRIETER-SPIRO, M. (1997). *Sklaven, Köche und Hetären: Das Dienstpersonal bei Menander. Stellung, Rolle, Komik und Sprache*. Stuttgart.

KRONASSER, H. (1960). 'Κολο-, "groß"'. *Sprache*, 6: 172–8.

KRONAUER, U. (1954). *Der formale Witz in den Komödien des Aristophanes* (Diss. Zurich). Oberwinterthur.

KUDLIEN, F. (1970). 'Hippokrateszitate in der altgriechischen Komödie?'. *Episteme*, 5: 279–84.

KÜHNER, R. (1841). 'Excursus I: De formis γίγνομαι et γίνομαι, γιγνώσκω et γινώσκω', in id., *Xenophontis opera omnia: Vol. II continens de Socrate commentarios*. Gotha, 481–3 = 2nd edn. (Gotha and Erfurt, 1858), 505–8.

—— and BLASS, F. (1890, 1892). *Ausführliche Grammatik der griechischen*

Sprache I: Elementar- und Formenlehre, 2 vols. Hanover and Leipzig (repr. Darmstadt, 1966).

KÜHNER, R., and GERTH, B. (1898, 1904). *Ausführliche Grammatik der griechischen Sprache II: Satzlehre*, 3rd edn., 2 vols. Hanover and Leipzig.

LABIANO ILUNDAIN, J. M. (2000). *Estudio de las interjecciones en las comedias de Aristófanes*. Amsterdam.

LADEMANN, W. (1915). *De titulis Atticis quaestiones orthographicae et grammaticae* (Diss. Basel). Kirchhain.

LAGERCRANTZ, O. (1898). *Zur griechischen Lautgeschichte*. Uppsala.

LAMAGNA, M. (1998). 'Dialogo riportato in Menandro', in García Novo–Rodríguez Alfageme (1998), 289–302.

LANDFESTER, M. (1967). *Die Ritter des Aristophanes: Beobachtungen zur dramatischen Handlung und zum komischen Stil des Aristophanes*. Amsterdam.

LANGENDOEN, D. T. (1968). *The London School of Linguistics: A Study of the Linguistic Theories of B. Malinowski and J. R. Firth*. Cambridge, Mass.

LANZA, D. (1979). *Lingua e discorso nell'Atene delle professioni*. Naples.

LASCU, N. (1969). 'Intorno ai nomi degli schiavi nel teatro antico'. *Dioniso*, 43: 97–106.

LATTE, K. (1968). *Kleine Schriften*. Munich.

LATTIMORE, R. (1979). 'Optatives of Consent and Refusal', in G. W. Bowersock, W. Burkert, and M. C. J. Putnam (eds.), *Arktouros: Hellenic Studies Presented to Bernard M. W. Knox*. Berlin, 209–16.

LAUTENSACH, O. (1896). *Grammatische Studien zu den griechischen Tragikern und Komikern I: Personalendungen*. Programm Gotha.

—— (1899). *Grammatische Studien zu den griechischen Tragikern und Komikern: Augment und Reduplikation*. Hanover and Leipzig.

—— (1911). *Die Aoriste bei den attischen Tragikern und Komikern*. (Forschungen zur griechischen und lateinischen Grammatik, 1). Göttingen.

—— (1912). 'Der Gebrauch des Aor. Med. und Aor. Pass. bei den attischen Tragikern und Komikern'. *Glotta*, 3: 221–36.

—— (1916). 'Grammatische Studien zu den attischen Tragikern und Komikern: Konjunktiv und Optativ'. *Glotta*, 7: 92–116.

—— (1917). 'Grammatische Studien zu den attischen Tragikern und Komikern: Optativ [und Imperativ]'. *Glotta*, 8: 168–96.

—— (1918). 'Grammatische Studien zu den attischen Tragikern und Komikern [Imperativ: Nachtrag]'. *Glotta*, 9: 69–94.

—— (1921). 'Grammatische Studien zu den attischen Tragikern und Komikern: Infinitive und Partizipien'. *Philologus*, 77: 46–76, 228–55.

LEE, E. T. (1993). 'The ἰαμβικὴ ἰδέα from Iambic Poetry to Attic Old Comedy'. Diss. Yale (*DA* 54/06: 2139; UMI order-no. 9331551).

LEECH, G. N., and SHORT, M. (1981). *Style in Fiction: A Linguistic Introduction to English Fictional Prose*. London.

LEEMAN, A. D. (1963). *Orationis Ratio*. Amsterdam.

LEGRAND, P.-E. (1910). *Daos: Tableau de la comédie grecque pendant la période dite nouvelle (Κωμῳδία Νέα)* (Annales de l'Université de Lyon, NS 2.22). Lyon and Paris.

LEJEUNE, M. (1993). 'Le nom de mesure λίτρα: Essai lexical'. *REG* 106: 1–11.

LESNÝ, V. (1923). 'Staroperský verš v Aristofanových *Acharnských*', in *Sborník prací filologických F. Grohovi*. Prague, 66–8.

LEUMANN, M. (1949). 'μέν und μήν, δέ und δή'. *MH* 6: 85–9; repr. in id., *Kleine Schriften* (Zurich, 1959), 229–34.

—— (1977). *Lateinische Laut- und Formenlehre*. Munich.

LEVER, K. (1952/3). 'Poetic Metaphor and Allegory in Aristophanes'. *CW* 46: 220–3.

LEWIS, D. M. (1955). 'Notes on Attic Inscriptions, II 23: Who Was Lysistrata?'. *ABSA* 50: 1–12; repr. in id., *Selected Papers in Greek and Near Eastern History*, ed. P. J. Rhodes (Cambridge, 1997), 187–202.

LILJA, S. (1979). 'Animal Imagery in Greek Comedy'. *Arctos*, 13: 85–90.

LITTLEFIELD, D. J. (1968). 'Metaphor and Myth: The Unity of Aristophanes' *Knights*'. *Studies in Philology*, 65: 1–22.

LITTRÉ, E. (1844). *Œuvres complètes d'Hippocrate*, vol. iv. Paris.

LLOYD-JONES, H. (1978). 'Ten Notes on Aeschylus, *Agamemnon*', in R. D. Dawe, J. Diggle, and P. E. Easterling (eds.), *Dionysiaca: Nine Studies in Greek Poetry by Former Pupils, Presented to Sir Denys Page on his Seventieth Birthday*. Cambridge, 45–61.

—— (1979). *Aeschylus: Oresteia, Agamemnon* (trans. with notes). London.

LOBEL, E. (1959). *The Oxyrhynchus Papyri: Part XXV*. London. (On 2426–9: pp. 1–44).

LOEPFE, A. (1940). *Die Wortstellung im Griechischen erklärt an Stücken aus Platon und Menander*. Diss. Fribourg.

LONG, T. (1986). *Barbarians in Greek Comedy*. Carbondale and Edwardsville.

LÓPEZ EIRE, A. (1986). 'La lengua de la comedia aristofánica'. *Emérita*, 54: 237–74.

—— (1991). *Ático, koiné y aticismo: Estudios sobre Aristófanes y Libanio*. Murcia.

—— (1993). 'De l'attique à la koiné', in C. Brixhe (ed.), *La Koiné grecque antique*, i: *Une langue introuvable?* (Études anciennes, 10). Nancy, 41–57.

—— (1996*a*). 'L'influence de l'ionien-attique sur les autres dialectes épigraphiques et l'origine de la koiné', in C. Brixhe (ed.), *La Koiné grecque antique*, ii: *La concurrence* (Études anciennes, 14). Nancy, 7–42.

López Eire, A. (1996*b*). *La lengua coloquial de la comedia aristofánica*. Murcia.
—— (1997*a*). 'À propos de l'attique familier de la comédie aristophanienne', in Thiercy–Menu (1997), 189–212.
—— (1997*b*). 'Lengua y política en la comedia aristofánica', in id. (ed.), *Sociedad, política y literatura: comedia griega antigua. Actas del I Congreso Internacional*. Salamanca, 45–80.
—— (1998*a*). 'Sobre el ático coloquial de la comedia aristofánica', in López Férez (1998), 137–75.
—— (1998*b*). 'El texto de la comedia aristofánica como texto de una representación dramática', in García Novo–Rodríguez Alfageme (1998), 229–50.
López Férez, J. A. (ed.) (1995). *De Homero a Libanio (Estudios actuales sobre textos griegos II)* (Estudios de filología griega, 2). Madrid.
—— (ed.) (1998). *La comedia griega y su influencia en la literatura española* (Estudios de filología griega, 3). Madrid.
Lorenz, A. O. F. (1864). *Leben und Schriften des Koers Epicharmos nebst einer Fragmentensammlung*. Berlin.
Lottich, O. (1881). *De sermone vulgari Atticorum maxime ex Aristophanis fabulis cognoscendo*. Diss. Halle.
Lowe, J. C. B. (1999). 'Pseudolus' "Intrigue" Against Simo'. *Maia*, 51: 1–15.
LSJ (1940) = H. G. Liddell and R. Scott, *A Greek–English Lexicon* (9th edn. by Sir Henry Stuart Jones). Oxford.
Lucas, D. W. (1968). *Aristotle: Poetics*. Oxford.
Luck, G. (1965). 'Elemente der Umgangssprache bei Menander und Terenz'. *RhM*, NF 108: 269–77.
Luppe, W. (1975). Review of Austin (1973). *GGA* 227: 179–206.
MacCary, W. T. (1969). 'Menander's Slaves: Their Names, Roles, and Masks'. *TAPhA* 100: 277–94.
—— (1970). 'Menander's Characters: Their Names, Roles, and Masks'. *TAPhA* 101: 277–90.
—— (1972). 'Menander's Soldiers: Their Names, Rôles, and Masks'. *AJPh* 93: 279–98.
McClure, L. (1999). *Spoken like a Woman: Speech and Gender in Athenian Drama*. Princeton.
MacDowell, D. M. (1971). *Aristophanes: Wasps*. Oxford.
—— (1990). *Demosthenes: Against Meidias (Oration 21)*. Oxford.
—— (1995). *Aristophanes and Athens: An Introduction to the Plays*. Oxford.
McLeish, K. (1977). '*Φύσις*: A Bawdy Joke in Aristophanes?'. *CQ*, NS 27: 76–9.
Macleod, M. D. (1970). 'A Rare Use of *νή* in Menander and Lucian'. *CR*, NS 20: 289.

—— (1981). 'Two Names From the *Dyscolos*'. *Glotta*, 59: 160–4.

Mactoux, M. M. (1978/9). 'Le système sémantique des termes désignant les esclaves chez Aristophane'. *Index*, 8: 219–21.

—— (1999). 'Esclaves-femmes dans le corpus d'Aristophane', in F. Reduzzi Merola and A. Storchi Marino (eds.), *Femmes-esclaves: Modèles d'interprétation anthropologique, économique, juridique* (Diáphora, 9). Naples, 21–46.

Malinowski, B. (1923). 'The Problem of Meaning in Primitive Languages', in C. K. Ogden, I. A. Richards, *et al.*, *The Meaning of Meaning: A Study of the Influence of Language upon Thought and of the Science of Symbolism.* London, 451–510 = 10th edn. (London, 1949), 296–336.

Maquieira Rodríguez, H. (1987). 'Sobre la dicotomía semántica *ἀγαθός–κακός* en Menandro'. *Ítaca*, 3: 99–109.

Marcovich, M. (1971). '*Μέγας* Is Not *mutuniatus*'. *CPh* 66: 262.

Margoliouth, D. S. (1887). 'Arist. *Ach.* 100'. *CR* 1: 204.

Marston, V. (1973). 'Aristophanes' Use of Obscenity'. Diss. Ohio State University (*DA* 34/12: 7727; UMI order-no. 7411010).

Martina, A. (1997). *Menandri Epitrepontes*, vol. i. Rome.

Martín de Lucas, I. (1996). 'Los demonstrativos con *-ί* epidíctica en Aristófanes'. *Emérita*, 64: 157–71.

Marzullo, B. (1953). 'Strepsiade'. *Maia*, 6: 99–124.

—— (1970). 'L'interlocuzione negli "Uccelli" di Aristofane'. *Philologus*, 114: 181–94.

Mastromarco, G. (1987). 'La parabasi aristofanea tra realtà e poesia'. *Dioniso*, 57: 75–93.

Mattingly, H. B. (1977). 'Vocabulary Change and Epigraphic Dating'. *Mnemosyne*, 4th ser. 30: 66–9.

Mawet, F. (1983). 'La formation nominale dans l'*Assemblée des Femmes* d'Aristophane'. *Glotta*, 61: 182–92.

Mayser, E. (1938). *Grammatik der griechischen Papyri aus der Ptolemäerzeit I: Laut- und Wortlehre, 2. Teil: Flexionslehre*, 2nd edn. Berlin.

—— rev. Schmoll, H. (1970). *Grammatik der griechischen Papyri aus der Ptolemäerzeit I: Laut- und Wortlehre, 1. Teil: Einleitung und Lautlehre*, 2nd edn. Berlin.

Meerwaldt, J. D. (1928). 'De sermonis puerilis apud ignotum quendam comicum ratione et usu'. *Mnemosyne*, NS 56: 202–6.

Meier-Brügger, M. (1992). *Griechische Sprachwissenschaft*, 2 vols. (Sammlung Göschen, 2241–2). Berlin.

Meillet, A. (1965). *Aperçu d'une histoire de la langue grecque*, 8th edn. rev. O. Masson (Études et commentaires, 55). Paris.

Meineke, A. (1839). *Fragmenta comicorum Graecorum.* Berlin.

Meisel, J. M. (1977). 'Linguistic Simplification: A Study of Immigrant

Workers' Speech and Foreigner Talk', in Corder–Roulet (1977), 88–113.

MEISTERHANS, K., rev. SCHWYZER, E. (1900). *Grammatik der attischen Inschriften*, 3rd edn. Berlin.

Menandrea (1960) = *Menandrea: miscellanea philologica* (Pubblicazioni dell'Istituto di filologia classica e medievale, 13). Genoa.

MENCKEN, H. L. (1963). *The American Language: An Inquiry into the Development of English in the United States*, 4th edn. abridged by R. I. McDavid, Jr. and D. W. Maurer. London.

MÉNDEZ DOSUNA, J. (1993). 'Metátesis de cantidad en jónico-ático y heracleota'. *Emérita*, 61: 95–134.

METTE, H. J. (1965). 'Der heutige Menander'. *Lustrum*, 10: 5–211.

—— (1966). 'Nachtrag zu: Der heutige Menander'. *Lustrum*, 11: 139–43.

—— (1968). 'Zweiter Nachtrag zu: Der heutige Menander'. *Lustrum*, 13: 535–68.

—— (1971/2). 'Menander 1966–1973'. *Lustrum*, 16: 5–80.

MEYER, G. (1923). *Die stilistische Verwendung der Nominalkomposition im Griechischen: Ein Beitrag zur Geschichte der Διπλᾶ ὀνόματα* (*Philologus*, Suppl. 16.3). Leipzig.

MICHAËL, C. A. (1981). *Ὁ κωμικὸς λόγος τοῦ Ἀριστοφάνους*. Athens.

MICKEY, K. (1981). 'Dialect Consciousness and Literary Language: An Example from Ancient Greek'. *TPhS* 35–66.

MIKOŁAJCZYK, R. (1979). 'Formy deminutywne imion własnych w komediach Arystofanesa'. *Eos*, 67: 221–31.

MILLER, H. W. (1942). 'Three-Word Iambic Trimeters in Aristophanes'. *CPh* 37: 194–5.

—— (1944). 'Repetition of Lines in Aristophanes'. *AJPh* 65: 26–36.

—— (1944/5). 'Conversational Idiom in Aristophanes'. *CW* 38: 162–3.

—— (1945*a*). 'Comic Iteration in Aristophanes'. *AJPh* 66: 398–408.

—— (1945*b*). 'Aristophanes and Medical Language'. *TAPhA* 76: 74–84.

MILLER, N. (1987). *Menander: Plays and Fragments*. London.

MITSDÖRFFER, W. (1954). 'Das Mnesilochoslied in Aristophanes' *Thesmophoriazusen*: Die Parodie einer tragischen Monodie'. *Philologus*, 98: 59–93.

MOLES, J. L. (1979). 'A Neglected Aspect of *Agamemnon* 1389–92'. *LCM* 4: 179–89.

MOLITOR, M. V. (1969). 'A Prosopographical Study of Aristophanes' Comedies'. Diss. Princeton (*DA* 30/11: 4958; UMI order-no. 7008383).

MÖLLENDORFF, P. VON (1995). *Grundlagen einer Ästhetik der alten Komödie: Untersuchungen zu Aristophanes und Michail Bachtin*. Tübingen.

MONTEIL, P. (1963). *La Phrase relative en grec ancien: Sa formation, son* *développement, sa structure des origines à la fin du Ve siècle A.C.* (Études et commentaires, 47). Paris.

MOORHOUSE, A. C. (1947). 'The Meaning and Use of μικρός and ὀλίγος in the Greek Poetical Vocabulary'. *CQ* 41: 31–45.

MORENILLA-TALENS, C. (1985). 'Procedimientos fónicos de estilo en Aristófanes'. *Estudios Clásicos*, 27 (89): 39–59.

—— (1987). 'Wort- und Klangresponsionen bei Aristophanes'. *Philologus*, 131: 32–49.

—— (1988). 'Ein Beitrag zum Studium der Metaphern bei Aristophanes: *Thesmophoriazusen* 49–62'. *Eranos*, 86: 160–2.

—— (1989). 'Die Charakterisierung der Ausländer durch lautliche Ausdrucksmittel in den *Persern* des Aischylos sowie den *Acharnern* und *Vögeln* des Aristophanes'. *IF* 94: 158–76.

MORGAN, J. D. (1986). '*Μαρικᾶς*'. *CQ*, NS 36: 529–31.

MORPURGO DAVIES, A. (1987). 'The Greek Notion of Dialect'. *Verbum*, 10: 7–28.

—— (1997). 'Particles in Greek Epigraphical Texts: The Case of Arcadian', in Rijksbaron (1997), 49–73.

MORRIS, W. (1960). 'The Syntax of the Dative Case in Aristophanes'. Diss. Johns Hopkins.

MOULTON, C. (1979). 'The Lyric of Insult and Abuse in Aristophanes'. *MH* 36: 23–47.

—— (1981). *Aristophanic Poetry* (Hypomnemata, 68). Göttingen.

MUECKE, F. (1998). 'Oracles in Aristophanes'. *Seminari romani di cultura greca*, 1.2: 257–74.

MÜLLER, A. (1913). 'Die Schimpfwörter in der griechischen Komödie'. *Philologus*, 72: 321–37.

MÜLLER, D. (1974). 'Die Verspottung der metaphorischen Ausdrucksweise durch Aristophanes', in U. Reinhardt and K. Sallmann (eds.), *Musa iocosa: Arbeiten über Humor und Witz, Komik und Komödie der Antike, Andreas Thierfelder zum 70. Geburtstag*. Hildesheim, 29–41.

MURPHY, C. T. (1938). 'Aristophanes and the Art of Rhetoric'. *HSPh* 49: 69–113.

—— (1955/6). 'A Survey of Recent Work on Aristophanes and Old Comedy'. *CW* 49: 201–11.

—— (1972). 'A Survey of Recent Work on Aristophanes and Old Comedy'. *CW* 65: 261–73.

NESSELRATH, H.-G. (1990). *Die attische Mittlere Komödie: Ihre Stellung in der antiken Literaturkritik und Literaturgeschichte* (Untersuchungen zur antiken Literatur und Geschichte, 36). Berlin.

—— (1993). 'Parody and Later Greek Comedy'. *HSPh* 95: 181–95.

NEVOLA, M. L. (1990/3). 'Meccanismi comici nelle *Nuvole* di Aristofane'. *Museum Criticum*, 25/8: 151–74.

NEWIGER, H. J. (1957). *Metapher und Allegorie: Studien zu Aristophanes* (Zetemata, 16). Munich.
—— (1975). 'Bibliographie', in id. (ed.), *Aristophanes und die alte Komödie* (Wege der Forschung, 265). Darmstadt, 487–510.
—— (1980). 'War and Peace in the Comedy of Aristophanes'. *YCS* 26: 219–37.
NICHOLS, J. (1980). 'Pidginization and Foreigner Talk: Chinese Pidgin Russian', in E. C. Traugott, R. Labrum, and S. Sheperd (eds.), *Papers from the 4th International Conference on Historical Linguistics*. Amsterdam, 397–407.
NICKAU, K. (1993). 'Zum Verbalaspekt der Imperative in Aristophanes' *Acharnern* 1097–1142'. *Glotta*, 71: 158–66.
NIEDDU, G. F. (1989). 'Una "boccetta" da ricomprare: Nota ad Aristoph. *Ran.* 1227–29 e 1235–37'. *A&R*, NS 34: 97–104.
NOËL, M.-P. (1997). 'Mots nouveaux et idées nouvelles dans les "Nuées" d'Aristophane'. *Ktèma*, 22: 173–84.
NÖTHIGER, M. (1971). *Die Sprache des Stesichorus und des Ibykus*. Zurich.
NUSSBAUM, M. (1994). 'Platonic Love and Colorado Law'. *Virginia Law Review*, 80: 1515–1651.
O'DALY, G. J. P. (1985). 'Clytemnestra and the Elders: Dramatic Technique in Aeschylus, *Agamemnon* 1372–1576'. *MH* 42: 1–19.
O'REGAN, D. E. (1992). *Rhetoric, Comedy, and the Violence of Language in Aristophanes'* Clouds. New York.
OHLERT, K. (1912). *Rätsel und Rätselspiele der alten Griechen*, 2nd edn. Berlin.
OLIVA, C. (1968). 'La parodia e la critica letteraria nella commedia postaristofanea'. *Dioniso*, 42: 25–92.
OLIVIERI, A. (1939). 'Il comico Alessi di Thurii'. *Dioniso*, 7: 279–95.
OLLIER, F. (1933). *Le Mirage spartiate: Étude sur l'idéalisation de Sparte dans l'antiquité grecque de l'origine jusqu'aux Cyniques*. Paris.
OLSON, S. D. (1992). 'Names and Naming in Aristophanic Comedy'. *CQ*, NS 42: 304–19.
—— (1998). *Aristophanes: Peace*. Oxford.
OPELT, I. (1975). 'Schimpfwörter bei Lysias', in *Scritti in onore di Giuliano Bonfante*. Brescia, ii. 571–84.
OSMUN, G. F. (1952). 'Dialogue in the Menandrean Monologue'. *TAPhA* 83: 156–63.
—— (1953). 'Dialogue Technique in Menander'. Diss. Michigan (*DA* 13/03: 384; UMI order-no. 0005079).
—— (1953/4). 'Building Up Comic Steam'. *CJ* 48: 85–9.
—— (1954). 'A Note on the Vocabulary of Menander'. *CPh* 49: 188–9.
PADUANO, G. (1978). 'Citazione ed esistenza (Menandro, *Aspis* 407 sgg.)'. *RCCM* 20: 1055–65.

PAGANELLI, L. (1978/9). '*Blepyros* nome parlante (Aristoph. *Eccl.* 327)'. *Museum Criticum*, 13/14: 231–5.

PAGE, D. L. (1941). *Select Papyri*, vol iii: *Poetry*. London.

PAIS, C. T. (1966). 'O trovão e o relâmpago nos processos de harmonia imitativa de Aristófanes'. *Alfa*, 9: 169–74.

PALUMBO STRACCA, B. M. (1991/2). 'Il megarese e il beotico nella testimonianza di Aristofane: Problemi di vocalismo'. *Helikon*, 31/2: 395–406.

PANAGL, O. (1983). '*Pheidippides*: Etymologische Überlegungen zu einem aristophanischen Personennamen', in Händel–Meid (1983), 297–306.

PARISE, N. F. (1989). 'Libbre e bronzo librale nell'Italia antica', in G. Pugliese Carratelli (ed.), *Italia omnium terrarum parens*. Milan, 581–99.

PARKER, R. (1983). *Miasma*. Oxford.

PASCUCCI, G. (1959). '*κινητιᾶν* (Men. *Dysc.* 462)'. *A&R*, NS 4: 102–5.

—— (1971). 'Novità lessicali nell'ultimo Menandro', in *Studi filologici e storici in onore di Vittorio De Falco*. Naples, 209–25.

—— (1972). 'Novità lessicali nell'ultimo Menandro, II: Le novità lessicali del *Sicyonius*, della *Samia* e dello *Scutum*', in *Studi classici in onore di Quintino Cataudella*, 4 vols. Catania, ii. 137–53.

PEARSON, A. C. (1917). *The Fragments of Sophocles*, vol. i. Cambridge.

PELLIZER, E. (1990). 'Outlines of a Morphology of Sympotic Entertainment', in O. Murray (ed.), *Sympotica: A Symposium on the Symposion*. Oxford, 177–84.

PENELLA, R. J. (1973). '*Κῳδάριον* in Aristophanes *Frogs*'. *Mnemosyne*, 4th ser. 26: 337–41.

—— (1974). '*Κῳδάριον*: A Comment'. *Mnemosyne*, 4th ser. 27: 295–7.

PENNEY, J. H. W. (1988). 'The Languages of Italy', in J. Boardman *et al.* (eds.), *The Cambridge Ancient History*, 2nd edn. Cambridge, iv. 720–38.

PEPPLER, C. W. (1902). *Comic Terminations in Aristophanes and the Comic Fragments I: Diminutives, Character Names, Patronymics*. Diss. Baltimore.

—— (1910). 'The Termination -*κός*, as Used by Aristophanes for Comic Effect'. *AJPh* 31: 428–44.

—— (1916). 'The Suffix -*μα* in Aristophanes'. *AJPh* 37: 459–65.

—— (1918). 'Comic Terminations in Aristophanes: Part IV'. *AJPh* 39: 173–83.

—— (1921). 'Comic Terminations in Aristophanes: Part V'. *AJPh* 42: 152–61.

—— (1933). 'Durative and Aoristic'. *AJPh* 54: 47–53.

PERPILLOU, J. L. (1984*a*). 'Signifiées clandestins ou le poêle et le tisonnier'. *RPh*, 3rd ser. 58: 53–62.

PERPILLOU, J. L. (1984*b*). 'La diphtongue αι en Attique'. *Glotta*, 62: 152–7.

PERUSINO, F. (1989). *Platonio: La commedia greca*. Urbino.

PETERSMANN, H. (1971). 'Philologische Untersuchungen zur antiken Bühnentür'. *WS*, NF 5: 91–109.

PFEIFFER, R. (1949). *Callimachus*, vol. i. Oxford.

—— (1968). *History of Classical Scholarship: From the Beginnings to the End of the Hellenistic Age*. Oxford.

PFEIFFNER, P. E. (1931). *Die Götteranrufungen in den Werken der drei Tragiker, in der Komödie des Aristophanes und in den Dialogen Platos und Xenophons*. Diss. Fribourg.

PHILLIPS, E. D. (1959). 'The Comic Odysseus'. *G&R*, NS 6: 58–67.

PICKARD-CAMBRIDGE, A. (1962). *Dithyramb, Tragedy and Comedy*, 2nd edn. rev. T. B. L. Webster. Oxford.

—— (1988). *The Dramatic Festivals of Athens*, 2nd edn. rev. J. Gould and D. M. Lewis, repr. with suppl. and corr. Oxford.

PIETERS, J. T. M. F. (1946). *Cratinus: Bijdrage tot de geschiedenis der vroeg-attische comedie* (Diss. Amsterdam). Leiden.

PLACES, E. DES (1934). 'Style parlé et style orale chez les écrivains grecs', in *Mélanges Bidez* (Annuaire de l'institut de philologie et d'histoire orientales, 2). Brussels, 267–86.

PLASSART, A. (1913). 'Les archers d'Athènes'. *REG* 26: 151–213.

PLATNAUER, M. (1960). 'Prodelision in Greek Drama'. *CQ*, NS 10: 140–4.

PLATTER, C. (1993). 'The Uninvited Guest: Aristophanes in Bakhtin's "History of Laughter"'. *Arethusa*, 26: 201–16.

PÖHLMANN, E. (1971). 'Die ABC-Komödie des Kallias'. *RhM*, NS 114: 230–40.

POLAND, F. (1914). 'Zur Charakteristik Menanders'. *Neue Jahrbücher für das klassische Altertum, Geschichte und deutsche Literatur*, 17: 585–96.

POMPELLA, G. (1996). *Lexicon Menandreum*. Hildesheim.

POST, C. R. (1913). 'The Dramatic Art of Menander'. *HSPh* 24: 111–45.

POST, L. A. (1938). 'Dramatic Uses of the Greek Imperative'. *AJPh* 59: 31–59.

POULTNEY, J. W. (1936). *The Syntax of the Genitive Case in Aristophanes*. Baltimore.

—— (1963). 'Studies in the Syntax of Attic Comedy'. *AJPh* 84: 359–76.

PRAG, A. J. N. W. (1985). *The Oresteia: Iconographic and Narrative Traditions*. Warminster.

—— (1991). 'Clytemnestra's Weapon Yet Once More'. *CQ*, NS 41: 242–6.

PRATO, C. (1968). *Tirteo*. Rome.

—— (ed.) (1983). *Ricerche sul trimetro di Menandro: Metro e verso*. Rome.

PRAUSE, O. (1876). *De particulae πρίν usu tragico et Aristophaneo*. Diss. Halle.

PRETAGOSTINI, R. (1976*a*). 'Dizione e canto nei dimetri anapestici di Aristofane'. *SCO* 25: 183–212.

—— (1976*b*). 'L'episodio di Caronte (Aristoph. *Ran.* 180–270)'. *A&R*, NS 21: 60–6.

—— (ed.) (1993). *Tradizione e innovazione nella cultura greca da Omero all'età ellenistica: Scritti in onore di Bruno Gentili*. Rome.

PROVOLO, G. (1960/1). 'Note sull'uso delle particelle in Menandro'. *AIV* 119: 183–219.

PUCCI, P. (1961). 'Aristofane ed Euripide: Ricerche metriche e stilistiche'. *Memorie della classe di scienze morali e storiche dell'Accademia Nazionale dei Lincei*, 358 (8th ser., 10.5): 273–423.

—— (1987). *Odysseus Polutropos: Intertextual Readings in the* Odyssey *and the* Iliad. Ithaca, N.Y.

RADT, S. (1985). *Tragicorum Graecorum Fragmenta 3 (Aeschylus)*. Göttingen.

RAFFAELLI, R. (1984). 'Nomi di *senes* nei prologhi plautini', in C. Questa and R. Raffaelli, *Maschere, prologhi, naufragi nella commedia plautina*. Bari, 85–99.

RAMALHO, A. DA COSTA (1952). *Διπλâ ὀνόματα no estilo de Aristófanes*. Coimbra.

RAU, P. (1967). *Paratragodia: Untersuchung einer komischen Form des Aristophanes* (Zetemata, 45). Munich.

RAWSON, E. (1969). *The Spartan Tradition in European Thought*. Oxford.

REHRENBÖCK, G. (1987). 'Bemerkungen zum Wortschatz des Pherekrates'. *WS* 100: 47–68.

RICCA, D. (1989). 'Gli avverbi deittici di luogo in Platone e Aristofane'. *L&S* 24: 57–88.

RICHARDSON, L. J. D. (1961). 'The Origin of the Prefix *Bou-* in Comedy'. *Hermathena*, 95: 53–63.

RICOTILLI, L. (1984). *La scelta del silenzio: Menandro e l'aposiopesi*. Bologna.

RIJKSBARON, A. (1994). *The Syntax and Semantics of the Verb in Classical Greek: An Introduction*, 2nd edn. Amsterdam.

—— (ed.) (1997). *New Approaches to Greek Particles* (Amsterdam Studies in Classical Philology, 7). Amsterdam.

RISCH, E. (1974). *Wortbildung der homerischen Sprache*, 2nd edn. Berlin.

RIX, H. (1976). *Historische Grammatik des Griechischen*. Darmstadt.

—— (1998). *Lexikon der indogermanischen Verben*. Wiesbaden.

ROBERTSON, M. (1982). '*Ληκύθιον* and *αὐτοκήκυθος*'. *JHS* 102: 234.

RODRÍGUEZ-NORIEGA GUILLÉN, L. (1992). 'Algunas notas sobre los adjetivos compuestos en Epicarmo', in J. Zaragoza and A. González Senmartí, *Homenatge a Josep Alsina: Actes del X^è simposi de la Secció catalana de la SEEC I*. Tarragona, 109–13.

ROSEN, R. M. (1984). 'The Ionian at Aristophanes, *Peace* 46'. *GRBS* 25: 389–96.

—— (1988). *Old Comedy and the Iambographic Tradition* (American Classical Studies, 19). Atlanta, Ga.

—— (1989). 'Euboulos' Ankylion and the Game of Kottabos'. *CQ*, NS 39: 355–9.

—— (1999). 'Comedy and Confusion in Callias' *Letter Tragedy*', *CPh* 94: 147–67.

ROSENKRANZ, M. L. (1964). 'Gli "atticismi" negli scoli ad Aristofane'. *Helikon*, 4: 261–78.

ROSENMEYER, P. A. (1992). *The Poetics of Imitation: Anacreon and the Anacreontic Tradition*. Cambridge.

ROSENMEYER, T. G. (1955). 'Gorgias, Aeschylus, and *Apate*'. *AJPh* 76: 225–60.

ROSENSTRAUCH, H. (1961). 'Parodia językowych badań sofistów w *Chmurach* Arystofanesa'. *Eos*, 51: 45–54.

—— (1964). 'Odczasownikowe twory zakończone na -*μα*, -*μός*, -*σις* u Menandra'. *Eos*, 54: 56–67.

—— (1967). *Studia nad językiem Menandra*. Wroclaw.

ROSSI, L. E. (1977). 'Un nuovo papiro epicarmeo e il tipo del medico in commedia'. *A&R*, NS 22: 81–4.

ROSSUM-STEENBEEK, M. VAN (1998). *Greek Reader's Digests? Studies on a Selection of Subliterary Papyri*. Leiden.

ROTHWELL, K. S. (1990). *Politics and Persuasion in Aristophanes'* Ecclesiazusae (*Mnemosyne*, Suppl. 111). Leiden.

RUCK, C. (1975). 'Euripides' Mother: Vegetables and the Phallos in Aristophanes'. *Arion*, NS 2: 13–57.

RUIJGH, C. J. (2001). 'Le *Spectacle des lettres*: comédie de Callias (Ath. X 453c–455b), avec un *excursus* sur les rapports entre la mélodie du chant et les contours mélodiques du langage parlé', *Mnemosyne*, 4th ser. 54: 257–335.

RUTHERFORD, W. G. (1881). *The New Phrynichus: Being a Revised Text of the* Ecloga *of the Grammarian Phrynichus*. London (repr. Hildesheim, 1968).

SACHTSCHAL, B. (1908). *De comicorum Graecorum sermone metro accommodato*. Diss. Breslau.

STE. CROIX, G. E. M. DE (1972). *The Origins of the Peloponnesian War*. London.

SANDBACH, F. H. (1970). 'Menander's Manipulation of Language for Dramatic Purposes', in Turner (1970), 111–43.

—— (1972). *Menandri reliquiae selectae*. Oxford (2nd edn. 1990).

SARATI, E. (1996). 'In margine al testo di Eupoli: note di lingua e di stile'. *Aevum antiquum*, 9: 107–33.

SARDIELLO, R. (1983*a*). 'I trimetri di tre parole nelle commedie di Aristofane e di Menandro', in *Studi Adamesteanu* (1983), 155–64.

—— (1983*b*). 'Le "soluzioni" nel trimetro Menandreo', in Prato (1983), 37–161, 344–51.

SCHIFFMAN, H. F. (1991). 'Swiss-German Diglossia'. *Southwest Journal of Linguistics*, 10 (1): 173–88.

SCHINCK, AE. (1873). *De interiectionum epiphonematumque apud Aristophanem vi atque usu*. Diss. Halle.

SCHLESINGER, A. C. (1936). 'Indications of Parody in Aristophanes'. *TAPhA* 67: 296–314.

—— (1937). 'Identification of Parodies in Aristophanes'. *AJPh* 58: 294–305.

SCHMID, F. (1954). *Die Deminutiva auf -ιον im Vokativ bei Aristophanes*. Diss. Zurich.

SCHMID, W. (1887–96). *Der Atticismus in seinen Hauptvertretern*, 4 vols. Stuttgart.

—— and STAEHLIN, O. (1929–48). *Geschichte der griechischen Literatur* (Handbuch der Altertumswissenschaft, 7.1), 5 vols. Munich.

SCHMIDT, V. (1977). *Dorismen im Corpus Hippocraticum*, in R. Joly (ed.), *Actes du colloque hippocratique de Mons (22–26 sept. 1975)*. Mons, 49–64.

—— (1978). 'Ein vermutetes Epicharm-Fragment bei Galen'. *ZPE* 30: 13–17.

SCHMITT, R. (1984). 'Perser und Persisches in der alten attischen Komödie', in *Orientalia J. Duchesne-Guillemin emerito oblata* (Acta Iranica, 23). Leiden, 459–72.

SCHMOLL, U. (1958). *Die vorgriechischen Sprachen Siziliens*. Wiesbaden.

SCHNEIDER, H. (1996). *Der anonyme Publikumskommentar in Ilias und Odyssee*. Münster.

SCHOLTZ, A. (1997). 'Ἐραστὴς τοῦ δήμου: Erotic Imagery in Political Contexts in Thucydides and Aristophanes'. Diss. Yale (*DA* 58/04: 1266; UMI order-no. 9731070).

SCHUCHARDT, H. (1909). 'Die Lingua Franca'. *Zeitschrift für romanische Philologie*, 33: 441–61.

SCHULTZ, W. (1912). *Rätsel aus dem hellenischen Kulturkreise*. Leipzig.

SCHWEIGHÄUSER, J. (1802*a*). *Athenaei Naucratitae Deipnosophistarum libri XV: Tomus secundus*. Strasburg.

—— (1802*b*). *Animadversiones in Athenaei Deipnosophistas: Tomus tertius*. Strasburg.

SCHWYZER, E. (1923). *Dialectorum Graecarum exempla epigraphica potiora*. Leipzig.

—— (1939). *Griechische Grammatik I: Allgemeiner Teil, Lautlehre, Wortbildung, Flexion* (Handbuch der Altertumswissenschaft, 2.1.1). Munich.

SCHWYZER, E., and DEBRUNNER, A. (1950). *Griechische Grammatik II: Syntax und syntaktische Stilistik* (Handbuch der Altertumswissenschaft, 2.1.2). Munich.

SEAFORD, R. (1977/8). 'The "Hyporchema" of Pratinas'. *Maia*, 29: 81–94.

—— (1984). *Euripides: Cyclops*. Oxford.

SECKNUS, G. (1927). *Untersuchungen zu religiösen Formeln und sonstigen Stellen religiösen Inhalts in den Komödien des Terenz*. Diss. Erlangen.

SEGAL, C. P. (1962). 'Gorgias and the Psychology of the Logos'. *HSPh* 66: 99–155.

SELVERS, F. (1909). *De mediae comoediae sermone*. Diss. Münster.

SENGER, J. H. (1888). 'Aristophanes' Use of the Preposition'. Diss. Berkeley.

SENS, A. (1991). 'Not I, but the Law: Juridical and Legislative Language in Aristophanes' *Ecclesiazusae*'. Diss. Harvard (*DA* 52/05: 1738; UMI order-no. 9132035).

SÉRIOT, P. (ed.) (1996). *Langue et nation en Europe centrale et orientale du XVIII*[ème] *siècle à nos jours* (Cahiers de l'ILSL, 8). Lausanne.

SETTI, G. (1885). 'Il linguaggio dell'uso comune presso Aristofane'. *Museo italiano*, 1: 113–30.

SHAPIRO, H. A. (1994). *Myth into Art: Poet and Painter in Classical Greece*. London.

SHIPP, G. P. (1979). *Modern Greek Evidence for the Ancient Greek Vocabulary*. Sydney.

SHLYAKHOV, V., and ADLER, E. (1995). *Dictionary of Russian Slang*. Hauppauge, N. Y.

SIER, K. (1992). 'Die Rolle des Skythen in den *Thesmophoriazusen* des Aristophanes', in C. W. Müller, K. Sier, and J. Werner (eds.), *Zum Umgang mit fremden Sprachen in der griechisch-römischen Antike* (Palingenesia, 36). Stuttgart.

SIFAKIS, G. M. (1971). *Parabasis and Animal Choruses*. London.

SIHLER, A. L. (1995). *New Comparative Grammar of Greek and Latin*. New York.

SILK, M. S. (1990). 'The People of Aristophanes', in C. B. R. Pelling (ed.), *Characterization and Individuality in Greek Literature*. Oxford, 150–73.

—— (2000*a*). *Aristophanes and the Definition of Comedy*. Oxford.

—— (2000*b*). 'Aristophanes Versus the Rest: Comic Poetry in Old Comedy', in Harvey–Wilkins (2000), 299–315.

SISTI, F. (1991). *Menandro: Epitrepontes*. Genoa.

ŠKILJAN, D. (1996). 'La langue entre symboles et signes: le cas serbo-croate', in Sériot (1996), 305–28.

SLATER, N. W. (1985). *Plautus in Performance: The Theatre of the Mind*. Princeton.

—— (1993). 'Space, Character, and 'Ἀπάτη: Transformation and Transvaluation in the *Acharnians*', in Sommerstein *et al.* (1993), 397–415.

SLAVITT, D. R., and BOVIE, P. (1998). *Menander: The Grouch, Desperately Seeking Justice, Closely Cropped Locks, The Girl from Samos, The Shield.* Philadelphia.

SLINGS, S. R. (1992). 'Written and Spoken Language: An Exercise in the Pragmatics of the Greek Sentence'. *CPh* 87: 95–109.

—— (1993). 'Figuren en wat daarvoor doorgaat'. *Lampas*, 26: 20–37.

—— (1997). 'Figures of Speech and their Lookalikes: Two Further Exercises in the Pragmatics of the Greek Sentence', in E. J. Bakker (ed.), *Grammar as Interpretation: Greek Literature in its Linguistic Context.* Leiden, 169–214.

SMITH, R. H. (1992). 'Language Behavior in Old and New Comedy: Some Applications of Discourse Analysis to a Study of Aristophanes' "Clouds" and Menander's "Dyskolos"'. Diss. Princeton (*DA* 53/01: 142; UMI order-no. 9216820).

SNELL, B. (1979). 'Lekythion'. *Hermes*, 107: 129–33.

SOBOLEWSKI, S. (1890). *De praepositionum usu Aristophaneo.* Moscow.

—— (1891). *Syntaxis Aristophaneae capita selecta: de sententiarum condicionalium temporalium relativorum formis et usu.* Moscow.

SOLMSEN, F. (1908). 'Ein dorisches Komödienbruchstück'. *RhM*, NS 63: 329–40.

SOMMERSTEIN, A. H. (1980*a*). 'The Naming of Women in Greek and Roman Comedy'. *Quaderni di storia*, 11: 393–418.

—— (1980*b*). 'βινεῖν'. *LCM* 5: 47.

—— (1987). 'The Theatre Audience, the Demos, and the *Suppliants* of Aeschylus', in C. B. R. Pelling (ed.), *Greek Tragedy and the Historian.* Oxford, 63–79.

—— (1989*a*). *Aeschylus: Eumenides.* Cambridge.

—— (1989*b*). 'Again Klytaimestra's Weapon'. *CQ*, NS 39: 296–301.

—— (1992). 'Old Comedians on Old Comedy'. *Drama*, 1: 14–33.

—— (1995). 'The Language of Athenian Women', in De Martino–Sommerstein (1995), ii. 61–85.

—— (1996). *Aeschylean Tragedy.* Bari.

—— (1998). *Aristophanes: Ecclesiazusae.* Warminster.

—— (1999). 'The Anatomy of Euphemism in Aristophanic Comedy', in F. De Martino and A. H. Sommerstein (eds.), *Studi sull'eufemismo.* Bari, 181–217.

—— (forthcoming *a*). 'Monsters, Ogres and Demons in Old Comedy', in C. Atherton (ed.), *Monsters and Monstrosity in Greek and Roman Culture.* Bari.

—— (forthcoming *b*). 'The Anger of Achilles, Mark One: Sophocles' *Syndeipnoi*', in id. (ed.), *Shards from Kolonos: Studies in Sophoclean Fragments.* Bari.

Sommerstein, A. H., Halliwell, S., Henderson, J., and Zimmermann, B. (eds.) (1993). *Tragedy, Comedy and the Polis: Papers from the Greek Drama Conference Nottingham, 18–20 July 1990*. Bari.

Southard, G. C. (1970). 'The Medical Language of Aristophanes'. Diss. Johns Hopkins (*DA* 31/09: 4745; UMI order-no. 7026724).

Spyropoulos, E. S. (1974). *L'Accumulation verbale chez Aristophane: Recherches sur le style d'Aristophane*. Thessaloniki.

Stanford, W. B. (1950). 'On the Ὀδυσσεὺς αὐτόμολος of Epicharmus'. *CPh* 45: 167–9.

Staples, D. (1978). '*Πέα πτερόεντα*: Plot and Metaphor in Aristophanes'. Diss. Boston University (*DA* 39/05: 2915; UMI order-no. 7819832).

Steiger, H. (1888). *Der Eigenname in der attischen Komödie*. Diss. Erlangen.

Stepanov, N. I. (1987). 'Menandri *Aspis*, v. 439–464 (kommentarij)'. *Philologia Classica (Leningrad)*, 3: 156–9.

Stephanopoulos, T. (1983). 'Drei alt- und neugriechische Babywörter'. *Glotta*, 61: 12–15.

Stephanus, H. (1865). *Thesaurus Graecae Linguae*, 3rd edn. rev. C. B. Hase *et al*. Paris.

Stevens, P. T. (1937). 'Colloquial Expressions in Euripides'. *CQ* 31: 182–91.

—— (1945). 'Colloquial Expressions in Aeschylus and Sophocles'. *CQ* 39: 95–105.

—— (1976). *Colloquial Expressions in Euripides* (Hermes Einzelschriften, 38). Wiesbaden.

Stewart, D. J. (1968). '*Nous* in Aristophanes'. *CJ* 63: 253–5.

Stone, L. M. (1978). 'The Obscene Use of *μέγας* in Aristophanes'. *AJPh* 99: 427–32.

Storey, I. C. (1987). 'Old Comedy 1975–1984'. *EMC* 6: 1–46.

—— (1992). '*Δέκατον μὲν ἔτος τόδ'*: Old Comedy 1982–1991'. *Antichthon*, 26: 1–29.

Studi Adamesteanu (1983) = *Studi in onore di Dinu Adamesteanu*. Galatina.

Suárez de la Torre, E. (1998). 'Observaciones sobre la presencia de la mántica en la comedia griega', in López Férez (1998), 177–201.

Sutton, D. F. (1983). 'Dithyramb as Drama: Philoxenus of Cythera's *Cyclops* or *Galatea*'. *QUCC* 42: 37–43.

Swoboda, M. (1971). 'De soliloquiorum in antiquo dramate ab Aeschyli temporibus usque ad Terentium adhibitorum munere scaenico'. *Eos*, 59: 57–76.

Szemerényi, O. J. L. (1987). 'Etyma graeca VI (33–34)'. *Minos*, 20–2: 569–80.

Tacho-Godi, A. (1965*a*). 'O nekotorych osobennostjach jazyka i žanra komedii Menandra "Diskol" ("Nenavistnik")'. *Voprosy klassičeskoj filologii*, 1: 42–74.

—— (1965*b*). 'Sintaksis složnogo predloženija v komedii Menandra "Diskol" v svjazi s obščimi problemami sintaksisa'. *Voprosy klassičeskoj filologii*, 1: 75–96.

—— (1965*c*). 'Die Alltagslexik in Menanders *Dyskolos*', in F. Zucker (ed.), *Menanders* Dyskolos *als Zeugnis seiner Epoche*. Berlin, 85–102.

TAILLARDAT, J. (1956). 'Calembours sur des noms propres chez Aristophane (*Guêpes* 1414; *Paix* 864; *Assemblée des femmes* 1101)'. Summary in *REG* 69: viii–x.

—— (1961). 'À propos des images d'Aristophane'. *IL* 13: 70–4.

—— (1965). *Les Images d'Aristophane: Études de langue et de style*, 2nd edn. Paris.

—— and ROESCH, P. (1966). 'L'inventaire sacré de Thespies: L'alphabet attique en Béotie'. *RPh*, 3rd ser. 40: 70–87.

TAPLIN, O. (1977*a*). 'Did Greek Dramatists Write Stage Instructions?'. *PCPhS*, NS 23: 121–32.

—— (1977*b*). *The Stagecraft of Aeschylus*. Oxford.

—— (1983). 'Tragedy and Trugedy'. *CQ*, NS 33: 331–3.

—— (1986). 'Fifth-Century Tragedy and Comedy: A *Synkrisis*'. *JHS* 106: 163–74.

TEODORSSON, S.-T. (1974). *The Phonemic System of the Attic Dialect 400–340* B.C. (Studia Graeca et Latina Gothoburgensia, 32). Göteborg.

—— (1978). *The Phonology of Attic in the Hellenistic Period* (Studia Graeca et Latina Gothoburgensia, 40). Göteborg.

—— (1987). 'Boeotian and Attic: Vowel Development Related?' *Verbum*, 10: 199–209.

TEYKOWSKI, H. (1940). *Der Präpositionsgebrauch bei Menander*. Diss. Bonn.

THIERCY, P. (1993). 'Les odeurs de la *polis* ou le "nez" d'Aristophane', in Sommerstein *et al.* (1993), 505–26.

—— and MENU, M. (eds.) (1997). *Aristophane: la langue, la scène, la cité* (Le Rane, 20). Bari.

THOMPSON, D. J. (1988). *Memphis under the Ptolemies*. Princeton.

THREATTE, L. (1980). *The Grammar of Attic Inscriptions*, i: *Phonology*. Berlin.

—— (1996). *The Grammar of Attic Inscriptions*, ii: *Morphology*. Berlin.

THUMB, A. (1901). *Die griechische Sprache im Zeitalter des Hellenismus: Beiträge zur Geschichte und Beurteilung der Koine*. Strasburg (repr. Berlin, 1974).

—— and KIECKERS, E. (1932). *Handbuch der griechischen Dialekte: Erster Teil*, 2nd edn. Heidelberg.

TODD, O. J. (1932). *Index Aristophaneus*. Cambridge, Mass.

TOLMAN, H. C. (1906). 'A Conjectural Persian Original of Aristophanes, *Acharnians*, 100'. *TAPhA* 37: xxxii f.

TREU, K. (1983). 'Zu den Sklavennamen bei Menander'. *Eirene*, 20: 39–42.

TREU, M. (1999). *Undici cori comici: Aggressività, derisione e tecniche drammatiche in Aristofane*. Genoa.

TURASIEWICZ, R. (1981). 'Konotacja terminu καλὸς κἀγαθός w komediach Arystofanesa'. *Eos*, 69: 21–9.

—— (1986). 'Zakres znaczeniowy ἀστεῖος w komedii Arystofanejskiej'. *Eos*, 74: 205–16.

TURNER, E. G. (ed.). *Ménandre: Sept exposés suivis de discussions* (Entretiens Hardt, 16). Vandœuvres-Geneva.

—— (1980). 'The Rhetoric of Question and Answer in Menander', in J. Redmond (ed.), *Themes in Drama II: Drama and Mimesis*. Cambridge, 1–23.

—— (1976) (with an additional note by E. W. Handley). 'A Fragment of Epicharmus? (or "Pseudoepicharmea"?)'. *WS*, NF 10: 48–60.

UCKERMANN, W. (1879). *De Aristophanis Comici vocabulorum formatione*. Diss. Marburg.

VALCKENAER, L. K. (1739). *Ammonius*. Leiden.

VALDMAN, A. (1977). 'L'effet de modèles culturels sur l'élaboration du langage simplifié (foreigner talk)', in Corder–Roulet (1977), 114–31.

—— (1981). 'Sociolinguistic Aspects of Foreigner Talk', in M. G. Clyne (ed.), *Foreigner Talk* (International Journal of the Sociology of Language, 28). The Hague, 41–52.

VERBAARSCHOT, G. (1988). 'Dialect Passages and Text Constitution in Aristophanes' *Acharnians*'. *Mnemosyne*, 4th ser. 41: 269–75.

VERDENIUS, W. J. (1981). 'Gorgias' Doctrine of Deception', in G. B. Kerferd (ed.), *The Sophists and Their Legacy: Proceedings of the Fourth International Colloquium on Ancient Philosophy* (Hermes Einzelschriften, 44). Wiesbaden, 116–28.

VETTA, M. (1993). 'La voce degli attori nel teatro antico', in Pretagostini (1993), ii. 703–18.

VICKERS, M. (1989*a*). 'Alcibiades on Stage: *Thesmophoriazusae* and *Helen*'. *Historia*, 38: 41–65.

—— (1989*b*). 'Alcibiades on Stage: Aristophanes' *Birds*'. *Historia*, 38: 267–99.

VRIES, G. J. DE (1966). 'Remarks on a Greek Form of Address (ὦ τᾶν)'. *Mnemosyne*, 4th ser. 19: 225–30.

—— (1973). 'Mystery Terminology in Aristophanes and Plato'. *Mnemosyne*, 4th ser. 26: 1–8.

WACHTER, R. (1991). 'The Inscriptions on the François Vase'. *MH* 48: 86–113.

WACKERNAGEL, J. (1888). 'Miszellen zur griechischen Grammatik'. *KZ* 29: 124–52; repr. Wackernagel (1953–79), i. 627–55.

—— (1907). 'Hellenistica'. Göttingen: Programm zur akademischen Preisverteilung; repr. Wackernagel (1953–79), ii. 1034–58.

—— (1914). 'Akzentstudien III: Zum homerischen Akzent'. *Nachr. Kön. Ges. Wiss. Göttingen, Philol.-histor. Klasse*: 97–130; repr. Wackernagel (1953–79), ii. 1154–87.

—— (1916). *Sprachliche Untersuchungen zu Homer*. Göttingen; pp. 1–159 repr. from *Glotta*, 7 (1916), 161–319.

—— 'Zu den altpersischen Stellen in Aristophanes' *Acharnern*'. *IF* 39: 224; repr. Wackernagel (1953–79), iii. 1657–8.

—— (1928). *Vorlesungen über Syntax mit besonderer Berücksichtigung von Griechisch, Lateinisch und Deutsch: Zweite Reihe*, 2nd edn. Basel.

—— (1953–79). *Kleine Schriften*, 3 vols. Göttingen.

WALKER, R. J. (1894). 'Doric Futures in Aristophanes'. *CR* 8: 17–21.

—— (1906). '"Doric" Futures: Aristophanes and Plato'. *CR* 20: 212–13.

WALTZ, P. (1911). 'Sur les sentences de Ménandre'. *REG* 24: 5–62.

WEBER, P. (1884–5). *Entwickelungsgeschichte der Absichtssätze*, 2 vols. Würzburg.

WEBSTER, T. B. L. (1974). *An Introduction to Menander*. Manchester.

WERNER, J. (1969). 'Aristophanische Sprachkunst in den Fröschen (V. 1–30)'. *Philologus*, 113: 10–23.

—— (1983). 'Nichtgriechische Sprachen im Bewußtsein der antiken Griechen', in Händel–Meid (1983), 583–95.

WERRES, J. (1936). *Die Beteuerungsformeln in der attischen Komödie*. Bonn.

WEST, M. L. (1968). 'Two Passages of Aristophanes'. *CR*, NS 18: 5–8.

—— (1970). 'Three Greek Baby-Words'. *Glotta*, 47: 184–6.

—— (1974). *Studies in Greek Elegy and Iambus*. Berlin.

—— (1977). 'Tragica I'. *BICS* 24: 89–103.

—— (1982). *Greek Metre*. Oxford.

—— (1990*a*). *Aeschyli tragoediae cum incerti poetae Prometheo*. Stuttgart.

—— (1990*b*). 'Colloquialism and Naïve Style in Aeschylus', in Craik (1990), 3–12.

—— (1992). *Ancient Greek Music*. Oxford.

WEST, S. (1988). 'The Transmission of the Text', in A. Heubeck, S. West, and J. B. Hainsworth, *A Commentary on Homer's Odyssey I*. Oxford, 33–48.

WHATMOUGH, J. (1952). 'On "Triballic" in Aristophanes (*Birds* 1615)'. *CPh* 47: 26.

WHITMAN, C. H. (1969). '*Ληκύθιον ἀπώλεσεν*'. *HSPh* 73: 109–12.

WILAMOWITZ (1895) = U. von Wilamowitz-Moellendorff, *Euripides: Herakles*. Berlin (3rd edn. 1921; repr. Darmstadt, 1959).

WILAMOWITZ (1902). 'Lesefrüchte'. *Hermes*, 37: 321–32 = Wilamowitz (1935–72), iv. 157–68.

—— (1907). 'Zum Menander von Kairo'. *Sitzungsberichte Akad. Berlin*, 860–72 = Wilamowitz (1935–72), i. 249–70.

—— (1922). *Pindaros*. Berlin.

—— (1925). *Menander: Das Schiedsgericht (Epitrepontes)*. Berlin.

—— (1935–72). *Kleine Schriften*, 6 vols. Berlin.

WILES, D. (1991). *The Masks of Menander: Sign and Meaning in Greek and Roman Performance*. Cambridge.

WILLCOCK, M. M. (1987). *Plautus: Pseudolus*. Bristol.

WILKINS, J. (2000). *The Boastful Chef: The Discourse of Food in Ancient Greek Comedy*. Oxford.

WILSON, A. M. (1974). 'A Slang Sense of *φορμός* to be Inferred from Aristophanes?'. *Mnemosyne*, 4th ser. 27: 297–8.

WILSON, J. R. (1971). '*Τόλμα* and the Meaning of *τάλας*'. *AJPh* 92: 292–300.

WIT-TAK, T. M. DE (1967). *Lysistrata: Vrede, vrouw en obsceniteit bij Aristophanes*. Diss. Groningen.

—— (1968). 'The Function of Obscenity in Aristophanes' *Thesmophoriazusae* and *Ecclesiazusae*'. *Mnemosyne*, 4th ser. 21: 357–65.

WRIGHT, F. W. (1911). *Studies in Menander*. Baltimore.

—— (1912). 'Oaths in Menander: Supplementa'. *CPh* 7: 250.

—— (1913). 'Iuraiuranda et personae Menandreae'. *CR* 27: 52.

WÜST, E. (1950). 'Epicharmos und die alte attische Komödie'. *RhM*, NF 93: 337–64.

ZAGAGI, N. (1995). *The Comedy of Menander: Convention, Variation and Originality*. London and Bloomington, Ind.

ZANETTO, G. (1999). 'Aristofane e il lessico della politica', in F. Conca (ed.), *Ricordando Raffaele Cantarella: Miscellanea di studi*. Milan and Bologna, 257–70.

—— (2001). 'Iambic Models in the Comedy of Aristophanes', in Aloni *et al.* (2001), in press.

ZARAGOZA, J. (1964). 'Usos del infinitivo en Aristófanes en función del estilo', in *Actas del II Congreso español de estudios clásicos*. Madrid, 144–9.

ZIMMERMANN, B. (1992*a*). 'Forschungsbericht: Griechische Komödie'. *Anzeiger für die Altertumswissenschaft*, 45: 161–84.

—— (1992*b*). *Dithyrambos: Geschichte einer Gattung* (Hypomnemata, 98). Göttingen.

—— (1992*c*). 'Hippokratisches in den Komödien des Aristophanes', in J. A. López (ed.), *Tratados hipocráticos (Estudios acerca de su contenido, forma e influencia). Actas del VII Coloquio internacional hipocrático*. Madrid, 513–25.

—— (1994). 'Forschungsbericht: Griechische Komödie'. *Anzeiger für die Altertumswissenschaft*, 47: 1–18.

—— (1997). 'Parodie dithyrambischer Dichtung in den Komödien des Aristophanes', in Thiercy–Menu (1997), 87–93.

ZINI, S. (1938). *Il linguaggio dei personaggi nelle commedie di Menandro*. Florence.

ZUCKER, F. (1955). 'Formen gesteigert affektischer Rede in der griechischen Tragödie'. *IF* 62: 62–77.

Index of Passages

Index of Greek

General Index